Also by Martin Bulmer

SOCIAL RESEARCH ETHICS (editor, 1982)
CENSUSES, SURVEYS AND PRIVACY (editor, 1979)
SOCIAL POLICY RESEARCH (editor, 1978)
ESSAYS ON THE HISTORY OF BRITISH SOCIOLOGICAL RESEARCH (editor, 1984)
THE CHICAGO SCHOOL OF SOCIOLOGY (1984)
SOCIAL RESEARCH IN DEVELOPING COUNTRIES (editor, with D. P. Warwick, 1983)
THE USES OF SOCIAL RESEARCH (1982)
SOCIAL RESEARCH AND ROYAL COMMISSIONS (editor, 1980)
MINING AND SOCIAL CHANGE: DURHAM COUNTY IN THE TWENTIETH CENTURY (editor,1978)
WORKING CLASS IMAGES OF SOCIETY (editor, 1975)

SOCIOLOGICAL RESEARCH METHODS

An Introduction

SECOND EDITION

Edited by

Martin Bulmer

Senior Lecturer in Social Administration
The London School of Economics and Political Science

MACMILLAN

First edition 1977
Reprinted 1979, 1983
Second edition 1984

ISBN 0 333 37345 6
ISBN 0 333 37346 4 pbk

Published by
Higher and Further Education Division
MACMILLAN PUBLISHERS LTD
London and Basingstoke
Companies and representatives
throughout the world

Filmsetting by Vantage Photosetting Co Ltd Eastleigh and London

Printed in Hong Kong

Contents

Contributors ix
Preface xi
Introduction: Problems, Theories and Methods in Sociology – (How) Do They Interrelate? 1
MARTIN BULMER

Part One

SOCIOLOGICAL THEORY IN EMPIRICAL RESEARCH

1 Facts, Concepts, Theories and Problems 37
MARTIN BULMER

Part Two

SOCIAL-SURVEY RESEARCH

2 Introduction and Further Reading 53
MARTIN BULMER
3 The Meaning of Relationships in Social-Survey Analysis 65
MORRIS ROSENBERG
4 Problems with Surveys: Method or Epistemology? 82
CATHERINE MARSH

Part Three

UNOBTRUSIVE MEASURES

5 Introduction and Further Reading 105
MARTIN BULMER

6 The Use of Archival Sources in Social Research 113
E. J. WEBB, D. T. CAMPBELL, R. D. SCHWARZ AND L. SECHREST
7 Why Don't Sociologists Make More Use of Official Statistics? 131
MARTIN BULMER

Part Four

HISTORICAL SOURCES

8 Introduction and Further Reading 155
MARTIN BULMER
9 The Relevance of History to Sociology 162
JOHN H. GOLDTHORPE
10 The Historical Study of Family Structure 175
MICHAEL ANDERSON
11 Class Structure in Early Twentieth-century Salford 192
ROBERT ROBERTS

Part Five

INTERPRETATIVE PROCEDURES

12 Introduction and Further Reading 209
MARTIN BULMER
13 Of Sociology and the Interview 215
MARK BENNEY AND EVERETT C. HUGHES
14 Asking Questions (And Listening to Answers) 225
IRWIN DEUTSCHER
15 Concepts in the Analysis of Qualitative Data 241
MARTIN BULMER

Part Six

THEORY, METHOD AND SUBSTANCE

16 Introduction and Further Reading 265
MARTIN BULMER
17 The Category of Pragmatic Knowledge in Sociological Analysis 276
W. BALDAMUS

18 Two Methods in Search of a Substance 294
LEWIS A. COSER

Notes and References 309
Bibliography 321

Contributors

MICHAEL ANDERSON	Professor of Economic History, University of Edinburgh
W. BALDAMUS	Professor Emeritus of Sociology, University of Birmingham
The late MARK BENNEY	British author and social scientist
MARTIN BULMER	Senior Lecturer in Social Administration, London School of Economics and Political Science
DONALD T. CAMPBELL	Albert Schweitzer Professor of Social Science, Syracuse University
LEWIS A. COSER	Distinguished Professor of Sociology, State University of New York, Stony Brook
IRWIN DEUTSCHER	Professor of Sociology, University of Akron
JOHN H. GOLDTHORPE	Official Fellow in Sociology, Nuffield College, Oxford
The late EVERETT C. HUGHES	Professor Emeritus of Sociology, University of Chicago and Brandeis University
CATHERINE MARSH	Lecturer in Social and Political Sciences, University of Cambridge
The late ROBERT ROBERTS	Teacher in H.M. Prison Service and in adult education in north-west England

MORRIS ROSENBERG — Professor of Sociology, University of Maryland at College Park

E. J. WEBB — Professor, Graduate School of Business, Stanford University

Preface to the Second Edition

The first edition of this book was produced seven years ago because sociological method was a relatively underdeveloped area from a teaching point of view, and there was a need for new perspectives on it. The material included was intended to encourage reflection, discussion and debate about research methods in sociology, even if the particular *gestalt* of the research process which it adopted did not command universal assent. The first edition was generally well received and used widely in undergraduate and graduate courses on research methodology. A revised edition is therefore timely.

Why does method matter as part of the education and professional competence of a contemporary sociologist? Students and teachers of sociology alike spend most of their academic time talking about the nature and interpretation of social reality. In doing so, accounts of social life are derived from our own social experience as members of a society, and from our location within social structures in that society. Through our families, our peers, our institutional memberships, our interests and our first-hand experiences we play social roles, are socialised into particular patterns of behaviour, and absorb a wide range of socially formed values, beliefs and attidudes. In another and more important sense, however, most sociological knowledge is knowledge at second hand, not derived from our own immediate experience. The social reality being talked is 'out there', beyond the confines of the educational institution in which the academic discourse is being carried on.

For accounts of this real world, student and teacher alike rely to a considerable extent upon the published researches of sociologists and other social scientists, as well as upon more general sources such as the press, television and radio, films, historical and literary sources, and material deriving from governments, interest groups and other voluntary organisations.

These different accounts of society and its parts vary considerably in their adequacy from a scientific standpoint. All are of potential value in social research, but many of the more accessible – for example, popular journalism and novels – are also the least systematic and potentially more unreliable in their portrayal of particular social groups or social processes. This book is concerned with sociological research methods, and its purpose is to examine the means by which the sociologist gains *systematic, reliable* and *valid* knowledge about the social world 'out there', and to indicate some of the ways in which this knowledge is used in the formulation of sociological explanations.

What follows should stimulate the reader to think about some of the main methodological problems in sociology. The book is intended as a source of ideas about sociological research methods which the reader must take up, work out and develop in his or her own work. It aims to convey a sense of what is involved in the process of research, and the practical problems encountered in producing sociological explanations. This volume does not provide an account of a single, unified, cut-and-dried research method because, contrary to what some texts suggest, it does not exist. The emphasis here upon contrasting methodological statements about key issues is deliberate, as a way of pointing up central questions and trying to convey a sense of the complexity of the processes of sociological research.

The title of this book has sometimes seemed a slight misnomer. It is centrally concerned, not with research methods alone, but with the integral connections (which suffuse the best sociological work) between theory, method and substance (the title of the last part of the book). The original conception of the book arose partly from the isolation of many research-methods courses from the main theoretical and substantive concerns of sociologists, and a belief that the connections between theories and methods need to be emphasised more in teaching. It also stemmed from dissatisfaction with the formalism of many research-methods textbooks, which tend to portray research like good military planning, whereas autobiographical accounts of the research process suggest that this is not how it is actually carried out.

A secondary emphasis is upon different *styles* of sociological research. Much writing about methodology (often from widely differing standpoints) gives the impression that one particular style (or cluster of styles) of research is to be preferred to other styles, about which critical comments are made. This is particularly true about those at either end of the quantitative/qualitative continuum, who sometimes display an intolerance, indeed bigotry, toward styles of research which do not accord with their own view of proper procedure. In what follows the *variety* of approaches to research is emphasised.

Teaching methods of social research sometimes seem to defy adequate solution at both undergraduate and graduate levels, since there are so many different aspects to it and it involves both academic and practical knowledge. What experienced sociologists have to say about their research work therefore has an important role in such teaching; this is also why this book takes the form of a reader. It provides an *introduction* to sociological research methods; it does not provide cut-and-dried answers. The scope and coverage of this book are inevitably selective; particular importance therefore attaches to the suggestions for further reading provided, which make it possible to follow up issues raised and fill some of the gaps. Nevertheless, certain specific omissions should be noted, in case the reader wonders why they are not included.

This collection is not primarily orientated to the detailed discussion of measurement and the quantitative analysis of social data, although Parts 2, 3 and 4 of this book are concerned with these subjects to some extent. This emphasis is deliberate. A number of excellent available texts deal with the contribution of statistical methods to sociology (e.g. Blalock [1960]; Weiss [1968]; Mueller *et al.* [1970]; Loether and McTavish [1974]; Bailey [1978]; Walizer and Wienir [1978]; Backstrom and Hursh-Cesar [1981]). A large and growing literature deals with the analysis of quantitative data at various levels of sophistication (e.g. Zeisel [1968]; Blalock and Blalock (eds) [1968]; Blalock (ed.) [1972]; Heise [1975]; Tukey [1977]; Fienberg [1977]). To add to either would be superfluous.

Nor is this book aiming to describe in detail the different tools of research used by sociologists; it is rather concerned with overall research strategy. Thus although one paper on interviewing appears in Part 5, the large literature on this subject (e.g. Hyman [1954]; Richardson [1965]; Bingham [1959]; Gorden [1975]) and on questionnaire construction (e.g. Payne [1951]; Oppenheim [1966]) is not touched on. Excellent textbook discussions are also available.

Two other omissions, solely for reasons of space, are perhaps more regrettable. Discussion of general methodological issues, as by Durkheim in *The Rules of Sociological Method* [1964] and by Max Weber in *The Methodology of the Social Sciences* [1949], is an indispensable part of studying methods of research. These issues are alluded to in the Introduction and in Part 6, but properly require a much more detailed treatment than has been possible here. Secondly, no attention is given to important ethical and political questions concerning social research. These enter into research in many ways: in the ethical commitment of the researcher in the field (cf. Barnes [1963]; Filstead [1970, Part 6]); in the political aims and ethical consequences of social research (cf. Horowitz [1967]; Rainwater and Yancey [1967]; Sjoberg (ed.) [1968]; Barnes [1980]; Bulmer (ed.) [1982]; Beauchamp [1982]); in the social and intellectual context within which research is carried on (Hughes [1959]; Bramson [1961]; Tiryakian (ed.) [1971]; Payne [1981]; Abrams *et al.* [1981]); and in the need to develop an adequate theory of social research, of the relation between the methodology of social research and its objects. Another book would be required to deal with these fully. Nor does the increasingly salient issue of the utilisation of research receive any attention here, and on this the reader must look elsewhere (cf. Bulmer [1978]; Lindblom and Cohen [1979]; Scott and Shore [1979]; Weiss [1980]; Bulmer [1980c]; Bulmer [1982]).

It is not clear, at least in Britain, that sociological method is any more strongly developed than it was seven years ago. A recent review of the teaching of the subject to postgraduates (Bulmer and Burgess (eds) [1981]) struck a rather pessimistic note, though there are a considerably larger number of British books about research methods today than there were seven years ago. A number of these are referred to in the further reading provided for each section of this book.

Acknowledgements

I am indebted to Valerie Campling, who typed the revised manuscript, and to Steven Kennedy of Macmillan, who suggested revising the first edition. It will be obvious throughout how much I have continued to draw on the writings of others about methods of sociological research, as well as on personal contacts with sociologists in Britain and the United States, too numerous to mention. In the suggestions for further reading and in the notes and references, I have attempted to indicate some of these sources. The first edition owed a good deal to the stimulus of colleagues in the Department of Sociology and Social Administration at the University of Durham before 1974 as well as specifically to the comments of Professors W. Baldamus and J. H. Westergaard. Since then the experience of working briefly in the Office of Population Censuses and Surveys, teaching research methods at the London School of Economics, and rather more extensive contact with sociology in the United States, has reinforced my belief in the importance of high quality methodological work. There is still scope for great improvement in this respect in Britain, which is one reason why it seems to me that a second edition is justified.

London, December 1983 MARTIN BULMER

Introduction: Problems, Theories and Methods in Sociology – (How) Do They Interrelate?

Martin Bulmer

Consider social facts as things (E. Durkheim).

Sociology is a science which attempts the interpretive understanding of social action in order thereby to arrive at a causal explanation of its course and effects (M. Weber).

Society does indeed possess objective facticity. And society is indeed built up by activity that expresses subjective meaning. It is precisely the dual character of society in terms of objective facticity and subjective meaning that makes its reality *sui generis* (P. Berger and T. Luckmann).

The Relation of Sociological Theory to Empirical Research

What constitutes sociological knowledge? This question has lain at the heart of discussions about sociological inquiry ever since Durkheim's classic *The Rules of Sociological Method* was published in 1895. How it is answered has implications for sociology's status as a scientific or humanistic discipline, for the activity of sociology itself, and for the explanatory power (and ultimately the effectiveness in the real world) of sociological propositions. Succeeding generations of sociologists have argued out, analysed and re-analysed the problems which it raises, and proposed new solutions to them. However one regards *The Rules* as an account of the logic of social inquiry, it is a landmark in the history of sociological methodology and a reference point for all subsequent debates. The attempt in it to weld empirical inquiry to theoretical concerns, and to illuminate and test theoretical propositions by confrontations with empirical data, provides a model for disciplined sociological work which is still pertinent today. Its significance lies above all in the guidance it provides for the conduct of empirical sociology, emphasising both theoretical and empirical elements *and their necessary interconnection.* As a methodological statement, it sharply demarcates empirical descriptive work (sociography) from empirical-theoretical work (sociology).

The history of empirical social research in general is of course much older (cf., Glaser [1959]; Lazarsfeld [1961]; Oberschall [1965 and 1972]; Kent [1982]). Sociology forms part of a much larger movement of social fact-gathering, government and private statistical inquiry, and survey research, many of whose most distinguished figures were British. William Farr, Sidney and Beatrice Webb, Charles Booth and Seebohm Rowntree, for example, carried out pioneering social investigations which considerably influenced both the subject-matter and character of British sociology. Yet such inquiries were primarily sociographic rather than sociological, concerned with gathering social facts to illuminate contemporary policy issues. In the last quarter of the twentieth century, sociology is more ambitious. 'Scientific method' is not understood simply as meticulous and painstaking collection and analysis of data, but involves a concern with theoretical problems and an urge to *explain* social phenomena through theoretical work.

The value of descriptive research, establishing the 'facts' of a particular situation, is not to be denied. The social characteristics of British people voting for the Labour Party since 1945, the proportion of the English working class who were church-attenders in 1851, or the proportion of blacks in non-manual occupations in the United States of America in 1970 are all important items of data. Their significance for the sociologist does not lie in the data themselves, however, for the world is a vast sea of potential data in which one would swim aimlessly in perpetuity (or drown) without criteria for selecting and organising the data. These criteria are provided by the *problems* and *theories* derived from sociology.

Descriptive research is important, and has played and continues to play a particularly significant role in the formulation of social policy. The empirical *sociologist,* however, does not set out only to gather 'the facts' about social life, although this may be important in preparing the ground for what is to follow. The sociologist setting out to grasp the complexity of social interaction and social process is himself seeking both to *understand* and *explain* social phenomena (not merely to describe them), and is interpreting the world, moreover, through a frame of reference of some kind, even if this is based on the view that 'the facts speak for themselves'. Doing sociological research, as Durkheim stressed, necessarily involves *theory* as well as the strategies and techniques of empirical investigation.

Any simplistic view of social research as a superior kind of fact-gathering is quite misleading, even if descriptive research is admitted to have a useful limited role to play. This is to confuse sociography with sociology. 'The more a piece of sociological research resembles a collection of facts, no matter how comprehensive, complete or accurate they might happen to be, the less is its scientific significance' (Bierstedt [1949]. A second and related point concerns the theoretical complexity of knowledge about society. Sociology is concerned with understanding the nature of 'social action', 'social relationships' and 'social structure', and in so doing to explain particular problems in theoretically adequate terms. Yet the operationalisation of these theoretical constructs in the course of empirical work is at best exceedingly complex, and the relationship between items of data and theoretical propositions is often very difficult to establish. What for example constitutes a 'fact' about social structure? What counts as a social action or a social relationship? Assuming we have identified a particular action as a social action, how do we interpret and understand the social actions of other people? Do we take account – in behavioural terms – of what they *do*, or of what the actors themselves say they are doing, or what we (i.e. the sociologists) say they are doing? Like the proverbial chicken and egg, data and the interpretation of data are inextricably bound up together. To conceive of one without the other is to deprive sociology of its theoretical core.

A third difficulty is the intractability of explaining social phenomena. Some advocates of the superiority of fact-gathering suggest that the social sciences 'progress by collecting facts which provide generalisations which, in turn, can be taken together to provide higher generalisations . . . social theory is simply an array of concepts which are used for the description of social facts which, when brought together in certain ways, provide causal explanations, or better still, meaningful correlations' (P. S. Cohen [1968] p. 242). As Cohen points out, this view is quite unsatisfactory. The social sciences have not, with the partial exception of economics, achieved the remarkable breakthroughs of the natural sciences in being able to formulate general laws from which to predict successfully the course of social development even on a small scale and under limiting conditions. Without entering into the debate about the status of the social sciences as *sciences*, it is reasonable to claim that the explanation of social behaviour is an exceedingly complex matter which requires the most careful procedures and theoretical sensitivity.

On the other hand, the opposite tendency to approach the study of society in purely theoretical terms, to view sociology as a branch of applied philosophy rather than an empirical discipline, may have most unfortunate consequences. Theory *and* empirical inquiry are necessary for sociological inquiry to flourish and bear fruit. Theory without the reality-testing which empirical research provides can be an increasingly barren and fruitless exercise, more akin to medieval theology than to modern social science. As well as theory, sociology involves method. Since the terms 'method', 'research methods' and 'methodology' are used widely and indiscriminately in discussing sociological research, an initial definition of terms is useful.

(1) *General methodology* denotes the systematic and logical study of the general principles guiding sociological investigation, concerned in the broadest sense with questions of how the sociologist establishes social knowledge and how he can convince others that his knowledge is correct.

It involves 'the consideration of the general grounds for the validity of scientific propositions and systems of them' (Parsons [1937] p. 24). As such it has clear and direct links to the philosophy of social science, itself a subject of specialist study by philosophers.

(2) *Research strategy or research procedure* refer to the way in

which one particular empirical study is designed and carried ou. what notions about the task of sociological research are embodied in the approach used, what type of research design is used, and which particular combination of available research techniques is employed.

(3) *Research techniques* are the specific manipulative and fact-finding operations which are used to yield data about the social world. Examples include the use of questionnaires or interview schedules to elicit people's social characteristics, beliefs, and attitudes, the use of official statistics, and the use of historical documents.

The term 'methodology' (as in Max Weber's *The Methodology of the Social Sciences*) commonly (although not invariably) refers to general considerations of the first type; it is here qualified by the adjective 'general' to make quite clear what is meant. 'Research methods' commonly (although not invariably) refers to the more concrete and specific activities of (2) and (3), which are here separately distinguished.

The available literature varies widely in its degree of specificity, from the most general (as in Durkheim's *The Rules of Sociological Method*) to the most specific detail about how to employ a particular research technique. The present work is strongly committed to an attempt to *integrate* these three different aspects of sociological research methods. Choice of research strategy and research techniques is rarely independent of a general methodological standpoint; conversely the use of a particular strategy or technique may have important implications for the general grounds for the validity of scientific proposions. Choice of research technique is dictated by research strategy; but strategy is constrained by the techniques which are available and which are feasible (cf., Sjoberg and Nett [1968]; Denzin [1970; new ed. 1978]; Ford [1975]).

Nevertheless sociological research, as research, is primarily committed to establishing systematic, reliable and valid knowledge about the social world. This involves a commitment to empirical investigation and the use of research strategies and techniques to that end. The material which follows is intended to illuminate the use of such strategies and techniques *in sociological research*. It is worth making this point because in some senses, research strategies and techniques are independent of the academic disciplines with ssociated. Social surveys, official statistics and re available to anyone to use and exploit (given social survey sufficient resources to do so). ods tend to be associated with particular academic – the social survey, for example, with sociology, social ministration and political science – but there is nothing inevitable about this. Unfortunately research methods are sometimes taught as if they were a set of skills, rather like those of cookery or vehicle maintenance, which can be learnt and applied regardless of context. It is a principal thesis of this book that this is a misleading way of presenting research methods, which should always be viewed in the context of the problems and theories which they are used to illuminate.

If this is the aim how can the research process be conceptualised? If it is not *simply* a matter of deploying certain standard skills (although this is certainly involved) how is it structured? One account which is widely propagated presents research by analogy with a military campaign, with a set series of stages which must be passed through from start to finish. Such a campaign is said, ideal-typically, to have the following stages:

(1) Research design: the specification of the problem, conceptual definitions, derivation of hypotheses to test, definition of the population to be studied etc.

(2) Sampling: the selection of the units of a population for study, the construction of a sampling frame, the drawing up of the sample etc.

(3) Questionnaire construction: the design and pre-testing and revision of the research instrument (commonly a questionnaire or interview schedule) intended to elicit the data required for the study.

(4) Data collection, by means of the research instrument, done either by the researcher himself or by hired hands.

(5) Coding, measurement and data analysis of the results, typically in quantitative form.

(6) Data interpretation and report writing: the drawing of conclusions about the original theoretical hypotheses.

Clearly such an account is very useful so far as it goes. All research work has a beginning, a middle and an end, and those whose job it is to do social research must know how to set about it. A clear idea of how to plan and execute a particular piece of larg scale research using quantitative procedures is very useful and necessary knowledge.

As a paradigm for discovery and understanding in the processes of social research, however, the account is less adequate. It tends to reduce the conduct of research to the technical operations performed at each stage of the research process (e.g. sampling, questionnaire construction, data analysis). While understanding of these techniques is necessary for the successful conduct of research, it is not sufficient. The model does not give an adequate picture of the play of the unexpected in social research, whether in the direction of theory building or in the course of data collection. Social research, judged by accounts written by its practitioners, is rarely like a well-conducted military campaign, and although most projects pass through a series of stages, these need not correspond exactly to those postulated in the model. How far, moreover, are the written accounts of research results reconstructions of the process of investigation after the event in terms of an ideal of inquiry which is rarely in practice followed? ((cf. Hammond [1964]; Weiss [1968] Ch. 16.)

A second weakness of the account of research in terms of stages is that it assimilates all social research to the model of survey research. While it is true that many sociological investigations use survey-research methods, this is not a reason for propounding a model of stages which proceeds as if *all* research is of a unitary kind. For example, historical researches and those based on extended fieldwork are not preliminary to survey research in logical terms (as is sometimes argued) but are in some senses alternatives. This is clear from the extracts included later in the book.

Thirdly the model of stages underemphasises the problematical nature of data *collection* in sociological research. Textbook treatments of interviewing in large-scale social surveys tend to underplay the problematical status of social inquiry itself as an activity (e.g. Smith [1972]). Gathering data is not merely a question of contacting respondents, establishing a degree of 'rapport' with them, and administering in an unbiased fashion a set of well-designed questions intended to tap the relevant aspects of their attributes, behaviour and attitudes. The researcher, after all, is in interaction with those people who are the subjects of his study. As Benney and Hughes emphasise in the paper later in the book (Chapter 13), the interview is the art of sociological sociability. Sociologists do not ıce like military strategists; they are rather sup- upon their respondent's good will. The interac- :her and subject is a delicate and fine one which ..ure of inquiry. Data collection is the Achilles' ...ological research, a point returned to later. To see ..rch as a series of stages underplays this weak point.

The *practice* of theorising will be discussed in detail in the last part of the book. It is, however, implicit throughout, and several chapters highlight the ways in which theory and method intertwine through *all* stages of the research process. Here it is desirable to move on, to consider models of research design in sociological research. This will highlight further why a model of all types of research in terms of stages is not entirely plausible – or at least why an approach in terms of *problems* poses certain methodological issues more sharply.

Research Design

The most widely accepted views of the logic of social-research design emphasise the importance of attempting to approximate to the logic of experimental design (Stouffer [1950]; Blalock [1964, 1970]; Campbell and Stanley [1963]). This entails, as an ideal type, the identification of causal relationships between independent and dependent variables by the division of a population into an experimental group and a control group, its observation over time, and the identification of the effects of the exposure of the experimental group only to the test variable. The structure of such inquiry is represented diagrammatically in Figure 1.

	Before	Exposure to test variable	After
Experimental group		✓	
Control group		✗	

FIGURE 1 *The logical structure of experimental research*

Sociologists, as distinct from social psychologists, do not (with a few exceptions) conduct experimental research on the model of the physical sciences. The reasons for this are evident – the ethical and moral considerations militating against conducting experiments upon human populations are so strong that such experiments as are carried out tend to be concerned with socially trivial issues. However, because social research does not correspond *in form* to experimental procedure, it does not follow that experimental logic is inapplicable. Non-experimental design attempts to identify causal relationships by satisfying three criteria:

(a) the association or correlation between two or more variables must be shown to occur in such a way that it holds in various situations under varying conditions;
(b) the correlation between the variables at (a) must be shown to be genuine, and not to be due to extraneous, intervening or antecedent variables which would suggest that the relationship was either spurious or contingent upon other factors being present;
(c) the time-order of occurrence of the variables must be known so that their temporal priority may be determined.

More detailed consideration is given to these issues in the paper by Rosenberg on social-survey analysis. In relation to the experimental ideal, several variant types of design may be distinguished, based on one or more of the four cells in Figure 1. Some research consists of a study of one group at one particular point in time, a case study. A second is the static group comparison. Data is collected at one point in time from two or more groups which differ in their exposure to a particular variable (e.g. entry into higher education). This is shown in Figure 3. An attempt is then made to make causal inferences by comparing those with one characteristic (e.g. have entered university or a polytechnic) with those without that characteristic, in relation to other characteristics which may have an independent effect (social class of parents, type of school or college,

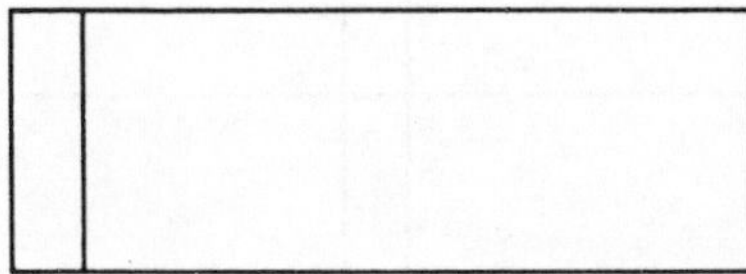

FIGURE 2 *The single case study*

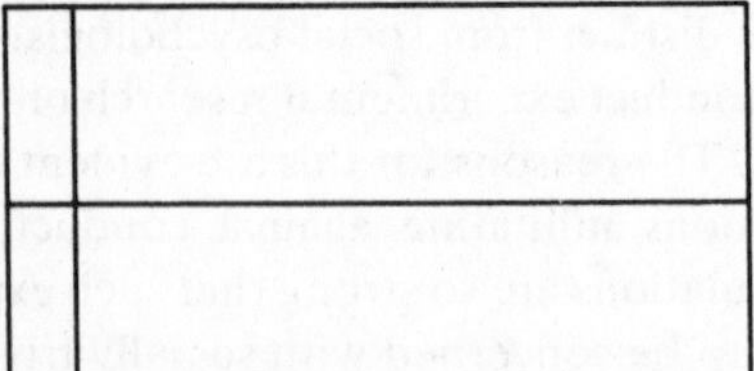

FIGURE 3 *The static group comparison*

motivation of student etc.). The problem is to determine how much of the observed difference (between those entering and not entering higher education) is due to the effect of these test variables, and how much is due to the influence of other extraneous factors in the selection of the individuals comprising the two groups.

A further and major disadvantage of this approach is that it is cross-sectional, depending upon data collected at one point in time. Researchers have therefore attempted to assess change over time (and the temporal priority of variables in relation to each other) by studying a sample at one point in time, and then another sample at another point in time. Logically this has the form in relation in the original experimental model shown in Figure 4.

One then attempts to make inferences about the effect of test factors (e.g. parents' social class, type of school) from differences between the two samples (e.g. in proportions going into higher education) and from changes in the two samples over time. The problem here is first to identify whether people actually changed in some respect over time – because the two groups are entirely different – and secondly to know whether the two samples differed in certain respects. We do not know this, so the observed change might not be due to the influence of a test factor but to the effects of this (unknown and uncontrolled) variation.

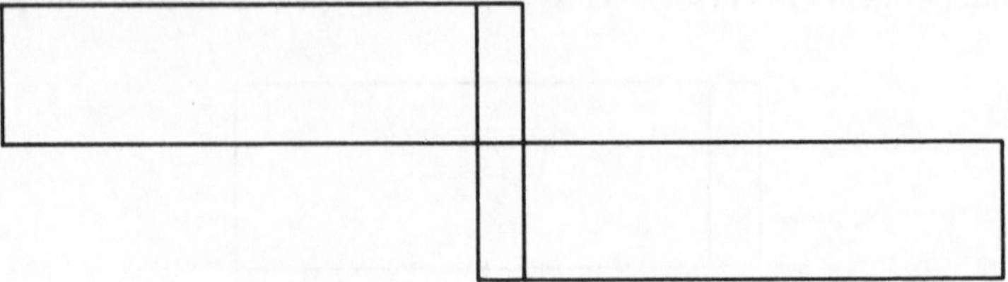

FIGURE 4 *Comparison of different populations at two points in time*

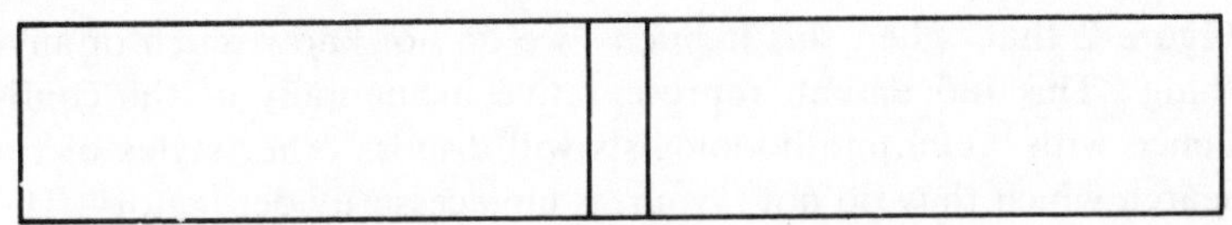

FIGURE 5 *The longitudinal study*

The longitudinal study which follows a selected group of individuals over time can to some extent overcome this problem. It has the logical form shown in Figure 5.

This design provides the possibility of comparing changes in identifiable individuals over time, and the possibility of meeting the criticism of the previous design that it cannot identify *who* actually changes in some respect. However it still does not resolve the problem of spurious or contingent correlation. Even though time-order of occurrence is fairly tightly controlled, the problem remains of showing, if co-variation occurs, which variables produced the result and whether it is possible to exclude the influence of other variables.

Several of the papers which follow are particularly concerned with problems of research design. Rosenberg, for example, on social-survey analysis clarifies the initial steps to be taken in a static group comparison using survey data. Anderson's paper on the history of family structure criticises those who have sought to supply a missing time dimension by conjecture; he emphasises the need for a proper historical grounding.

Mainly for resource reasons, however, most empirical studies in sociology are either of a single case or a static group comparison (Figure 2 or 3). Is the experimental model an impossible ideal toward which social scientists strive? Well-formulated research is obviously designed to advance understanding and produce explanations, but the gap between ideal and practice is so wide that undue emphasis upon experimental logic may divert attention from other fruitful avenues. *The Affluent Worker* study (Goldthorpe *et al.* [1968–9]), for example, involved an ingenious design for the specification of a 'critical case' by which to test the theory of embourgeoisement. It hardly fits very readily into the framework outlined above.

In-depth studies of particular social milieux, considered in Part 5 of this book, do not fit readily into the model either. Stouffer ([1950] p. 357) commented on the type of design represented in

Figure 2 that 'when this happens, we do not know much of anything'. This judgement, representative incidentally of the confidence with which methodologists will dismiss other styles of research which they do not favour, is unnecessarily derogatory. The logic of 'naturalistic' social inquiry has been stated among others by Denzin (1971) and Schatzman and Strauss ([1973] Ch. 1). It is linked to the procuedure known as 'analytic induction', discussed in Chapter 15, emphasising the interplay of theory and method. The theoretical ideas of the sociologist do not feed into and emerge out of the operations of multi-variate analysis, but develop from immersion in field situations. The naturalist grounds his propositions in empirical observations, formulates theoretical propositions from these observations, and tests them by further observation.

Such a research design proceeds from a somewhat different starting-point to that of experimental logic. It emphasises not so much a model of society in terms of causal variables, as a research commitment to come to grips with the natural social worlds in which people interact. To render those worlds intelligible from the point of view of a theory grounded in the attitudes and behaviours of those studied, its focus is upon the social construction of reality and the ways in which social interaction reflects actors' unfolding definitions of their situation. Man is subject as well as object in this type of research. As David Matza has pointed out ([1969] p. 8), 'naturalism claims fidelity to the empirical world. In the empirical world, man is subject and not object, except when he is likened to one by himself or by another subject. Naturalism must choose the subjective view, and consequently it must combine the scientific method with the distinctive tools of humanism – experience, intuition and empathy.'

In generalising about social research, including historical sociology, no one, single, all-embracing model for research design is satisfactory. The overall research enterprise is characterised more adequately by its concern with problems than it is by an excessive devotion to a remote experimental ideal.

Research Strategies

It will by now be apparent that the organisation of the core of this book is not centred on a model of research as a series of ideal-typical stages, nor as following a single standard research design. Rather it takes as its starting-point the interplay of problems, theories and methods in sociological research and asks: what *styles* of sociological work are most widespread and admired? How does each style stimulate the sociological imagination! How does it bring theory and evidence together? What types of research design does it employ? What sort of data does it use? How reliable and valid is the evidence it produces?

In terms of the threefold distinction made earlier, the focus is upon research strategies and procedures, rather than upon research techniques or general methodology. Both of them are discussed, but the emphasis is upon the particular crystallisation of theory and method which takes place when a research study is undertaken. Such an emphasis upon the *practice* of sociology may do as much justice to the varieties of sociological research as an account which concentrates upon the formal characteristics of research as an activity.

The four styles of research distinguished are:

(1) *Social survey research*, the most extensively used strategy in social inquiry and the one most closely identified with sociology. The emphasis here is placed upon its *analytic* potential to address theoretical problems.

(2) *Unobtrusive measures*, the use of pre-existing data sources for analytic ends.

(3) *Historical sources*, the use of the methods and materials of the historian, both quantitative and non-quantitative, for sociological ends, including a discussion of personal documents.

(4) *Interpretative procedures*, using a variety of techniques (including extended field-work in a single milieu) to provide understanding of social structure and process from the actor's point of view.

This classification is not exhaustive, although the four types probably cover the main approaches used in nine-tenths of sociological research monographs. Specific exclusions, largely for reasons of space, are experimental research designs (Greenwood [1945]) (cf. Figure 1); secondary analysis of survey and other data (Boudon [1969]; Hyman [1972]); content analysis (Berelson [1952]; North [1963]; Krippendorf [1980]); and network analysis (Mitchell [1969]). More advanced developments in survey analysis and interpretative work are not covered, for reasons explained shortly.

Cross-cultural comparative research is not examined (except indirectly in Part 4) since its scope is so vast and the methodological problems it throws up so diverse. Sociological research is an exceedingly complex activity which can be examined from a number of different standpoints. Complete coverage from any of these is virtually impossible, and the present work is no exception.

The four styles of research are analytic abstractions or ideal types, whose purpose is heuristic in order to clarify the ways in which the sociologist brings theory and method together.

It is not suggested that different strategies are not combined in particular investigations – because they often are – nor that the different strategies are not complementary. The purpose of setting out the different strategies is to explore the ways in which sociologists make choices between different research strategies (to the extent that they do) and what influences them in making such choices. There has been among sociologists a continuing debate about the fruitfulness of different styles of research, so that there is nothing like the consensus which appears to have been reached in academic psychology over the experiment as a paradigm for research design, with a few extreme critics isolated outside the consensus. In any particular substantive area it is possible to point to a number of instances where similar subjects have been studied using quite contrasting strategies.

How are such choices made? Clearly some people prefer one particular style to another. Judged simply in terms of use, social survey research has the largest following, and is most widely employed. Consider the following observation on the subject.

'Sociology is rapidly becoming synonymous in many quarters with survey research. Worse still, many *sociologists* are equating empirical research with survey research. I first expressed my objection to this some time ago (Bechhofer [1967]), but this may be a good place to repeat it. The survey is an excellent way of acquiring certain kinds of information, but it is limited and almost certainly over-used' (Bechhofer [1973] pp. 74–5). Many standard textbooks take this preference for granted, considering primarily survey research and commenting on the weaknesses of methods mainly in relation to other sources such as case studies, personal documents or unobtrusive measures. A short controversy in the 1950s, however, suggested that preference alone is insufficient. Becker and Geer, in a well known article [1957], suggested that participant observation was to be preferred to interviewing in a number of respects – its sensitivity to language, its ability to probe difficult topics, its involvement in events – and that one could say (in certain limited respects) that one method was 'better' than another. Martin Trow [1957] sharply disagreed, saying that it was not a question 'of the general and inherent superiority of one method over another, on the basis of some intrinsic qualities it presumably possesses'. Support for Trow's view has also come from Zelditch [1962], Reiss [1968], Sieber [1973] and Mitchell [1983].

Trow's case rested on the argument that the most widely accepted view among social scientists is that different kinds of information about man and society are best gathered in different ways, and that the research problem under investigation properly dictates the methods of investigation.

> Every cobbler [he wrote] thinks leather is the only thing. Most social scientists, including the present writer, have their favourite research methods with which they are familiar and have some skill in using. And I suspect we mostly choose to investigate problems that seem vulnerable to attack through these methods. But we should at least try to be less parochial than cobblers. Let us be done with the arguments of participant observation *versus* interviewing – as we have largely dispensed with the arguments for psychology *versus* sociology – and get on with the business of attacking our problems with the widest array of conceptual and methodological tools that we possess and they demand.

The sociologist's *problem* is therefore clearly of central importance to the question of how choices between different research strategies are made. A clarification of the term 'problem' is therefore required, and then an examination of how problems and methods, and problems and theories, interrelate, since the three form a trinity at the heart of the sociological enterprise.

The Nature of Sociological Problems

Theory and method do not co-exist in the abstract, in a vacuum. They are brought together and tied together by a commitment to tackle a certain sociological problem. What then *is* a problem? As the quotation from Trow suggests, it is something of a cliché of informal exchanges among fellow social researchers that their work is centred on 'problems', and theories and methods are selected as appropriate to the problem under investigation. But there exist very few specifications of what this formulation actually means. What are its implications for the selection of areas and topics of study? What are its consequences for the level, range and cumulative power of theoretical propositions? What are its corrolaries so far as choice of research strategy and research technique are concerned? What follows seeks to explore, in a preliminary and very general way, some aspects of this confusion. In so far as theory and method are brought together through a focus on 'problems', the discussion is pertinent to the wider issues of the relationship between sociological theory and empirical research.

One influential account of what is meant by a 'problem' is provided by R. Dahrendorf [1958, 1968]. What matters is that sociologists should regain a sense of puzzlement about the world. Many sociologists, Dahrendorf argues, have lost the simple impulse of curiosity, the desire to solve riddles of experience, the concern with problems. At the beginning of every sociological investigation there has to be a fact or set of facts which is puzzling to the investigator; for example, that children of businessmen prefer professional to business occupations; or that there is a higher incidence of suicide among upwardly mobile persons than among others; or that left-wing parties in predominantly Catholic countries of Europe seem unable to get more than 30 per cent of the popular vote. All these sets of facts invite the question: why? Problems require explanations; explanations require assumptions and hypotheses; hypotheses require testing by further facts; testing often generates new problems.

As a further elaboration of this theme, Dahrendorf distinguishes ([1968] Ch. 10) between *questions* and *problems*. Questions are of our own making, we can answer them if we like, they are timeless. Problems are those issues with which life confronts us, they are timebound, it is a condition of our existence that we solve problems. All the great theories of social science, in this view, were stimulated by problems.

The objections to this formulation are twofold. Although the question/problem distinction is suggestive, it is not clear to what extent the work of classic social theorists could be said necessarily to be stimulated by problems rather than questions. Some were all of the time and all were part of the time. But is it the case that Weber's analysis of the world religions, Simmel's work on forms of sociability or Durkheim's study of the elementary forms of the religious life were produced to solve problems requiring solution as a condition of existence? More generally, puzzlement about the world may be a necessary but it is not a sufficient condition for granting a particular conundrum problematic status. There are different kinds of puzzlement, and the relationship between questions or problems and research is not entirely clear-cut.

Indeed R. K. Merton [1959], in his paper 'Notes on Problem-finding in Sociology' in *Sociology Today*, argues that Dahrendorf's formulation is altogether too simple. It is not just a matter of adding 'why?' to a set of facts, because not every question of this kind involves a scientific problem. Problem-finding in sociology is more complex.

A justification for a 'why?' question having problematic status must be put forward to the 'court of social scientific opinion'. This is the way in which questions are weeded out and the flow of scientifically trivial questions is curbed. It is very difficult to state exact criteria, but sociologists do this all the time when teachers decide what to teach, investigators decide what to research, scholars referee papers for journals, editors of journals decide what to publish and so on.

Merton discerns two main justifications for according a 'why?' question the status of a problem. First, idle curiosity, where knowledge is a self-contained end in its own right. Possible practical consequences of increasing knowledge are not denied, but they are ignored. Second, practical curiosity, where the case for a 'why?' question is that its answer will help men to achieve values other than knowledge itself – values of health, comfort, safety, efficiency, justice, etc. Again a justification in terms of practical curiosity does not rule out a problem throwing important light on sociological questions pertaining to pure knowledge. A theoretical rationale and a practical rationale for a sociological question may be, and indeed often are, quite consistent. On the other hand in some situations emphasis on one may hinder the other.

The main limitation of this perceptive account is that the discussion of idle and practical curiosity is abstracted from its social context. In what situations did idle or practical curiosity develop? In which historical periods did they complement or conflict with each other? The relationship of sociological problem formation to other movements of thought is not explored. How far can one abstract the development of a discipline from the social milieu in which it exists?

A more refined analysis of different types of problem in social science has been provided by Scott Greer [1969]. Greer, albeit somewhat sketchily, distinguishes three kinds of problem that have lain behind much sociological work. First, and most obviously, sociologists have been concerned with *policy problems*. These are problems of everyday life in society, of social concern and importance in a direct sense. The urge to inquire into such problems very often arises from the impulse to bring social reality closer into accord with certain sets of values. For example, the study of the incidence of poverty in Britain, from Charles Booth to Peter Townsend, has been concerned both with the extent and distribution of low incomes in the population, and with practical measures which might be taken to alleviate the condition of those with such low incomes. In the United States the social indicators movement which W. F. Ogburn initiated in the 1920s had a similar objective of providing background information on the basis of which action could be taken (cf. Carley [1981] pp. 1–21).

At the same time sociologists who are concerned with policy problems have become involved in their theoretical explanation. From the publication in 1918 of *The Polish Peasant in Europe and America* onwards, the sociology of social policy has had a pronounced theoretical bent.

A second source of sociological problems of a different order has lain in the *philosophy of history* or *social philosophy*. Here are to be found problems of great range and scope, many of them as old as human history. The contents of a book like Robert Nisbet's *The Sociological Tradition* [1967] provides a good example of the kinds of concepts and theories to which this source has given rise: community, authority, status, the sacred, alienation. 'Community' provides a good example both of the fruitfulness of this kind of problem formulation and of the awkward dilemmas for empirical work which it poses. One of the perennial difficulties for those working in the area of community studies is the penumbra of evaluation which surrounds the central concept in the field. Is the analysis of *community* more concerned with establishing the conditions under which *Gemeinschaft* will persist, or with the delineation of particular empirical instances of local social interaction? What is one explaining in pointing to the persistence of *Gemeinschaft*-based relations in the modern world? (cf. Bell and Newby [1972]). A different example of the influence of the philosophy of history upon sociology is the Marxist tradition which has provided a powerful stimulus to the study of the nature of social stratification and differentiation, the relations between social classes, the nature of alienation, and the moving forces of social change (cf. Bottomore [1975]).

A third source of sociological problems has been intrinsic in the discipline itself, arising out of questions posed by previous pieces of sociological work. Much debate in the philosophy of social science centres around the question of whether the social sciences are cumulative in the new knowledge which they produce. Whether or not sociology cumulates knowledge in the way that physics does (and the evidence supporting such a view is not very strong), there is undoubtedly *some* cumulative effect within the discipline which is apparent in conflicts between existing theories, conflicts between empirical findings and theoretical propositions, and gaps in empirical support for particular sets of hypotheses. A classic example of such an issue is the Weberian debate over the reasons for the development of capitalism in Western Europe, and why it had developed there when it was not developed by the ancient civilisations of India or China. Notably Weber's argument in *The Protestant Ethic and the Spirit of Capitalism* – that there was a necessary relationship between a particular kind of Protestant ethic and the spirit of capitalist enterprise – has provoked debate and further research of great intrinsic importance to sociologists and economic and social historians.

Greer emphasises that over a period of time there is a tendency for public problems to lead on to policy problems and these in turn to become scientific problems.

> One may postulate a natural history of social science specialities. Out of interest couched in the folk frame of reference develops a public problem; defined as capable of solution, it becomes a policy problem. Then, as systematic inquiry is stimulated, it is subjected to the control of the research cycle, moving toward the status of an intrinsically scientific problem. The same is true of problems generated by social philosophy. While, as Merton has

suggested, American social scientists have been more stimulated by policy problems and European scholars by those derived from the philosophy of history, both kinds lead to the same end: the basic research problem, the search for structure and changes in structure, whose results have caught the attention of practical men or philosophers, leading them to identify 'problems'.

The virtue of Greer's formulation of the nature of 'problems' is that it gives due weight to the independent influence of social philosophy and the philosophy of history as well as to sources in policy and scientific domains. And it incorporates a preliminary attempt to locate socially the changing nature of problem-definition in western social science. It is only a very rough outline, but it seems one of the more cogent accounts of the sources of 'problems' to have been produced to date.

The Interrelation of Problems, Theories and Methods

The range of problem sources is thus very wide, emphasising the importance of the underlying theoretical impulses to empirical inquiry and the widely divergent reasons which lead people to do sociological research. To identify a problem, however, is only the initial step. A problem is a problem is a problem. What are we to do with it? What operations are involved in bringing theory and method to bear upon a problem? How do theory and method relate to each other in the process? What are the criteria for deciding which theories, and which methods, are appropriate to a particular problem? This is the nub of the puzzlement created by the conventional wisdom which insists that problems, theories and methods are related to each other.

Several different answers have been proposed. The first, shown in Figure 6, is that methods are properly conceived of as tools which one uses to sort out which particular set of theoretical ideas most adequately explains the problem one is concerned with. Methods are the essentially unproblematical centre-piece or linchpin of inquiry. In this formal account methods make the wheel of social science go round.

The inadequacy of this formulation lies in its lack of guidance as to *which* methods to employ to establish the connections. Although

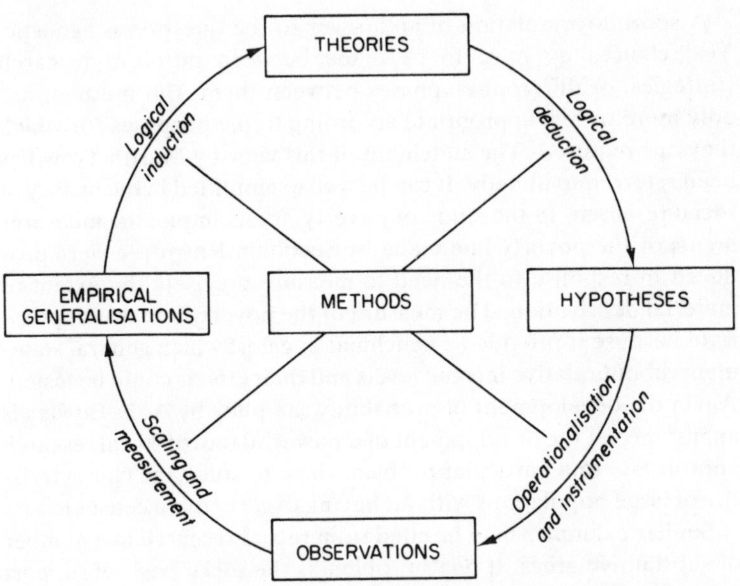

FIGURE 6 *The components and process of scientific sociology (after Wallace [1969] p. ix)*

rightly emphasising systematic procedures as a necessary condition for regarding sociology as an activity the results of which are open to the scrutiny of others, it does not identify what manner of sampling, which strategies of data collection or what modes of analysis to employ. Nor does it indicate whether or not there are any significant connections between *theory* and methods, treating each in a formal manner confined to its own particular box or boxes. This point is further discussed below.

The discussion of research in terms of a model of stages also tends to treat methods as unproblematical. The primary emphasis is upon initial research design and sampling, followed by progression to succeeding stages. Implicitly the model is that of a large-scale survey, with well codified procedures and a framework in which the choice of strategy is already predetermined, although a number of consequent decisions about choice of particular techniques will have to be taken. Theory is fed in at the beginning and comes out confirmed or falsified at the end. Studying methods is essentially a matter of knowing how to handle to different stages of research.

A second formulation of an answer to the question is agnostic. Yes, choices do have to be made between different research strategies, or different emphases between them. But methods are only more or less appropriate according to the purposes for which they are required. The statement of this view by Martin Trow has been referred to already. It can be well exemplified in the history of social research. In the study of poverty, for example, the measurements of the poverty line made by Seebohm Rowntree were produced in response to the need to measure precisely the extent of material deprivation. The measure of the poverty line was appropriate because it provided a benchmark against which general statements about relative income levels and their effects could be tested. Again the development of probability sampling by A. L. Bowley is an instance of the development of a powerful tool of social research appropriate to a particular problem (how to study the characteristics of large populations without having to carry out a census).

Similar examples may be cited from recent research in a number of substantive areas. If one's problem is the social basis of support for particular political parties, extensive social survey research is likely to be suitable approach, and intensive case studies rather ineffective (cf. Butler and Stokes [1969]). Conversely if one's problem is the nature of informal relationships within formal organisations, and the nature of cliques and in-groups, intensive study using participant observation would be likely to be the most effective way of gaining useful knowledge and a social survey relatively unproductive (cf. Dalton [1959, 1964]). Many problems require a combination of strategies. In the study of trade-union government in *Union Democracy* (referred to in the further reading for Part 2) a social survey formed only part of the inquiry, and Lipset and his co-workers also drew on historical sources dealing with the union, records held by the union bureaucracy, and intensive interviewing of an open-ended kind with union leaders. In *Patterns of Industrial Bureaucracy* (referred to in the further reading for Part 5) Gouldner and his team used both a period of extended field-work in the gypsum plant and relatively systematised interview schedules to talk to underground miners and surface workers. In a well-known British community study of Banbury by Margaret Stacey [1960], intensive participant observation by three research workers living in the town was supplemented by analysis of records, intensive interviewing, and a sample survey of one in five of the local population.

Thus different strategies are often combined in particular studies. How this is done depends on the nature of the problem.

Yet there do seem to be limits to the usefulness of such a formulation. In the study of poverty, for example, both survey research and very detailed personal accounts gathered by the use of intensive strategies are available. What in this instance is appropriate to what? Is the quantitative survey data the real thing and the life histories just adding a touch of colour? Or do the intensive studies attempt a theoretical explanation of the phenomenon, while the survey provides mainly descriptive material? Moreover in the attempt to identify the *causes* of poverty is there a connection between the type of account produced and the kinds of methods used to establish the validity of that account? Valentine's critique [1968] of theories of the culture of poverty in general, and the work of Oscar Lewis in particular [1961, 1967], suggests not so much agnosticism about the relationship between methods and problems as that there may be a considerable degree of fit between the use of particular strategies and the adoption of particular theoretical stances.

This is borne out by certain work in other substantive areas. J. D. Douglas's work on *The Social Meanings of Suicide* provides an almost total contrast to Durkheim's *Suicide* in terms of both research strategy and initial general methodological standpoint (see further reading for Part 3). Less striking but significant differences are provided by studies of delinquency (Hirschi [1969]; Becker [1963]); of differential educational achievement (J. W. B. Douglas [1964]; Hargreaves [1970]); of formal organisations (Dalton [1959]; Blau and Schoenherr [1971]; and of the student experience in medical school (Merton *et al.* [1957]; Becker *et al.* [1961]). There appears to be more to choice of strategy than simply suitability to the problem being investigated.

This is underlined when a third view is considered, that theory determines or strongly influences method. The theoretical formulation and specification of a problem tends to determine the method which is used to investigate it; hence the discussion of methods of social research has no independent significance. The view derives some support from problems whose origin lies in the philosophy of history, but it is implicit in much sociological inquiry. The reason for this rests in the complexity of theoretical and empirical constructs which sociologists use to make sense of the world. Concepts like community, bureaucratisation, social cohesion and class consciousness pose difficult problems for making the transition from theoretical statement to research measurement. (For an example see Bulmer (ed.) [1975]). Even empirically derived concepts like crime, mental illness, witchcraft or the Mafia are not without significant theoretical overtones.

Much effort in empirical social research has been devoted to devising *indicators* of theoretical concepts; the paper by Paul Lazarsfeld on evidence and inference in Part 2 provides a classic example of this procedure in survey research. The measurement of key empirically derived variables such as occupation, income, housing, religion and locality have been usefully reviewed in British symposia edited by Stacey [1969], Gittus [1972] and Burgess (ed.) [1984]. The relation between concepts and indicators is further discussed in Part 1 and in Chapter 15.

Yet the difficulties remain substantial. Symbolic interactionist critics such as Blumer [1956] question whether social phenomena can be reduced to variables in the standard way practised by survey researchers. Critics who argue from a standpoint nearer to pure theory hold that certain constructs do not lend themselves to empirical investigation, an example being the concept of *alienation*. Both J. Horton [1964] and S. M. Lukes [1967] have criticised attempts to develop this strand in social and political thought through empirical research. Attempts by several social scientists (notably Blauner [1964]) to establish operational definitions of alienation and determine its extent among particular groups have been criticised as conceptually unclear or operationally suspect or both. Those who write about research methods are inclined to neglect the possibility that there may be discontinuities as well as continuities between theory and method, extreme criticisms being couched in the spirit of e. e. cummings:

> . . . who cares if some one-eyed son of a bitch
> invents an instrument to measure spring with.

If some theorists doubt whether methods have their own independent status, in a different formulation the methodologists assert their own superiority: method determines or tends to determine theory and even the problem selected for study. Scientific method, not theory, is the foundation of inquiry. The argument that the tail should not wag the dog may seem surprising. There can be few disciplines where the technical apparatus *determines* the conduct of inquiry. Methods are a necessary, but not a sufficient, condition for intellectual advance. Why should sociology (or some sociologists) claim to be different?

One reason may be the relative sparsity of sociological studies of particular phenomena, and hence the importance invested in those studies which are carried out and published. If particular combinations of theory and method are seen to be fruitful, and if a method produces convincing findings, the method may be recognised as valid. It then may become a model for future investigations of the same topic. American studies of community power, for example, attempting to answer such questions about local political control as 'Who runs this town?' were for some years polarised between two different theoretical schools, the elitist and the pluralist. Elitist accounts (such as that of Floyd Hunter [1953]) argued that local social elites should be analysed as part of a wider system of social stratification. The methods they used to establish this were 'reputational' – i.e. asking people (or key people) who they thought held positions of power in the community. In this way the local elite was identified. On the other hand pluralist accounts (such as those of Polsby [1963], Dahl [1964] and others) emphasised the need to break down the original question into at least three parts (who participates? who gains and loses? who prevails in decision-making?) and to attempt to answer such questions by means of the analysis of particular *issues* and *decisions* within the community. The elitist approach, based on reputational methods, produced a pyramidal analysis of local power structures. The pluralist approach, based on decision analysis, produced an account in terms of the factional/coalitional/amorphous nature of local community power. The different theoretical interpretations are at least in part the product of differing research methods used.

A second attraction of the doctrine derives from the power and elegance with which particular frameworks can be used to array data. The Oxford social mobility study for example (Hope [1972]) starts from the idea that individuals and collectivities exist in a 'stratification space' in which they lie at certain distances from each other along certain dimensions. The research seeks to use this framework, up to then little more than a series of images, as a theory-neutral way of measuring the nature and extent of social mobility. 'If technique is to be an adequate servant of sociology [it is argued], then the needs of the various analytic methods must be clearly recognised and allowed for in the collection and organisation of data.' Techniques may be used to answer theoretical problems, but

> in order to overcome the ever-present danger that technical limitations will set bounds to the substantive questions which we might pose and, further, in order to exploit the power of analytic processes to sharpen and clarify our theorising, we have sought to bend the analytic methods to our purposes and to use them as a resource for elaborating and systematising our thinking about social stratification . . . One of the failures of the sociology of stratification has been its refusal to push its imagery to its logical conclusion. Sorokin, for instance, makes considerable play with images of social distance, and the height, gradation and profile of occupational stratification. Writing his first edition of *Social Mobility* half a century ago, he may be forgiven for not realising the analytical potential of his analogies. It is time to take them quite literally to clarify the problems, if not plan the collection of data, by geometrical explication (Hope [1972] pp. 2, 6).

A further and probably dominant reason for this standpoint is the growth of research technology. Lewis Coser in Chap. 18 points out that American graduate schools 'tend to produce young sociologists with superior research skills but with a trained incapacity to think in theoretically-innovative ways'. This is due to the growth of advanced techniques for the analysis of quantitative data, such as regression and path analysis, which have moved the frontiers of quantitative methodology well beyond the tabular procedures described in this book (cf. Mullins [1975]). The difficulty, as Coser argues, is that methods become the independent and substantive issues the dependent variable. 'Not only the choice of technique but even the choice of problem tends to be determined by what is quick and easy rather than by theoretical considerations or an evaluation of the questions that are raised. Moreover, the uses of a sophisticated technological and methodological apparatus gives assurance, but often deceptive assurance, to the researcher'.

'The hypertrophy of method at the expense of substantive theory' is demonstrated by other tendencies. Coser particularly criticises also ethnomethodology for its exclusive insistence upon one particular dimension of reality and one particular mode of analysis, communicated through particularistic codes which effectively restrict access to all but insiders. He argues that preoccupation with method has led to the neglect of significance and substance. Neither advanced quantitative techniques nor esoteric qualitative ones provide 'substantive enlightenment . . . about the social structures in which we are enmeshed and which largely condition the course of our lives'. Sociology will not advance if it degenerates into 'congeries of rival sects and specialist researchers'.

The second, third and fourth views so far identified – that methods are chosen as appropriate to problems, that theory determines research strategy, and that research strategy determines theory – all have a certain contingent plausibility. What is lacking, however, is any convincing account of the relationship between problems and theories and *general* methodology (as defined at the outset). A fifth view of the sociological trinity is therefore that the sociologist's choice of methods is influenced by the way in which he conceptualises social reality, and the epistemological principles which underline those conceptions. These conceptualisations are in turn linked to his or her theoretical standpoint. Therefore theory and general methodology interrelate. General methodology, in turn, tends to determine research strategy.

A number of contrasting instances of this kind of pattern of influence through general methodology may be cited. These include explanations couched in terms of the social structural determinants of action, as opposed to the interpretative understanding of its subjectively meaningful nature; system and action types of explanation (Dawe [1970]); holist and individualist approaches (O'Neill [1973]); synchronic as against diachronic forms of explanation, and so on. In relation to research procedure, Denzin [1970] has stated the argument as follows. Research methods represent lines of action toward the empirical word, and the use of particular strategies implies different lines of action. Each research method reveals peculiar elements of symbolic reality. Social surveys for example dictate a stance toward the invariant and stable features of social reality, while participant observation assumes a reality continually in change and flux. The meanings attached to the interpretation of reality by sociologists are never likely to be totally in agreement. Methods are rather like a kaleidoscope; depending on how they are approached, held and acted toward, different observations will be revealed. Fundamental elements of symbolic interaction are embedded in the act of sociology itself.

What Denzin does not bring out adequately is the degree of fit (which varies) between different general methodological positions, and the adoption of particular research strategies. The degree of fit between Durkheim's *Rules* and *Suicide* and modern survey research has been emphasised by Selvin in a well-known article [1965b]. The partnership between Merton and Lazarsfeld at Columbia University represented a link between a particular theoretical stance and a particular style of research. Less well recognised but equally strong has been the link between Chicago symbolic-interactionism and research strategies based on extended fieldwork.

The diversity and multiplicity of methods available to the sociologist – and the variety of possible interrelationships between theory and method – reflect the complexity of the social world, the difficulty which the sociologist has in coming to grips with it conceptually and empirically, and to a certain extent different general methodological perspectives upon it. The insoluble nature of the quest for a single, unified, paradigmatic sociological method is a consequence of this. Some of the strains of contemporary sociology arise from the tensions which this can produce, particularly perhaps between the desire to be technically competent on the one hand and at the same time philosophically sophisticated on the other. The research strategies consonant with the principles enunciated in Durkheim's *The Rules of Sociological Method* are familiar and well codified. But which strategies (if any) are most consonant with the methodological ideas expressed by Max Weber in the first chapter of *Wirtschaft und Gesellschaft*? That the answer is less clear-cut is both important and indicative. Choice of methods, as R. H. Turner ([1967] p. xxi) has hinted, may be influenced by the subjective appeal which they have. 'A scholar's choice of methods depends upon the character of the findings he finds most useful or intuitively most satisfying.'

Triangulation

The drawing of distinctions between different styles of research runs the danger, already emphasised, of reifying the distinction between them and implying that each may be a self-contained and alternative method of social inquiry. This is the opposite of the true state of affairs. Different styles of research complement each other, and can fruitfully be used in conjunction with one another.

One conclusion to be drawn from the discussion so far is that open-mindedness about selection of research strategy in a particular inquiry is of great importance. Michael Anderson brings this out very clearly in discussing both quantitative and descriptive data sources in Chapter 10. Coser in Chapter 18 makes a similar point: 'Sociology is not advanced enough solely to rely on precisely measured variables. Qualitative observations of a small universe can provide theoretical leads that may at a later stage become amenable to more refined statistical treatment'. The dangers of technological complexity have been noted by Heise (in Costner (ed.) [1974] p. 2), who urges sociologists to 'avoid the development of a statistical sub-discipline asymptomically insulated from the realities of small-sample research in real situations'.

Another conclusion is the need to articulate the grounds on which choices are made between different strategies. It is clear that different strategies imply giving different weights to the criteria of representativeness, reliability and validity. The great strength of social-survey research and official statistics is in terms of the coverage of a population either completely in a census or within calculable margins of sampling error in a sample census or a survey using random sampling. Interpretative procedures tend to be weak in this respect, an argument frequently used against case studies.

Some years ago Zelditch [1962] demonstrated that there were different routes to obtaining different types of information. Frequency distribution might be best obtained by enumerators and samples, but incidents and histories were more illuminatingly studied by direct observation, and institutionalised norms and statuses by interviewing informants. There was no one 'best' method, and each method had its strengths and weaknesses. Different styles of research are not concretely different types of study, but analytically different aspects of a common mode of inquiry, social research.

More recently, Sieber has emphasised the limitations of treating different styles of research as alternatives. They can and frequently are combined within a single study.

> The integration of research techniques within a single project opens up enormous opportunities for mutual advantage in each of the three major phases – design, data collection and analysis. These mutual benefits are not merely quantitative . . . but qualitative as well – one could almost say that a new style of research is born of the marriage of survey and fieldwork methodologies (Sieber [1973]).

The value of 'methodological marriages' (Warwick [1983]) is apparent, not least because the weaknesses of one style may be balanced against the strengths of another style.

The reliability of particular research techniques and measuring instruments – the extent to which they yield a consistent result when used on more than one occasion or by different people – has also been studied closely. A great deal of work, particularly on subjects like attitude measurement, has been devoted to improving the reliability of research techniques and one of the advantages of survey research is that its tools have been demonstrated to be reliable to a far greater extent than those involved in other types of research.

However, reliability alone is not sufficient. No matter how good a result is achieved in terms of consistency, this does not affect whether a technique taps the *theoretical* dimensions specified in the problem. The *validity* of knowledge produced by different means – the extent to which empirical research yields knowledge about the construct which it purports to depict – is less easily determined yet repays attention. A philosophical and epistemological rather than simply a technical problem, validity is inescapable. LaPiere's classic study [1934] of attitudes in relation to action was one of the first pieces of methodological research which showed the kinds of difficulties and contradictions with which sociologists may be faced. In his study LaPiere found an almost total contradiction between observed behaviour in hotels and restaurants towards a Chinese couple with whom LaPiere travelled the United States, and expressed attitudes towards receiving Chinese at the same hotels and restaurants elicited subsequently by means of a mail questionnaire.

Later research has examined both the problem of the relation between attitudes and behaviour and the validity of the results of questionnaire and interview research. The findings of the latter have shown the extent to which the results of research can, within limits, vary according to the attributes of interviewer and respondent and their interaction. Race, age, sex, social status, religion and personality have all been shown to influence the pattern of responses in social surveys (Hyman [1954]; Kahn and Cannell [1957]; Phillips [1971]). Social psychological research by Friedman [1967] and Rosenthal [1966] has shown how the expectations of the researcher may quite unintentionally affect the results of laboratory experiments using human subjects. Deutscher [1972, 1973] has argued that these effects are to be expected since people will tend to adjust their sentiments and acts to those of others in the same situation. The chapter by Deutscher in Part 5 raises the question of the extent to which linguistic comparability can be assumed in sociological inquiry. Are there 'universes of meaning' within which members share a common medium of discourse? Or are there parts of a society with their own languages and understandings where the sociologist who assumes linguistic comparability may become badly unstuck?

Evidence about the validity of data collected by interviews and questionnaires, cross-checked against other data, is inconclusive. Verbal reports of attributes or behaviour show a fairly high degree of consistency with other evidence in some cases (for example, voting) but much lower in others (for example, self-reporting of deviant behaviour (Phillips [1971]; Nettler [1974])). Intervening variables of importance include the time elapsed, nature of the information and the circumstances in which it is collected. A considered judgement turns crucially on what degree of inconsistency is acceptable. A most respected model of advanced methodology, for example Blau and Duncan [1968], reveals in an appendix that a pilot study of data validity comparing survey data on recall of parental occupation with the same information in the census produced only a 70 per cent consistent response. Further research is clearly required into the validity of different types of data, a subject on which historians (as Anderson's paper suggests) have much of value to contribute in view of their continual experience of dealing with imperfect, intractable and potentially invalid sources.

The debate over the value of official statistics, joined in Chapter 7, also shows the importance of testing through methodological research the validity as well as the reliability of data gathered in different ways. In that area sociologists have been too ready to impute invalidity, and to abandon certain types of data, inappropriately, on *a priori* grounds.

The organisation of the remainder of the book is designed to bring out the interplay of problems, theories and methods in the context of the choices which may be made between different research strategies. Several papers consider questions about the validity of data, notably Webb *et al.* in Part 3 on unobtrusive measures and Benney and Hughes and Deutscher in Part 5 on interpretative procedures, in addition to Anderson already mentioned. However, the aim of this collection is not to suggest that one or other strategy is superior. Four distinctive types of research are emphasised because such differences in style do exist in the way that research is carried out. The choice between them is resolved, however, not by plumping for one in particular, but by combining different strategies and techniques in different ways – by triangulating.

This odd term, first propounded by Campbell and Fiske [1959] and made more widely known by Webb (Webb *et al.*, [1966]), refers to the attempt to strengthen the validity of empirical evidence in social science by reliance on more than one approach. When a hypothesis can survive the confrontation of a series of complementary methods of testing, it contains a degree of validity unattainable by a hypothesis tested with the more constricted framework of a single method. J. Galtung also enters a plea for 'a norm of research that gives low degrees of confirmation to propositions confirmed for one type of data collection only, and a much higher degree of confirmation when multi-dimensional approaches to the data problem are made use of ([1967] p. 450).

Denzin [1970] further develops these arguments for methodological triangulation, whose basic feature is the combination of two or more different research strategies in the study of the same empirical units. Such an approach complements one in terms of the interrelationships of problems, theories and methods. For in answer to the question of which of several available strategies will be best for a particular research problem, the answer is that there is no best method either in general or for a particular problem (cf. Bulmer [1972]). All methods have their strengths and weaknesses. Better to ask which *combination* of strategies will be most adequate and most fruitful.

The test of successful triangulation lies in the value of the explanations produced in a particular piece of research. Research involves engagement with the empirical world, not reliance on a self-contained rationalism. Coser's critique of certain trends in

American sociology in the last chapter, which refers to 'congeries of rival sects' echoes the comments of Bernstein ([1973] p. 154) on the state of the sociology of education in Britain.

> In a subject where theories and methods are weak, intellectual shifts are likely to arise out of the conflict between *approaches* rather than conflicts between explanations, for by definition most explanations will be weak and often non-comparable, because they are approach-specific. The weakness of the explanation is likely to be attributed to the approach, which is analysed in terms of its ideological stance. Once the ideological stance is exposed then all the work may be written off. Every new approach becomes a social movement or sect which immediately defines the nature of the subject by redefining what is admitted, and what is beyond the pale, so that with every new approach the subject starts almost from scratch.

Of course research and inquiry suffer. Evidence for the resulting problems in British sociology is contained in Bulmer and Burgess (eds) [1981].

It is ironic that sociology has moved so far in the direction of diversity of approaches that it has weakened its capacity to confront different types of explanation. Sociologists are concerned with the *understanding* and *explanation* of social phenomena, and the capacity to provide satisfactory explanations of sociological problems provides a touchstone for the evaluation of the fruitfulness of particular combinations of problem, theory and method. Different analyses of the same or similar problems can be confronted with one another; the same or similar problems can be investigated in the same inquiry using different methods. Different analyses of the same phenomena can be confronted with one another. In the absence of a sociological paradigm, conflicting perspectives may be evaluated from the point of view of their capacity to explain.

Du choc des opinions
Jaillit la vérité

Part One

Sociological Theory in Empirical Research

1 Facts, Concepts, Theories and Problems

Martin Bulmer

Perception without conception is blind; conception without perception is empty (I. Kant).

Sociology is often a puzzle to those who come into contact with it for the first time. What are its defining characteristics? To some, particularly in Britain, sociology is identified with social investigation. Charles Booth, Seebohm Rowntree and other figures in the Pantheon, rather than Herbert Spencer or L. T. Hobhouse, are seen as having established the subject and started a distinctive indigenous tradition (cf. Bulmer [1985]). To others sociology appears primarily as a theoretical or philosophical concern dealing with highly abstract and difficult concepts and propositions, using special (often obscure) language and addressing a narrow audience of fellow-professionals.

Neither view is satisfactory not accurate. The accumulation of social facts in twentieth-century industrial society is a major undertaking. Sociography, social surveys and social arithmetic flourish, often with powerful State backing. Most of those who collect such data are (in Britain at least) not socialists, and do not regard themselves as sociologists but rather as social statisticians, demographers, social policy-makers or social researchers without a particular disciplinary adherence. *Sociology* on the other hand is both, at one and the same time an empirical and a *theoretical* discipline. Sociological work represents an attempt to bring theory and data together in a fruitful conjunction. What is meant by those who insist that sociology is both a theoretical and empirical activity at one and the same time? The theme runs through sociological writing of the past generation to a remarkable extent; C. Wright Mill's attack on both 'abstracted empiricism' and 'grand theory' is perhaps the best known. Can the striving to study the social world empirically – to find out what is going on 'out there', to measure social phenomena, to get inside social situations not usually open to outsiders, to discover *regularities* in social affairs – be reconciled with an adequate theoretical account which seeks to understand and explain the phenomena under consideration? The materials presented in this book are intended to suggest that it can, and how it can, and to convey a sense of what theoretically informed research and inquiry involve.

As a first step the role of theory has to be clearly established. Empiricism – the doctrine that factual knowledge alone is enough for social understanding – is *not* enough, plausible though the claims of its proponents may be. A mode of social inquiry which produces social facts bereft of theory may be worth while in a number of respects – particularly for policy-making in government – but lacks direction. Conversely, theory alone is empty. The pitfalls of an excessive rationalism – the development of *a priori* mental constructs into self-contained intellectual systems without any necessary empirical reference – are that the crucial test of the usefulness and correctness of a theory which empirical data provide is lacking (Bierstedt [1949]).

> As an epistemological doctrine empiricism has nowhere received the philosophic support which would justify its exclusive use in the social sciences. The ultimate logical consequences of a pure empiricism are either Berkeleian idealism or solipsism. It can be demonstrated on purely logical grounds that observation and experiment are never sufficient for the construction of generalisations, laws, and principals in any of the sciences, except in cases where the universe of data is so limited as to allow for a complete induction. . . . The more a piece of sociological investigation resembles a collection of facts, no matter how comprehensive,

> complete and accurate they might happen to be, the less is its scientific significance. . . . A survey or a census, no matter what its intrinsic merit or utility, does not constitute or contribute to a science expect in its function as a laboratory for testing the tools of research and as a source of data upon which to construct rational scientific theory. *The Polish Peasant in Europe and America* is a sociological classic not because of what it tells us about Polish immigrants but because of what it tells us about human social behaviour. Few contemporary sociologists are interested in the Polish peasant; all are interested in *The Polish Peasant* (Bierstedt [1949]).

Empiricism – the doctrine that empirical data *alone* are a sufficient condition for knowledge about society – is probably now on the defensive. Particularly powerful attacks upon it by philosoph of science have demonstrated its inadequacy, and the necessity for problems and hypotheses to be an integral part of social inquiry (Popper [1957, 1972]; Nagel [1961]; Brown [1963]). Rationalism, to the extent that it involves disinterest in or indifference to empirical evidence, probably has a wider appeal currently. The scope and generality or rationalist propositions have a seductive appeal, yet an attachment to theory divorced from empirical inquiry becomes ultimately solipsistic. As Herbert Blumer [1954] has aptly put it,

> contemporary social theory shows grave shortcomings. Its divorce from the empirical world is glaring. To a preponderant extent, it is compartmentised into a world of its own, inside of which it feeds on itself. . . . For the most part it has its own literature. . . . When applied to the empirical world, social theory is primarily an interpretation which orders the world into its mould, not a studious cultivation of empirical facts to see if the theory fits. In terms both of origin and use, social theory seems in general not to be geared into its empirical world.

Sociologists show little inclination to forget the founding fathers and continue to draw upon them extensively for theoretical inspiration (for three examples cf. Nisbet [1967], Giddens [1971] and Poggi [1972]). Yet the founding fathers – Marx, Weber and Durkheim in particular – were far from being committed to a non-empirical rationalism. Indeed both their own work and that of their successors has been concerned to explore particular problems by means of empirical inquiry – Marx on the structure of capitalist society, Weber on the world religions, Durkheim on suicide, for example. How can the link to the classics be continued, and yet the thrust of empirical inquiry be maintained? A variety of approaches has been adopted, including an emphasis on deductive theory-construction (Zetterberg [1965]; Stinchcombe [1968]; Dubin [1969]); the generation of formal theory from particular case studies (Glaser and Strauss [1967]); and the continuing exploration of theoretical ideas derived from the classics. It is this last strand which is often overlooked. Contemporary sociology is still profoundly influenced, often in subtle and indirect ways, by the theoretical inheritance it carries with it; this is true of substantive empirical research and its methodology despite appearances to the contrary. For instance the influence of George Simmel on American sociology was wide-ranging and productive of a great deal of empirical research (cf. Levine *et al.* [1976]). Much of the effect was indirect, through graduate study and the experience of sociologists such as Robert Park who had themselves studied in Germany, but it left its mark. Traces of the ideas of Simmel and of Marx, Weber and Durkheim are particularly evident in the chapters by Goldthorpe, Benney and Hughes, Baldamus and Coser. If sociologists hesitate to forget their founders it is because their influence is still strongly felt in problem-formulation.

From Durkheim onwards, sociologists have wrestled with these difficulties. One particular influential view has enjoyed a certain vogue. The argument that sociology will progress by focusing upon 'stepping stones into the middle distance' or 'theories of the middle range' has been widely advocated, notably by T. H. Marshall [1963] and R. K. Merton [1957]. Marshall's view, first adumbrated in 1946, was that sociology stood at a crossroads. Which way was to be taken?

> I do not recommend the way to the stars; sociologists should not expend all their energies climbing in search of vast generalizations, universal laws, and a total comprehension of human society as such. They are more likely to get there in the end if they don't try to get there now. Nor do I recommend the way into the sands of whirling facts which blow into the eyes and ears until nothing can be clearly seen or heard. But there is a middle way which runs

> over firm ground. It leads into a country whose features are neither Gargantuan nor Lilliputian where sociology can choose units of study of a manageable size – not society, progress, morals and civilization, but specific social structures in which the basic process and functions have determined meanings. . . . The search for what I have called stepping stones in the middle distance has been pursued by many of those who have embarked upon sociological inquiry. . . . Durkheim. . . . Max Weber . . . , Karl Mannheim (Marshall [1963] pp. 22–3).

Robert Merton's 'theories of the middle range' had a similar objective in view.

> One major task today is to develop special theories applicable to limited ranges of data – theories, for example, of class dynamics, of conflicting group pressures, of the flow of power and the direction of interpersonal influence – rather than to seek at once the 'integrated' conceptual structure adequate to derive all these and other theories. The sociological theorist *exclusively* committed to the exploration of high abstractions runs the risk that, as with modern decor, the furniture of his mind will be sparse, bare and uncomfortable (Merton [1957] p. 9).

In Merton's case there is the added implication that in order to become a mature science sociology has to reach beyond and forget its founding fathers in order to establish a coherent and integrated body of contemporary theory. The suggestion has several merits and has commended itself to many of those trying to bring about a meeting of the more abstract and more concrete elements in sociological inquiry, but only in certain fields – such as social psychology and organisation theory – has the advice been taken to heart.

What passes for theory in contemporary sociology takes many forms. Merton suggested [1957] that six different types of work were conflated under the term 'theory':

(1) general methodology and the logic of scientific procedure
(2) general sociological orientations, broad postulates indicating merely the types of variables to be taken into account.
(3) the analysis of sociological concepts

(4) *post factum* sociological interpretations
(5) empirical generalisations
(6) sociological theory proper.

Particular confusion attends the conflation of the third and sixth types, concepts and theories proper. Concepts are a necessary part of sociological theory, but they are not sufficient. Some aspects of social research are more susceptible to codification and formulisation than others. Selection of units of study, methods of collecting (both quantitative and qualitative) data, and means of assessing the reliability of data so produced, have all received much attention. Other aspects of research – the initial delicate stages of problem-formulation and research design, the fraught phase of writing-up – either have been neglected or treated in terms of formulae (e.g. the logic of experimental design) whose applicability to at least some types of social research is in doubt.

The realm of concepts falls clearly in the latter category. Analysis of the role of concepts in empirical social research remains to a very considerable extent underdeveloped, both a symptom and a cause of the gulf which continues to separate sociological theory from sociological research. Despite a number of important attempts to bridge the gulf, it is fair to say that in the available literature on how to do research, the awkward problems of the formation and justification of concepts are rapidly passed over to get to more tractable fields like sample design or questionnaire construction. Not that sociologists neglect the analysis of concepts. At the theoretical and meta-theoretical levels enormous effort is devoted to the dissection and explication of terms, the results of which appear in series with titles such as *Key Concepts in the Social Sciences*. The better measurement of variables is the separate concern of those who do empirical research, the results appearing in volumes with titles such as *Key Variables in Social Research* (Stacey [1969]; Gittus (ed.) [1972]; Burgess [1984b]). What is chiefly remarkable at the present time is how little one type of work informs the other.

Whatever the excesses of conceptual analysis in contemporary sociological theory the explicit use of concepts is one of the most important characteristics differentiating sociology from purely idiographic activities such as narrative history or ethnography. Concepts perform several functions in sociology. They provide a means of summarising and classifying the formless mass of social data. In Myrdal's words, 'Concepts are spaces into which reality is fitted by analysis' (Myrdal [1961] p. 273). One aim of conceptual analysis is commonly to make explicit the character of phenomena subsumed under a concept. Concepts, too, provide a degree of fixity or determinateness in making observations in social science. As L. J. Henderson put it, 'A fact is a statement about experience in terms of a conceptual scheme' (quoted in Parsons [1970] p. 830). Put slightly differently, concepts specify routes which may be followed in analysing phenomena. 'Concepts mark out paths by which we may move most freely in logical space. They identify nodes or junctions in the network of relationships, termini at which we can halt while preserving the maximum range of choice as to where to go next' (Kaplan [1964] p. 52).

Concepts in themselves are not theories. They are categories for the organisation of ideas and observations. In order to form an explanatory theory, concepts must be interrelated. But concepts do act as a means of storing observations of phenomena which may at a future time be used in a theory. Similarly while concepts are distinct from observations, the formation of concepts is a spur to the development of observable indices of the phenomenon subsumed under the concept. Concepts, then, mediate between theory and data. They form an essential bridge, but one which is difficult to construct and maintain.

One of the most significant difficulties, which has much exercised philosophers of science, in *the paradox of categorisation.* Where do concepts come from in the first place, and what provides the justification for the use of particular concepts? 'If my categories of thought determine what I observe, then what I observe provides no independent control over my thought. On the other hand, if my categories of thought do not determine what I observe, then what I observe must be uncategorised, that is to say, formless and nondescript – hence again incapable of providing any test of my thought. So in neither case is it possible for observation, be it what it may, to provide any independent control over thought. . . . Observation contaminated by thought yields circular tests; observation uncontaminated by thought yields no tests at all (Scheffler [1967] pp. 13–14).

It is sometimes argued that attempts to reconstruct the logic or psychology of concept-formation are wasted, by comparison with engaging in conceptual analysis through empirical research. As

Lazarsfeld has observed, 'One cannot write a handbook on "how to form fruitful theoretical concepts" in the same way as handbooks are written on sampling or questionnaire construction' (Lazarsfeld [1972] p. 226). Systematic reflection about the task of concept formation may, however, throw light on the problem, intractable though it is. For the paradox of categorisation is a very real one, indeed it is inescapable. Concept-formation in the analysis of sociological data proceeds neither from observation to category, nor from category to observation, but in both directions at once and in interaction. The distinctive character of concepts in empirical social science derives from this dual theoretical and empirical character. The process is one in which concepts are formed and modified *both* in the light of empirical evidence *and* in the context of theory. Both theory and evidence can exercise compelling influence on what emerges. The use of concepts to analyse qualitative data is further discussed in Chapter 15.

Many of the theoretical concepts which sociologists use – social class, social cohesion, religious belief, bureaucratisation, power – are complex, intricate and rich in meaning. (For one example, 'deprivation', see Bulmer [1982] pp. 52–8.) They do not lend themselves easily to being reduced to their elements, specified in terms of indicators and measured; yet if social scientists are to exploit the explanatory potential of large-scale survey research, using representative sampling and quantitative techniques to investigate causal relationships, this is a necessary step along the road. Theoretical terms have to be translated into research instruments.

What happens in actual research? What are the stages of concept formation? The first stage in the development of any concept is that of *imagery*. The researcher has an intuitive general idea of the kind of construction which is of interest. Some disparate phenomena may have been perceived as having some underlying characteristic in common, or he may have observed some empirical regularities and be trying to explain them.

The second stage is *the logical analysis of the components of the concept.* If one is analysing a concept such as occupational aspiration it is necessary to sort out the different dimensions within the overall concept, decide which parts may be regarded as distinct (and which are interrelated) and reduce the number of dimensions to manageable proportions. For example, in a study of children's job aspirations, are occupational fantasies, children's desires and realistic aspirations for jobs three distinct components or reducible to two categories (Ford [1969] p. 52)?

The third stage is *the translation of the concept into empirical operations* to 'get at' the phenomenon in terms of which one's research hypothesis is formulated. Thus Ford operationalised occupational aspirations by means of four questions distinguishing: (a) the job a child 'wanted' to do when he or she left school; (b) the job a child 'expected' to do when he left school; (c) the job a child expected to be doing ten years in the future; and (d) the 'fantasy' choice of job given a completely free situation (Ford [1969] p. 52).

The choice of indicators to measure underlying concepts requires care:

> The fact that each indicator has not an absolute but only a probability relation to our underlying concept requires us to consider a great many possible indicators. The case of intelligence tests furnishes an example. First, intelligence is divided into dimensions of manual intelligence, verbal intelligence and so on. But even then there is not just one indicator by which an aspect of intelligence such as imaginativeness can be measured. We must use many indicators to get at it (Lazarsfeld [1958] p. 103).

An early decision has to be made whether the concept is unidimensional or multi-dimensional. If the former, operationalisation involves developing some kind of *scale* which will permit one to differentiate the degree to which this concept is present. If it appears to be multi-dimensional, as in Ford's study of occupational choice or in the measurement of intelligence, the procedure of *typological classification* allows one to determine what relationships one must observe and correlate before the individuals or groups can be classified. One common criterion for the inclusion of items as for measuring the same concept is whether or not they inter-correlate:

> When social scientists use the term 'measurement', it is in a much broader sense than the natural scientists do. For instance if we are able to say that one department in a company has higher morale than another, we would be very pleased with ourselves and we would say that he had performed a 'measurement'. We would not worry that we cannot say that it is twice as high or only 20 per cent higher. This does not mean that we make no efforts to

arrive at measurements in the traditional sense, with a precise metric. Some success has been achieved, but these efforts are only beginning and they represent merely a small part of measurement activities in the broader sense (Lazarsfeld [1958]).

The development of concepts is thus a critical phase of research, but does not in itself constitute a theory seeking to understand and explain social phenomena. Such a theory consists of a set of propositions stating a relationship between two or more properties, whose characteristics are defined in terms of concepts. The propositions form a deductive system from which statements may be derived and empirically tested.

An example of such a theory is Durkheim's explanation of the low suicide rate in Spain (Durkheim [1951] pp. 152–79):

(1) In any social grouping, the suicide rate varies directly with the degree of individualism (egoism)
(2) The degree of individualism varies with the incidence of Protestantism
(3) Therefore, the suicide rate varies with the incidence of Protestantism
(4) The incidence of Protestantism in Spain is low
(5) Therefore, the suicide rate in Spain is low.

One common way of conceptualising theoretical relationships in social research is in terms of variables.

> No science deals with its objects of study in their full concreteness. It selects certain of their properties and attempts to establish relations among them. The finding of such laws is the ultimate goal of all scientific inquiries. But in the social sciences the singling out of relevant properties is in itself a major problem. No standard terminology has yet been developed for this task. The properties are sometimes called aspects or attributes, and often the term 'variable' is borrowed from mathematics as the most general category. The attribution of properties is interchangeably called description, classification or measurement (Lazarsfeld [1958]).

The key importance of research design in empirical investigation, touched on in the Introduction, lies in anticipating the analytical questions which the investigator will seek to ask of the data, in relation to theory, and planning the inquiry in such a way from the outset that it can yield useful answers to these questions (cf. Stouffer [1950]; Homans [1964]). Facts, concepts and theories are bound up with each other as part of the cloth of sociological investigation.

Where do *problems* fit in? Max Weber, in a classic statement, emphasised that 'it is not the "actual" interconnections of "things" but the conceptual interconnections of problems which define the scope of the various sciences' [1949] p. 68). One fruitful way forward is to ask what sorts of problems sociologists address themselves to and how this relates to the type of theory they employ.

A useful classification distinguishes between policy problems, problems in social philosophy, and problems intrinsic to developing scientific disciplines (Greer [1969] pp. 8–18):

> The policy problem was the first sort to be attacked empirically, for its resolution must be in empirically testable terms. It is the problem of everyday life in the society, a problem of practical urgency. Its salience is clear in the general concern with social and clinical problems and the industries (social welfare, psychiatry) that have emerged to deal with them. Much of the public acceptance of the social sciences today comes from the average citizen's concern with poverty, race relations, mental illness and crime....
>
> The second source of problems for social science is in the philosophy of history, or more broadly social philosophy. Here we find intellectual problems of great scope, many as old as the history of human thought. In the most general terms, new elements, unknown in their implications, must be fitted into the given context of the culture, reconciled with the known. Such problems grow out of the effort to integrate, in one map of the world, newly discovered regions and continents of knowledge and/or belief....
>
> The third origin of problems in the social sciences is in the emerging questions raised by previously accumulated propositions. These are questions intrinsic to the discipline: they may have significance for policy or social philosophy, but that is not their significance for the scientist. The plotting of 'learning curves' may be useful to the teacher, but the research psychologist is concerned with the general theory of learning. Such problems, requiring previously formalised theories, come later in the development of a science than policy problems (which may

reflect the vocabulary of the folk culture and the assumptions of causation prevalent in everyday life) or problems of social philosophy (which may rest upon unsystematic and unproven beliefs about history and the nature of society).

The range and diversity of what passes for theory in contemporary sociology is due on no small measure to the very wide range of problems with which it is concerned. The diversity of problems to which sociologists address themselves suggests both a convincing account (albeit in outline) of the growth of social-science interest in problems and a means of reconciling different views of the aims and interests of sociologists. One of the reasons why 'middle-range theory' has failed to be the universal panacea it was purported to be is that its definition of a sociological problem, tending to exclude the philosophy of history, was too narrow.

The implications of this diversity of problem-sources is one of the issues explored in the remainder of the book. An over-narrow conception of 'problem' may possibly have restricted the past development of sociological research methods, just as it widened the gulf between general theory and middle-range theory. Problems, theories and methods are necessarily bound up together and are not separable in the *practice* of sociological investigation.

In a sense, of course, no sociologist's work can be purely theoretical or non-empirical in character. We are all social beings, we all incorporate our own social experience into our scholarly work, as Wright Mills emphasised [1959]. Nevertheless the view of theory taken here is that it is necessarily bound up with empirical inquiry of a systematic and explicit kind, going well beyond our own experiences. The *problem* with which the sociologist starts partially determines the type of theory which is used, and the way in which theory, concept and fact fit together. The basic commitment, however, is clear, which the rest of this book seeks to exemplify:

> The aim of theory in empirical science is to develop analytic schemes of the empirical world with which the given science is concerned. This is done by conceiving the world abstractly, that is, in terms of classes of objects and relations between such classes. Theoretical schemes are essentially proposals as to the nature of such classes and of their relations where this nature is problematical or unknown. Such proposals become guides to

investigation to see whether they or their implications are true. Thus, theory exercises a compelling influence on research – setting problems, staking out objects, and leading inquiry into asserted relations. In turn, findings of fact test theories, and in suggesting new problems invite the formulation of new proposals. Theory, inquiry and empirical fact are interwoven in a texture of operation with theory guiding inquiry, inquiry seeking and isolating facts, and facts affecting theory. The fruitfulness of their interplay is the means by which an empirical science develops (Blumer [1954]).

Further Reading

(1) L. Coser, *Masters of Sociological Thought: Ideas in Historical and Social Context*, 2nd edn (New York: Harcourt Brace Jovanovich, 1977). An encyclopedic and erudite intellectual and social biography of the most influential figures in the sociological Pantheon. Although necessarily compressed, it sets out the essential elements of a broad range of classical sociological theory and provides many clues to the varieties of problem which have underlain the development of the subject.
(2) C. Wright Mills, *The Sociological Imagination* (New York: Oxford University Press, 1959). An influential statement of the humanistic significance of sociology, a critique of the polarisation between pure theory and pure empiricism, and a manifesto for the social relevance of a critical sociology. The Appendix 'On Intellectual Craftsmanship' is particularly illuminating.
(3) R. K. Merton, *Social Theory and Social Structure*, 2nd edn (New York: Free Press, 1957) – Introduction (pp. 3–16); 'The Bearing of Sociological Theory on Empirical Research' (pp. 85–101); 'The Bearing of Empirical Research on Sociological Theory' (pp. 102–20). A classic discussion of the relationships between sociological theory and empirical research, including a powerful statement of the case for 'theories of the middle range'. Merton contrasts two kinds of approach to sociology. On the one hand there are the theoretical generalisers who say 'We do not know whether what we say is true, but it is at least significant'. On the other hand there are the radical empiricists whose motto is 'This is demonstrably so, but we cannot indicate its significance'. Is there a middle path between these two extremes?
(4) B. G. Glaser and A. L. Strauss, *The Discovery of Grounded*

Theory (London: Weidenfeld & Nicolson, 1967). A controversial and stimulating restatement and elaboration of the approach to theorising known as 'analytic induction', first developed by Znaniecki [1934]. The authors argue that theorising must be grounded in the data, experiences and categories of empirical research. Theory is not an *a priori* construct, but concepts and hypotheses emerge in the course of an inquiry. Although the chapter discussing 'theoretical sampling' is actively misleading, the rest of the book is a worth-while attempt to say something new about theory and research in relation to each other. The book is best read in conjunction with the author's empirical study of the way in which medical staff treat terminal patients in hospital, *Awareness of Dying* (Chicago: Aldine, 1965).

(5) G. V. Zito, *Methodology and Meanings: Varieties of Sociological Inquiry* (New York: Praeger, 1975). Reviews a number of different styles of research, arguing that social research is primarily a search for meanings. A stimulating essay comparing different ways of tackling the research task.

(6) Nicholas Bateson, *Data Construction in Social Surveys* (London: Allen & Unwin, 1984). A thoughtful discussion of problems of social measurement and the way in which data categories are framed in social research. Though focused upon social surveys, it has wider relevance to the problem of crossing the gap between concepts and indicators. It provides an interesting contrast between the more critical stance taken to measurement in Cicourel [1964].

Part Two

Social-Survey Research

2 Introduction and Further Reading

Martin Bulmer

> Research sociologists, in their driving effort to get the facts, tend to forget that (besides methodology) the distinctive offering of sociology to our society is sociological theory, not only researched description. Indeed, the market, corporate and government fact-finding agencies can easily outdo any sociologist in researched descriptions through sheer resources, if they care to. Where the sociologist can help is by providing theory that will make the research relevant (Glaser and Strauss [1967] pp. 30–1).

The social survey dominates empirical social research in Western industrial societies. A very large proportion of social research is carried out using these methods, and the majority of textbooks on research methods devote most attention to aspects of research design, sampling, data collection and analysis for social surveys. The social survey in its modern form is largely a British invention being first developed in the classical poverty surveys by Charles Booth on London ([1889–1902]; also Simey and Simey [1960], Pfautz [1967]) and Seebohm Rowntree in York ([1902]; also Briggs [1961]). Sampling techniques were first employed by A. L. Bowley in a study carried out in 1912 in a study of social conditions in four English towns, enormously increasing the usefulness of surveys because they enabled inferences to be made about a population, within calculable margins of error, from a sample of only a very small fraction of that population (Bowley [1915]). Developments during the present century have carried on this tradition which is particularly closely linked to social policy and social administration in all its aspects (Abrams [1951]; Moser and Kalton [1971] Ch. 1).

Two broad types of social survey may be distinguished, the *descriptive* and the *analytical.* The former is much the more common, particularly in Britain. Descriptive surveys are designed to portray accurately the characteristics of particular individuals, situations or groups (in terms of behaviour, attitudes and dispositions to act), and to determine the frequency with which such behaviour or attitudes occur in the population being sampled. Analytic surveys are concerned to test hypotheses about the relationships between variables in order to understand and explain a particular social phenomenon (Selltiz *et al.* [1965] Chs 3, 4). The distinction is not a hard and fast one, but it can usually be clearly made. In particular a very large amount indeed of descriptive social-survey research is carried on outside academic settings by people who do not regard themselves as sociologists and whose research is often not informed by theoretical considerations at all.

Historically there has been a considerable divergence between those whose primary interest in social surveys is statistical and technical, and those whose interests are more theoretical and sociologically oriented (cf. Abrams [1968] pp. 13–30, 136–43). Many of the developments in British survey work in the twentieth century have come from statisticians from Bowley onwards, while until 1950 sociologists were so few in number that there was not the impulse to follow theoretical lines of inquiry through survey work.

In part because of the close identification of empirical British sociology with sociography, some theoretically influential works have been sharply critical of a tendency to sacrifice 'theoretical clarity for the sake of obtaining easily quantitative data' or a concern 'merely with providing accurate data in the service of social reforms or administration' (Rex [1961] pp. 40–1). In this respect there is a marked difference between Britain and the United States, where a more sophisticated view of social survey research as contributing to analysis of the causes of social behaviour has developed. (cf. Marsh [1982], esp. pp. 37–47). This is reflected here in Chapter 3 by Morris Rosenberg and in other texts such as Hirschi and Selvin [1967], Blalock (ed.) [1972] and Heise [1975].

More surprisingly Popperian ideas seem to have had a relatively slight impact on the practice of survey research in Britain. A large number of studies still espouse either an unexamined inductivism (cf. Medawar [1969]) or what Stinchcombe has called [1970] 'Marxified Fabianism'. Britain lags behind seriously in the exploitation of the *analytic* potential of social surveys (cf. Selvin [1965a]). Standard introductory texts are largely American. Moser and Kalton [1971] and Galtung [1967] are the principal exceptions.

Paul Lazarsfeld, one of the leading practitioners of social scientific survey research, early acknowledged their drawbacks:

> The limitations of survey methods are obvious. They do not use experimental techniques; they rely primarily on what people say and rarely include objective observations; they deal with aggregates of individuals rather than with integrated communities; they are restricted to contemporary problems – history can be studied only by the use of documents remaining from earlier periods. In spite of these limitations survey methods provide one of the foundations upon which social science is being built. The finding of regularities is the beginning of any science and surveys can make an important contribution in this respect. For it is necessary that we know what people usually do under many and different circumstances if we are to develop theories explaining their behaviour (Lazarsfeld [1949]).

A common misconception about the usefulness of social-survey research in studying one's own society is that there is nothing to be found out. This ranges from the scepticism of the man in the street about the benefits of research to academic objections about 'proving the obvious'. Peter Worsley, for example, writes in the foreword to his major work on *The Third World* [1964] that he:

> deliberately eschewed writing a work which proves that working-class children have less opportunity to become Cabinet Ministers than children from public schools, or that millions of people in Britain are still poor. Investigations of this kind are very necessary, since the obvious is very often denied or neglected. But they are *not* intellectually challenging. They are, rather, demonstrations of what is abundantly evident from everyday experience and from rich documentation. The obvious, however, is often assiduously proved.

This is all very well, but what are the criteria for distinguishing between what is obvious and what is not? What happens if there is a conflict between one person's view of 'the facts' and someone else's? An elegant review by Lazarsfeld many years ago of *The American Soldier*, a study of the U.S. Army during World War II directed by Samuel Stouffer *et al.* [1949], brought out very clearly the role which sociological research can play in producing findings which are not obvious at all, and indeed may contradict what is the received opinion or conventional wisdom.

Lazarsfeld emphasised the peculiar problems faced by the social sciences in studying social phenomena:

> The world of social events is much less 'visible' than the realm of nature. That bodies fall to the ground, that things are hot or cold, that iron becomes rusty, are all immediately obvious. It is much more difficult to realise that ideas of right and wrong vary in different cultures; that customs may serve a different function from the one which the people practising them believe they are serving; that the same person may show marked contrasts in his behaviour as a member of a family and as a member of an occupational group. The mere description of human behaviour, of its variation from group to group and of its changes in different situations, is a vast and difficult undertaking. It is this task of describing, sifting and ferreting out interrelationships which surveys perform for us. And yet this very function often leads to serious misunderstandings. For it is hard to find a form of human behaviour that has not already been observed somewhere. Consequently if a study reports a prevailing regularity, many readers respond to it by thinking 'of course that is the way things are'. Thus from time to time the argument is advanced that surveys only put into complicated form observations which are already obvious to everyone.
>
> Understanding the origin of this point of view is of importance far beyond the limits of the present discussion. The reader may be helped in recognising this attitude if he looks over a few statements which are typical of many survey findings and carefully observes his own reaction. A short list of these, with brief interpretative comments, will be given here in order to bring into sharper focus probable reactions of many readers. (References are handled the following way. The first and second volumes of

The American Soldier are referred to by (A) and (B) respectively.)

(1) Better educated men showed more psycho-neurotic symptoms than those with less education. (The mental instability of the intellectual as compared to the more impassive psychology of the man-in-the-street has often been commented on.) B, p. 439.

(2) Men from rural backgrounds were usually in better spirits during their army life than soldiers from city backgrounds. (After all, they are more accustomed to hardships.) A, p. 94.

(3) Southern soldiers were better able to stand the climate in the hot South Sea Islands than Northern soldiers. (Of course, Southerners are more accustomed to hot weather.) A, p. 175.

(4) White privates were more eager to become non-coms than Negroes. (The lack of ambition among Negroes is almost proverbial.) A, p. 583.

(5) Southern Negroes preferred Southern to Northern white officers. (Isn't it well known that Southern whites have a more fatherly attitude toward their 'darkies'?) A, p. 581.

(6) As long as the fighting continued, men were more eager to be returned to the States than they were after the German surrender. (You cannot blame people for not wanting to be killed.) B, p. 561.

We have in these examples a sample list of the simplest types of interrelationships which provide the 'bricks' from which our empirical social science is being built. But why, since they are so obvious, is so much money and energy given to establish such findings? Would it not be wiser to take them for granted and proceed directly to a more sophisticated type of analysis? This might be so except for one interesting point about the list. *Every one of these statements is the direct opposite of what actually was found.* Poorly educated soldiers were more neurotic than those with high education; Southerners showed no greater ability than Northerners to adjust to a tropical climate; Negroes were more eager for promotion than whites; and so on. (The references following the above statements indicate where the evidence for the true findings can be located.)

If we had mentioned the actual results of the investigation first, the reader would have labelled these 'obvious' also. Obviously something is wrong with the entire argument of 'obviousness'. It should really be turned on its head. Since every kind of human reaction is conceivable, it is of great importance to know which reactions actually occur most frequently and under what conditions; only then will a more advanced social science develop (Lazarsfeld [1949] pp. 379–80).

The American Soldier was not a compendium of 'facts' about the characteristics of the American army in World War II. It is an *analytic* study seeking to understand and explain features of army life and organisation, not simply to describe them. As Durkheim stressed, doing sociological research necessarily involves *theory* as well as the strategies and techniques of empirical investigation. What then does this mean for the sociological uses which are made of surveys for analytic purposes?

One central problem of analytic surveys is the specification of key theoretical concepts in order to make them researchable. This is a general problem in research which was discussed in the previous chapter. A second, more particular, problem in survey research is how to disentangle the interrelationships of variables in order to make causal inferences. This is discussed in Chapter 3 by Morris Rosenberg.

He provides an introduction to the complexities of survey analysis and the use of survey data to enhance sociological understanding. His account emphasises how much the interpretation of survey data, far from being a purely mechanical or technical activity, requires the exercise of the sociological imagination. The tracing out of a pattern of interrelationship between variables involves the systematic examination of the logical possibilities which can follow from one's hypotheses, and a confrontation of ideas with evidence.

Consider a (highly oversimplified) example. Survey data indicates that there is a positive association between the amount of education someone has received in the past and the income which they currently receive from employment (e.g. Abrams [1964]). Does this imply that education is a 'cause' of income differentials in the population? Moreover since in Britain there is a strong association between social class of origin and educational level reached (cf. Douglas [1964, 1968]), what does this finding imply about the relationship between social class of origin and present income? The complexity of this type of analysis is apparent if we consider the two

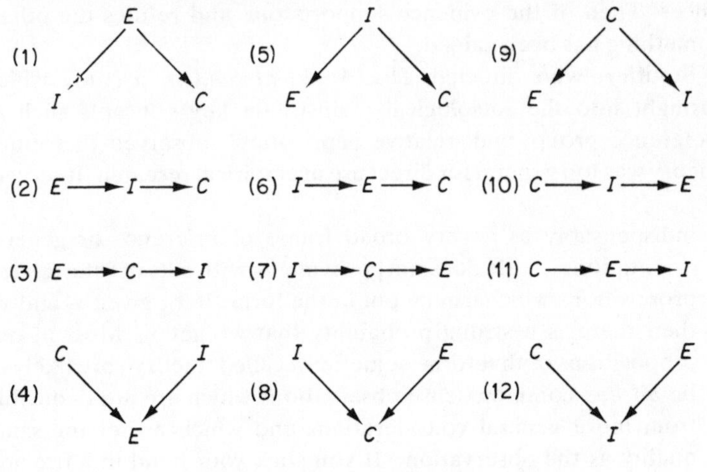

FIGURE 7

variables in Figure 7, education (E) and income (I), in relation to the third variable, social class of origin of the person concerned (C). Logically there are at least twelve possible patterns of interrelationship.

The introduction of *time* into the relationship serves to eliminate a number of these alternatives. Current income could not be a determinant of past education or social class of origin, nor social class of origin a result of past education (since it is temporally prior). This reduces the number of possible interrelationships to three – (9), (11) or (12). It is then the task of further analysis to determine whether class of origin or educational level, singly or together, is the determinant; if other factors (e.g. age) could account for the result; and (if the relationship does hold) whether it is causal or maturational (e.g. night following day).

The social investigator needs to consider carefully *at the outset of a piece of research* what are the theoretical questions to which an answer is sought. The importance of research design, discussed in the Introduction, is apparent here. Social research, survey research especially, is costly. Every study needs to be related to a more general body of theoretical ideas. One needs to look particularly for situations where two equally plausible hypotheses deducible from more general theory lead to the expectation of different consequences. Then, if the evidence supports one and refutes the other, something has been gained.

Stouffer, who directed *The Americal Soldier*, a study which brought into the sociological mainstream key concepts such as 'reference group' and 'relative deprivation', observed that much theory was too general for direct use in empirical research. It served

> indispensably as a very broad frame of reference or general orientation. . . . [It does not] provide us with sets of interrelated propositions which can be put in the form: If x_1, given x_2 and x_3, then there is a strong probability that we get x_4. Most of our propositions of that form, sometimes called 'theory', are likely to be *ad hoc* common-sense observations which are not deducible from more general considerations and which are of the same quality as the observation, 'If you stick your hand in a fire and hold it there, you will get burned' (Stouffer [1950] p. 359).

The aim of rendering theory more precise and testable is one which sociological survey researchers have pursued vigorously, with notable success in some areas such as social stratification and social mobility. Several excellent accounts of this method of theory-development have been given (cf. Blalock [1964], Hirschi and Selvin [1967], Rosenberg [1968], Heise [1975], Hellevik [1984]). In this type of analysis, social process and social change are conceptualised in terms of production. Formally stated, 'if *X* is a cause of *Y*, we have in mind that a change in *X* produces a change in *Y* and not merely that a change in *X* is followed or associated with a change in *Y*' (Blalock [1964] p. 9). The task of sociological inquiry is to identify the causal antecedents of regularities in social behaviour. The starting-point may be a theoretical one – how may one account for variation in incomes? – or it may be an observed empirical association between two variables (in this case, education and income). The proper role of inquiry lies in its contribution to the *verification* of theoretical proportions under controlled conditions in which precision, reliability and validity are guaranteed by the use of scientific procedures.

If at an earlier stage British sociology was in danger of being too empiricist, in the sense of believing that 'the facts speak for themselves', the opposite error is now more likely to be committed, the belief that it is possible to gain knowledge about society without rigorous empirical evidence in support of theoretical propositions. One source of this strand in contemporary British sociology has been philosophical doubts that have generated scepticism about the value of survey research (on different and often conflicting grounds) (see, for example, Atkinson [1968], Filmer *et al.* [1972] Chs 3 and 5, Hindess [1973]). A recent spirited defence of the survey method has been mounted by Marsh, who in chapter 4 considers the basis of these criticisms and also sets out the logical structure of survey data. In a recent monograph (Marsh [1982]) she takes the argument further, showing that surveys are capable of producing results which are both causally adequate and adequate at the level of meaning. The method is a valuable one which cannot be dismissed in the light fashion of its critics.

Further Reading

Methodology

The discussion here and the extracts are introductory; they are intended to raise certain issues and highlight sometimes neglected aspects of survey research in sociology. There is no substitute, however, for familiarity with all stages in the design and execution of a social survey, including sampling, design of the interview schedule, interviewing, coding of results and analysis. Excellent textbooks are available, three being particularly useful:

D. P. Warwick and C. Lininger, *The Sample Survey: Theory and Practice* (New York: McGraw-Hill, 1975), provides a well-balanced discussion of all aspects of the survey research process.
C. A. Moser and G. Kalton, *Survey Methods in Social Investigation* (London: Heinemann, 1971), provides particularly good coverage of sampling, data collection and statistical implications in the conduct of large-scale survey research.
M. Bulmer and D. P. Warwick (eds), *Social Research in Developing Countries: Surveys and Censuses in the Third World* (New York and Chichester, Sussex: Wiley, 1983), focuses upon data collection in Third World surveys, thereby highlighting many of the features and problems of survey research in the developed world.

From the standpoint of sociological theorising, four sources are of particular use:

(1) M. Rosenberg, *The Logic of Survey Analysis* (New York: Basic Books, 1968). The best single discussion of the procedures to follow in order to achieve understanding through 'variable analysis'. Lucid, elegant, making minimal statistical demands, it provides a comprehensive introduction to the subject of this section.
(2) Ottar Hellevik, *Introduction to Causal Analysis: Exploring Survey Data by Crosstabulation* (London and Boston: Allen & Unwin, 1984). A clear and straightforward introduction to the analysis of percentage tables of survey data, in order to draw out the causal relationships to be found in them.
(3) Nigel Gilbert, *Modelling Society: An Introduction to Loglinear Analysis for Social Researchers* (London and Boston: Allen & Unwin, 1981). Loglinear analysis is a relatively new technique for the analysis of tabular data. Gilbert provides an introduction to the procedure which avoids mathematical complexity and demonstrates its relevance to testing theoretical ideas.
(4) Catherine Marsh, *The Survey Method: The Contribution of Surveys to Sociological Explanation* (London and Boston: Allen & Unwin, 1982). A spirited defence of survey research against its sociological critics, arguing that surveys can provide the kind of evidence needed to test social theories. Questions the view that particular research procedures necessarily commit those who use them to a particular theory of knowledge or view of human nature. Contains a good critique of public opinion polling and its misuses.

Empirical studies

(1) S. M. Lipset, M. Trow and J. S. Coleman, *Union Democracy* (Glencoe: Free Press, 1956). A landmark in industrial and political sociology which examines the internal political organisation of the International Typographical Union in New York City. It set out to investigate why the I.T.U. was an exception to Michels's 'iron law of oligarchy', and produced a convincing and original explanation. Lipset provides an intellectual biography of the study in Hammond (ed.) ([1964] pp. 96–120) which throws interesting light on the canons of the hypothetic-deductive method. Methodologically *Union Democracy* is valuable in exemplifying unfolding survey analysis (although other kinds of data collection were used as well), for its discussion of significance tests and for its triangulation of problems and methods.
(2) J. H. Goldthorpe, D. Lockwood, F. Bechhofer and J. Platt, *The Affluent Worker: Industrial Attitudes and Behaviour*; *The Affluent*

Worker: Political Attitudes and Behaviour; *The Affluent Worker in the Class Structure* (Cambridge: Cambridge University Press, 1968, 1968, 1969). A major three-volume British study of the theory of working-class 'embourgeoisement' by means of research on affluent manual workers in the car-manufacturing town of Luton. Relevant for its careful identification of the theoretical problem, the elegant research design and choice of Luton as a 'critical case' by which to test the theory and for the means by which the concepts of 'embourgeoisement' and 'class' are empirically specified and investigated.

(3) J. W. B. Douglas, *The Home and the School* (London: MacGibbon & Kee, 1964; paperback, London: Panther, 1967). This study of inequality of educational opportunity in Britain is drawn from a longitudinal study of a cohort of children born in March 1946 and follows them from ages five to eleven. It provides a mine of information on the social correlates of educational performance at primary school and, because of its longitudinal design, permits control of the time factor and teasing out of causal relationships between social background and educational performance in a way not usually possible in cross-sectional survey designs.

(4) T. Hirschi, *The Causes of Delinquency* (Berkeley: University of California Press, 1969). An illuminating attempt to state and test by empirical research three contrasting theories of the causation of juvenile delinquency: the strain, the control, and the cultural deviance perspectives. Hirschi's analysis, using tabular methods, is based on a major questionnaire survey completed by 4,000 San Francisco high-school students. This work exemplifies a rigorous hypothetico-dedective approach to survey analysis.

(5) G. W. Brown and T. Harris, *The Social Origins of Depression: A Study of Psychiatric Disorder in Women* (London: Tavistock, 1978). A classic study of the social determinants of health demonstrating a high degree of sociological sophistication in design, measurement and analysis of a complex phenomenon. Particularly interesting for the way in which survey data are used to test a model and theory of the onset of depression in working-class women.

(6) Glen H. Elder, Jr, *Children of the Great Depression: Social Change in Life Experience* (Chicago: University of Chicago Press, 1974). A major sociological and historical study of a small cohort of American children born in 1920–1 and followed up from 1931 in a longitudinal study. Elder has re-analysed the data from the archives

and collected more of his own to examine in a theoretically fruitful way the consequences of the Great Depression of the 1930s. The study particularly examines the effects of social class and of economic deprivation in youth on family structure, social experience and personality, adult values and career. The study is unusual both for its fertile and elegant use of cohort analysis, and for taking a *single* antecedent independent variable – the differential effects of the Depression – and looking at its social effects on a number of dependent variables. (A more usual design is to look at the effects on a single dependent variable (e.g. voting, fertility, educational performance) of a number of independent variables.)

3 The Meaning of Relationships in Social-Survey Analysis*

Morris Rosenberg

The first step in the analysis of survey data is to examine the relationship between two variables. Such a relationship, however, may have many different meanings. In a formal sense there are three possible meanings which a relationshp between two variables may have:[1]† (1) *Neither* variable may influence the other; such relationships are termed *symmetrical.* (2) *Both* variables may influence one another; these are *reciprocal* relationships. (3) *One* of the variables may influence the other; the term *asymmetrical* is applied to this type of relationship. It is useful to consider some of the different types of symmetrical, reciprocal and asymmetrical relationships appearing in research.

Symmetrical Relationships

A symmetrical relationship, as noted, assumes that neither variable is due to the other. We may find, for example, that people who do well on verbal tests also do well on mathematics tests. But we would

* Chapter 1, 'The Meaning of Relationships', from *The Logic of Survey Analysis*, by Morris Rosenberg, © 1968 by Basic Books Inc., Publishers, New York.

† Notes and References begin on page 309.

not assume that the mathematical ability is responsible for the verbal ability, or vice versa. It is a matter of indifference whether we say that people who are high on verbal skills tend to be high on mathematical skills or that people who are high on mathematical skills tend to be high on verbal skills.

Symmetrical relationships, while generally of lesser theoretical significance than asymmetrical relationships, are often valuable in understanding social processes. It is thus relevant to consider five types of symmetrical relationships.

The first and most obvious type of symmetrical relationship is one in which both variables are viewed as *alternative indicators of the same concept.* One finds, for example, that there is a relationship between palmar perspiration and heart pounding. Both these symptoms may be interpreted as signs of anxiety; neither variable would be viewed as the cause of the other. Similarly if there is an association between contributing to the community chest and freedom in lending money to friends, this relationship might be interpreted as one between alternative expressions of the disposition of generosity. If one finds an association between the statements, 'I seldom feel blue', and 'I often feel depressed and discouraged', one is almost certain that this relationship is due to the fact that these are alternative symptoms of depression.

It is obvious in such cases that it makes no difference how one phrases the relationship. One might say that people whose palms perspire are more likely to experience heart pounding or that people who experience heart pounding are more likely to have palmar perspiration. There is no logical reason for assigning priority to either symptom.[2]

A second type of symmetrical relationship is one in which the two variables are *effects of a common cause.* The presence of a relationship between hay fever and the size of the corn crop does not mean that one causes the other. It simply means that the same favourable climatic conditions that promote corn production also promote the growth of ragweed. Similarly one generally finds a relationship, among nations, between the level of medical practice and the frequency of air travel. But it is not that medicine keeps pilots alive or that aeroplanes enable doctors to travel more quickly. Both are consequences of the conditions which have produced the scientific and technological revolutions of recent times, revolutions which find expression in diverse aspects of human behaviour.

It is conventional to describe relationships between variables which are consequences of a common cause as 'spurious', and to dismiss the result as trivial or meaningless. This conclusion is not invariably justified. For example it is implicit in Durkheim's analysis that societies which have a restitutive form of justice will be characterised by a high level of egoism in the population.[3] There is no reason to believe, however, that the form of justice is responsible for the level of egoism or that the level of egoism has influenced the nature of the legal system. Durkheim suggests that each of these social phenomena is an outgrowth of the division of labour. To understand this fact is surely to have an improved understanding of these social phenomena.

Such relationships may thus point to the diversity of consequences of some common cause. The relationship is, however, symmetrical since neither variable is essentially responsible for the other.

A third type of symmetrical relationship is one involving the *functional interdependence* of the elements of a unit.[4] Thus there is a correlation between the presence of a heart and the presence of lungs: where one is found, the other appears; where one is absent, so is the other. This relationship is based on the fact that the various parts of the total organism perform distinctive functions, thus enabling the unit to survive. But one organ does not 'cause' the other, although all the parts are dependent on one another in order for each to perform its task.

The concept of 'bureaucracy' is a case in point. One might find, for example, that organisations characterised by formal, abstract, impersonal rules tend to have an elaborate system of hierarchical ranks. It is not that the rules or the ranks cause one another, but that both are indispensable elements in the functioning of the total system.

A closely related type of symmetrical relationship is one in which elements are associated as *parts of a common 'system' or 'complex'*. They are not, however, functionally interdependent, for the elements are often arbitrary. There may be an association between joining the country club and attending the opera. Both practices are elements of a class 'style of life', encompassing a variety of interests, attitudes, values and behaviour which develop out of communicative interaction. But these practices are not indispensable for the unit; they may easily be supplanted by other practices; they are dependent solely upon acceptance by the relevant group.

Such relationships are especially characteristic of cultural practices. Where one finds hamburgers, one also tends to find hot dogs; people who eat lasagna are more likely to eat minestrone; the public burning of blankets is associated with the public destruction of coppers. Such associations shed light on the elements of a whole which hang together for arbitrary reasons. There is, of course, no causal link between the two variables.

Occasional ambiguity arises in deciding whether a relationship is functional or reflects parts of a larger complex. In a sense both represent the 'organismic-holistic' approach. A functional relationship, however, implies an entity in which the various parts play a role indispensable to the operation of the totality. The human body, a machine, a group, an organisation all illustrate a functional interrelationship of parts.

A 'joint complex', on the other hand, reflects a series of elements that hand together for essentially normative reasons. The elements are, however, socially relevant and it is important to know what they are. That people who drink martinis tend to patronise concert halls reflects no interdependence between these two practices (such practices might change without doing violence to the complex), but simply indicates that these are components of a certain 'style of life'. The sociologist is necessarily interested in such life styles or cultural complexes and such symmetrical relationships may thus be of great interest.

Finally, of course, some symmetrical associations are simply *fortuitous*. The fact that there is an association between proportion of orientals and consumption of rice is simply an accident of history and geography. The fact that there is a rough chronological relationship between rock 'n' roll music and the onset of the space age does not mean that one is in any sense responsible for the other or that they both are associated with a common source (although the imaginative thinker may be capable of establishing such a link). There may be a temptation to see in such correlations the subtle hand of causation or association with a common variable, but one must always acknowledge the possibility of coincidence. The child who has misbehaved and who later accidentally stubs his toe may interpret this sequence of events as divine retribution, but whether it is causal or coincidental remains an imponderable.

It is important to be explicit about the interpretation of a symmetrical relationship, for such interpretations are often susceptible of further test. For example if one interprets a relationship as reflecting an association between two indicators of a common concept, this assumption can often be tested through scaling techniques, factor analysis or other internal consistency procedures. If on the other hand one interprets the relationship as representing two separate consequences of a common cause, then this assumption can often be tested through control on a test factor. Similarly finding that there is a relationship between two indicators of a common concept sheds light on the range and diversity of manifestations of a phenomenon. The finding that two consequences are attributable to a common cause can tell us something about the importance of that cause in accounting for a wide range of social phenomena. The finding that a relationship is based on the functional contribution of two elements to a social unit may often shed light on the structure and operation of the unit. Finally if a relationship represents the concordance of elements in a system or complex, then it may be of considerable descriptive value in clarifying the nature of the complex.

While symmetrical relationships may not generally match the theoretical significance of asymmetrical relationships in social research, they none the less often make important contributions to understanding. It would thus represent a theoretical loss to present such findings simply as descriptive results without attempting to interpret them. The interpretation would ordinarily suggest, however, that elaboration is *not* a useful next step.

Reciprocal Relationships

One frequently encounters relationships in social research in which it is not immediately possible to specify which is the independent (causal) and which the dependent (effect) variable, but in which causal forces are none the less in operation. This is the case in which the two variables are reciprocal, interacting and mutually reinforcing; one might describe this pattern as one of 'alternating asymmetry'.

Probably the classical illustration of a reciprocal relationship is that between the temperature and the thermosatat. The temperature influences the action of the thermostat, and the thermostat influences the temperature in the room, in an endless cyclical process. The *present* relationship is due to the mutual effects of both variables; each is cause and each is effect. The engineering concepts 'feedback' and 'servomechanisms' illustrate this type of relationship.

Such reciprocal relationships are extremely common in survey research. One finds, for example, that Republicans tend to be exposed to Republican communications and Democrats to Democratic communications. It is apparent that the causal influence between exposure and political affiliation operates in both directions. Republican convictions cause one to select Republican messages, and Republican messages reinforce one's Republican convictions. Again one might find a relationship between alienation and low social status. Low status may alienate one from the societal value system, and alienation may cause behaviour which results in low status. Similarly one may find a relationship between investments and profits. A company which makes profits increases its investments, which increases its profits, which increases its investments. The elucidation of such mutually reinforcing processes may contribute substantially to the understanding of social phenomena.

We have described this pattern of asymmetry as alternating because, as Blalock notes:

> Probably most persons agree that *A* cannot be a cause of *B* and *B* simultaneously a cause of *A*. Yet we may wish to speak of *X* and *Y* being 'mutual causes', or we allow for 'reciprocal' causation. What we usually mean would be something like this: a change in *X* produces a change in *Y*, which in turn produces a further change in *X* at some later time, which produces a still further change in *Y*, and so on. Symbolically
>
> $$X_{t0} \longrightarrow Y_{t1} \longrightarrow X_{t2} \longrightarrow Y_{t3} \longrightarrow X_{t4} \longrightarrow \ldots.$$
>
> An increase in the level of unemployment might lead to fewer retail sales at a somewhat later time. This, in turn, could lead to further unemployment, and so on.[5]

The reciprocal type of relationship thus stands somewhere between the symmetrical and the asymmetrical types. It is symmetrical in the sense that one cannot say which variable is cause and which effect, which independent and which dependent. At the same time it is asymmetrical in the sense that each variable is continuously affecting the other. In such cases, of course, one might speculate as to a 'primal cause', but it is an open question whether this can be considered the independent variable. For example, one may find a relationship between a husband's hostility toward his wife and her hostility toward him. Perhaps his hostility has caused him to behave disagreeably toward her; this behaviour arouses her hostility, which causes her to respond with equal unpleasantness, which increases his hostility etc. One might say that the primal cause was his original hostility. But after this has been going on for some time it is no longer the original cause but the unpleasant behaviour of each toward the other which arouses their mutual hostility. The relationship is one of alternating asymmetry. It is sufficient to know that the chicken and egg are responsible for one another without confronting the problem of which came first.[6]

Asymmetrical Relationships

The core of sociological analysis is to be found in the asymmetrical relationship. In this type of relationship we postulate that one variable (the independent variable) is essentially 'responsible for' another (the dependent variable). If younger people go to the movies more, it is apparent that it is some aspect of their age which is responsible for the movie attendance since there is no way in which going to the movies can make one young. Asymmetrical relationships thus propel one into the vital scientific area of causal analysis.[7]

Thus far we have used the concept of causation rather loosely, employing it in its common-sense meaning of one variable being 'responsible for' another. Causation, however, has a more restricted meaning. We speak of a cause when an external influence produces a change in some unit. The term 'produces' is crucial in this definition, for it implies that an efficient external agent exercises an isolable power on the unit. Causes have properties of uniqueness, isolability, productiveness, invariability, unidirectionality etc.[8] which are by no means characteristic of many asymmetrical relationships in social science.

It is generally assumed that causal analysis is the basic approach of the scientific method. This is a misconception. The scientist is interested in explanation and understanding (as well as prediction and control); causation is only one of several ways of producing this explanation and understanding.

Bunge notes: 'There are many ways of understanding, that is, of answering why-questions, the disclosure of causes being but one of such ways. . . . Causality is not a sufficient condition for understanding reality, although it is quite often a component of scientific explanation. . . . Scientific explanation is, in short, explanation by laws – not necessarily explanation by causes.'[9] One need merely note such formulae as 'energy equals one-half of mass times the square of velocity', or 'electrical resistance equals current divided by pressure', to recognise that these non-causal statements (neither side of the equation 'causes' the other) are of enormous scientific value.

Causation, in fact, is but one type of *determination*.[10] Determination involves a *necessary connection* between two variables; a causal relationship represents but one among a much larger number of types of necessary connections among variables.[11]

Since the material available to the survey analyst is a correlation, on what basis does he decide which is the determining (independent) variable and which the determined (dependent) variable? The key criterion for understanding the direction of determination appears to be *susceptibility to influence*. If one finds a relationship between sex and political interest, it is obvious that one's level of political interest cannot determine one's sex; the influence can only be in the other direction. If older people are politically more conservative, their conservatism surely did not make them old; it can only be that their age, in some sense, is responsible for their conservatism.

Two factors are basically involved in deciding on the direction of influence of the variables: (1) the time order, and (2) the fixity or alterability of the variables.

The importance of the time sequence has been universally emphasised. Since something that happened later cannot be responsible for what happened earlier, it follows that the variable which is temporally prior must always be the determinant or independent variable. If one finds a relationship between the way children have been toilet-trained and their adult personalities, the adult personalities cannot be responsible for the toilet-training experiences. 'If, for instance, we relate length of engagement with subsequent marital happiness, the length of engagement comes earlier in the time order. If we relate parole breaking to some conditions of a criminal's adolescence, the latter again is prior in the time sequence.'[12]

The time factor, while important, is not an infallible guide in determining the direction of determination. If someone is born both black and poor, and remains that way throughout his life, neither variable has temporal priority. Yet there is no doubt whatever that race is the determining variable. It is not that race came first, in the temporal sense, but that race is not subject to change, whereas income is. Similarly if one finds a relationship between education and television viewing, it is difficult to establish any temporal priority; during the years of education one watched television, and during the years of watching television one went to school. Time thus does not tell the tale. Yet the direction of determination is clear. It is easy to see how level of education may determine one's preference for certain kinds of programmes, but it is much less likely that preference for certain kinds of programmes will importantly determine one's educational level.

These observations suggest the second criterion of determinacy, namely the *fixity, permanence* or *alterability* of the variables. Sociology employs a number of such fixed variables, for example sex, race, birth order, national origin. The variable of age, while not unchangeable, is not subject to influence by any power. Similarly, if blacks are more alienated than whites,[13] it is evident that the alienation cannot be responsible for the race. If Italians feel they have less control over their government than Americans,[14] the attitudes toward the government cannot be responsible for their nationality. Race and national origins are fixed uninfluenceable properties.

Certain important sociological variables are relatively, but not absolutely, fixed properties of the individual. Social class, religion and rural-urban residence are of this nature. As a consequence some element of reciprocity may enter into an asymmetrical relationship; that is the dependent variable may have some influence on the dependent variable. For example consider the relationship between social class and organisational membership. While one's social class generally determines one's organisational membership, it is possible that some people may join organisations to 'meet the right people' and thereby achieve acceptance into the higher reaches of the status system. Or consider the well-documented relationship between religion and political affiliation. While religion must generally be considered the determinant, it is conceivable that a man might change his religion to agree with his political affiliation (an ambitious Protestant running for office in a heavily Catholic neighbourhood might 'convert').

Does this mean that if it is at all possible for the dependent variable to influence the independent variable then one can no longer treat the relationship as asymmetrical? This appears to be the position taken by Srole and his colleagues,[15] who argue that only the unalterable variables – age, sex, parental socio-economic status etc. – can be treated as independent determinants of mental health, whereas no direction of determination can be made for the *relatively* fixed variables in which some elements of reciprocity is possible.

Such a position strikes us as excessively rigid. Survey research must allow for *the dominant direction of influence* of variables. If one finds that a man's religion is related to his mental health, one may reasonably suggest that religion is the dominant influence although there undoubtedly are cases in which a man's mental health may cause him to change his religion. Similarly the fact that joining an organisation may help one to rise in the status hierarchy should not blind one to the fact that it is the social class which overwhelmingly is responsible for the organisational membership.

The failure to accept this view is actually seen by some as a drawback to the causal principle. According to Bunge:

> A severe shortcoming of the strict doctrine of causality is that it disregards the fact that all known actions are accompanied or followed by reactions, that is, that the effect always reacts back on the input unless the latter has ceased to exist. However, an examination of real processes suggests that there are often *predominantly* (though not exclusively) uni-directional $C \longrightarrow E$ (cause leads to effect) actions. Causality may be a good approximation in cases of extreme asymmetry of the cause and the effect, that is, when there is a strong dependence of the effect upon the cause, with a negligible reaction of the output upon the input and, of course, whenever the cause has ceased existing.[16]

Needless to say, the analyst must give due consideration to the possibility of reciprocal interaction in his interpretation. The decision regarding the dominant direction of influence may either be made on the basis of panel data or on logical or theoretical grounds. So long as the dominant direction of influence can be specified and defended, it is legitimate to interpret one's relationships as asymmetrical and determinative.

Types of asymmetrical relationships

Unless one is engaged in purely descriptive research, the analyst wishes to interpret his relationship in order to reveal its theoretical implications. The particular interpretation he applies to his data will as we shall see have important implications for his further data analysis. It is thus worth considering the types of asymmetrical relationships which the sociologist is likely to encounter in his research.

One type of relationship involves an association between *a stimulus and a response.* This would be the most directly causal type of determinant. One might examine the effect of rainfall on the price of wheat, or the threat of war on civilian morale. Such relationships may be mediate or immediate (and they are rarely perfect), but they refer to the influence of some external stimulus upon a particular response.

In order to infer a stimulus–response relationship, it is essential that those exposed to the stimulus and those not exposed are reasonably comparable in other respects. For example a study was conducted in England to determine the effects of television on children.[17] One might, for example, compare the study habits of children who did or did not have television sets in the home, but this would be questionable since these homes might differ in ways other than the possession of a set. In the early 1950s, however, some British communities had television stations and others did not. The investigators thus took the TV owners in the community with TV reception and matched them on age, socio-economic status and sex with those in the community without reception. This procedure enabled them to test the effects of television on the children.

The stimulus–response type of relationship encounters peculiar difficulties in social research because of the principle of selectivity. One could not, for example, compare the attitudes of those who have or have not seen a specific film and attribute the difference to the effect of the film, since those who have chosen to see the film may differ in their initial attitudes from those who have not. Some years ago, for example, Hollywood produced an antiprejudice film entitled *Gentleman's Agreement.* If one had studied the prejudice levels of those who had or had not seen the movie one could not attribute the difference to the film, since it is likely that unprejudiced people sought it out and prejudiced people avoided it. If, however, there is a basis for believing that the two comparison groups are approximately equivalent, or if panel data are available, then it is possible to interpret the relationship as reflecting an association between a stimulus and a response.

Another type of asymmetrical relationship involves an association between *a disposition and a response.* A disposition refers not to a state or condition of the individual, but to a tendency to respond in a certain way under designated circumstances.[18] For example when we characterise a rubber band as 'elastic' or sugar as 'soluble', we mean that they are capable of being stretched or dissolved, not that they actually are stretched or dissolved. Similarly when we characterise a man as a 'liberal' we do not mean that he is manifesting liberal inclinations at any particular moment, but that he *would* respond liberally if the appropriate circumstances arose.

Such disposition, it may be noted, are not 'stimuli' in the sense of some external force impinging on an object and producing a certain effect. It is not that some people hear a lecture and others do not, but that some people *have* a certain attitude, trait or personality quality and others do not. Under certain circumstances the disposition will give rise to the behaviour.

Along with 'properties' (to be discussed shortly), dispositions constitute the main type of concepts employed in research. These include: *attitudes* (toward liberalism, toward economic systems, toward political candidates); *abilities* (musical skill, artistic talent, athletic prowess): *reflexes* (eye-blink, Babinski reflex, heat or cold sensitivity); *habits* (brushing teeth, eating at a certain time, watching a recurrent television programme); *values* (belief in democracy, equality, success); *drives* (sex, food, belongingness, self-actualisation); '*personality traits*' (authoritarianism, compulsiveness, depression); or 'powers' or 'tendencies' generally.

A very prominent type of research analysis thus considers the relationship between a disposition as the independent variable, and behaviour (verbal or otherwise) as the dependent variable. One might for example find a relationship between liberalism and vote, prejudice and discrimination, extroversion and joining groups, intelligence and test performance, valuation of success and striving for good grades etc. Such relationships tend to be unidirectional and asymmetrical.

Most relationships between dispositions and responses are fairly straightforward. There is, however, a special type of disposition–response relationship which appears to be a partial redundancy but which is often enlightening and theoretically fruitful. This is the case of a relationship between a broad variable and a more specific variable which is encompassed by it. One would probably find for example that authoritarianism (measured, let us say, by the F-scale)[19] is associated with inordinate respect for power. Since the concept of authoritarianism includes as one of its several elements (or part of its syndrome) attitudes toward power, one would say that the association is due to a larger concept embracing a smaller one.

Or consider the following example. One finds an association between a generalised attitude of misanthropy (distrust of people) and attitudes toward certain specific aspects of the democratic process, for example the beliefs that the mass of the people are capable of reaching rational political decisions, that political figures are responsive to the will of the people, that people must be restrained by law etc.[20] While there may be an element of tautology in such a relationship, the result is by no means trivial or irrelevant. If a person has a general disdain or hatred of human nature, then when confronted with those aspects of a political system which presuppose certain qualities of human nature he will tend to respond in terms of his general attitude. Thus the democratic ideology is based on certain fundamental assumptions of man – that man is generally rational, that his elected representatives are responsive to him, that he is capable of guiding his own political destiny without degenerating into anarchy, chaos or ineffectuality. A man's basic attitude toward human nature may thus meaningfully bear on his attitudes toward a political system in so far as the general attitude is implicated in the political attitude. Otherwise expressed, the political attitude is a specific expression of the general attitude.

Similarly Lott and Lott show that the California E (ethnocentrism) scale is related to the 'judgements about the relative superiority of one's own country as compared with another'.[21] The broader disposition thus helps one to understand the specific expression of it.

A third type of asymmetrical relationship is one involving a *property*[22] of the individual as the independent variable, and a disposition or act as the dependent variable. A property may be distinguished from a disposition in being a relatively perduring characteristic which is not dependent upon circumstances for its activation. In the realm of objects we might say that solubility is a disposition of a lump of sugar, but its shape, size, weight and colour are its properties. Size and shape are not qualities that an object 'can be' or 'tends to be'; they refer to what an object 'is'.

So it is when one studies people. Such qualities as sex, race, religion, rural-urban residence, age, marital status, nationality, hair colour, eye colour etc. may be thought of as properties of the individual. A person is a male, a white man, an American, a first child, irrespective of what he does or what happens to him. This is quite different from calling a man 'politically liberal'. He is 'liberal' in the sense that he carries around in him this potential or tendency which may or may not be activated, but not as a firm property, such as his sex, size, nationality etc.

The relationship between a property and a disposition or act is probably the central type of relationship in social research. The relationships between race and alienation, region of country and voting behaviour, age and conservatism, class and anomie, religion and authoritarianism, sex and vote – all these are examples of the relationships of properties as independent variables, and dispositions or behaviour as dependent variables.

As we observed earlier the reason properties will almost invariably be treated as the determinant factors in such relationships is that they are either strongly or absolutely resistant to influence. It may be noted, however, that they are 'determinants' in a rather different sense from a precise stimulus. To say that a particular political speech makes one more Democratic is surely different from saying that 'Catholicism' makes one more Democratic.

A fourth type of asymmetrical relationship is one in which the independent variable is essentially a *necessary precondition* for a given effect. For example one may find a relationship between a nation's level of technological development and the possession of nuclear weaponry. The technological development does not 'cause' the nuclear weaponry; it only makes it possible. Some technologically advanced nations do not possess atomic bombs. Technology is thus a necessary but not a sufficient condition for creating the dependent variable. It is not causal in the sense of 'forcing' or 'producing' the result.

Similarly it is generally true that there is a relationship between a free and mobile labour force and a particular stage of capitalist development. Marx believed that a free labour force was an essential condition for the development of capitalism – capitalism could not develop without it – but was not solely responsible for capitalism. Marx interpreted such diverse events as the enclosure movement in England and the Civil War in America as events establishing the free labour precondition for capitalism.

A fifth type of asymmetrical relationship is one involving an *immanent* relationship between the two variables. Such a relationship derives from the fact that qualities inherent in the nature of an organism give rise to certain consequences. For example the sociologist of organisation would probably find a relationship between size of bureaucracy and amount of red tape; he would not say that the bureaucracy causes the red tape but that red tape is immanent in bureaucracy. It is inherent in the nature of bureaucracy that it establishes abstract impersonal rules which cannot adequately adapt to the diverse concrete situations which fall under its rubric. It is also inevitable in the nature of authority and tenure that the bureaucrat will tend to become more concerned with strict adherence to the rules than with effecting the purposes for which the rules were designed. Hence the phenomenon of red tape. It is not that one factor causes the other, but that the dependent variable arises out of the independent variable.

Michels' contention that organisation leads to oligarchy implies a similar determinative sequence.[23] Michels' reasoning, briefly stated, is as follows: Many organisations, such as socialist political parties or labour unions, are created under the aegis of the democratic ideology. The membership bands together, democratically choosing its leaders. In the course of time, however, the leadership develops specialised and expert knowledge of their jobs as, say, union leaders. They also lose their original skills as plumbers and cigar makers, which increases their desire to remain union leaders. At the same time the membership develops feelings of familiarity with, and respect for, the leadership, and accepts their decisions. Eventually the membership becomes uninterested and apathetic, thus making it easier for the leaders to maintain their positions.

On the basis of this analysis, Michels erected his 'iron law of oligarchy'. All organisations originally motivated by a democratic impulse eventually degenerate into oligarchies. It is not that the nature of the organisation 'causes' oligarchy, but that the democratic organisation inevitably becomes *oligarchical.* One may say that oligarchy is immanent in organisation.

A sixth type of asymmetrical relationship is one involving an association between *ends* and *means*. The relationship is interpreted as purposive; it is based on the fact that the means contribute to the ends. Thus to cite Bunge's example, there is a relationship between the building of nests by birds and the survival of the young; the nest building is a means for insuring that survival.[24] Similarly there is a relationship between standardisation in industry and production costs. Standardisation is a means of reducing costs.

This type of relationship appears with considerable frequency in social science. One might find for example that there is a relationship between hard work and success, amount of studying and school grades, national aggressive aims and expansion of military forces, investment and profits, care for personal appearance and marriage rate and so on. In each case the means serve the end.

Since such relationships are viewed as purposive the question arises: In whose mind does the purpose reside? Thus the bird builds her nest on the basis of instinct, not with the conscious purpose of insuring the survival of the species. People who are hard-working may end up successful even if this was not their particular goal. On the other hand a nation with expansionist aims will intentionally enlarge its military establishment, just as a student who aspires to be accepted by the college of his choice may decide to concentrate on his school-work. In some cases then the purpose may be in the mind of the actor, whereas in other cases it is inferred by the analyst.

This leads to the problem of whether the ends determine the means or whether the means determine the ends. Both are possible: a person with a goal will select the means best suited to attain it; conversely certain behaviour may lead to certain ends. How then can one decide whether it is the ends or the means which is the independent variable?

One rule of thumb is that if the purpose resides in the mind of the actor then the ends determine the means; man can plan and he selects his behaviour in accord with its contribution to his goals. It is the goal of increased profit that induces the businessman to invest; he would not do so otherwise. On the other hand if the purpose resides in the mind of the investigator, then the means determine the ends and are the independent variables. The ascetic, this worldly, work-dedicated orientation of the early Calvinist was a response to the unbearable uncertainty posed by the riddle of salvation, but it was indispensable to the growth of capitalism. In this case the means gave rise to the end.

It is apparent from the foregoing discussion that there are many possible 'meanings' of relationships. Hence when a survey analyst examines a two-variable relationship, his first task is to assign meaning to it and to do so as explicitly as possible. For one thing, the particular meaning he assigns to the relationship generally determines the next step in his analysis. For another, the theoretical contribution of the finding will depend on the framework within which it is viewed. The first question he must pose then is: Is the relationship to be viewed as symmetrical, reciprocal or asymmetrical; if asymmetrical, which is the independent (determinative) variable and which the dependent (effect) variable?

As we have observed, symmetrical relationships may contribute importantly to scientific understanding in showing that the variables may be indicators of a common concept, in showing the related consequences of a common cause, in revealing the functional relationships among variables and in showing the concordance of elements in a social complex. Similarly the understanding of reciprocal relationships is of great value in clarifying the dynamic nature of social processes. Finally asymmetrical relationships may be enlightening in revealing how stimuli may effect responses, how dispositions may influence behaviour, how properties may influence dispositions or behaviour, how necessary preconditions may be responsible for consequences, how variables may be immanent in structures and how ends and means are associated. Each type of interpretation makes its distinctive contribution to the understanding of social phenomena, and all should be given due consideration in the analysis of survey data.

While symmetrical, reciprocal and asymmetrical relationships all have theoretical significance, the process of elaboration is undertaken only with *asymmetrical relationships.* The type of asymmetrical relationship most commonly investigated in sociology is one between a *property* as the independent variable, and a *disposition or act* as the dependent variable. The relationships between race and vote, age and mental health, class and self-values are illustrative. Once the decision is made that the relationship is asymmetrical, one then introduces a third variable into this two-variable relationship in order to understand it better.

4 Problems with Surveys: Method or Epistemology?*

Catherine Marsh

It may seem untimely to start worrying about the philosphical basis of survey research at a time when the main difficulty facing any of us is most probably getting cash to do the research at all. However, perhaps for that very reason, arguments, which are declaring that survey research is after all perhaps not on a very sound epistemological footing are gaining currency; I was forced to reflect hard on the process of decision-making in large-scale organisations when the S.S.R.C. suddenly discovered in 1975, when funds were beginning to dry up, that it had changed its mind on the importance of survey research and decided to close the S.S.R.C. Survey Unit. Many of those arguments and arguments since have made vague references to unease about survey research as a method applicable to producing sociological theory, and some of them I think touch chords in all of us when we consider what contributions to sociological theory have actually been made by survey research.

The trouble is that there are two bogeys to be dealt with at once. The first and most serious is the anti-scientism prevalent in most British sociology today which charges all scientific attempts at the construction of social theory 'positivist', and which holds that

*Reprinted from *Sociology*, vol. 13, no. 2, May 1979, pp. 293 – 305.

technical errors are the result of this philosophical mistake. But the second is the existence of a certain amount of positivist thinking among survey researchers which allows the former confusion to persist.

I am not going to defend the scientific method as such here; that is too large a task. But I hope to relieve it, and surveys as part of it, from the accusation of positivism. I shall do this by examining first what constitutes survey research as a particular type of research method and what are the problems peculiar to it.

I then further want to consider whether these problems are intrinsic philosophical problems which place absolute constraints on the method, or whether they are technical problems which are in principle capable of a solution. It is my contention that, behind the war-cry of positivism, attacks that have been parading as fundamental criticisms of the epistemological basis of survey research have very often been either criticisms of a practical technical nature – i.e. criticisms of bad survey research, which all of us would want to agree with I'm sure – or have raised problems to do with the problem of *any* kind of data collection in social sciences, which stem from the problem that the subject matter of our research is conscious, communicates in a language whose meaning is not capable of unique determination, and is capable of changing very rapidly. This is a problem for any social scientist, from the experimenter to the ethnographer, and is not confined to surveys.

My comments will be restricted to surveys which are designed to provide evidence for particular sociological theorising. Part of the opprobrium attaching to surveys has come from the fact that their form is similar to that utilised by the public opinion pollster and the market researcher, both of whom are more concerned with predictive ability than with explanation and understanding of the phenomena they study. The polling conception of survey research has often tended to rub off on the sociologist conducting a survey. This has tended to produce two types of results. One response is for the sociologist to treat the subjects from whom she collects information as proxy sociologist, to provide the explanations for their own behaviour that she cannot provide. Another response is that the sociologist acts as something not far removed from a lobbyist, aggregating individual opinions and presenting them, as if their meaning and importance was self-evident. But those developing social theory also may survey individuals by means of interviews, and collect reports of behaviour, beliefs and attitudes (although as I shall show there is no reason why a survey should not systematically directly observe people); for the academic, the responses are *data* whose role is subservient, to act as evidence for the theoretical end point they are pursuing. For such use, it is important to understand the vital differences between self reported behaviour, beliefs and attitudes; many criticisms of survey research have been correct to unmask the illicit assumption that verbal behaviour of various kinds gives good access to behaviour outside the interview. It is vital to realise that in a sociological survey, individuals are approached for information because that is the most efficient way to gain it (it is not always even that, unfortunately). They are usually asked to give reports on their behaviour and their beliefs and attitudes are sought.

Practitioners in this area must be clear themselves about the fundamental nature of what they are doing and the limits and possibilities in using this particular method. Survey researchers have probably all got some vague negative justification for survey research in their heads which amounts to a knowledge that the other styles of research that are open to sociologists are in practice inadequate. For most areas of inquiry the style of research that is based on experimentation is not possible both on practical and ethical grounds. Yet the 'ethnographic style' of research, if I may so generalise about all those various attempts to apply the method of *verstehen* to small-scale situations by intensive immersion in one area, is somehow not rigorous enough to allow its theories to be subjected to any real constraint in the world beyond the researcher, nor is it capable of producing data over a large enough range of situations to allow the scope or generality of its theories to be tested.

I hope to show in this chapter that the drive for rigour and objectivity in our research methods does not commit us to a positivist bandwagon, although I concede that most of the textbook discussions of the subject would not allow one to make the distinction.

The Survey as a Method of Testing Hypotheses

I want to define a survey as any inquiry which collects pieces of information, by whatever method, over a range of different cases, and arranges the information about those cases as variables; variables therefore must have the property of providing one unique code for every case. The common strategy for the survey researcher who has collected a case by variable matrix of data of this form is to consider the relationship of the variables, either over the whole of the matrix or in subgroups.

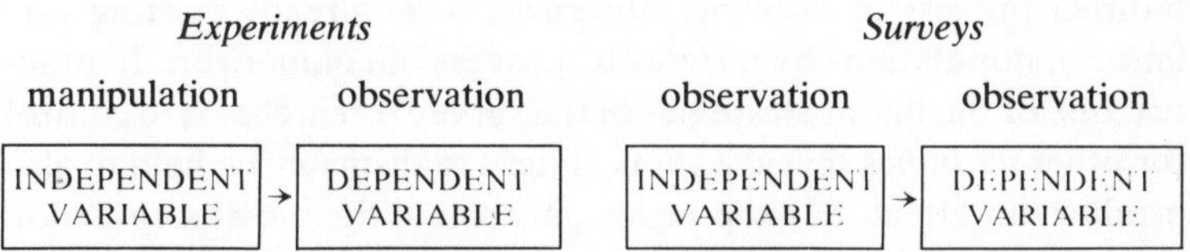

FIGURE 8 *Logically distinct ways of testing causal hypotheses*

Figure 8 summarises the two ways known to me of testing hypotheses about social processes. The experimenter 'does something to' her subjects (and usually also 'does not do something to' a set of controls) and looks to see what effect *manipulating* variance in the independent variable has on the depndent variable. Within the limits defined by the laws of probability (if the subjects have been randomly allocated into experimental group and control group) she can be sure that it is what she did to the independent variable that has produced any variance she observes in the dependent variable.

But the survey researcher has only made a series of observations; to be sure, as we shall come on to argue, these cannot be seen just as passive reflections of unproblematic reality, but they must be logically distinguished from the manipulation that the experimenter engages in. The only element of randomness in the survey design comes in random selection of cases; *random sampling is not the same as random allocation into control and experimental groups.* The survey researcher may have a theory which leads her to suspect that X is having a causal effect on Y. If she wants to test this, she has to measure X and Y on a variety of different subjects and infer from the fact that X and Y covary that the original hypothesis was true. But unlike the experimenter, she cannot rule out the possibility *in principle* of there being a third variable prir to X and Y causing the variance in both; the experimenter knows that the relationship is not spurious in this technical sense because she knows exactly what produced variance in *X* – *she* did. In common with the experimenter, the survey researcher cannot know how *X* produces an effect on *Y*; it may do it directly, or it may work through intervening variables.

In other words, in survey research the process of testing causal hypotheses, central to any theory-building endeavour, is a very indirect process of drawing inferences from already existing variance in populations by a rigorous process of comparison. In practice one of the major strategies of the survey researcher is to control for other variables that she thinks might realistically be held to also produce an effect, but she never gets round the purist's objection that since she did not measure everything and control for everything (as the experimenter did by randomisation) she has not definitively established a causal relationship.

Furthermore, although having panel data across time certainly helps with the practical resolution of the problem of how to decide which of one's variables are logically prior to which others, it does not solve this logical difficulty that in principle any relationship which one finds may be explained by the operation of another unmeasured factor. And since we are talking about the application of survey research for the elaboration of sociological theory, we can also see that when the subject matter is conscious human beings who are capable of anticipating future occurrences in their actions, knowing that something occurs before something else is no guarantee that it caused it rather than that it was caused by it. (Take for example the relationship between exam performance at O and A level and later jobs taken up among British schoolgirls; there is now quite strong evidence to suppose that the early maturity thesis is quite wrong and that girls, although starting out slightly more capable than boys at getting O level passes, have by A level stage anticipated their later job possibilities and set their horizons lower).

It is this logical structure which is intrinsic to survey methodology. The data could come from observation, from fixed-choice responses to a postal questionnaire, from content analysis of newspapers or from post-coding tape-recorded depth interviews. The important thing is that there is more than one case and that variation between cases is considered systematically. I shall come on later in the chapter to argue that the charge of positivism has most bite when applied to some views of structured questionnaires. However, the logical status of a survey is that is is one of two possible ways to test causal hypotheses.

The Essence of Positivism

We are not quite ready to answer the critics who claim that survey research has an inherently positivist bia, however, for we must lay our cards on the table about what constitutes the essence of this philosophy which has almost become a synonym for crassness in common sociological parlance. Kolakowski [1972] defines positivism as a philosophy which says nothing about the origin of knowledge but which aims to provide a demarcation between the knowledge that deserves the name science and that which does not. Although he admits that his intellectual history of positivism has an element of arbitrariness to it inasmuch as he discusses protagonists of this philosophy who with one exception, did not apply this label to themselves, nevertheless he extracts from the wide variation in positivist philosophy four elements which he considers sum up its essence:

(1) the rule of phenomenalism, which asserts that there is only experience, and which rejects all abstractions be they 'matter' or 'spirit';
(2) the rule of nominalism, which asserts that words, generalisations, abstractions are linguistic phenomena and do not give us new insight into the world;
(3) the separation of facts and values;
(4) the unity of the scientific method.

Obviously all four of these prescriptions have implications if applied to development of sociological theories.

(1) and (2) assert that all knowledge is limited to experience, and that it is impossible to go beyond this to some deeper reality; while historically the development of these postulates about knowledge served a useful purpose in refuting the idealism of the old theological views of knowledge, they deny the possibility of cognitive knowledge. This would lead sociologists to deny the search for underlying personality or social structures which have got dynamics which affect the world as perceived but which themselves are not *directly* perceivable. I stress this: positivism is correct in asserting that evidential criteria have to be sought in our sense perceptions of the world, but incorrect in asserting that theories flow directly from these sense perceptions. Indeed, the opposite is the case: without theory, perceptions are meaningless.

(3) would make sociology a purely technical endeavour collecting

enough facts about the world to inform any value position wanted. If we accept this postulate, then the only thing that can go wrong in the process of research is that facts are somehow wrongly reported or perceived. The notion that categories used are inevitably based on a theoretical position and value position is denied by the positivist.

(4) of course asserts the unity of the scientific method on the basis of the first three postulates. Taken out of context it is not objectionable; indeed, I have just argued that there are only two ways to test casual hypothesis in any scientific endeavour. But positivism is wrong in stressing an essential unity of the subject matter of the various sciences, and thus the similarity of causal factors; in the human sciences where the subject matter is social and conscious man, then intentions and motives become an important although not exhaustive component of causes. Moreover, there is no reason to suppose in the social world that any underlying determining social processes *themselves* do not change. This is the major reason why the positivist demand for cumulative empirical knowledge is not easily met.

It is the aim of any science to get at the causal relationships between things; this is precisely what the positivist cannot accept if she buys the first two postulates above, for concepts like necessity and mechanism are abstractions. She is forced to argue that the distinction between causation and correlation is a spurious one, for all that our sense perceptions tell us about is correlation.

Is Survey Research Inherently Positivistic?

I stress the word 'inherently' because I would be the first to concede that very large amounts of research in the survey style, as in the laboratory experimental style or the ethnographic style, have accepted the first three postulates of the philosophy that I have argued are unacceptable as the basis of rational knowledge.

Consider Figure 9 as a summary of the points that I made earlier about needing to distinguish between problems in principle and technical, corrigible problems, and needing to distinguish between data collection and data analysis. The distinction between data collection and analysis is clearly not a temporal one which says that data collection comes before data analysis; this can be illustrated by

		NATURE OF PROBLEM	
		PHILOSOPHICAL	PRACTICAL
AREA OF PROBLEM	DATA COLLECTION	e.g. reactivity	e.g. choice of words for a question
	ANALYSIS	e.g. casual inference	e.g. level of analysis

FIGURE 9 *A typology of 'problems' in sociological research*

thinking about the process of coding, which is at once both a method of selecting and collecting information and at the same time is a method of the most primary kind of analysis of that information. I am simply arguing that the problems at the philosophical level of validity, which relate to how to collect valid data and how to draw valid inferences from it, are distinct.

If my earlier argument was correct that the characteristic of survey research was that it was a particular approach to the problem of causality, then a charge of positivism should be found in the problems located in the bottom left-hand box of Figure 9. The argument should be that drawing causal inferences from cross-sectional data, from already existing variation, is unsound because it follows one of the first three epistemological principles outlined.

There are certainly large difficulties associated with drawing causal inferences from snapshots organised in this form, or even from motion pictures: but the procedure is only positivistic if one tries to claim that theory has no role in ordering the variables and assessing the significance of the coefficients. Those who think that there is an automatic way of deciding on the substantive causal significance of a finding through doing a test of significance on a correlation coefficient are certainly wide open to the charge of overt positivism. The question is whether survey research can be used by those who believe that there are processes at work in reality, but not obvious to the observer, to be uncovered by him by means of theory construction and test.

The answer is complex. We cannot order variables in our survey without recourse to a theory about the way the world works, and that theory itself will certainly not have derived from cross-sectional observations. This is not the place to discuss the origins of theories about the world, but in my view they do not spring from passive observations and correlation of attributes of those observations. The results of a survey do not lead to any automatic conclusions about the world which will guide either conservative cabinet ministers or revolutionaries in how to go about achieving their objectives. But they do provide a test (more importantly they often provide the *only* test) of a theoretical hypothesis if the theory is made explicit.

An Example to Illustrate This

Nichols and Armstrong in a book called *Workers Divided* [1976] described their depth study of a chemical plant in the West of England and the workers who work in it; unfortunately, although there is much of potential value in this book, it is overshadowed by a complete refusal to discuss methodology. They don't even tell us whether they did their interviews in the factory or in the pub after work. For two authors who say they reject the survey method (owing to their confusion of the same with fixed format questionnaires) because it is incapable of reflecting in a sensitive fashion the complexities and subtleties of working-class thought and ideology, this silence is stunning. Who knows what subtle pressures are at work when the researcher, obviously a committed 'leftie', is buying the drinks?

Although you have to extract the hypotheses from the text with a pickaxe, there are several interesting ideas lurking which could be formalized into hypothetical conditions preventing the development of class solidarity. Taking one of Nichols's chapters from early on in the book, he suggests in effect that one would expect to find a negative relationship between solidarity and

- the management collection of trade union dues
- shift working
- national as opposed to plant wage bargaining
- existence of contract labour on site
- 'massified capital' and complex organisational structures
- management sophistication

These are all suggestions that he culled from his depth study at one particular workplace, BUT THEY STILL REQUIRE CORROBORATION. The only way I know of getting even partial information to back up these extremely interesting hypotheses is through systematically comparing plants around the country with different situations regarding our hypothesised conditions, to see if there is indeed systematic variation in solidarity. Now just doing a survey of a series of plants and observing variations of this kind certainly would not enable us to draw causal inferences relating the conditions to the development of solidarity, but within the context of a theory which says why these things might be expected to happen, we can use the observations as a limited test. We have to be clear that the test is limited by the fact that it is based on passive observations of the world, rather than manipulation which attempts to change the world in some way.

We may accept a limited version of the Popperian thesis of asymmetry between corroboration and refutation. If we did indeed find a correlation where we expected, even after we had controlled for everything else which we thought was a candidate for making the relationship a spurious one, we would still not wish to call this proof of our theory. But if we failed to find a relationship at all, we would be tempted to consider this a refutation. I call this a limited version of the Popperian idea because there is always still the theoretical possibility of a third variable acting as a 'suppressor', to use the Columbia terminology: we may fail to find a relationship because sex may be acting to suppress the relationship between shift working and lack of solidarity. It might be that women do less shift work, but are also slower to develop solidaristic class consciousness (there is little evidence that this is the case, I hasten to say), and this is hiding an overall negative relationship between shiftwork and class consciousness when you hold sex constant. None the less, I think that we have to say that a persistent failure to establish correlation after searching long and hard for possible suppressor variables must be taken as a refutation of the theory which gave rise to the hypothesis.

We are forced to admit that this procedure of inferring causality is fraught with danger, and outside the framework of a developed theory is pointless and uninteresting.

Practical Problems of Data Analysis

The example of *Workers Divided* leads us very naturally to consideration of another problem of survey research. Those who have charged it with the accusation of positivism have often found it very difficult to decide whether it committed the atomist fallacy of tearing individuals from their social location and failing to situate them in their social structural setting, or whether the real crime was the aggregative holist fallacy of thinking that there was anything inherently meaningful in characteristics of whole groups or whole societies. Apart from being rather contradictory, there are aspects of both these criticisms that should be located in the bottom righ-hand box of Figure 9, namely, practical difficulties of data analysis. There is nothing intrinsic to the logic of survey research that dictates the level of analysis, the unit under consideration. The unit has most commonly been the individual, since it is a relatively straightforward procedure to collect information from individuals. None the less, many surveys treat households, firm, or geographical territories or even whole societies as their basic unit of analysis.

Realising that this is a practical, technical problem, should make practitioners using this method of research reflect very hard about the theory that they are testing, for there are many dangers which surround one when trying to infer features of one level from properties measured at another (Robinson [1950]; Alker [1962]). Hauser [1970] argues that most features of collectivities are, in fact, interpreted as short-hand for properties of individuals, and great care should be taken to measure the original individual properties. He shows, in an entertaining spoof of a respectable-scientific-paper, the dangers associated with inferring a *meaning* to the correlation between the proportion of girls in a school and the educational aspirations of the girls and boys in it. One strand of positivist thinking has historically been associated with holism, and a failure to provide an explanation at the level of mechanism: the mistake of most survey researchers seems to be atomism, however. As Blau [1957] argued in his paper on the methodology of analysing organisations as a whole, 'Quantification, so important for providing evidence in support of generalisations, has often produced an artificial atomism of the organised social structures under investigation'. While I would disagree with Blau's attribution of quantification as the cause (the fact that individuals can speak in answer to questionnaires where organisations cannot seems far more cogent an explanation), I would agree with his diagnosis of the sickness.

The cure is for researchers to think a lot harder about the possible ways in which the distributions in the variables they study might be being generated; Blau was one of the first people to demonstrate that survey research could be used to distinguish between truly individual effects and what he calls 'structural effects', where aggregated individual properties have effects on other individuals. Survey data on individuals can be aggregated to provide contextual measures also.

Let me illustrate this again with the same example of a hypothesised relationship between shift-working and the lack of development of class solidarity. If we found a relationship, it could mean:

(1) that working shifts made individuals less likely to develop solidaristic consciousness, regardless of what other people in the factory did:
(2) that when many people in the plant were on shift work, the whole plant failed to develop solidaristic consciousness, but that was not more true for shift-workers than for others:
(3) that the existence of shift-work in the plant made the shift-workers more conscious but this was outweighed by the effect it had on the other staff in whom it produced the effect of complacency.

And of course there could be complex interactions of these effects. Surveys, if properly designed, can investigate the existence of contextual effects of this kind. There is no need *post hoc* to rationalise explanations for how such a negative correlation between shift-working and class consciousness came about. If these explanations can be anticipated, with some careful thought and with advice about some of the very complex statistical questions about inference and degrees of freedom associated with different levels of analysis, a study could be designed of several factories and workers within those factories to illuminate some of these interesting questions (Davis *et al.* [1961]).

It would appear that the work of the Columbia School sociologists (e.g. Lazarsfeld [1959]) and other European successors, like Boudon [1971] is little known to English sociologists who are engaged in survey research; and it clearly is unknown to those who argue that there is something inherent in survey research which commits you to a particular level of analysis, even though they cannot make up their mind what that is.

Variables

Finally, we must discuss some of the difficulties which arise from converting individual information to variables and thereafter analysing these either in the whole dataset or in specific subgroups. Blumer's call [1956] for what he terms 'generic' variables (I would prefer to call them variables with real definitions) in social sciences is well taken. But it is important not to blame the process of trying to make one's categories explicit and systematic by 'fitting' reality to variables for the substantive and theoretical paucity of the categories themselves. I have defined a variable as a parameter which has got one unique value for every case and which varies across the population; numbers are usually assigned to the categories in the process of coding, but these categories need reflect no more than a nominal scale of measurement. In other words, all that this criterion for survey research is saying is that when we are talking about characteristics, we must minimally be able to differentiate between the characteristic being present and it being absent. Coding something as a variable 'measured' at a nominal level is doing no more than describing it, making the rules for description in this manner as explicit as possible. Variables are thus simply the result of following through coding rules – they need to be interpreted theoretically before they can be utilised in theory construction. Baldamus [1976, p. 125] has pointed out that a large proportion of what passes for sociological explanation is merely taking an interesting variable that one would like to 'explain' and correlating it with half a dozen background variables, like age, sex, class, education, religion and so on. This approach results in atheoretical sociology and impossibly boring journal articles.

But the fault is not to be laid at the door of converting complex and rich reality into variables. The fault is the crudity of the way in which things like education are measured, owing to the even greater crudity in the way it is theorised. We do not know whether to measure length of schooling, qualifications, type of institution or attributes of teachers or other pupils, because we have not got a sufficiently specific theory about the importance of various aspects of education. The fact that almost any variable you care to name will produce a zero-order correlation with these background variables reflects the fact that the variables are standing as a simple, miserable proxy for vast and complexly interwoven social institutions.

However, there are difficulties here, because not all the variables are of the same type. Lazarsfeld and Menzel [1961] provided an excellent classification for different types of individual properties: these are –

absolute properties which are unique to the individual (e.g. age),
relational properties which express the relationship of one individual to another (e.g. marital status),
comparative properties which derive from a comparison of one individual with another (e.g. sibling order),
contextual properties which are formed by associating the individual with the value of his collectivity (e.g. generation).

Causal interpretation of these variable types is very different, since to give a causal explanation is to assert that a change in one variable produces a change in another one, and change in these variable types differs in its implication for other people. If we explain militancy by the absolute variable age, we could just be describing our sample by saying that the older respondents were less militant. But if we wished to give a causal interpretation of this, we would say that the older a person becomes, the less militant she becomes, and we would also be free to say that if the age structure of the population changed such that mean age increased, then we might expect mean militancy to decrease. But if we think age is standing as proxy for the contextual variable of generation membership individual changes are impossible, but changes in mean value of militancy could be said to have been caused by generational movement. Similarly, if job satisfaction is held to be an absolute property, individual and average changes in it will produce individual and average changes in militancy. But it could plausibly be argued that it is derived from comparing one's own situation with that of others. If one individual's job satisfaction increases, it is bound to mean that someone else's decreases, and thus shifts in average job satisfaction are conceptually impossible and this group causal interpretation cannot be given.

Finally, on the subject of variables, what do we do with those aspects of reality which are important *constants* in human behaviour, which do not vary at all? State power might be considered as something that would fit with the example we have been using of factors affecting the development of class solidarity. Just because something is a constant at the time when we want to measure it, does not mean that it cannot change. Moreover, although state power itself might be a constant itself, it might interact with other variables, especially variables tapping aspects of political consciousness, in producing an effect. Our causal model would be an inaccurate reflection of reality if it did not take this into account.

To sum up, if correlational analysis is used to test theories which link variables in a causal model, then survey research has a contribution to make to the development of scientific theories. We have noted that the idea of cause in our models may not be interpretable in the sense that changing *X* would necessarily bring about a change in *Y*, but this is not because the explanation being put forward is not causal. It is because the actual variables being used in the model are not necessarily open to the technical manipulation that would allow the situation to change.

Problems of Data Collection – the Scheduled Questionnaire

But we cannot ignore completely the fact that historically the survey method of investigation has been linked with the use of a fixed format questionnaire which is designed so that the transformation of the information on it to computer cards is reasonably fast and straightforward. And it is in the arena of the use of standardised questioning that the charge of positivism has bitten deepest. So I should like to devote the rest of this paper to a consideration of the dangers and difficulties attached to the use of fixed format questions – in other words, of communicating with individuals under fairly controlled conditions. These are questions that affect all sociological research which collects its data this way, not just surveys; you do not escape the difficulties by pretending that you can extract unproblematic information yourself in a pub over a pint of beer.

It is impossible to avoid the problem that asking people questions, as an instrument of measurement, itself 'reacts' upon the person who is being asked the question, and affects the response. Positivism attempts to deny this inherent reactivity; the positivist claims that it is possible to ask unbiased questions, and to get at the truth. This idea of 'absolute truth' lying waiting for a sociologist with keen sense perception and good measuring instruments to tap is absurd. It suggests that perceptions can be atheoretical and value-free, the third postulate. These notions are highly problematic, but they have currency.

In an otherwise sensible book on questionnaire design, Stanley Payne [1951] defines an unbiased question as one which does not itself affect the answer. What is this supposed to mean? Does it mean that the answer would be an utterance that the same person might have made spontaneously? Clearly not, for any utterance is spoken for a reason, with intention of communicating something: spontaneously there is no reason why people surveyed should desire to convey this information without a reason. The definition is absurd, for we ask questions precisely in order to elicit utterances slanted in a particular way.

Payne continues: 'One thing has always stumped researchers, and will stump us for a long time to come: having observed different results with different types of questions on the same subject, we still cannot agree on which of the different results comes nearest the truth.' With a definition of truth like this, who wonders at researchers getting stumped? We learn, as we read the (pitifully meagre) literature on question formulation, that you do indeed increase the proportion of people who are prepared to answer negatively to a question by the addition of 'or not' at the end of the question regardless of the subject matter. We learn that the addition of a neutral category in an attitude question which explicitly allows people to remain uncommitted decreases the proportion of those who will endorse the positively phrased items whatever the question. What does this mean? Is one response more true than the other? Certainly not, for different questions were asked: questions are live communications and different questions will convey different intentions of what it is that the researcher wants to the respondent. Our task is to make sure that the intention that is conveyed is the one that we wish to convey, and is not a question about social desirability of something. And certainly every question will not convey precisely the same intention to each respondent, but we shall return to that. We need to know a lot more about what the effect of changing the wording of questions is – we need to know more about the interaction that goes on between interviewer and respondent in the interview situation, so that the interviewer is capable of effectively conveying the researcher's intentions. We must reject Moser and Kalton's [1971] prescription of the search for the 'individual true value' (the ITV) which our methods measure with a greater or lesser degree of precision.

What is the implication of this position? Does it rule out the use of the fixed format question? In my opinion, the main conclusion of adopting a position of this kind is that questionnaire design is a very complex task in interpersonal communication, especially if it is designed to stand up to being handled via a third party, namely, an interviewer who did not herself frame the question. It means that before a fixed form for the question can be settled on, piloting various versions of the question and depth interviewing of respondents and interviewers about what they thought the question meant absolutely must occur. Cicourel [1964] does not knock any dents in fixed-choice questions at all by pointing out the validity of the questions rests on the skills of interpersonal communication of those involved with translating those questions into variables. We must be quite explicit about this and not pretend that the meaning of any of the questions that we ask is self-evident.

But we must also not forget why we bother going to all the trouble of getting a standardised format of communication: it is difficult enough to fully understand the reactivity of this highly controlled situation without multiplying it unduly by changing the question wording also.

Let us return to the question of assuming unity of meaning. Cicourel argues that for a fixed form of question to produce valid answers, the question and the answer would have to be in everyday language not altered by 'particular relevance structures'.

Taylor [1978] criticises the attempt to consider as data 'the subjective reality of individuals' beliefs, attitudes, values, as attested by their responses to certain forms of words'. He believes that questionnaire items are fundamentally incapable of considering 'social reality as characterised by intersubjective and common meanings'.

To the extent that critics in the hermeneutic tradition have made us aware of the centrality of language in many (although by no means all) social interactions, they have performed a very useful function in forcing us to be sensitive to possible ambiguities in the words we choose to frame our questions in and the coding schemes we use for decoding the meanings of the respondents. There is no doubt that there are many sitting targets for this kind of criticism in much social science. The field of opinion and attitude research is notorious for its blindness to the subtleties of meaning in the questions – it is well known that the general public is strongly in favour of the democratic right to withhold one's labour in an industrial dispute, but draws the line at strikes. There is the ever-present danger of artifacts, and the question creating the response rather than 'eliciting' it. (Marsh [1979]).

To the extent that criticisms such as these direct the survey researcher towards painstaking piloting of questionnaires, using all the complex skills of a human interviewer to negotiate in a depth interview about the complex meanings involved in respondents' answers, the criticism has been constructive and useful. But, by and large, this has not been the direction of such criticism. The quote from Taylor above illustrates that he believes that fixed format questions can never achieve an understanding of social reality 'as characterized by intersubjective and common meanings', and he is a sufficiently hard-line interpretativist to believe that these common meanings exhaustively constitute the social world.

There are several criticisms one could raise against this point of view. The most obvious is that the social world is clearly *not* simply constituted through language. To be sure, the meaning of the words that we use is inherently problematic. Philosophers who discuss the problems of meaning recognise that the meaning of some words has to be assumed *a priori* as unproblematic so that the meaning of others may be discussed, in order that the 'hermeneutic circle' may be broken. The empirical recommendations for research of authors such as Cicourel [1964], who refuse to draw the line at any point over this question of meaning is inevitably sucked into a never-ending circle of negotiation and interpretation. The empirical product of the social science that espouses this view (aptly described by Goldthorpe's characterisation as 'DIY linguistics') has not managed to escape from the problems that it has itself identified. And one could argue, against Cicourel, that at one level it is precisely systematic variation in 'particular relevance structures' that we are interested in. A good question will often be one that gets at the appropriate relevance structure, if you like.

Let me illustrate this first with a question about attitudes. If we ask people their opinion on the EEC, it is quite clear that they will not all have the same idea of what the EEC actually is, nor will it be relevant to all of them in the same way. But presumably this is what we would think accounted for differences in their responses to the question; indeed, it is hard to think what else could account for differences, for the EEC itself is not a variable. It makes no sense to talk of response error to a question of this kind. If we ask a question that elicits what has been called a 'social desirability response', we have got to see this as an error in the question, not the respondent.

The danger comes in using words whose ambiguity is unintended and unknown: the meaning of the question to different respondents is varying according to contextual factors that we may be unaware of. But it is important to remember that the most likely result of this ambiguity will be to produce seemingly more random data, obscuring real relationships, rather than leading us into mistaking true relationships which in fact just stem from differences in meaning.

Moser and Kalton [1971], who define response error as deviation from the ITV, admit that there are some difficulties with this conception:

> It is true that many questions are not so simple and – for instance – with opinion questions – it would often be difficult to define the ITV. However, this difficulty is beside the point here.

The difficulty is not beside the point. It highlights precisely what is wrong with the positivist conception of truth.

But I might have had a more difficult a time, and Moser and Kalton [1971] an easier one, with something 'harder' like the number of rooms in a respondent's house. Here the notion that there is a correct answer that is independent of the question, the interviewer or the respondent, would seem attractive. And yet the post-census survey which checked on the accuracy of census completion discovered that the definition of a room was not common to all respondents. Some called their landing a room if they did their cooking on it. But my point is that this is a failure in the adequate communication of the intention behind the question, not a 'response error'. The respondent did not err; she merely told the census division something incidentally interesting about the way people define room space. We want the *answer* to vary according to the particular relevance structure, which is here the number of rooms as defined by the census division; but we want the question to invariably communicate the way in which the relevance is to be considered.

Now it may be that there are some intentions that we may have as sociologists which cannot be adequately communicated to respondents. Sennett and Cobb [1973] pointed out that sociologists often act as though the syndrome of denial of particularly painful psychological events had not been discovered, for they expect respondents to be able to convey to them the most inner of feeling states. This means that different techniques must be developed, like the semantic differential, which communicate the question at a less conscious level.

We must not confuse an impossible attempt to achieve 'absolute truth' through asking unbiased questions, with the aim of being objective in our quest for truth, through trying to be as rigorous as possible in the way in which we draw conclusions from observations we make about the world, what people say and how they behave; such objectivity stems mainly from making explicit the rules of coding we use.

What is the practical implication of this discussion of reactivity? Most importantly, it means that although studies which shine light on interviewer variance or response instability have got a positive aspect in that they force the research to be aware of the fact that the instrument she is using is a highly reactive one, it is no solution to just use the knowledge to increase one's confidence intervals around one's population estimates as Moser and Kalton recommend. Interviewer variance and test–retest results merely point to the existence of ambiguity through their *net* effects. We must as sociologists be concerned with the whole of the situation, and understand why some interviewers are communicating different intentions to other ones. In order to do this, we will have to investigate thoroughly what intensions they are in fact conveying, and this is something we should be looking at even with stable questions and no interviewer variance. The meaning of a stable response is certainly not self-evident, as Cicourel correctly points out.

But, in summary, this is a problem that any researcher who, if forced to collect data in this way, will have to face. Very many experiments have as the measurement of the dependent variable a fixed-choice question to the subjects of the experiment. And certainly most depth field studies advance through the medium of language. These studies do not avoid the problems although perhaps they are much less likely to be able to clearly say the extent of them.

Conclusion

I have been concerned to make a distinction between philosophical problems and technical problems, between problems inherent in analysis and problems in data collection. The purpose of making these is to avoid misidentifying the source of many of the problems that exist in survey research today. Crude data-dredging and false notions of truth and bias have allowed some of the critics of survey research to call the method inherently positivist. We must be clear that there is an alternative and valid way to approach the problem of causal inference and objectivity in social science which survey research can be part of.

We have to clear up these problems in order to tackle the bigger one, which is defending the scientific approach to an understanding of human affairs. We do not need to support a very strong version of the sociology of knowledge to feel sure that funding bodies will be casting around at the moment for ways to save money, and arguments about the inherent uselessness of survey research will gain an ear. We have to be clear about why these arguments are wrong.

Part Three

Unobtrusive Measures

5 Introduction and Further Reading

Martin Bulmer

> Today, the dominant mass of social science research is based upon interviews and questionnaires. We lament this over-dependence upon a single, fallible method. Interviews and questionnaires intrude as a foreign element into the social setting they would describe, they create as well as measure attitudes, they elicit atypical roles and responses, they are limited to those who are accessible and will co-operate, and the responses obtained are produced in part by dimensions of individual differences irrelevant to the topic at hand. . . . This [work] directs attention to social science research data *not* obtained by interview and questionnaire. Some may think this exclusion does not leave much. It does. Many innovations in research method are to be found scattered throughout the social science literature. Their use, however, is unsystematic, their importance understated (Webb [1966] p. 1).

Social surveys involve interaction between researcher and the subjects of research, with all the problems this creates for the validity of the measuring instruments being used. Why not, as an alternative, use *existing* sources of social data which have already been collected for other purposes? For, as Paul Lazarsfeld noted, 'man is a data producing animal. Wherever he goes, he leaves certain kinds of data – court records, tax records, school records, birth and death records, and the like. This leads to the possibility of using existing institutional data as indicators of complex social trends and relationships.'

In Britain for example a very wide range of statistical information is available from pre-existing sources, much of it collected as an aid to government policy-making. The decennial census (described in Benjamin [1970] and Hakim [1982]) provides information for the whole country on population, fertility, migration, country of birth, household and family structure, economic activity, housing, education, journey to work and other topics, at various levels of geographical aggregation from the whole society at one extreme to enumeration districts with a population of a few hundred at the other. While much census data is published, even more remains unpublished, all of it an enormous reservoir for the intrepid social researcher.

Registration data – on births, marriages and deaths – is also collected on a national basis and has been extensively used (in conjunction with census data) by demographers studying the characteristics and dynamics of population structure.

Statistical records of the main operational government departments – for example in the employment, health and social service fields – provide a further most important source of social data covering many of the major fields of sociological inquiry. Much of this data is published, and Edwards [1974], used in conjunction with the current issue of *Social Trends*, provides a guide to what is available. Its American equivalent is *Social Indicators III* [1980].

Not strictly a pre-existing source, but effectively so for the purposes of an individual social researcher, are the results of large-scale continuous social surveys carried on for the government by the Social Survey Division of O.P.C.S. The *Family Expenditure Survey* (*F.E.S.*) on income, expenditure and income maintenance; the *International Passenger Survey* (*I.P.S.*) on international migratory movements; and the *General Household Survey* (*G.H.S.*) on a large number of social topics including population, employment, housing, education and health (*G.H.S.* [1972, 1975]) all provide invaluable material for the investigation of particular topics. In the United States the *Current Population Survey* (*C.P.S.*) conducted by the Bureau of the Census is one source, but the most widely used survey for secondary analysis is the N.O.R.C. *General Social Survey* (*G.S.S.*) (cf. Glenn *et al.* [1978]).

All these sources are used extensively in research practice, yet when *methods* of research are discussed, the use of available sources are less fully considered. The purpose of Part 3 is therefore to highlight the existence and usefulness of unobtrusive measures for sociological inquiry. Their advantages are clearly considerable. In coverage and representativeness the data is often much better than an individual researcher can achieve. Registration data and some census data are available on a 100 per cent basis, other census topics for 10 per cent of the population. Compared to most other surveys, the *F.E.S.*, *G.H.S.*, and *G.S.S.* have very much larger samples and therefore permit finer analysis of particular interrelations of variables.

Moreover pre-existing data is by definition already collected, and there is no need for the researcher to devote great resources to data collection on his own account. Government departments in particular have resources available on a scale which dwarfs any facilities which even a large-scale academic research project can muster.

To use pre-existing sources, too, is a non-reactive method of research. It does not involve the researcher or one of his staff intruding into a social situation to conduct an interview or distribute a questionnaire. As Webb *et al.* [1966] emphasised, the reactive effects of survey research have important consequences for the validity of the data which they yield. Unobtrusive measures are non-reactive, which argues powerfully in their favour.

A further considerable advantage of existing sources is that they provide a means for triangulating data, of supplementing other methods and of trying to counteract the weaknesses of each method singly by multiple perspectives upon a particular problem. If a proposition can be confirmed by two or more independent methods the uncertainty of its interpretation can be substantially reduced.

The two extracts include in this section are intended to highlight different points. The piece by Webb *et al.* discusses a number of examples of the use of registration data in research, the ways in which particular sources were located and used and the methodological adequacy of such sources for the social scientist using them after the event of their collection. The arguments and criticisms which they deploy are applicable more widely to the use of available statistical sources of all kinds.

'Why don't sociologists make more use of official statistics?' is a critique of the current conventional wisdom in British sociology that official statistics are so flawed as to be worthless as valid social data. To be sure, unobtrusive measures, like any other kind of data, are fallible and imperfect. Indeed in certain respects they may be more insidious because of their seeming completness and representativeness. 'At the outset, the student must expect disappointment. Sociologists must rely to a considerable degree on data collected by other men for other purposes.... In practice the problem remains largely that of adapting to social science ends statistics which, from the point of view of the sociologist, are a by-product of administrative and organisational activity' (Halsey (ed.) [1972] pp.2–3).

The theoretical inadequacy of available data can be serious. Official statistics of the provision of many social services, for example, yield little information on the quality or adequacy of such services, of the extent to which they meet particular needs. The Registrar-General's concept of social class and what sociologists refer to as social class have by no means the same meaning, although they may appear similar. Classifications used in official series often change over time, not necessarily in a way which can be detected. Classifications of similar phenomena (e.g. families and households) in different series may be different and so prevent comparison. Classification in terms of a particular variable in which one is interested for research may be missing altogether (for example, the black population may not be readily identifiable from the census).

The interpretation of available statistics requires caution on account of the errors which may have entered into their collection, throwing doubt on their reliability or validity. Because of their importance the further reading is orientated partly to critical examination of the limitations of available sources. Types of error are usefully discussed by Morgenstern [1963]. Problems of conceptual definition and the interpretive understanding of social action are central to Douglas's study of suicide [1967], which presents a major critique, on theoretical and methodological grounds, of the Durkheimian tradition. Criminal statistics have also been the subject of continuing controversy, discussed in Wiles's paper [1975].

There is, however, the danger of concluding from some of these discussions that official statistics are so flawed as to be of little sociological value. This is a mistake. Phenomenological critiques are by no means generally accepted; they have, for example, been attacked by Hindess [1973] from a distinctive conceptualist and rationalist standpoint, as well as from more mainstream points of view. Official statistics of crime and deviance undoubtedly present special problems; the discussion of key indicators in other areas of social research such as family and household, occupation, housing and locality (Stacey [1969], Gittus (ed.) [1972], Burgess (ed.) [1984]) does not suggest that official sources are generally vitiated by error and invalidity, although they do indeed suffer from the imperfections noted earlier. Chapter 7 considers these issues in considerable detail, maintaining that negative criticism has been pushed much too far.

Moreover the test of exploring relationships by means of unobtrusive measures demonstrates associations which appear to be significant. Is the relationship between social class and mortality (Preston [1974], Townsend and Davidson [1982]), which has persisted in Britain since the data were first analysed in 1911, not a real relationship despite undoubted difficulties in recording and coding occupation data and matching census and registration records? 'The pay-off comes only when ingenuity leads to new means of making more valid comparisons. In the available grab-bag of imperfect research methods there is room for new uses of the old.' (Webb *et al.* [1966] p. 182.)

Further Reading

Empirical sources

(1) A first-rate source of descriptive statistics about British society is *Social Trends* (London: H.M.S.O., annually). It provides a comprehensive summary of available official statistics on social topics produced each year by the Government Statistical Service. Each issue also includes a number of articles; in 1975 the social commentary on social-class differences in Britain is of considerable sociological interest.

(2) The nearest American counterpart is *Social Indicators III* [1980] (Washington, D.C.: U.S. Government Printing Office for the Bureau of the Census, 1980), a compendium of social and economic data about the state of American society at the beginning of the 1980s. See also the special issue of *The Annals of the American Academy of Political and Social Science* (vol. 453,

January 1981), ed. Conrad Taeuber, 'Social Indicators: American Society in the Eighties'. (see also Annals [1978]).

(3) On a world scale the *World Development Report*, published annually since 1978 for the World Bank by Oxford University Press, provides an excellent summary of the very wide variations in economic and social conditions between different countries in the world. For a discussion of some of the methodological problems involved in such international comparisons see M. D. Morris, *Measuring the Condition of the World's Poor* (New York and Oxford: Pergamon Press for the Overseas Development Council, 1979).

(4) A. H. Halsey (ed.), *Trends in British Society since 1900* (London: Macmillan, 1972), throws its net rather wider than *Social Trends* to cover non-governmental statistical sources, and to treat more directly sociological topics such as urbanisation, immigration, religion and social mobility, building in an historical dimension. P. Abrams (ed.), *Work, Urbanism and Inequality: U.K. Society Today* (London: Weidenfeld & Nicolson, 1978), uses official and other data to analyse urban structure, work, the division of labour, deviance and elite groups from a sociological point of view.

(5) Angus Campbell, *The Sense of Well-Being in America: Recent Patterns and Trends* (New York: McGraw-Hill, 1981), reports on studies of subjective life satisfaction. Alex C. Michalos, *North American Social Report: A Comparative Study of the Quality of Life in Canada and the U.S.A. from 1964 to 1974* (Dordrecht: D. Reidel, 5 vols, 1980–2), is as its title implies a compendious general survey. A valuable example of the theoretical and policy uses of social indicators is provided by U.S. Commission on Civil Rights, *Social Indicators of Equality for Minorities and Women* (Washington, D.C.: U.S. Commission on Civil Rights, 1978).

(6) In the United States, secondary analysis of major surveys is not uncommon. A good example is provided by the primary research of James S. Coleman *et al.*, *Inequality of Educational Opportunity* (Washington, D.C.: U.S. Government Printing Office, 1966), which led to several reviews and reanalyses to test their conclusions. The most useful sources to consult are F. Mosteller and D. P. Moynihan, *On Equality of Educational Opportunity* (New York: Random House, 1972), and C. Jencks *et al.*, *Inequality* (New York: Basic Books 1972 and Penguin Books, Harmondsworth, 1973), which was the result of a major secondary analysis project.

(7) R. Layard *et al.*, *The Causes of Poverty* (Royal Commission on the Distribution of Income and Wealth, Background Study no. 5) (London: H.M.S.O., 1978), perceptively analyse the determinants

of low incomes in Britain by means of secondary analysis of data from the General Household Survey.
(8) P. Townsend and N. Davidson, *Inequalities in Health: The Black Report* (Harmondsworth: Penguin Books, 1982), demonstrate the continuing differences in life chances between different social groups in Britain, largely using statistics drawn from official sources, including registration and census data and the *General Household Survey.*

Methodology

The use of unobtrusive measures in social research is much less well codified and systematised than the use of social-survey methods. Despite the enormous amount of source materials available their exploitation and use have rarely been systematically considered other than by demographers. There is now, however, a growing literature which may be consulted.

(1) C. Hakim, *Secondary Analysis in Social Research* (London and Boston: Allen & Unwin, 1982), provides a comprehensive introduction to the U.K. Census and to large multi-purpose surveys such as the *F.E.S.* and the *G.H.S.* as sources of data for secondary analysis.
(2) E. J. Webb, D. T. Campbell, R. D. Schwarz and L. Sechrest, *Unobtrusive Measures: Non-reactive Research in the Social Sciences* (Chicago: Rand McNally, 1966). A compendious survey of data obtained from archives, physical traces and hidden observation in several social-science disciplines. It is prefaced by an incisive discussion of reactivity between the social researcher and his subjects through consideration of problems of the internal and external *validity* of measuring instruments. Contains a valuable discussion of methodological triangulation.
(3) O. Morgenstern, *On the Accuracy of Economic Observations*, rev. edn (Princeton University Press, 1963). A classic discussion of sources of error in economic statistics which is without parallel in other social sciences. Many of the points made in Part I, however, are applicable also to pre-existing social data. Watch out for the example of the Bulgarian pigs!
(4) M. Carley, *Social Measurement and Social Indicators* (London and Boston: Allen & Unwin, 1981), provides an introduction to the use of official data in the form of social indicators to measure the state of a society and change in that society from one point of time to another. Much of the book is devoted to discussing the difficulties to which this gives rise.

The analytic use of official statistics in sociology has been most widespread – and most controversial – in the study of deviance and crime.

(5) E. Durkheim, *Suicide* (London: Routledge, 1951), remains *the* classic study using available data. Its methodology has been usefully explicated in an article by Selvin (1965b).
(6) J. D. Douglas, *The Social Meanings of Suicide* (Princeton, N.J.: Princeton University Press, 1967), discusses Durkheim's work in historical context, and goes on to argue that the official statistics which he and others used are highly unreliable. An alternative approach in terms of the study of the social meanings of suicidal actions is proposed. The debate has been carried on in Britain between Atkinson [1968, 1971, 1973] and Bagley [1972, 1974].
(7) P. Wiles, 'Criminal Statistics and Sociological Explanations of Crime', in W. G. Carson and P. Wiles (eds), *The Sociology of Crime and Delinquency in Britain*, vol. 1: *The British Tradition* (London: Martin Robertson, 1975) pp. 198–219, provides an introduction to the question of the accuracy of published crime figures. Kituse and Cicourel [1963], Cicourel [1968], Nettler [1974] Chs 3 and 4 and Sparks *et al.* [1978] contain a fuller discussion.
(8) M. J. Hindelgang, T. Hirschi and J. G. Weis, *Measuring Delinquency* (Beverly Hills: Sage, 1981), reports on a major American study to assess the adequacy of officially recorded and self-reported data on delinquent behaviour.

6 The Use of Archival Sources in Social Research*

E. J. Webb, D. T. Campbell, R. D. Schwarz and L. Sechrest

Possibly a wife was more likely to get an inscribed tablet if she died before her husband than if she outlived him.

The tablet cited here is a tombstone and the quotation is from Durand's [1960] study of life expectancy in ancient Rome and its provinces. Tombstones are but one of a plethora of archives available for the adventurous researcher, and all social scientists should now and then give thanks to those literate record-keeping societies which systematically provide so much material appropriate to novel analysis.

The purpose of this chapter is to examine and evaluate some uses of data periodically produced for other than scholarly purposes, but which can be exploited by social scientists. These are the ongoing continuing records of a society, and the potential source of varied scientific data particularly useful for longitudinal studies. The data are the actuarial records, the votes, the city budgets and the communications media which are periodically produced and paid for by someone other than the researcher.

* Eugene J. Webb *et al.*, *Unobtrusive Measures*, © 1966 by Rand McNally College Publishing Company, Chicago, pp. 53–65, 82–7.

Besides the low cost of acquiring a massive amount of pertinent data, one common advantage of archival material is its non-reactivity. Although there may be substantial errors in the material, it is not usual to find masking or sensitivity because the producer of the data knows he is being studied by some social scientist. This gain by itself makes the use of archives attractive if one wants to compensate for the reactivity which riddles the interview and the questionnaire. The risks of error implicit in archival sources are not trivial, but, to repeat our litany, if they recognised and accounted for by multiple measurement techniques, the errors need not preclude use of the data.

More than other scholars, archaeologists, anthropologists and historians have wrestled with the problems of archival data. Obviously they frequently have little choice but to use what is available and then to apply corrections. Unlike the social scientist working with a contemporaneous problem, there is little chance to generate new data which will be pertinent to the problem and which will circumvent the singular weakness of the records being employed.

Naroll [1962] recently reviewed the methodological issues of archives in his book *Data Quality Control.* His central argument focuses on representative sampling. Does the archaeologist with his 1,000-year-old pottery shards or the historian with a set of 200-year-old memoirs really have a representative body of data from which to draw conclusions? This is one part of 'Croce's problem'. Either one is uncertain of the data when only a limited body exists, or uncertain of the sample when so much exists that selection is necessary.

Modern sampling methods obviate the second part of the problem. We can know, with a specified degree of error, the confidence we can place in a set of findings. But the first part of Croce's problem is not always solvable. Sometimes the running record is spotty and we do not know if the missing parts can be adequately estimated by a study of the rest of the series. That is one issue. But even if the record is serially complete, the collection of the secondary sources impeccable and the analysis inspired, the validity of the conclusions must rest on assumptions of the adequacy of the original material.

There are at least two major sources of bias in archival records – selective deposit and selective survival. They are the same two concerns one meets in dealing with physical-evidence data.

Durand's study of the ancient Roman tombstones illustrates the selective-deposit concern. Does a study of a properly selected sample of tombstones tell us about the longevity of the ancient Romans, or only of a subset of that civilisation? Durand, as noted, suggests that the timing of a wife's death may determine the chance of her datum (CCCI–CCCL) being included in his sample. It is not only the wives who die after their husbands who may be under-represented. There is, too, a possible economic or social-class contaminant. Middle- and upper-class Romans were more likely to have tombstones (and particularly those that survived until now) than those in the lower reaches of Roman society. This bias is a risk to validity to the degree that mortality rates varied across economic or social classes – which they probably did. The more affluent were more likely to have access to physicians and drugs which, given the state of medicine, may have either shortened or lengthened their lives. It is to Durand's credit that he carefully suggests potential biases in his data and properly interprets his findings within the framework of possible sampling error.

This same type of sampling error is possible when studying documents, whether letters to the editor or suicide notes. We know that systematic biases exist among editors. Some try to present a 'balanced' picture on controversial topics regardless of how unbalanced the mail. With the study of suicide notes the question must be asked whether suicides who do not write notes would have expressed the same type of thoughts had they taken pen in hand. Any inferences from suicide notes must be hedged by the realisation that less than a quarter of all suicides write notes. Are both the writers and non-writers drawn from the same population?

The demographer cannot get new Romans to live and die; the psychologist cannot precipitate suicides. And therein is the central problem of historical data. New and overlapping data are difficult to obtain from the same or equivalent samples. The reduction of error must come from a close internal analysis which usually means fragmenting the data into subclasses and making cross-checks.

An alternative approach is feasible when reports on the same phenomenon by different observers are available. By a comparative evaluation of the sources, based on their different qualifications, inferences may be drawn on the data's accuracy (Naroll [1960]; Naroll [1961]). In examining an extinct culture for example one can compare reports made by those who lived among the people for a long period of time with reports from casual visitors. Or there can be a comparison of the reports from those who learned the indigenous language and those who did not. For those items on which there is consensus, there is a higher probability that the item reported is indeed valid. This consensus test is one solution to discovery of selective deposit or editing of material. It does not eliminate the risk that all surviving records are biased in the same selective way; what it does do is reduce the plausibility of such an objection. The greater the number of observers with different qualifications, the less plausible the hypothesis that the same systematic error exists.

Sometimes selective editing creeps in through an administrative practice. Columbus kept two logs – one for himself and one for the crew. Record-keepers may not keep two logs, but they may choose among alternative methods of recording or presenting the data. Sometimes this is innocent, sometimes it is to mask elements they consider deleterious. In economic records, book-keeping practices may vary so much that close attention must be paid to which alternative record system was selected. The depreciation of physical equipment is an example. Often deliberate errors of record-keeping policy can be detected by the sophisticate. At other times the data are lost forever (Morgenstern [1963]).

One more example may serve. A rich source of continuing data is the *Congressional Record*, that weighty but sometimes humorous document which records the speeches and activities of the Congress. A congressman may deliver a vituperative speech which looks, upon reflection, to be unflattering. Since proofs are submitted to the congressman, he can easily alter the speech to eliminate his peccadilloes. A naïve reader of the *Record* might be misled in an analysis of material which he thinks is spontaneous, but which is in fact studied.

A demurrer is entered. Even if the data were originally produced without any systematic bias that could threaten validity, the risk of their selective survival remains. It is no accident that archaeologists are pottery experts. Baked clay is a 'durable artefact' that cannot be digested and decays negligibly. Naroll [1956] comments that artefacts survive because they are not consumed in use, are indifferent to decay and are not incorporated into some other artefact so as to become unidentifiable. Discrete and durable, they remain as clues, but partial clues; other evidence was eaten, rotted or re-employed. Short of complete destruction, decay by itself is no problem. It only becomes one when the rate and distribution of decay is unknown. If known it may become a profitable piece of evidence – as Libby's [1963] work with radio-carbon dating shows.

For the student of the present, as well as of the past, the selective destruction of records is a question. Particularly in the political area, the holes that exist in data series are suspect. Are records missing because knowledge of their contents would reflect in an untoward way on the administration? Have the files been rifled? If records are destroyed casually, as they often are during an office move, was there some biasing principle for the research comparison which determined what would be retained and what destroyed?

When estimating missing values in a statistical series, one is usually delighted if all but one or two values are present. This gives confidence when filling in the missing cells. If the one or two holes existing in the series have potential political significance, the student is less sanguine and more suspicious of his ability to estimate the missing data.

Actuarial Records

Birth, marriage, death. For each of these, societies maintain continuing records as normal procedure. Governments at various levels provide massive amounts of statistical data, ranging from the national census to the simple entry of a wedding in a town-hall ledger. Such formal records have frequently been used in descriptive studies, but they offer promise for hypothesis-testing research as well.

Take Winston's [1932] research. He wanted to examine the preference for male offspring in upper-class families. He could have interviewed prospective mothers in affluent homes or fathers in waiting rooms. Indeed one could pay obstetricians to ask, 'What would you like me to order?' Other measures, non-reactive ones, might be studies of adoption records, the sale of different layette colours (cutting the data by the class level of the store), or the incidence of 'other sex' names – such as Marion, Shirley, Jean, Jerry, Jo.

But Winston went to the enormous data bank of birth records and manipulated them adroitly. He simply noted the sex of each child in each birth order. A preference for males was indicated, he hypothesised, if the male-female ratio of the last child born in families estimated to be complete was greater than that ratio for all children in the same families. With the detail present in birth records, he was able to segregate his upper-class sample of parents by the peripheral data of occupation and so forth. The same auxiliary data can be employed in any study to serve as a check on evident population restrictions – a decided plus for detailed archives.

This study also illustrates the time-sampling problem. For the period studied, and because of the limitation to upper-class families, Winston's measure is probably not contaminated by economic limitations on the absolute number of children, a variable that may operate independently of any family sex preference. Had his study covered only the 1930s, or were he making a a time-series comparison of economically marginal families, the time factor could offer a substantial obstacle to valid comparison. The argument for the existence of such an economic variable would be supported if a study of the 1930s showed no sex difference among terminal children but did show significant differences for children born in the 1940s.

Economic conditions are only one of the factors important to errors due to timing. Wars, depressions and acts of God are all events which can pervasively influence the comparisons of social-science data. The subjective probability of their influence may be awkward to assign, yet the ability to control that influence through index numbers and other data transformations is a reasonable and proper practice.

There are many demographic studies of fertility levels in different societies, but Middleton [1960] showed a shrewd understanding of archival sources in his work. He developed two sets of data: fertility values expressed in magazine fiction, and actuarial fertility levels at three different time periods. For 1916, 1936 and 1956 he estimated fertility values by noting the size of fictional families in eight American magazines. A comparison with the population data showed that shifts in the size of fictional families closely paralleled shifts in the true United States fertility level.

Middleton had a troublesome sampling problem. Since only a small number of magazines continued publication over the period from 1916 to 1956, was the group of eight long-term survivors a proper sample? This durable group may not have been representative, but it was quite proper. The very fact that these eight survived the social changes of the forty years argues that they probably reflected the society's values (or those of a sufficiently large segment of the society to keep the magazine economically alive) more adequately than those which failed. The issue was not one of getting a representative sample of all magazines, but, instead, of magazines which printed material that would have recorded more faithfully the pertinent research information.

Christensen [1960] made a cross-cultural study of marriage and birth records to estimate the incidence of premarital sex relations in different societies. He simply checked off the time interval between marriage and birth of the first child – a procedure which showed marked differences in premarital conception, if not in activity among cultures. His study illustrates some of the problems in cross-cultural study. The rate of premature births may vary across societies, and it is necessary to test whether this hypothesis can explain differences. Data on the incidence of premature births of later-born children in each society permit this correction. A population problem to be guarded against in these cross-cultural studies, however, is the differential recording of births, marriages and the like. There are many societies in which a substantial share of marriages are not formally entered in a record-keeping system, although the parties initially regard the alliance to be as binding as do those in other societies where records are more complete. The incidence in Mexico of 'free-union' marriages is both extensive and selective – more prevalent among working classes than other groups (Lewis [1961]).

Simple marriage records alone were used by Burchinal and Kenkel [1962] and Burchinal and Chancellor [1962]. The records were used as a handy source by Burchinal and Kenkel [1962] to study the association between religious identification and occupational status. The records provided a great body of data from which to work, but also posed a sampling question. Are men about to be grooms a good base for estimating the link between religion and occupation? The small cadre of confirmed bachelors is excluded from the sample universe, and depending upon the dates of the records studied there can be an interaction between history and groomdom.

A later study by Burchinal and Chancellor [1963] took the complete marriage and divorce records of the Iowa Division of Vital

Statistics for the years 1953 and 1959. From these records the authors compared marriages of same-religion and mixed-religion pairs for longevity. As might be expected, they found mixed marriages to be significantly shorter-lived than same-religion ones. Of the mixed marriages, those partners who described themselves as Protestants without naming a specific affiliation showed the highest divorce rate.

It might be well to note that such data may be contaminated by self-selection error. Persons entering mixed marriages may be more unstable or more quick to see divorce as a solution. Such people might not increase the chances of a durable marriage by choosing a mate of the same religion.

These same marriage records could be employed as tests of functional literacy. Taking a time series of marriage records, what is the proportion of people signing 'X' at varying points in history?

Of all the marriage-record studies, probably none is more engaging than Galton's [1870] classic on hereditary genius. Galton used archival records to determine the eminence of subjects defined as 'geniuses' and additional archives to note how their relatives fared on eminence. Few scientists have been so sensitive as Galton to possible error in drawing conclusions, and, in a section on occupations, he notes that many of the judges he studied postponed marriage until they were elevated to the bench. Even so, their issue of legitimate children was considerable. In Stein and Heinze's [1960] summary: 'Galton points out that among English peers in general there is a preference for marrying heiresses, and these women have been peculiarly unprolific' (p. 87). And on the possible contaminant of the relative capacities of the male and female line to transmit ability:

> the decidedly smaller number of transmissions along the female line suggests either an 'inherent incapacity in the female line for transmitting the peculiar forms of ability we are now discussing,' or possibly 'the aunts, sisters and daughters of eminent men do not marry, on the average, so frequently as other women.' He believes there is some evidence for this latter explanation (p. 89).

Galton [1872] even used longevity data to measure the efficacy of prayer. He argued that if prayer were efficacious and if members of royal houses are the persons whose longevity is most widely and continuously prayed for, then they should live longer than others. Data showed the mean age at death of royalty to be 64.04 years, men of literature and science 67.55 years and gentry 70.22 years.

Another pioneering study, Durkheim's *Suicide* [1951], shows an active exploration of archival source possibilities. He concluded that 'the social suicide rate can be explained only sociologically' (p. 299) by relating suicide levels to religion, season of the year, time of day, race, sex, education and marital status, doing all of this for different countries. All of these variables were obtained from available archives, and their systematic manipulation presaged the morass of cross-tabulations that were later to appear in sociological research.

Wechsler [1961] integrated three different classes of archival data in his correlational study of the relationships among suicide, depressive disorders and community growth. He went to the census for data on population change, to mental illness diagnoses in hospital records and to the vital statistics of the state to get the suicide incidence.

Another study employing death records is Warner's [1959] work, *The Living and the Dead.* Death and its accoutrements in Yankee City were the subject of this multimethod research. Warner consulted official cemetery documents to establish a history of the dead and added interviewing, observation and trace analysis as aids to his description of graveyards. 'Their ground and burial lots were plotted and inventory was taken of the ownership of the various burial lots, and listings were made of the individuals and families buried in them' (p. 287).

His findings are of interest for what they say of response tendencies in the laying down of physical evidence. Here the response tendencies, and the way in which they vary across social-class groups, become the major clues to the analysis. Warner found the social structure of Yankee City mirrored (if this be the proper verb) in the cemetery; he found evidence on family organisation, sex and age differentiation, and social mobility. For example the father was most often buried in the centre of the family plot and headstones of males were larger than those of females. In some cases Warner found that a family which had raised its social status moved the graves of their relatives from less prestigious cemeteries to more prestigious ones.

Tombstones would be an interesting source of data for comparative analysis of different cultures. In matriarchal societies for example is the matriarch's stone substantially larger than the husband's? Does the husband get a marker at all? What are the differences in societies with extended versus nuclear family structures?

Warner's findings tie in with Durand's [1960] study of ancient Rome. In both studies, the relative dominance of the male was demonstrated by the characteristics of the tombstones.

A more recent commentary on tombstones comes from Crowald [1964] who wandered through Moscow's Novo-Devich cemetery, noting the comparative treatment of old tsarists and modern communists. After noting that over Chekhov's grave a cherry tree is appropriately blooming, he states:

> the cemetery also tells a quieter, more dramatic tale. Climbing out of some weedy grass is the washboard-sized marker of Maxim Litvinov, once a Stalin foreign minister and the wartime Soviet envoy to America. His mite of a marker reminds what happened to those who fell from Stalin's favour (p. 12).

Just as in ancient Rome, the timing of a wife's death makes a difference in the nature of the tombstone. Here this potential contaminant is used as a piece of evidence.

> Novo-Devich does show, too, that things have changed in Russia since Stalin. For example, there is the great marble monument to Rosa Kaganovich. She was the wife of Lazar Kaganovich, the Stalin lieutenant booted from power in 1957 by Premier Nikita S. Khrushchev. Kaganovich is in full disgrace, but he fell after Stalin died. So his wife, who died in 1961, still got her big place in the cemetery. Fresh flowers decorate her marble (p. 12).

These objects are just big and small pieces of stone to the uninformed, but to the investigator who possesses intelligence on those buried and relates it to the stones, the humble and grandiose memorials are significant evidence.

In Rogow and Lasswell's [1963] discussion of 'game politicians' they note:

> his relations with his immediate family were not close; indeed his wife and children saw less of him during his active life than certain

> key individuals in his political organisation. As a result he is remembered less by his family than by the state which he dominated for so many years. His grave in the family plot is unattended, but his statue stands in front of the state capitol building (p. 48).

And for a novelistic treatment of what remains behind, there is Richard Stern's [1960] commentary on Poppa Hondorp.

> The obituaries were Poppa Hondorp's measure of human worth. 'There's little they can add or subtract from you then,' was his view. Poppa's eye had sharpened over the years so that he could weigh a two-and-a-half-inch column of ex-alderman against three-and-a-quarter inches of inorganic chemist and know at a glance their comparative worth. When his son had one day suggested that the exigencies of the printer and make-up man might in part account for the amount of space accorded a deceased, Poppa Hondorp had shivered with a rage his son knew he should never excite again. 'Don't mess with credoes', knew young Hondorp, so the obituaries were sacrosanct: the *Times* issued mysteriously from an immaculate source (p. 24).

Frequently one has a choice among different archival sources, and a useful alternative are directories, whether of residents, association members or locations. Ianni [1957–8] elected to use city directories as the primary source of data in his study of residential mobility. An analysis of these directories over time allowed him to establish the rates of mobility and then relate these mobility indices to the acculturation of ethnic groups.

It is obviously a tedious task to perform such an analysis, and the work includes a high amount of dross. If possible such mobility levels might be more efficiently indexed by access to change-of-address forms in the post office. But the question here becomes one of population restriction. Is the gain in efficiency that comes from use of change-of-address forms worth the possible loss in completeness of sampling? The answer comes, of course, from a preliminary study evaluating the two sources of data for their selective characteristics.

For some studies, more selective directories are indicated, and the inclusion of a person in a directory serves as one element in the researcher's discriminations. *Who's Who in America* doesn't print everybody's name, nor does *American Men of Science*. W. H. Clark [1955] used both of these sources in his 'A Study of Some of the Factors Leading to Achievement and Creativity with Special Reference to Religious Scepticism and Belief'. Boring and Boring [1948] used *American Men of Science* to choose the psychologists studied in their useful article on the intellectual genealogy of American psychologists. Fry [1933] had earlier used *Who's Who in America* in a study entitled 'The Religious Affiliations of American Leaders'. (See also Lehman and Witty [1931].)

Fry's work showed that if one depends on the editors of such directories for selective inclusion, one must also rely on the individuals listed for complete reporting. All of the problems associated with self-report are present, for the individual has a choice of whether or not he will include all data, and whether he will report accurately. The archive serves as an inexpensive substitute for interviewing a large sample of subjects stratified along some known or unknown set of variables. Fry found that a 1926 religious census showed 3.6 per cent of the general population to be Jews, while only .75 per cent of the entries in *Who's Who in America* were listed as Jews. Does this mean that Jews are less distinguished, are discriminated against in being invited to appear in the directory or is there selective reporting by the Jews of their religion? Fry gave a partial answer to the question by a check of another directory – *Who's Who in American Jewry*. He found 432 persons in this directory who had reported no Jewish affiliation in *Who's Who in America*, thereby raising the Jewish percentage to 2.2. By raising the question of another plausible hypothesis for a comparison (3.6 per cent of the population compared with .75 per cent in the directory), he structured a question which was testable by recourse to a second archival source highly pertinent to the hypothesis.

Babchuk and Bates [1962] employed the membership list of the American Sociological Association in their work 'Professor or Producer: The Two Faces of Academic Man'. After first procuring a list of all sociology Ph.D.s for a given period from the *American Journal of Sociology*, they referred to four different membership directories of the A.S.A. for a measurement of the degree of identification with the profession. A number of persons in the sample never became affiliated with the Association; this fact was interpreted as meaning that such persons lacked an 'orientation to [the] discipline' (p. 342).

Kenneth Clark [1957] used the American Psychological Association's directory in his study of the psychological profession. For any study extending over a long time period, the A.P.A. directory can be frustrating. As the number of psychologists grew, the detail in the individual listings shrank. Thus the number of items on which a complete time series could be produced were reduced as tighter and tighter editing took place. The measuring instrument was constant in its content for only a few pieces of information. The change in the number of available categories of information is a detectable shift in the quality of the measure. Other changes, such as increasingly difficult requirements for membership or individuals responding to the greater bulk of the directory by writing more truncated listings, may change the character of the instrument in a less visible way and produce significant differences which are, in fact, only recording artefacts.

Digging into the past, Marsh [1961] obtained the names of 1,047 Chinese government officials from the government directories of 1778 and 1831–79. He then correlated the ranks of the officials with the time required to reach a particular rank and with other factors such as age and family background. If there was no differential recording, one may conclude with Marsh that the rich get there faster.

Data Transformations and Indices of the Running Record

Because the class of data cited in this chapter is drawn from continuous records which typically extend over long periods of time and all the extraneous events of history are at work to threaten valid research comparisons, there is a great need for transformation.

Perhaps the most obvious threat to valid comparisons is the change in the size of the population. The population increase has meant that the absolute values of actuarial and allied data are relatively useless. In studies employing election records, for instance, the absolute number of votes cast provides an inadequate base for most research purposes. It would give Mr Nixon little comfort, we are sure, to know that he garnered more votes in 1960, as a loser, than did any preceding winning candidate except Eisenhower. Similarly the absolute number of entries associated with population level has changed over time. This secular trend in the data is often best removed. Thus Ianni [1957–8] had to construct a relative index of residential mobility over time, and DeCharms and Moeller [1962] transformed patent production to an index tied to population.

Time also works its effect by a change in the composition of a critical group. The number of congressmen in the House of Representatives may stay relatively stable over a long time period, but the characteristics of these congressmen change – and in changing produce a set of rival hypotheses for some investigator's explanation of a research comparison. The Supreme Court ruling on reapportionment of the House (to reflect population distribution more adequately) meant substantial changes in the aggregate voting behaviour of the House, influencing the decisional setting for all congressmen, both those there before the change and the new members.

With known changes in composition, it may be necessary to segregate research findings by time periods in which relatively homogeneous external conditions held. This is a grosser correction than the more continuous correction possible for data linked to population. Even with population, though, the only thoroughly reliable data – the census totals – are produced only once every ten years. The accuracy of intervening estimates, whether from the Census Bureau itself or the highly reliable *Sales Management* magazine, are high but still imperfect.

The frailty of individual sets of records, which is discussed below, has caused many investigators to employ indices which combine several different types or units of information. The adequacy of such combinations rests, of course, on the degree to which the component elements are adequate outcroppings of the research hypothesis, as well as the degree to which appropriate weights can be assigned to the elements. Setting these questions aside, however, it is apparent that combined indices must be employed when an investigator lacks a theory so precise and subtle as to predict a single critical test, or when the theory's precision is adequate, no data exist for the critical test. For E. L. Thorndike's [1939] purpose in studying cities, there was no acceptable alternative to transforming such data as park area and property values into indices. And for MacRae [1954] and Riker and Niemi [1962], the unstable nature of a single vote by a congressman forced the construction of indices of samples of votes, which were hopefully a less ephemeral source for comparisons. MacRae needed a 'liberal index', Riker and Niemi an 'index of coalitions'. Because the individual unit was highly suspect as a sampling of the critical behaviour under study, the sampling has to be expanded. There occurs, too, the attendant questions of how the units are to be stated, weighted and combined.

One of the major gains of the running record, then, is the capability to study a hypothesis as external conditions vary over time. Such analysis demands that the investigator consider all possible transformations before making comparisons and also decide whether indices will provide a more stable and valid base for hypothesis testing. This requirement is not as pronounced in discontinuous archival records or among the observational and physical-evidence methods.

Overall Evaluation of Running Records

It should be obvious that we prize the potential for historical analysis contained in running records.

> The best fact is one that is set in a context, that is known in relation to other facts, that is perceived in part in the context of its past, that comes into understanding as an event which acquires significance because it belongs in a continuous dynamic sequence. (Boring [1963] p. 5).

If a research hypothesis, particularly for social behaviour, can survive the assaults of changing times and conditions, its plausibility is far greater than if it were tested by a method which strips away alien threats and evaluates the hypothesis in an assumptive one-time test. Validity can be inferred from a hypothesis' robustness. If the events of time are vacillating, as they usually are, then only the valid hypothesis has the intellectual robustness to be sustained, while rival hypotheses expire.

One pays a price in such time-series analysis, the necessary price of uncertainty. We again agree with that gentle stylist Boring [1963]: 'The seats on the train of progress all face backwards; you can see the past but only guess about the future' (p. 5). A hypothesis might not hold for anything but the past, but if the present is tested, and a new, possibly better, hypothesis produced, those same running records are available, as economical as ever, for restudy and new testing.

For all gains, however, the gnawing reality remains that archives have been produced for someone else and by someone else. There must be a careful evaluation of the way in which the records were produced, for the risk is high that one is getting a cut-rate version of another's errors. Udy [1964] wrote of ethnographic data:

> Researchers who use secondary sources are always open to the charge that they are cavalier and uncritical in their use of source materials and cross cultural analysis – particularly when large numbers of societies are used with information taken out of context – is particularly vulnerable to such criticism (p. 179).

At the beginning of this chapter we detailed the operating questions of selective deposit and selective survival of archives. Both these contaminants can add significant restrictions to the content and contributing populations of the archival materials. In the discussion of individual research studies, we have noted how roll-call votes, marriage records, reports of congressional speeches, letters to the editor, crime reports and other records are all subject to substantial population or content restrictions in their initial recording. To a lesser degree the selective survival of records can be a serious contaminant, and in certain areas such as politics it is always a prime question.

Those contaminants which threaten the temporal and cross-sectional stability of the data are controllable through data transformation and indexing methods – if they can be known. Happily one of the more engaging attributes of many of these records is that they contain a body of auxiliary data which allows the investigator good access to knowledge of the population restrictions. We have noted this for the absentee contaminant in congressional voting and the selective choice of cases in judicial proceedings. With the actuarial material on birth, marriage and death, it is often possible to find within the records, or in associated data series such as the census, information which will provide checks on the extent to which the research population is representative of the universe to which the findings are to be generalised.

If the restrictions can be known it is possible to consider the alternative of randomly sampling from the body of records, with a stratification control based on the knowledge of the population restriction. This is feasible for any of the records we have mentioned because of their massiveness. Indeed even if no substantial population contaminants exist, it is often advisable to sample the data because of their unwieldy bulk. Since usually they can be divided into convenient sampling units, and also frequently classified in a form appropriate for stratification, the ability to sample archival materials, particularly those in a continuous series, is a decided advantage for this class of data. The sampling of observations, or of traces of physical evidence, is markedly more difficult.

The population restrictions are potentially controllable through auxiliary intelligence; the content restrictions are more awkward. For all the varied records available, there may still be no single set, or combination of sets, that provides an appropriate test of an hypothesis.

Something of this content rigidity is reflected in Walter Lippmann's [1955] discussion of the 'decline of the west'. Lippmann writes of the turn of the century when

> The public interest could be equated with that which was revealed in election returns, in sales reports, balance sheets, circulation figures, and statistics of expansion. As long as peace should be taken for granted, the public good could be thought of as being immanent in the aggregate of private transactions (p. 16).

Yet many of the studies reported in this chapter have revealed the power of insightful minds to see appropriate data where associates only see 'someone else's' records. There is little explicit in patent records, city water-pressure archives, parking-meter collection records or children's readers to suggest their research utility. It required imagination to perceive the application, and a willingness to follow an unconventional line of data collection. Imagination cannot, of course, provide data if none are there. Our thesis is solely that the content limitations of archival records are not as great as the social scientists bound by orthodoxy thinks.

There is no easy way of knowing the degree to which reactive measurement errors exist among running archival records. These are second-hand measures and many of them are contaminated by reactive biases, while others are not. The politician voting on a bill is well aware that an observer in the gallery made a note of the tic in his left eye when his name was called to vote. The records contributed by the person or group studied – the votes, the speeches, the entries written for directories – are produced with an awareness that they may be interpreted as expressive behaviour. Thus those errors that come from awareness of being tested, from role elicitation, from response sets and from the act of measurement as a change agent are all potentially working to confound comparisons. With other data, such as the reports of presidential press conferences and census figures, the investigator has the additional bias of possible interviewer error passed along.

For data collected by a second party, by someone other than the producer (birth and death records, weather reports, power failures, patents and the like), the risk of awareness, role or interviewer contaminants is present but low. The main problem becomes one of instrument decay. Has the record-keeping process been constant or knowably variant over the period of study? For example suicides in Prussia jumped 20 per cent between 1882 and 1883 – it may be that response sets on the part of the record-keepers, or a change in administrative practice, threatens valid comparisons across time periods or geographic areas. To know of this variation is extremely difficult, and it represents one of the major drawbacks to archival records.

In summary the running archival records offer a large mass of pertinent data for many substantive areas of research. They are cheap to obtain, easy to sample, and the population restrictions associated with them are often knowable and controllable through data transformations and the construction of indices. But all content is not amenable to study by archival records, and there is an ever-present risk that reactive or other elements in the data-producing process will cause selective deposit or survival of the material. Against this must be balanced the opportunity for longitudinal studies over time, studies in which one may test a hypothesis by subjecting it to the rigour of evaluation in multiple settings and at multiple times.

7 Why Don't Sociologists Make More Use of Official Statistics?*

Martin Bulmer

Who nowadays reads Ogburn, Steinmetz or Morgenstern? Few British sociologists, one may surmise. Indeed, there is today relatively little interest in the potentialities of official statistics for sociological analysis, with a few notable exceptions (Halsey (ed.) [1972]; Westergaard and Resler [1975]; Reid [1977]; Abrams [1978]). This is partly due to an unfortunate disinclination to undertake large-scale empirical research; partly due to an exaggerated suspicion of social measurement; and partly due to an excessive distrust of officially-produced numerical data. We do not read or honour Ogburn (who more or less invented social indicators), Steinmetz (who coined the word 'sociography') or Morgenstern (economist and author of one of the finest critiques of error in official data [1963]) because there is little interest in the sorts of data which they sought to exploit or the uses which they tried to make of them. This paper seeks to redress the imbalance by putting forward some arguments in favour of the use of official statistics.

Such an essay may seem rather quixotic. For some, undoubtedly, the argument is not necessary; its point is already accepted. For others, entrenched critical views of such data are unlikely to be

* Reprinted from *Sociology*, vol. 14, no. 4, November 1980, pp. 505–23.

moved by argument, since objections seem to be matters of methodological faith rather than experiences based on actual research. As Reid remarks [1977 p. ix] at the beginning of his useful compendium of social class data:

> It may be that presenting empirical data has become controversial in the light of the current debate in sociology between those who believe that data are the essence of the discipline, and those whose concerns lead them to question, or to reject, existing data. Much of this debate seems to stem from ignorance on both sides, due in large part to lack of readily available sources. The display of current knowledge in sociology is too well hidden; it is about time we all had a good look.

Official statistics *are* available, more pertinent to some sociological problems and less flawed than is commonly supposed. Indeed, as one nineteenth-century writer observed, Britain led the way.

> The social statistics of Germany and the rest of Continental Western Europe are, in comparison with those of England, wretchedly compiled. But they raise the veil just enough to let us catch a glimpse of the Medusa head behind it. We should be appalled at the state of things at home (i.e. Germany), if, as in England, our governments and parliaments appointed periodically commissions of inquiry into economic conditions; if these commissions were armed with the same plenary powers to get at the truth; if it was possible to find for this purpose men as competent, as free from partisanship and respect of persons as are the English factory inspectors, her medical reporters on public health, her commissioners of inquiry into the exploitation of women and children, into housing and food. Perseus wore a magic cap that the monsters he hunted down might not see him. We draw the magic cap down over eyes and ears as a make-believe that there are no monsters.

The writer was Marx in 1867 [1954 ed., p. 9].

Half a century later the pioneer British social investigator A. L. Bowley (Professor of Statistics at L.S.E. and best known as the originator of probability sampling in social survey research) was arguing for the exploitation of the official statistical materials which were readily available.

> If we can define the task of sociological measurement, determine what are the facts which it is essential to know, and derive a means of ascertaining them, half the task is accomplished. In my experience it is neither a long nor expensive business to get the main rough measurements of quantities, though no obvious data are to hand. Official information, imperfect and badly adapted for sociological purposes as it often is, generally suffices to show the magnitude, nature and locality of a problem; common knowledge, obtainable by conversation with those who have lived in close contact with its circumstances, will place it in fair perspective; while a rapid investigation by sample will give an approximation to detailed measurements. Very often this is all that is wanted. (Bowley [1915], p. 11. Cf. also Abrams [1968] pp. 140–2.)

Official Statistics in Sociology: Pro's and Con's

What are we talking about when dealing with 'official statistics'? Their scope can be gauged from two general surveys of British official statistics, the Central Statistical Office *Guide to Official Statistics* [1978], the first edition of which was justly awarded a Library Association prize for the best reference work in 1976, and G. F. Lock, *General Sources of Statistics* [1976].

Official statistics will be defined here as data from:

(a) administrative sources, collected as a by-product of administrative procedures, e.g. Department of Employment unemployment statistics, Home Office immigration statistics, etc.

(b) vital registration: statistics of births, marriages and deaths, collected by the General Register Offices (in England and Wales part of O.P.C.S.) as a by-product of the legal registration of those events.

(c) the population census, carried out at ten-yearly intervals by the Census Division of O.P.C.S. and by G.R.O. (Scotland). The next census will be in 1991. The most recent was in 1981. In 1966 there was a 10 per cent sample census. Full censuses planned for 1976 and 1986 were cancelled due to expenditure cuts.

(d) social survey data collected by the Government Social Survey (now the Social Survey Division of O.P.C.S.). This can be separated into

(i) data from large-scale continuous surveys such as the *General Household Survey (G.H.S.)* or the *Family Expenditure Survey (F.E.S.)*, and
(ii) data from specific *ad hoc* surveys on particular subjects.

Data from such sources are documentary in the sense that they are not collected by the investigator using them, and are pre-existing when he or she comes to use them. They are available to the investigator as printed documents and (in the case of (d) only), also in machine readable form through the S.S.R.C. Survey Archive. (The Archive also holds a set of 1971 Census small-area (S.A.S.) data). Most such data are aggregate data, with suitable safeguards to preserve individual anonymity. This is true, for example, of Census S.A.S. data. The only individualised data available for secondary analysis are data sets under (d) available from the Survey Archive. This paper is primarily concerned with published official statistics, and only secondarily with reanalysis of government survey data. How one defines 'secondary analysis' is anyway rather a tricky point, which will be glossed over. Nor is it intended to depreciate re-analysis of survey data as a strategy for both research and teaching, as Hyman [1972] and Glenn *et al.* [1978] have documented. But for the purpose of this argument, such secondary analysis of government surveys is a special case of the use of government statistics more generally. (For a discussion of both see Hakim [1982].)

Can one explain why such official statistics are *relatively* under-used in sociological research, compared to the use made of them by, for example, economists, demographers or geographers? One important factor is undoubtedly that the measurement of monetary units, vital events or spatial distance is inherently easier than much social measurement. Secondly, and related, measurement of key social variables (let alone sociological variables) may present exceptional difficulties, though these vary from one field to another. A third difficulty is that the coverage of key social variables in official statistics is often deficient, and since the researcher himself does not collect the data, there is little directly to be done to rectify the omissions. As Halsey observes, 'the problem remains largely that of adapting to social science ends statistics which, from the point of view of the sociologist, are a by-product of administrative or organisational activity' [1972, p. 3]. A fourth and very important reason for caution is the unknown reliability of data derived from official sources.

Fifth, and perhaps most significantly for the purposes of the paper, a strong general critique of official statistics has been developed from various standpoints by Kitsuse and Cicourel [1963], Cicourel [1964 and 1976], Douglas [1967], Hindess [1973], Wiles [1975] and many others. Wakeford's *Research Methods Syllabuses in Sociology Departments in the U.K.* [1979] shows that where official statistics are taught as part of undergraduate methodology courses, it is these works (and examples drawn from the study of suicide and social deviance) which are overwhelmingly referred to. The intellectual climate to which this leads is aptly caught in a review of Abrams's collection on British social structure:

> Richard Brown's lengthy chapter on work presents a wealth of empirical material. Changes in the occupational structure, income from different occupations, fringe benefits, unionization, illness and accidents at work, job satisfaction and recruitment to the labour market are all carefully and clearly analysed, in spite of the profusion of statistical tables (Berry 1978: 17).

It would be widely agreed that official statistics as sociological data are difficult, intractable and to be treated with even more suspicion than any other quantitative datum in social science. One benefit of a social science education should be the development of a healthy scepticism about any numerical datum, whatever its source. Current criticisms of official statistics among sociologists, however, go well beyond such scepticism, to suggest that certain kinds of official data are so vitiated with error and/or common-sense assumptions as to be not useful for research purposes.

For several reasons such a view is unacceptable. Firstly, there is no logical reason why awareness of possible serious sources of error in official data should lead to their rejection for research purposes. It could as well point to the need for methodological work to secure their improvement. Secondly, a great many of the more thoroughgoing critiques of official statistics relate to statistics of suicide, crime and delinquency, areas in which there are special problems of reliable and valid measurement, notoriously so. The specific problems encountered in these fields are not, *ipso facto*, generalisable to all official statistics whatever their content. Thirdly, cases of the extensive use of official data – for example, by demographers – do not suggest that those who use them are unaware of the possible pitfalls in doing so. The world is not made up just of knowledgeable sceptics and naïve hard-line positivists.

A fourth reason for scepticism is that some critiques of official statistics are undoubtedly simply special cases of the rejection of a place for any empirical evidence in sociology. As Michael Mann has remarked [1978], 'confusing empirical research with empiricism, most Marxian sociologists (unlike their counterparts in history and economics) do not utilize the results of government censuses or sample surveys. They also tend to ignore non-Marxist theoretical work even where an overlap exists with their own interests . . . [as a result they] are trapped by a disregard for data which restricts them to evaluating Marxist theories in terms of internal consistency and consistency with Marx, while ignorance of other theory condemns them to repeat debates already heard elsewhere'. Cicourel has objected that Hindess's well-known critique is based on 'the curious notion that knowledge is not derived from human experience. . . . He does not indicate how this utopian situation comes about whereby the researcher's ideas of how to construct his categories and interpret the responses of respondents to his questions in some cultural-historical context, is to be divorced from the experiences of all parties to the research and the organization and analysis of findings. . . . Those we interview or observe and our use of a classification system to subsume objects and events is not determined by a logarithm' (Cicourel [1976] pp. xvi–xvii).

A fifth objection to the wholesale rejection of official statistics is the suspicion that the gulf between the common-sense assumptions of statisticians and the theoretical constructs of sociology may not be quite as wide as is sometimes supposed. This is certainly suggested by a reading of some of the chapters of the volumes on 'key variables' edited for the B.S.A. by Margaret Stacey [1969], Betty Gittus [1972] and Robert Burgess [1984b]. Sixthly and finally, what is one to make of empirical regularities which regularly turn up in analyses of official statistics done by non-sociologists, for example, the social class gradient in mortality? Several others could be cited (*Social Trends 1975;* Reid [1977]). What, if official statistics are so flawed as to be unusable, does the demonstration of such a regularity mean?

The case for making greater use of official statistics in sociological research can be made in three ways: by showing that they produce substantively interesting findings; by showing that those who use them are deeply concerned about possible errors in their data; and by showing that the conceptual issues faced are not dissimilar to those faced by academic sociologists.

Significant Empirical Regularities

First, substantively interesting findings. This point should hardly need making. A compendium such as *Social Trends* is full of fascinating data about the state of contemporary British society, albeit largely collected and collated by non-sociologists. Are they doing a job which sociologists should be doing? Several have thought so, judging by the Halsey [1972] and Abrams [1978] edited volumes, the December 1978 issue of the *B.J.S.*, and the radical critique in Irvine *et al.* (eds) [1979]. It is worth recalling that Ogburn was so keen on this kind of work that during the early 1930s one issue per year of the *American Journal of Sociology* was devoted to a statistical survey of the United States, compiled under his editorship.

Despite damaging criticism of the validity of official statistics on crime and deviance, in at least two areas, the sociography of wealth and health, what we know about these phenomena in contemporary Britain is heavily dependent on the availability of official statistics. In these areas, criticism and reservation are a prelude to *using* the data, not discarding them. As Atkinson and others have shown (Atkinson [1972]; Atkinson and Harrison [1978]; Atkinson *et al.* (1978]; Royal Commission on the Distribution of Income and Wealth [1975–9]), the most reliable data on wealth distribution appear to be those contained in Inland Revenue estate duty statistics. These are superior to even the results of purpose-designed sample surveys of wealth such as the Oxford Savings Surveys of 1953 and 1954, even though the IR data only includes estates subject to estate duty and excludes an estimated 50 per cent of estates which fall below the threshold of this tax. A good deal of the work on the distribution of wealth has involved an examination of the quality of such data, but those who use them – predominantly economists – do not conclude that they are worthless. Westergaard and Resler, for example, recognise that data on wealth distribution is indicative rather than precise, but conclude that 'these uncertainties of estimation are not too important, however, by comparison with two outstanding facts. First, there is a heavy concentration of private property however the exact figures come out. The share of all personal wealth owned by just the richest 1 per cent of the adult population was probably near 30 per cent around 1970. . . . The second outstanding fact is the limited degree to which private wealth has become more widely diffused over time' ([1975] p. 109–10). Critical awareness is essential – as Rose *et al.* (1977) have demonstrated in relation to land tenure statistics – but without official statistics of wealth our knowledge of wealth distribution in contemporary Britain would be slight indeed.

For evidence on the 'life chances' of different social classes, sociologists and students of social medicine have typically relied on official statistics of various kinds. The classic source is the Registrar-General's *Decennial Supplement* on Occupational Mortality, in which mortality data from death registrations around the census period are linked to denominators taken from the population enumerated in the census to work out mortality rates. This yields data expressed as standardised mortality ratios as in Table 1.

TABLE 1

Male standardised mortality ratios, by social class, for England and Wales

Social Class	*1921–3 (age 20–64)*	*1930–2 (age 20–64)*	*1949–53 (age 20–64)*	*1959–63 (age 15–64)*	*1970–2 (age 15–64)*
I	82	90	98	76	77
II	94	94	86	81	81
III	95	97	101	100	104
IV	101	102	94	103	114
V	125	111	118	143	137
All social classes	100	100	100	100	100

Source: Registrar-General's Decennial Supplement, *Occupational Mortality 1970–2*, London, H.M.S.O., 1977, p. 174.

This is but one example. As one commentator put it, 'there is so much evidence demonstrating differences in mortality and morbidity between the social classes as defined by our Registrars-General that it is difficult to select from the evidence' (Brotherston [1976]). Blaxter [1976] has shown that not only do class differentials in mortality and morbidity persist (despite falling absolute rates at given ages) but that there are also persisting class differentials in health *care*. Hart [1980] has reached similar conclusions in a more extended analysis looking at class differentials in death rates, human development and decay, personal reports of sickness, and class differences in disease. Both Blaxter and Hart rely in their discussions of morbidity upon data from the *General Household Survey*, one of the most important sources of data on self-reported illness currently available. Even a severe critic of official statistics on health states that the *G.H.S.* 'can probably be regarded as the least unsatisfactory estimate of the state of health of the population' (Doyal [1979] p. 246).

Neither the wealth nor health data cited will be news to anyone. It is indeed sociologically rather commonplace, though raising some intriguing questions of explanation for further investigation. It is cited here not to provide new insights for the reader, but simply to point out that official statistics do produce findings which are substantively interesting and important. This is the first good reason why they are worth exploiting as a source of documentary data.

Technical Shortcomings: Error

Ah, the wise critic responds, official statistics tend to be so vitiated with error that if you rely on them to find interesting patterns of association, some at least of these associations will be due to errors in the data rather than 'real' relationships. One answer to this is that the strength of the relationships revealed – for instance, the degree of inequality of distribution of wealth – are so striking that they could not be accounted for by error terms. (Indeed, critics of the data sometimes argue that various errors or omissions from the statistics lead to *under*-statement rather than over-statement of the degree of concentration of wealth) (cf. Hird and Irvine [1979] p. 208). But the more substantial point that needs to be emphasised in response to those acutely aware and rightly so of the manifold deficiencies of official statistics, is that people whose job it is to compile such data are often aware of possible sources of error, and devote much attention to estimation of error and attempts to reduce or eliminate error. We come thus to the second good reason for taking official statistics seriously: awareness of error is not the prerogative of the sociological critic.

Consider the following quotation: 'The very notion of accuracy and the acceptability of a measurement, observation, description, count – whatever the concrete case might be – is inseparably tied to the use to which it is put. In other words, there is always a theory or model, however roughly formulated it may be, a purpose or use to which the statistic has to refer, in order to talk meaningfully about accuracy. In this manner the topic soon stops being primitive; on the contrary, very deep-lying problems are encountered, some of which have only recently been recognized.' The author is not a sceptical sociologist but a sceptical econometrician – Morgenstern [1963 p. 4] – who then proceeds to develop a brilliant analysis of the different sources of error in economic statistics. Error is defined as 'an expression of imperfection and of incompleteness in description' in scientific observation, thus avoiding some of the metaphysical difficulties one may encounter in defining error in terms of an 'individual true value' (Moser and Kelton [1971] pp. 378 ff.). No comparable analysis of the nature of error in social statistics exists. If it did, how likely is it that the author would conclude that 'a study of the entire complex of the accuracy of existing statistics is not only helpful but also indispensable in designing programmes for the collection of new, improved data. Since the process of producing statistics is for the most part continuous, i.e. an unending one, the practical significance of such studies is immediate' (Morgenstern [1963] p. 6). To what extent is this true of the contribution of sociologists in Britain? To my knowledge, our colleagues contribute relatively little to the deliberations of government statisticians as to how to improve their data.

Demography provides further examples of the sensitivity of social scientists to the possibility of error in data which, by comparison with other subjects, are highly reliable and complete. British data derived from birth and death registration, for instance, is probably amongst the highest-quality social data currently available. Yet demographers scrutinise and search out the weaknesses in the data they are using as a matter of course. A standard social demography textbook, Petersen's *Population* ([1975] chap. 2), deals in the same chapter with the sources of data and then with the chief sources of error in such data: errors in coverage; errors in classification; errors in recording; errors in processing; and then discusses ways of trying to reduce such errors.

The first of these sources of error – errors in coverage – provides an instructive example. Although population censuses are designed to produce a complete count of the population, in practice coverage is not quite complete and *under-enumeration* occurs. Though this is relatively small (a few percentage points overall at most for the total population), it can have serious consequences both for demographic work and for public policies which use census data as a basis for action (e.g. the allocation of government grants on a per-capita basis to local government). It is therefore instructive to find a thorough review of census under-enumeration – *America's Uncounted People* (Parsons (ed.) [1972]) – produced by a 15-strong committee of academic social scientists, including at least six sociologists – S. M. Miller (the chairman), Norman Bradburn, Leo Schnore, Lee Rainwater, Eliot Liebow and John I. Kitsuse. It it perhaps unfair to draw too close parallels between American and British social science (Sharpe [1978]) but it would seem rather unlikely that a collection of British sociologists of similar variety could be assembled to contribute such an analysis of the quality of data from the British census.

Consider, as a third instance, the data on social class and mortality reproduced in Table 1. This has been criticised by sociologists, most recently by P. Razzell [1977]. 'The overall figures on social class and mortality are notoriously unreliable, on the grounds that they involve the matching of two completely different sets of data (census and death registration), which are known to involve different bases for classifying social class. In addition, the overall definition has been changed from period to period, so that in the last occupational mortality official statistics, the number of people in social class V was reduced by nearly a half because of the exclusion of occupational categories considered to be semi-skilled.' One might wonder how 'notorious' is 'unreliable', and whether these are fresh insights. Far from it. They are in fact problems which were first identified by official statisticians working to analyse the occupational mortality data. Changes in the numbers of people in different social classes are identified both in recent official publications (e.g. Fox [1977] p. 11) and in Knight's [1967] analysis of changes in the occupational composition of social classes between censuses. The most recent *Decennial Supplement* contains a whole chapter entitled 'Limitations of the method of inquiry' (Registrar-General [1977] pp. 17–35), which discusses a variety of sources of error in the data. Both this chapter and Leete and Fox [1977, p. 3–4] treat the problem of comparability of reporting of occupation at registration and in the census, and report a matching study to test this. It took one per cent of fathers who had a child between census day (25 April) and 31 December 1971, and a comparison was made between the occupation reported for the father on the birth certificate with that reported by him in the census. Some 81 per cent of the sample were assigned to the same social class at both events; at birth registration 10 per cent were assigned to a higher social class, and 9 per cent to a lower social class. By this means, an attempt is made to measure the inconsistency of statements about occupation in two different sources of demographic data.

Criminal statistics, where sociological controversy waxes fiercest, provide a fourth case of attention to error. Despite the prevailing tendency to discount such data, there are notable examples of attempts both to use and to improve the quality of official data on crime. Baldwin and Bottoms's work on *The Urban Criminal* [1976] is an example of willingness to use such data, despite a clear awareness of the pitfalls of so doing, partly argued for on the grounds that such data appear to show significant regularities (e.g. in the distribution of offences between areas) which warrant further investigation. Sparks *et al's* surveys of victims of crime are a preliminary attempt to measure the extent of the 'dark figure' of unrecorded crime, so often quoted to justify the unreliability of criminal statistics. As they comment ([1978] p. 2), the 'dark figure' in the past 100 years has been rather like the weather. Criminologists have talked about it, but none of them did very much about it or attempted to measure its extent. Yet they show that an attempt at such measurement is feasible, despite the great methodological and conceptual problems.

In a more general review of statistics on crime, Nigel Walker has commented ([1971] p. 10) that 'the chief effect which books of social statistics have on many readers is to increase their scepticism about the possibility of basing any reliable inference on figures. ... The truth is less discouraging than that. Provided that one knows how the figures were compiled, and provided that one is able to use the sort of common sense that I have mentioned, plus a few rules that I shall explain, a number of interesting and useful inferences about crime and our penal system can be made'. Awareness of error and doubts about the validity and reliability of official statistics need not necessarily lead to rejecting their use for research purposes.

Conceptual Difficulties: Theory

If the technical difficulties associated with the use of official statistics are not as novel as some sociological critics seem to imagine, neither may the conceptual difficulties be quite so intractable as it sometimes supposed. There is more common ground between official statisticians and social scientists than is often apparent. This is in no way to under-estimate the enormous difficulties which there are in matching up official data with sociological concepts; almost every user of and commentator on such data is aware of them. The most trenchant recent statement of such difficulties, drawing on the Thorners's [1962] analysis of the Indian Census of 1951, argues that:

> the rational evaluation and utilization of statistics for scientific purposes must take account of the conceptual means for their production, that is, of the system of categories together with the instructions and elaborations in which they are specified. This means that it must depend on the theoretical interests of the science concerned (Hindess [1973] p. 45).

Hindess's own account, however, is severely flawed by an epistemological position which in some respects is a mirror-image of vulgar empiricism (using 'empiricism' in the sense of 'the facts speak for themselves', rather than its (frequent) misuse to mean 'empirical'). For he maintains that 'scientific experimentation is never reducible to some empiricist process of testing theory against essentially pre-theoretical observation. Still less is scientific knowledge reducible to human experience ... (official) statistics are the product of a determinate system of concepts' (Hindess [1973] p. 56). This very strong assertion of the irrelevance of empirical data to theory not only misuses the term 'empiricist', but claims that knowledge is *governed by* 'a determinate system of concepts'. This is surely over-determinist.

What characterises empirical social inquiry, in the first place, is that it is a *practical* activity in which social factors influence the actual production and development of the instruments of inquiry. 'The assignment of events and individuals into categories by officials is, nevertheless, much more than the mechanical operation of theoretical categories and technical instruments' (Miles and Irvine [1979] p. 123).

In the second place, to assert that concepts are purely and only theoretically given (or exclusively a matter of theoretical production) would seem to lead to an arid kind of scholasticism. It is also a serious misrepresentation, put forward on *a priori* philosophical grounds, of much empirical sociology. Caricatures of the latter do not serve any useful purpose. A great deal of sociological work is avowedly and fruitfully empirical while also being at the same time theoretical. Much sociology is not characterised either by vulgar positivism or by 'empiricism' in the sense of the absurd belief that facts speak for themselves. It is equally absurd, dare one say it, to maintain that 'theory speaks for itself'. The pitfall of an excessive rationalism (cf. Bierstedt [1949]) is that it leads to insistence on the *a priori* character of knowledge, to a belief that science is independent of the facts as observed, that it is somehow capable of deriving theorems of practical significance by pure thought. 'There is no way of making statements about the economic or any other world without some observation of reality, or what we take it to be, no matter how coarse or rudimentary our observations' (Morgenstern [1963] p. 302).

The most difficult questions arise, of course, in the *interplay between* categories and evidence, between concepts and empirical data. It is here that sociologists have in principle much to contribute to the work of official statisticians, since sociology at least aspires to be a nomothetic discipline in which concepts provide the key link between theory and evidence. Unfortunately, this potential sociological contribution to social statistics is all too easily sidetracked by either over-determinist claims for the theory-laden status of sociological knowledge, or over-simple political analyses which purport to show that 'official statistics form part of the process of maintaining and reproducing the dominant ideologies of capitalist society. . . . [O]fficial statistics are in fact a selection of data typically offering far less of use to the radical critic than the reactionary. . . . [T]he concepts employed serve to reinforce the arguments advanced by political and intellectual representatives of the ruling class.' (Miles and Irvine [1979] pp. 126–7.) Would that it were all so straightforward and reducible to the right political analysis and allegiance! In fact, theoretical and conceptual analysis is independent of political position. The study of social-class and health and wealth distribution, for instance, has probably done more to bring about a degree of social change than it has to bolster reactionary social policies. But the problems of defining 'social class', or 'health' or 'wealth' and then trying to measure them are to a large extent independent of one's politics. General categories pose autonomous *scientific* problems (Bulmer [1980a]).

The essential importance of the interplay between our general categories and our empirical observations of reality (or what we take to be reality) can be briefly demonstrated by looking at three familiar sociological concepts which also appear in official statistics. Occupation is the first. In Britain, the basic categories in terms of which we classify occupations are developed by official statisticians and administrators in the Department of Employment and O.P.C.S., who have produced C.O.D.O.T. [1972] and the *Classification of Occupations* (O.P.C.S. [1970]). Such basic conceptual work is necessary (if not sufficient) for the sociological analysis of work. Even if such categorisations are to some degree arbitrary and inevitably conceal as well as reveal differences, they form a basic building block for sociological analysis, as Brown has recently demonstrated in an analysis of work in Britain (see also Hakim [1980b]). Despite the acknowledged limitations of official data, such data can be used because occupation is a key concept, 'a socially structured and socially recognized set of work activities, the carrying out of which produces goods and/or services for which others would be willing to pay. It therefore implies both a place in the social division of labour and a potential or actual place in the market for goods or services' (Brown [1978] p. 56). There is a sufficiently close match between official statistician's 'commonsense' understandings of the meaning of occupation, and sociological uses of the concept, for the relationship between the two to be relatively unproblematic.

The scope for historical study of occupational structure using census data has been demonstrated in several studies, for instance, in papers by Bellamy [1978] and Hakim [1980a] through Davies [1980] has shown from the census how one occupation, nurses, during the nineteenth century there were significant changes in who were counted as nurses, how nurses were regarded, and their position in the social structure. Banks [1978] has provided an analysis of changing British social structure in the nineteenth century, starting from occupational data and using this to construct a 'social class' categorisation permitting him to discern changes over time.

The extent to which the more abstract concept of social class has been measured using occupational data is remarkable in British empirical sociology. Even though the theoretical content of 'social class' is far wider, the use of occupation as an empirical indicator of social class has been widely thought to be justified. Groupings of occupations take account of their level and type of rewards, their social standing, the education, training and skills needed and so on. 'Although no set of occupational categories can be regarded as a straightforward division of the population into 'classes' as a sociologist would understand that term, schemes of occupational grading probably come closest to grouping together those with similar 'life chances'. They are therefore the best available basis for exploring the differential impact of work for men and women's lives and social situations in our society (Brown [1978] p. 61).

With social class, however, one comes up against a paradox which an emphasis on the primacy of theoretical categorisation does not resolve. There is indeed a sharp theoretical divergence between official statisticians who have developed the Registrar-General's Social Class and Socio-Economic Group (S.E.G) classifications and sociologists interested in stratification. Reading Leete and Fox [1977] on the origins of the official concepts, one would scarcely be aware that the discipline of sociology existed, other than a footnote reference to David Glass. The most important influence upon official developments seems to have been socially-aware medical statisticians interested in mortality differentials, who tried grouping occupations together to see if there were any broader social differences (other than those between occupations) in mortality rates. There were, and the fact that such statistical differences persisted over time then provided the justification for continuing to use the Social Class classification. (Indeed, one reason for developing the S.E.G. classification after 1951 was the possible circularity in the Social Class classification, the ranking possibly being influenced by preconceived notions of health and behaviour which the groupings were then used to discover (cf. Benjamin [1968] pp. 41–2).)

Despite the theoretical divergence between official statisticians and sociologists, what is striking is the *empirical convergence*, in the sense of agreement that differences demonstrated in official statistics of social class are 'real' and socially significant. Such data are indeed not infrequently used in sociological work, as indicated earlier in the discussion of health inequalities. There is room for argument about the precise classification used, and the Hall-Jones and Hope–Goldthorpe scales have been developed as alternatives. Nevertheless, the Registrar-General's scales are used both as a basis for classification in empirical research and as the standard classification when official sources are used. In a sample of English locality studies the Registrar General's Social Class classification was used in one-half of those studies which made a social-class classification (Weinberg and Lyons [1972] pp. 54–5). Nichols also discerns considerable convergence between official, sociological and Marxist use of social-class concepts and data while arguing for a different, more theoretical level of analysis following Poulantzas (Nichols [1979]). Brown's [1978, p. 82] assessment is fairly typical: 'For discovering broad difficulties in the costs and rewards of work, they (official statistics by social class) are probably adequate.'

Facts do (or reality does) indeed kick sometimes. But the lesson is not that the 'facts speak for themselves'; they do not. It is rather that sociologists and official statisticians may have reached *some* convergence in their conceptualisation and measurement of social inequality, by different routes and from different theoretical presuppositions. A wide conceptual gap remains, but the area of common ground is sufficiently firm for sociologists to regularly use social-class derived from official sources, while official statisticians are willing to chance their arm at extended description of contemporary class differences, even though disavowing any sociological intent (*cf. Social Trends* 1975).

A different case, race and ethnicity, is that of another complex and intractable concept. Here we are provided with a good example of the negative influence of British sociological scepticism of official data, on a subject of potentially great importance for sociological analysis. To take but one example, William Wilson's *The Declining Significance of Race* [1978], a major contribution to the sociology of American race relations, is filled with tables of data comparing American blacks and whites using census returns, for example in terms of their occupational distribution, median income, degree of residential segregation, and so on. In Britain, the picture could not be more different, since such data is not available from the 1971

Census. However, it was proposed during 1978 that the forthcoming 1981 Census should include a direct question on each person's race or ethnicity: 'The Registrar-Generals are considering the reliability and acceptability of possible forms of a direct question on ethnic origins of the kind already asked in many other countries, such as the Caribbean countries of the Commonwealth, Canada and the U.S.A. The government believe that a question on race or ethnic origin should be asked . . . [B]efore a final decision is made, the government would wish to take into account the findings of the Registrar-Generals and of public opinion' (O.P.C.S. [1978] para. 25). In the voluntary test Census carried out in London Borough of Haringey in April 1979, one-half of heads of household were asked a direct question on race ethnicity.

In the event, a decision was taken to exclude such a question from the 1981 Census. What is clear is that the contribution of British sociologists to this potentially significant and sociologically important change in census content has so far been non-existent or largely negative. No professional representations have been made on the subject, while public comment by individual sociologists has pointed to the (undoubted) difficulties (if not impossibility) of framing such a direct question, and also the possible undesirability of asking such a question at all in the political climate over race and immigration of the late 1970s (Mack, [1978]). Such a question is indeed both technically difficult to ask (relying on self-identification in terms of predetermined categories) (cf. Sillitoe [1978a, b]), conceptually problematical and politically sensitive. There are genuine reasons for strong disagreement, and may be political grounds for opposing such a question. But it is curious, to say the least, that academic social scientists should be so ready with political pronouncements while having so little to say on the technical merits and demerits of such a question. This would appear to owe little to a belief in *a priori* theorising, and much more to scepticism about official data and lack of a desire to exploit such a data source as the census in the future (Bulmer [1980b]).

Two Ways Forward

There are many limitations to official statistics as well as a need for a healthy distrust of the 'facts' when these are in the form of official numerical data. Learning how very hard it is to get good data, however, need not lead to a retreat into total scepticism or theoretical scholasticism. Official statistics *can* be used to good effect in sociological research. There are, nevertheless, troublesome conceptual and theoretical issues which will not go away. Unlike economics or demography for example, the degree of fit between theory and official data tends to be poor. 'The selection of data for a publication such as *Social Trends* presents particular difficulties. In the economic field there is a set of coherent theories, linked conceptually by a common monetary unit ... The social field has not such theoretical ... unity' (*Social Trends 1975*, p. 9). Will sociology follow the path of economics? There economic statistics fit readily into models, and statistical data gathering and theoretical developments went on side by side. 'It would be untrue to say that the construction (of economic indicators) was completely based on economic theory. Theories were developed, but simultaneously and in parallel, series were selected for improved measurement, relationships between them and others were investigated and formalized, models were gradually built up, theories were improved in turn, and so forth' (Moser [1978] p. 208).

Two lines of development would seem to offer some scope for bringing official statistics into sociology to a greater extent than at present. One – following the example of Morgenstern in economics – would be greater sociological involvement in work on objective social indicators, a field of growing interest to official statisticians and to national government and international organizations. Despite its manifold difficulties (cf. Bulmer (ed.) [1978] pp. 201–67), such work does pose challenges both to official statisticians to be more conceptually sophisticated, and to sociologists to be more engaged in secondary social measurement. The most recent U.S. equivalent to *Social Trends, Social Indicators 1976*, was published with an accompanying journal issue (*The Annals*, 1978) containing analytical articles on the data in *Social Trends 1976* by a range of American social scientists. Nevertheless, the enterprise received a savaging in a major sociological review symposium (Ferris *et al.* [1978]), several critics pointing to the enduring mismatch between official categories and sociological concepts and theories. The challenge of trying to influence official work on social indicators is one which few British sociologists have cared to take up.

The aim of integrating social statistics and social theory is highly problematical, and less likely of solution than that in the case of economics statistics and economic theory. A different way forward, therefore, may lie in trying to integrate social statistics to a greater extent into sociological work. A good line of attack and hence the references to Marx, Ogburn, Bowley and Steinmetz at the outset – may be through the cultivation of 'sociography', in the sense of a concrete description of a society and its social structure. For example, the influence of the 'Chicago School' is quite widely felt in different branches of contemporary sociology. It is not always appreciated, however, the extent to which its knowledge of that city was derived from official statistical series. Data were drawn extensively from the census, and the famous *Local Community Fact Book* (Wirth (ed.) [1938]) looks to a modern eye like nothing so much as a set of small-area census data.

Indeed, Chicago sociologist Ernest W. Burgess has some claim to be called the midwife of modern census small area statistics, in which he took a keen interest from his arrival on the staff at Chicago in 1917. Burgess saw the availability of census data broken down for smaller areas of the city of Chicago as an essential prerequisite for its empirical study. At the time census data were produced either for the city as a whole, or for wards within the city whose boundaries changed considerably from one census to another due to gerrymandering and the securing of political advantage. Burgess pressed the U.S. Census Bureau very strongly in the 1920s to produce data for census tracts, small subdivisions of the city containing between 3000 and 8000 people, whose boundaries would remain unchanged from one census to another and thus permit reliable intercensal comparisons of local urban trends. He had the Census Bureau produce to his specification special extracts of data for Chicago tracts from the 1920 Census, and chaired the city-wide Chicago Census Committee set up in 1924 'to secure the collection and publication of census data according to relatively small permanent areas'. This work bore most direct fruit in two massive compendiums of census tract data about Chicago, for the 1920 Census (Burgess and Newcomb [1931]) and for the 1930 Census (Burgess and Newcomb [1933]), which are essentially census small area statistics. The interest of Chicago sociologists in such official data at this time is also shown by the fact that the City of Chicago conducted a special census of the whole city in 1934, the results of which were published within a year (Newcomb and Lang [1934]). It is clear that the idea of such a census originated with Burgess, and his close associate Charles Newcomb was its Director. The idea commended itself also to local politicians as a relief measure in the depression (providing local employment for enumerators).

The first *Local Community Fact Book* included in addition to census tract data descriptions of the area for which the data were presented, going beyond the simple presentation of statistics. (Further volumes of the series were produced based on 1940, 1950 and 1960 Census data for the city of Chicago.) Such data were regarded as essential for the development of the extensive Chicago programme of local community studies, and for the formulation of the theoretical ideas which underpinned the Chicago approach to urban sociology. The postulation of zones of activity differentiated broad areas of the city, while the census was used to distinguish 75 'natural areas' which were the areas used as a base to present the *Local Community Fact Book* data (cf. Hunter [1974] Chs 1 and 2). The 'natural areas', too, were the focus of intensive ethnographic investigation, so that a blending of aggregate quantitative material derived from field observation and life histories was achieved in a number of the monographs of the period.

The history of this aspect of Chicago sociology shows the fruitful uses which can be made of official data, and the central role which such data played at an early period in the history of modern empirical sociology, a role which it is nowadays easy to forget. (For a fuller discussion see Bulmer [1984].) Moreover, 'the sociography' and what is nowadays called 'ethnography' were carried on together and cross-fertilised each other. Though 'ethnography' is increasingly used to refer generally to qualitative field research using observational methods, its original meaning denoted the descriptive activities and results of social anthropological research. 'Sociography' denoted the descriptive activities of sociological research. It is rather ironical that the current (laudable) interest in the ethnography of industrial societies has not been matched by a similar interest in quantitative sociography using official statistics. The two in combination would be a powerful force for turning British sociology in the direction of doing more empirical research.

'Sociography' (which Steinmetz defined as 'the study of people and their component groups in all their diversity') is not synonymous with statistics. Indeed its early proponents Steinmetz and Toennies saw it as embracing both qualitative and quantitative observations (Oberschall [1965] pp. 51 ff.; Jacoby [1973] pp. 96 ff.; Heberle [1931], Steinmetz [1952], van Doorn [1956] pp. 191–202; Zijderveld [1966] pp. 116–24).

Such empirical studies combining ethnographic and official data might do much to bridge the gap which can devide quantitative from qualitative research. As Hans Zeisl [1933, p. 125] pointed out nearly half a century ago, bringing the two together is no easy task, though an objective to be worked towards. '[S]ociography has not achieved a synthesis between statistics and a full description of concrete observations, In work of impressive conceptualization – for instance, in *The Polish Peasant* – statistics are completely mission; inversely, the statistical surveys are often of a regrettably routine nature. The task of integration still lies ahead.'

Part Four

Historical Sources

8 Introduction and Further Reading

Martin Bulmer

> The more sociological history becomes and the more historical sociology becomes, the better for both. Let the frontier between them be kept open for two-way traffic (E. H. Carr [1961]).

> Although the logic and approach of science can and should be used in historical sociology, it is obvious that work in this field cannot validate hypotheses with the rigour normally associated with the concept of a science. That this is so should only highlight the challenge. No discipline can select its research problems solely from those which are easy to study with extant methods. Those sociological problems which lend themselves to experimentation, to rigorous quantification, to explicit testing of mathematical models, are now relatively easy to study. Those in which it is difficult to isolate variables, in which one must deal with numerous factors and few cases, require a high level of theoretical and methodological ingenuity (S. M. Lipset [1968] p. 52).

Are sociology and history distinct intellectual enterprises, and if they are, wherein does the difference lie? The traditional view which would distinguish an idiographic from a nomothetic discipline and the counter-argument that history and sociology are not separable activities point in different directions. The majority of sociologists *and* historians would probably consider that each does entail a different mode of analysing social reality, empirically if not logically, although there would be disagreement whether this difference lay in the subject-matter, the epistemological frame of reference, the role accorded to concepts and theory, the logic of explanation, the methods used to collect and analyse data or the criteria used to evaluate data. In any case there is little doubt that differences *within* each discipline are as significant as differences *between* the two disciplines, rendering extended discussion of the relationship in the abstract relatively unprofitable.

Yet the relationship does remain problematical because in Britain (although less so in France or in the United States) the links between sociology and history have remained fragmentary and uneasy. One of the minor misfortunes associated with the rise of sociology in Britain has been the degree of mistrust displayed toward it by some English historians (particularly at the ancient universities) and the consequent comparative lack of intellectual dialogue about the potentialities of sociological history and historical sociology. Although the situation has changed quite dramatically within the last ten years – a transition most notably signalled and encouraged by E. H. Carr's Trevelyan lectures – many traditional historiographers seem to see social science as a threat rather than a fructifying influence.

The late development of sociology in Britain may in part account for this history of tension. To some extent the inheritance of the tradition of political arithmetic and the absence of a coherent body of theory (such as that drawn on from economics by economic historians), which encapsulated the sociological approach, led to difficulties in establishing social history as an identifiable specialism within history. Notwithstanding the pioneer contributions of Tawney or Namier or the fertile influence of those working more or less explicitly within a Marxist framework such as Christopher Hill, E. J. Hobsbawm and E. P. Thompson, the direct application of sociological modes of analysis, *by historians*, to problems in the history of social structure has been unusual.

Hopefully this period is now past. As work done over the past ten to twenty years is appearing in print, in turn stimulating further research, there promises to be an increasingly fruitful relationship between sociology and history. Among historians Lawrence Stone, E. J. Hobsbawm, J. R. Vincent, E. P. Thompson and Asa Briggs exemplify this trend; among sociologists N. J. Smelser, J. A. and O. Banks and W. L. Guttsman for example have made important contributions to English historiography.

John Goldthorpe's useful short introduction (Chapter 9) to the relationship between the two disciplines touches on the philosophical origins of these differing views of the two subjects, and of the ways in which the disciplines have impinged upon one another. He emphasises both the extent to which history and sociology have drawn together and the need for critical examination of the methodological basis of historical sociology using secondary sources.

Michael Anderson (Chapter 10) demonstrates the potential of the 'new' quantitative historical sociology, using as sources enumeration books and other census data and parish registers. He shows how voluminous but unorganised data sets like these can yield a much more rigorous and structured picture of the social conditions and consequences of nineteenth-century industrialisation than had hitherto seemed possible. At the same time there is a continuing concern for the reliability and validity of the data so obtained. For 'there is a delusive clarity and apparent authority in the printed word or digit. But what is printed in a census volume or any other statistical publication represents the last operation in a long chain of data collection and collation, subject to error, omission and misinterpretation at every stage from the phrasing of the original inquiry to the proof reading of the printer's galleys' (Wrigley (ed.) [1972] p. 1). Similar problems arise with the use of historical sources as with unobtrusive measures (considered in Part 3) and these are further examined by Anderson and other contributors to the same symposium (Wrigley [1972]).

In addition, however, Anderson discusses in an illuminating way the use of non-quantitative historical sources – what he terms 'descriptive' data. This is important both because much sociological history is non-quantitative and because there is a tendency to denigrate qualitative data among those who are more quantitatively minded. Circumspection is indeed required, but if carefully used such sources can yield important insights into social conditions and social actors' own views of their situation.

At this point the discussion connects the use of life histories in cohort analysis and the consideration of interpretative procedures. The use of personal documents in sociology and history is of long standing, including autobiographies, diaries, letters and life histories (cf. Gottschalk [1947]). Their value has lain pre-eminently in yielding data about participants' views of social situations in which they were actively involved.

Autobiographies, diaries and letters have been a staple source for historians, particularly political historians, for a very long time. Rarely have such documents been available written by members of the working class, although a number of British examples provide very interesting material (cf. Burnett [1974]; Hudson [1972]; Ashby [1961]; Davies [1963]; Roberts [1971, 1976]). One such extract is included here, from Robert Roberts's autobiographical account [1971] of early twentieth-century Salford, across the Mersey from Manchester. Roberts's account is of particular interest not only in its own right but because of differences in interpretation with Richard Hoggart's autobiographical recollections of working-class life in Hunslet in *The Uses of Literacy* [1957]. Roberts subsequently [1976] wrote a more personal and autobiographical account of life in the classic slum.

Sociological life histories, from Thomas and Znaniecki [1918–20] and other Chicago sociologists onwards, have been used in the study of subjective social action, a use reargued by Denzin ([1970] Ch. 10). More recently there have been important reviews of the field by Bennett [1981], Bertaux (ed.) [1981] and Plummer [1983]. The historical sociologist, too, may go out to attempt to obtain first-person accounts of social conditions in past time from older members of the community. The recent growth of oral history (*Oral History* [1971]) in Britain is worth the attention of sociologists interested in historical research, for it involves the application of the life-history methods long used in sociology and anthropology to the study of the past. Since the appearance of Vansina's methodological critique [1965] there is no excuse for dismissing such techniques as of marginal importance. Moreover their utility has been demonstrated in several areas of historical research and the potential of the approach for sociological history would seem to be considerable.

A further type of historical sociology should be mentioned. Comparative historical sociology using secondary sources occupies an honoured place in the discipline, starting as it does from Max

Weber's monumental work. Relatively little concrete guidance is available, however, to someone undertaking this type of research (but see for example the bibliography by S. B. Garfin in Vallier (ed.) [1973] pp. 423–67). Yet the macrosociological and comparative study of institutions viewed in the round is an important part of empirical sociological inquiry. The two references to Barrington Moore and Smelser in the further reading [1969 and 1959] relate to this type of historical research.

But a distinctive research strategy or technique alone is not enough. New innovations in methods of quantitative and qualitative historical analysis do not in themselves generate fresh historical interpretations. The centrality of what E. H. Carr calls the 'hard core of interpretation' does not need labouring in a sociological work, yet it is not always reflected in the few available writings on methods in historical sociology. It is hard to relate the achievement of Max Weber or Marc Bloch to the several available texts which either advocate rather uncritically the application of quantitative methods to the study of the past or provide merely a nuts-and-bolts account of problems of documentary interpretation. As S. M. Lipset has emphasised [1968], strict verificationist canons can rarely be met in historical sociology, which proceeds by 'the method of the dialogue'. But this dialogue is one in which one interpretation is pitted against another and evaluated in the light of its theoretical consistency and empirical support. It is a dialogue about *problems* not about facts (however innovative the method of their discovery). It seems plausible to argue that the most fruitful relations between history and sociology stem less from the sharing of common methods than from the focus upon a common problem or problems.

Further Reading

Historical works

There is no substitute for the reading of a piece of historical research.

(1) E. H. Carr, *What is History?* (London: Penguin Books, 1968), is not a monograph but it is one of the most effective and insightful recent statements, by a great English historian, of the relationship between history and the social sciences. Originally delivered as a

series of lectures, Carr combines the cut and thrust of controversy with broad and comprehensive historical learning.

(2) M. W. Flinn and T. C. Smout (eds), *Essays in Social History* (London: Oxford University Press, 1974) contains many of the best shorter essays by social historians of English society which have appeared in recent years, including Eric Hobsbawm on social history and social theory. Neil Smelser on the Industrial Revolution, E. P. Thompson on time and work discipline, Asa Briggs on the language of 'class', and J. Foster on class in nineteenth-century towns.

(3) Michael Anderson, *Family Structure in Nineteenth-century Lancashire* (Cambridge: Cambridge University Press, 1971) is a work of meticulous historical sociology and a major study of the impact of English industrialisation upon family structure. It provides the substantive material to fill out the short methodological article reproduced here.

(4) Barrington Moore jun., *The Social Origins of Dictatorship and Democracy* (London: Penguin Books, 1969). Subtitled 'Lord and Peasant in the Making of the Modern World', the book provides an account and interpretation of the course of change from agrarian to industrial states, showing how the differing relationship between lord and peasant could have widely differing political consequences. Displaying an extraordinary grasp of the social histories of England, France, America, China and Japan, many regard this one of the finest works of comparative historical sociology to appear in recent years. For an incisive critique, however, see Dore [1969].

(5) Theda Skocpol, *States and Social Revolutions* (Cambridge: Cambridge University Press, 1979). A rigorous comparative historical analysis, with a sociological framework, of the French, Russian and Chinese revolutions. A major contribution to comparative historical sociology.

(6) H. Becker, 'Introduction' to C. Shaw, *The Jack Roller* (Chicago: University of Chicago Press, 1966) pp. v–xviii, is the best statement of the rationale of the use of personal documents in sociology and history to appear in recent years. The personal document by Shaw which it introduces is itself a good example of the genre.

Methodological

(1) Philip Abrams, *Historical Sociology* (Shepton Mallet, Somerset: Open Books, 1982). A wide-ranging and authoritative review of the relation between history and sociology and the main issues of theory and method which arise.

(2) S. M. Lipset and R. Hofstadter (eds), *Sociology and History: Methods* (New York: Basic Books, 1968). An American collection which illustrates the fertility and ingenuity of attempts to apply the techniques of sociology to the study of the past. Particularly useful because in the main historians have been reticent about their methods of research, not deeming it a subject worth talking about but rather something to be learnt by doing.
(3) Jennifer Platt, 'Evidence and Proof in Documentary Research', *The Sociological Review*, vol. 29 (1) (1981) pp. 31–66. A thoughtful examination of the criteria to be used in assessing documentary materials used by the sociologist, and an analysis of the ways in which their assessment differs from or is similar to the criteria used in relation to social survey research or participant observation.
(4) M. Bulmer, 'Sociology and History: Some Recent Trends', *Sociology*, vol. 8 (1974) pp. 137–50. An essay reviewing recent British work in sociological and demographic history. It discusses the relative merits of quantitative and qualitative approaches and emphasises the importance of *problems* as the criterion for choice of methods.
(5) N. J. Smelser, *Comparative Methods in the Social Sciences* (Englewood Cliffs, N.J.: Prentice-Hall, 1976). A major statement of the logic of comparative sociological inquiry, emphasising the centrality of theory. The first half of the book examines the comparative and historical work of de Tocqueville, Durkheim and Max Weber; the second considers problems of classification, measurement and causal analysis in more recent comparative studies. Ranging more widely than just historical sociology, the book complements Vallier [1971] and D. P. Warwick and S. Osherson (eds), *Comparative Research Methods* (Englewood Cliffs, N.J.: Prentice-Hall, 1973). The latter also includes papers by Deutscher [1968] and Mitchell [1965] referred to in Chapter 14.
(6) Theda Skocpol and Margaret Somers, 'The Use of Comparative History in Macrosocial Inquiry', *Comparative Studies in Society and History*, vol. 22 (2) (1980) pp. 174–97. A discussion of the logic of different types of comparative history. A brave attempt to grapple with the problem of large-scale sociological generalisation from historical materials.
(7) Ken Plummer, *Documents of Life: An Introduction to the Problems and Literature of a Humanistic Method* (London: Allen & Unwin, 1983). An extensive review of the use of life histories, oral history, letters, diaries, photographs, film and the novel as data for the sociologist, supplemented by a very extensive guide to further reading.

9 The Relevance of History to Sociology*

John H. Goldthorpe

During the relatively brief period in which sociology has been recognised as a legitimate form of intellectual endeavour, various attempts have been made to establish strict distinctions between sociology and the study of history in terms of both their logic and their method. None of these attempts has been demonstrably successful but certain of them have none the less been influential and must, I think, be taken into account in any discussion of the relationship between history and sociology, whether this is in terms of theory or of practice.

Perhaps the most forceful case which has been made out for creating a sharp dichotomy between history and sociology is that which rests on the distinction between 'idiographic' and 'nomothetic' disciplines.[1] This distinction, which has its origins in the thought of neo-Kantian philosophers such as Windelband and Rickert, was used initially in the attempt to demonstrate qualitative differences between history and other *Kulturwissenschaften* on the one hand and the various *Naturwissenschaften* on the other. An idiographic

*The Postscript, written in 1972, is published here for the first time. The first part of the chapter was originally published in *Cambridge Opinion*, no. 28 (1962) and is reprinted with the permission of the author and *Cambridge Opinion* magazine.

discipline such as history, it was held, was concerned with unique and particular events or instances which were studied for their own sake – for their intrinsic interest. By contrast a nomothetic discipline such as physics or chemistry was concerned with the formulation of general propositions through which it was sought to understand and explain the *class* of phenomena which constituted its subject matter. It is this distinction which has latterly been most often referred to by both historians and sociologists who, for whatever reasons, are anxious to maintain clear lines of demarcation between the studies which they pursue. Sociology has been placed along with the natural sciences in the nomothetic category as being an essentially generalising discipline, while the fundamentally idiographic character of history has been strongly upheld.

At the same time two further derived distinctions have frequently been utilised in order to supplement and clarify the main argument. Firstly it has been held that in his quest for general propositions about society the sociologist has necessarily to develop extensive conceptual schemes by means of which he may analyse and reduce to order the manifold diversities of man's social existence: the historian on the other hand, concerned as he is with individuals and events in all their idiosyncratic detail, is said to have little use for such general concepts but to be interested rather in developing ever more reliable and penetrating methods of ascertaining historical fact. In other words sociologist and historian are represented as working on quite different levels of abstraction; the essential tools of the former being instruments of theoretical analysis, those of the latter techniques for ferreting out all that is knowable about particular instances and occurrences. The second of the derived distinctions concerns the role played in the two disciplines by the category of time. The historian, it is argued, is typically engaged in tracing a chronological sequence of past events and with showing how certain events led on to others; time is thus a major dimension of his work. In contrast to this the sociologist is seen as being centrally concerned with the functional relationships which exist between the analytically separable elements in societies (or 'social systems') – time notwithstanding. The general propositions which he seeks are, when true, timeless and have no existential implications. Or to put the matter briefly 'historical propositions have a date; sociological propositions do not'.

In addition to attempts made on these lines to establish clear-cut *differentia* between history and sociology, there is one other fairly common argument to this end which also calls for attention. This argument appears to be advanced predominantly by sociologists who feel anxiety about their status as scientists and who are determined to safeguard this. It is to the effect that history and sociology are most decisively distinguished as disciplines not so much by the kind of propositions their practitioners seek to establish but rather by the kinds of methods the latter properly use in conducting their inquiries. In order to uphold this claim it is of course necessary strictly to delimit what may rightly be regarded as sociological method. In effect this usually implies defining this method in terms of (a) certain forms of field research, involving sampling, interviewing and systematic observation and (b) certain techniques for the quantification and statistical analysis of the data thus obtained. It is in this way then possible to maintain that since procedures of the kind in question are generally inapplicable to the study of the past, sociology and history represent quite different varieties of intellectual activity. The former, so the argument runs, seeks to be scientific in its methodology – that is, to follow the methods of the natural sciences: the latter on the other hand does not, and for the most part cannot, aspire to this because of the very nature of its subject matter; it has, rather, to rest content with methods of inquiry which give qualitatively inferior findings in terms of precision, completeness and objectivity alike.

Both of the cases which I have outlined for drawing strict lines of demarcation between history and sociology involve considerable difficulties. For example the distinction between idiographic and nomethetic disciplines is one which in the last analysis can scarcely be maintained. It is not easy to understand, among other things, how in a purely idiographic discipline one could ever be said to have knowledge (as opposed to experience) or anything at all, or how in a supposedly nomothetic one any consideration of the singular and non-recurrent is to be avoided.[2] Similarly the attempt to distinguish history from sociology on methodological grounds requires that sociology be virtually restricted to the study of present-day societies, and thus in fact results in the scope of the subject being defined by reference to a particular set of research techniques – a highly paradoxical and, one would have thought, unscientific state of affairs.

However so far as present purposes are concerned, the actual validity of the arguments in question is less relevant than the implications which they carry for the sociologist's appreciation of the uses of history in his own field of study. In this respect it would seem, not surprisingly, that where sociologists hold to the view that history and sociology are logically or methodologically distinct, or at least proceed as it they do, they tend to set a notably low estimation on the significance of history for their work.

Take for example the sociologist who sees as the major task confronting his discipline the building up of a logically articulated body of analytical categories on which may be based an entirely general theory of social systems. In creating these categories and in testing their usefulness empirically, historical material will in general be of no more value to him than any other kind of data about human societies and indeed may often have lower value than, say, survey data or ethnographical data because of its possible incompleteness or unreliability. For the sociologist concerned with theory which purports to be general – in other words *trans*historical – historical data are in fact of particular interest in one respect only; that is, in connection with the dynamic aspects of the theory, if such it possesses.

To develop and test general propositions about the process of long-term social change data are obviously required which have continuity over time; and since survey research is of fairly recent origin this usually means data produced by the conventional methods of the historian. A good illustration of historical data being employed by a sociologist for the purpose in question is afforded by Neil Smelser's recent study *Social Change in the Industrial Revolution*. Here Smelser uses a great deal of material from the industrial and 'social' history of Lancashire over the period 1770 to 1840 in order to provide an empirical test of a general theory of change in social systems through a process of structural differentiation – a theory which is in fact a segment of a wider theory of social action developed by Talcott Parsons and his associates. In essentials the procedure which Smelser follows is to show how his model of structural change can be successfully applied (a) to change in the Lancashire cotton industry, and then (b) to change in the family economy of the Lancashire working class. Although then two quite different institutional sub-systems are involved, both, Smelser can argue, conform to the same pattern of structural differentiation; in both cases the process of change can be explained in terms of the same dynamic model. Thus, Smelser can claim, the general applicability of his model is supported: so also is the generality of the wider theory of action from which the model derives – in the same way as this has been supported by earlier studies into such diverse matters as the behaviour of small groups, the socialisation of the child and the development of economic institutions.

Thus, for Smelser the data of history are of value simply as a useful kind of material with which to fill the 'empty boxes' of his transhistorical theory. He is not primarily interested in the Lancashire cotton industry and the Lancashire working-class family as providing a case study of for example the relationship between economic growth and the functions of the family in England during the Industrial Revolution, nor even in the context of some broader theory of, say, the process of industrialisation in the Western Europe. Essentially he is interested in these topics because they provide data which can be applied in testing a dynamic aspect of an absolutely general theory of social systems. In other words their specific historicity is of no particular importance to him.

For those sociologists who hold that basic methodological differences exist between history and sociology, historical data are of still smaller significance than for those who are concerned with general theory. Adherents of the view in question may accept that 'broad historical studies' have some general 'orientation' value for the sociologist[3] and their monographs may frequently be prefaced by a section on 'historical background'. But conventional historiography is nevertheless typically regarded as representing a mode of pre-scientific thinking about man and society which is quite superseded in the study of contemporary societies, thanks to the research techniques which are the proper instruments of the modern sociologist. In so far as these methodological purists do concern themselves with history, it is in fact chiefly to point out the inadequate empirical basis of much historical argument. Characteristic here is Paul Lazarsfeld's caustic remark that historians often make statements about public opinion 'which read like a Gallup release except, of course, that the tables are missing'.[4] Even in regard to the study of social change sociologists of the school in question are reluctant to make use of historical materials of a conventional kind. They would prefer, rather, to start from scratch, as it were, and to create their own kind of historical data by such means as 'follow-up' or 'panel' studies – that is, studies of particular social situations or groups (a community, an electorate, etc.) repeated at intervals over a period of time. Only in this way, they would argue, can data be obtained of a quality which will permit a profitable theoretical analysis of the processes and mechanisms of social change.

If, then, sociologists were entirely concerned either with developing general theory or with conducting research by means of 'survey' methods, the relevance of history to sociology could be little more than marginal. However there exists a further major tradition of sociological study – and indeed it may fairly be termed the 'classic' tradition – which stands in an entirely different relationship to history; the study of history is in fact one of the most important sources from which the tradition stems and necessarily remains in an intimate connection with it. In sociological inquiry which follows this tradition, the focus of interest is not primarily on those properties which may be taken as common for all societies but rather on the differing forms of structure and culture exhibited by particular societies at particular periods in their development. Or again in regard to dynamic aspects, the chief concern is not with establishing models of social change which are of universal applicability but more with understanding and explaning particular processes of change which can be delimited in geographical and historical terms. In other words sociologists who work in the classic tradition operate at a level of abstraction which is clearly below that required of those who are concerned with general theory; they operate, in C. Wright Mills's words, 'at the level of social-historical structures'.[5] At the same time, however, one should note that the perspectives of the 'classic' sociologist are far wider than those of sociologists who would define the scope of their subject in terms of modern methods of field research. Because of the limitations of the techniques to which they are wedded the latter are forced to restrict themselves largely to the study of social milieux (communities, work situations, local associations, etc.) considered statically or over very short-term periods. Without forsaking their techniques they are thus unable to appreciate or to explain how these social milieux have emerged from, and are conditioned by, the structure of the wider society in which they are set or how ongoing changes at the level of the milieux are related to changes at a societal level. To do this would entail a shift precisely to the classic mode of sociological analysis. It would mean thinking in terms of societies as developing structures or in other words it would call for the introduction of a historical dimension.

In one sense then the classic tradition stands in an intermediate position in the range of different types of inquiry which make up modern sociology. Its exponents do not have as their direct objective the formulation of entirely general sociological theory, but neither are they content with the description of social behaviour in small scale locales at certain points in time. Their central concern is with comprehending the variety which is revealed in the structure and culture of human societies, with establishing the limits and determinants of this variation and, in the context of this wider knowledge, with explaining how particular societies, or institutions within them, have developed in a particular way and why they function as they do.

In the pursuit of aims of this kind the special relevance of historical data is not difficult to appreciate. In the first place any attempt at a developmental approach will obviously require such data. For example whenever we speak of the transition from 'traditional' to 'industrial' society, or from the 'folk' to the 'urban' community or from 'familial' to 'bureaucratic' business enterprises, we are in effect using conceptions the validity of which can only be derived from historical study. Moreover the comparative method, which more than any other is fundamental to the classic tradition, is also in large measure dependent upon history. In order to explain patterns of variation in social structure and culture, comparisons between societies are clearly essential; and if the range of comparison is not to be severely restricted then societies of the past as well as of the present must undoubtedly be included in the analysis. For instance in an inquiry into the relationship between, say, dominant economic institutions and forms of social stratification, a comparison between modern Britain and feudal Britain might well be as important as one between modern Britain and modern Russia. Whatever materials there may be available on contemporary societies, advanced and primitive, the exponent of the comparative method cannot afford to neglect the store of information about man and society which the past has to offer. History is certainly his broadest, and probably also his richest, field of study.

Conceived, then, according to the classic tradition, sociology is in effect a historical discipline; the problems with which it is concerned cannot be approached – or even formulated – without the adoption of a historical perspective and the extensive use of historical materials. From this viewpoint no clear boundary of any kind is in fact to be discerned between history and sociology. They are seen rather as merging imperceptibly one into the other; differences between them in either their logic or their method are regarded as differences in degree not in kind.

The foregoing discussion thus leads up to a major issue in modern sociology – an issue which turns on the question of the relevance of history. On the one side are those who support what we may call the natural science view of sociology, whether the focus of their interest is on the formulation of general theory or on the development of stringent quantitative methods in empirical social research. So far as the members of this school are concerned, the uses of history in sociology are of no great significance and the two disciplines are treated as if they were clearly distinguishable. On the other side stand the defenders of what I have termed the 'classic tradition', holding firm to their conception of sociology as being inevitably rooted in the study of history. The former claim that if it is to be truly a science, sociology must have general theory, just as it must have instruments which permit precise measurement and analysis; in both theory and method history must be transcended. The latter reply that natural science does not necessarily provide an entirely appropriate model for social science and question the value both of attempts to establish transhistorical theory and of detailed studies of social milieux, however accurate, which leave out of account their societal and historical contexts; history will not be transcended.

The merits of this controversy are not easy to assess but one point, it would seem, can and should be made with some conviction; that is that little will be gained by those on one side of the argument denying in a dogmatic way the validity of the kind of sociology favoured by those on the other. It is for example futile and arrogant for methodological purists to seek to exclude from the literature of sociology all studies which do not match up methodologically to the standards which they have arbitrarily decreed: it is equally futile and arrogant for writers such as C. Wright Mills to claim that general theory in sociology is in principle impossible or to imply that modern quantitative methods in social research can be of use only in the study of trivial problems. The real scope for argument arises not over contentions such as these but over much more urgent questions concerning current strategy in sociological studies; that is, over questions of how, here and now, sociologists may best direct their efforts and resources.

In this connection I can here do no more than put forward a personal view. This is quite simply that studies on 'classic' lines remain of crucial importance to contemporary sociology and should be pursued much more extensively than they have been of late, at least in Great Britain and the United States. The reasons I would give for this view are the following. Firstly a deeper understanding is required of the range of variation possible in human societies, particularly in the ways in which they are integrated and change, before any significant advances in general theory are likely to be achieved. A major criticism of Parsonian general theory is in fact that it is not enough – that there are certain types of society to which it would not effectively apply. Secondly studies of a historical and comparative kind are necessary to act as frameworks into which detailed studies of social milieux can be fitted in a meaningful way. Modern research techniques would be far better exploited if particular milieux were singled out for intensive investigation not more or less by accident but because they appeared likely to have special significance in the context of some wider structural analysis. Thirdly studies which focus on patterns of variation in social structure and in culture, and even in 'human nature' itself, are those likely to be most helpful to us in our efforts to understand our own society and our own time. It is often through comparison with other worlds, historically as well as geographically distant, that our own social existence is made most intelligible.

As I see it then the tradition of historically orientated study must continue to form the core of sociology. If such a view is prejudicial to the scientific status of the discipline then so much the worse for that.

Postscript (1972)

In reading today what I wrote some ten years ago I am conscious of the extent to which my remarks were orientated, implicitly if not explicitly, towards issues which, while of some moment at the time in question, may now appear to be rather *passé*. In 1962 sociology was beginning its period of rapid expansion within British universities, and its relationship to longer-established but seemingly cognate disciplines was a matter of some controversy. Simultaneously the shock waves were crossing the Atlantic from the impact of

Wright Mills's *The Sociological Imagination* on the orthodoxy represented by Parsonian theory and Lazarsfeldian methodology. In both these connections the relevance of history to sociological inquiry was a question of crucial importance. The chief purpose of my paper was thus to state a position on this question in the context of the debates that were then in progress within the academic communities of Cambridge in particular and of British sociology more generally.

Ten years later I do not find that there is much in the paper that I would actually wish to retract. Nevertheless the fact that it was written so much under the influence of specific circumstances – together with the further fact that much has of course happened in sociology and in the world in the interim – means that the paper contains both emphases and undertones which I would not now want to introduce into the argument. Conversely there are certain points that I would now like to stress more heavily than I did in 1962 and some quite new ones that I would like to bring forward. Because of limitations of space, the comments that follow are rather allusive and the reader seeking further elaboration must turn to the various books and articles that are cited.

(1) I believe that now there is much less need than in 1962 to stress the importance of a historical perspective (and the impossibility of 'transcending' history) as a counter to aggressive, although naïve, championing of the idea of a 'natural science of society'. This idea has in fact lost ground considerably in the recent past as a result of the increasingly critical (but by no means merely negative) position that sociologists themselves have adopted towards both 'general theory' and methods of quantitative – especially survey – research. On the one hand one can trace growing scepticism about the explanatory or even heuristic value of structural-functional theory, based on the notion of a 'social system', whether this is of Parsonian or other provenance.[6] On the other one may note that while significant advances in techniques of quantitative analysis have been made, the whole question of the ways in which the data of such analysis are actually constituted has of late come under searching examination. More sophisticated approaches to quantification have given rise in particular to doubts as to the validity of much attitudinal and other 'subjective' data generated through the medium of highly structured questionnaires or interview schedules.[7]

One significant outcome of these developments is that now, from a theoretical and methodological standpoint alike, the concept of *social action* has assumed a new centrality. The importance – and at the same time the difficulties – of explaining social structure in terms of action (rather than of function) and of interpreting the meaning of action (as well as accounting for it causally) have returned to being major preoccupations of sociological analysis. Thus the divergence between the intellectual problems and perspectives of historians and sociologists now appears much less than it did at a time when scientific ambitions among the latter were at a peak, and the possibility of conducting the kind of dialogue between the two disciplines which proved so fruitful in Max Weber's day would once again seem real.[8]

(2) There is now less basis than previously for differentiating historians from sociologists by reference to the kinds of material with which they typically work and the ways in which they utilise their data. The last decade has seen the rapid development of new forms of social history – most notably of a broadly defined 'urban' history – which aim at investigating social structures and processes through the analysis of relatively large bodies of quantitative material derived from for example parish registers, trade directories and, most importantly, enumeration books and other census sources.[9] In handling such material, historians have come to draw heavily on techniques of data processing and analysis developed for the most part by sociologists; and one may add that they are now apparently also discovering more about the value of sociological concepts – if only in dealing with problems of the selection and organisation of data which become acute when the amount of potential 'raw material is quite vast. In turn the new social history should have positive consequences for sociology. The demonstration that historical data can be of a systematic quantitative kind seems likely to encourage sociologists to use such data not simply for contextual or essentially *illustrative* purposes, as they have mostly done hitherto, but further for the actual testing of specific hypotheses where questions of 'more' or 'less' are crucial. In particular there are clearly attractive possibilities here for the empirical investigation of various 'middle-range' theories concerning the long-term effects of industrialisation as – for example – on family structure, community and neighbourhood relations, and occupational and social mobility.[10]

(3) In 1962 it seemed salutary to urge that sociologists should not, out of methodological inhibition, confine themselves to the investigation simply of social milieux more or less statically conceived, and to stress the continuing importance of the classic tradition concerned with the study of total societies in the course of their historical development. Today when both 'macrosociological' and evolutionary or developmental perspectives are in fact attracting a renewed interest, I would feel that a rather more critical stance toward them is called for.

First it must be said that not a few present-day sociologists seeking to work in the classic tradition would be well served by rather more 'inhibition', particularly in their use of history as derived from *secondary* sources. Most ironically one may observe writers (for example on the New Left) who would be among the first to decry survey-based research as 'positivistic', themselves displaying at least as crude a positivism in treating the 'facts' contained in historical works as if they were something like stamps or butterflies to be diligently collected, arranged in attractive patterns and then displayed for admiration. But such facts must always be understood as simply *inferences* – the most interesting being usually the most complex and debatable – drawn from the 'relics' at the historian's disposal. The methodological basis of any kind of historical sociology wholly or largely reliant upon secondary sources should, I believe, be regarded as no less problematical and as requiring no less critical scrutiny than that, say, of the most ambitious mathematical or quantitative sociology.

Secondly, and giving yet greater cause for concern, one may note that certain varieties of present-day sociology which utilise an evolutionary or developmental approach reveal a dangerous uncertainty or obscurity on the matter of the relationship between historical and theoretical statements. In some instances it is evident enough that the aim is to demonstrate *empirically*, on the basis of historical materials, the existence of certain 'sequential' regularities in changes occurring in institutional and other social-structure forms.[11] Such an objective is in itself entirely legitimate, although it needs to be recognised that tracing historical patterns *post factum* does not amount to their theoretical explanation. In fact what is produced is a number of – more or less – interesting *explicanda* which then require theoretical attention as a separate undertaking. In other instances, however, historical and theoretical aims are seemingly fused, or at all events are confounded. That is to say that attempts are made to produce 'theoretical history' – or theories of social evolution or development – in the sense of constructions which purport to comprehend the principles or logic *immanent in* established sequential regularities, and thus to be able to go beyond these and to offer some grasp on the future.[12] For example such attempts clearly remain part of the programme of various forms of recently fashionable Marxism;[13] and, as I have argued elsewhere,[14] are certainly present, if for the most part covertly, in much current American writing on the themes of modernisation and industrialism. In some of this, one may add – and above all in the latest work of Parsons himself[15] – one encounters the last desperate but logical bid to revivify structural-functional theory with a marriage with a strongly 'pro-naturalistic' evolutionism. What must be strenuously objected to in all such endeavours is that their authors while advancing no defence against, and in fact largely ignoring, cogent attacks on the very idea of theoretical history (as presented by Popper and others[16]) still seek, in classic historicist fashion, to use their theories to lend a spurious scientific basis and objectivity to what can be shown to be ideological arguments.

As Robert Nisbet has observed, the problem that has from the first 'haunted' theories of social evolution and development has been that of how to make the historical record congruent with the immanent processes of change that are proposed.[17] A greater awareness of this record and of the way in which it is constituted may then be the most powerful safeguard that sociologists can have against further succumbing to the treacherous attractions that such theories offer.

10 The Historical Study of Family Structure*

Michael Anderson

Dahrendorf has noted that 'Sociologists still like to invent their history so as to lend profile to their statements about the present'.[1] To a remarkable extent this is still true of the sociology of the family. Until recently our knowledge of family life in the past was usually derived from one or more of three kinds of sources: novels, usually by middle-class writers; largely impressionistic writings, frequently reformatory or didactic in aim, by middle-class contemporaries; and anecdotes recounted to investigators by elderly respondents, some of which they in turn had heard from others even older than themselves. The first two were inevitably rather impressionistic and based on incomplete knowledge; in addition their didactic aims encouraged an emphasis on social pathology. Their evidence is almost certainly not therefore representative of the population as a whole.[2] The anecdotal sources are subject to all the well-known problems of long period recall which seem to blur away the harshness of the past and the sufferings of substantial minority groups and lead people to portray the past through rose-coloured (or occasion-

*Reprinted from E. A. Wrigley (ed.), *Nineteenth Century Society: Essays in the Use of Quantitative Methods for the Study of Social Data* (Cambridge: Cambridge University Press, 1972) pp. 47–55 and 77–81, with the permission of the publishers and the author.

ally grimy) spectacles. This bias in recall data on the family appears to be common to all cultures at all periods of history.[3]

All these sources, then, tend to give a picture of family and social life in the past which exaggerates in one direction or the other, which portrays the historical family either as highly integrated or, alternatively, as highly disrupted. Undue stress is inevitably laid on isolated cases which were almost certainly atypical. Little weight can be given to such sources taken alone as facts on which to base reliable generalisations.

And yet the sociology of the family, more than most branches of the discipline of sociology, is much preoccupied with change and with the impact of social changes on the family.

Thus for example a number of studies have suggested, mainly on the basis of the kinds of data considered above, that important changes have occurred in family life in Britain's towns over the past thirty or so years.[4] Our ideas of what went before are usually hazy in the extreme but often seem to include some images, based on scattered contemporary material and on our over-fertile imaginations, of stable rural communities, cohesive nuclear family systems and, perhaps, tightly knit kinship systems. Then there came sudden disruptions brought about by migration to the towns, factory work, squalid social conditions, until the situation gradually stabilised again into the relatively integrated 'traditional' working-class communities which some writers have suggested existed in the 1930s and before.[5] Laslett and his associates have already shown something of the falsity of the romantic picture of pre-industrial rural England,[6] but we have so far rather few studies which attempt to get at the facts about family structure in nineteenth- and early twentieth-century British towns.[7] If, however, we are to be able to say anything really useful about recent social changes then we must have much more 'hard' information about the past than we possess at present. Systematic historical research into family structure in past ages must therefore become an integral part of the sociology of the family.

Much of the work that is done in the field is focused on the impact of industrialisation and urbanisation on some aspect of family structure. Rigorous investigations of the course of changes in family structure in Britain over the past 400 years could make an important contribution to our theoretical knowledge of the effects of these social revolutions, for here we have the opportunity of studying the impact on a society of changes generated within that society on people with, comparatively speaking, a highly homogeneous culture regardless of their occupations and technology.

The nineteenth century provides an important focal point in any plan for systematic study of the impact of industrialisation on the British family, for it was above all in this period that Britain was transformed from a pre-industrial to an industrial society.

There is also one other more mundane but no less important reason to consider the study of family structure in nineteenth-century Britain as potentially fruitful. Particularly after 1841 data on at least some aspects of family life become very readily available in the census enumerators' books. At about the same time valuable descriptive sources suddenly blossom forth in evergrowing numbers.

This kind of research is obviously, then, important to the sociologist. And it is equally valuable to the historian. For example data obtained on the causes of variation in the age of marriage in the nineteenth century between different groups of the population and between different areas suggest support for the birth-rate theory of population growth in the eighteenth century.[8] Data on the roles played by kin and neighbours in crises, and on the important contribution made by the old in some areas to the standard of living of their married children by allowing young mothers to work, may well help to explain some of the variations in the loads of Poor Law Guardians in different parts of the country. Data on patterns of inheritance and land transfer between generations suggest the correctness of Habakkuk's suggestion[9] that the availability of a labour force not tied to the parental plot was at least one very important factor which made the industrial revolution in Britain possible at all.

In view of the importance of research in this area it is perhaps somewhat surprising that there should exist few published modern studies of any aspect of family life in the late eighteenth and in the nineteenth centuries. A certain amount is known about changes in the economic functions of the urban-industrial family from the work of Collier[10] and Smelser.[11] Margaret Hewitt has discussed the effect that a factory-working mother could have on the family as a domestic group.[12] Ivy Pinchbeck has reviewed more generally the roles of wives and mothers in the period of industrialisation.[13] A number of studies are now in progress or nearing completion using census enumerators' books to study the social structure of nineteenth-century towns and these will obviously throw up many facts and ideas which are highly relevant to the family sociologist.[14] Dorothy Crozier has concluded an important investigation into London middle-class family structure,[15] and some limited statistical data from a wider study of the whole population have also appeared.[16] The only completed study which to my knowledge has considered kinship and family cohesion in any rigorous manner is that of Foster, although mainly because this is incidental to his main purpose he has confined himself to a few tables and some stimulating discussion.[17] My own work[18] is therefore almost unique in its attempt to study the family and social change in one area of nineteenth-century urban England in detail although much of it should be seen as exploratory rather than as a definitive example of this kind of research. A major gap remains, then, to be filled.

This chapter suggests some of the possible ways of replacing by fact what is at present little more than folk myth. It is not concerned with the history of individual families, although such histories may be of great help in building up the overall picture.[19] The aim is rather to seek out and describe *patterns and uniformities* in the family life of certain sectors of the population taken as a whole.

The discussion relies heavily on my experience which has been based largely on a study of parent-child relationships and of people's relationships with kin outside the nuclear family. It would seem that these aspects of family structure will be the main concern of most future investigators since it is much more difficult to do any adequate study of husband-wife relationships in a historical context. Many of the principles and techniques discussed here would however, also be useful to those looking at other aspects of family life. I shall be concerned particularly to look at sources and techniques for the study of lower-class family structure, meaning by lower class that whole section of the population, 'the class of labourers and small shopkeepers',[20] which the Victorian middle class saw as so clearly differentiated from themselves. Students of middle-class and trade families also have at their disposal other valuable sources, notably wills and business records. Those interested in this area should therefore also consult the work of Dorothy Crozier.[21]

It is important that investigations of this kind are not confined to the family in isolation from its social setting, nor to only some of the many functions that the family in any society performs. Descriptions should have a wider scope, encompassing as far as is possible all behaviour that was in any way influenced by the individual's memberships in his family and kinship systems. Any aspect of family life, at home, in leisure time, at work or elsewhere, in which family members orientated their actions in any way be reference to their family memberships should potentially be considered as relevant for a full understanding of family structure and must be investigated if a full picture of the *significance* of family relationships is to be built up.

For beyond a first simple series of descriptions will lie for most students a more fundamental and unifying aim to assess *how important* family membership at different levels – membership of nuclear family, membership of different wider kinship groups – was to the members of any given society and group within that society. The aim then, even if it will often be only implicit or half formalised is to establish as far as possible, in a comparative perspective (comparative across the country, between countries, between groups at a point in time and over time) how important were relationships with parents, children and wider kin in influencing the life chances of members of that group or society.

If we are even to begin to approach this ultimate aim of assessing the importance of relationships, we must try to decide what we mean by 'important' and how we might try to assess it. Unfortunately there is a wide range of disagreement among sociologists on both these matters although a number of fruitful lines of action do seem to be emerging.[22]

For example it is now becoming clear that it is totally inadequate to confine one's attention simply to the study of patterns of residence. The sharing of a home and of obligations incurred by commensality is only one sphere of family activity and its significance can only be assessed in the context of a much wider review of all the functions provided by the family, and of the extent to which individuals see themselves overall as being dependent on family relationships. Two examples from Victorian Lancashire may help to illustrate this point.

Firstly a comparison of the proportion of young couples in the silk-weaving village of Middleton, Lancashire, who in 1851 shared a home with a parent, with the comparable figure for the town of Preston (6 per cent compared with 16 per cent), might suggest far stronger family bonds in Preston than in Middleton. This interpretation is almost certainly erroneous. In both these communities, relationships with parents were of very considerable importance for young married couples. In Middleton these couples were frequently highly dependent on their parents for employment and for the provision of a loom on which to work,[23] and there were strong normative pressures which would have made it very difficult to refuse to meet community-prescribed obligations to parents.[24] In Preston, if my interpretation is correct, both these pressures were much less but the young couples found their mothers very useful as baby minders while the young wife worked. In addition (and this must to some extent have been important in Middleton too) bonds of kinship were important for most of the population because relationships with kin provided the most effective social-welfare service available in the face of the crises which so frequently affects their lives.[25] Other forces were at work too in Preston. The town had a severe housing shortage and rents were high. This made it more difficult and less economical for young couples to set up in a home of their own, particularly one near their parents. In Middleton, on the other hand, while there is no evidence that there was any norm against this kind of sharing, such sharing was much less necessary. It would be a very rash man, therefore, who asserted on the basis of the figures cited above that relationships with kin were more important in Preston, let alone two and a half times as important.

Similarly, taken alone, the finding that in Preston in 1851 well over four-fifths of all boys aged 15 to 19 were living with their families of orientation in spite of high rates of immigration among single boys in this age group and the presence of considerable numbers of orphans, is only one indicator, and not necessarily a very good one taken alone, of the importance of family bonds to this group. Only by considering their relationships with the economic system, backed up by descriptive evidence on the content of their relationships with their parents, can it be established that this relationship was for some largely a matter of convenience. Indeed the extent of dependence and the degree of subjugation to parental authority of this group as a whole was rather low. Their high wages, earned as individuals in employment to which they had been often recruited without reference to their family membership, and the existence of alternative accommodation in the form of lodging houses, meant that if too great attempts were made to control them they could threaten to leave home and could if necessary back up this threat by going off to join others of their age group in the lodging houses. Contrast with this the situation of the son destined to inherit the family farm in Ireland or in the rural areas of Lancashire who was highly dependent for his whole future standard of living on inheriting the farm and was therefore highly dependent on his father. Yet in many areas he was, at the same age, more likely than his urban cousin to be living away from home, as a farm servant or labourer earning money to extend the family plot or gaining experience on other farms.[26]

It is essential, in short, to seek information over as wide a range of activities as possible. People in all societies face many different problems and require assistance from others in meeting them. Finding a home and domestic assistance are only two of these problems. One also needs to find a job, someone to care for one in old age, assistance in all kinds of crises – sickness or death of the wage-earner or mother or family member, unemployment, migration to a new community – and possibly quite simply someone to confide in and give advice. If the individual cannot solve these problems himself, and in as far as they are seen to be frequent or pressing, he must seek help from others. In most societies these others have usually been kin.

This leads on to the second emerging principle on the concept of importance of family relationships. Attention cannot simply be confined to the study of relationships with other family members.[27] The study of sources of assistance other than kin in the major problems areas of a person's life is also necessary. As a polar case, if there is no one but kin to help a man solve some crucial problem that life presents him then his family must be of overwhelming significance to him for if he terminates relationships with them he will die or suffer some serious deprivation.[28] This means, incidentally, that it is of particular interest to study what happens to those who have no relatives to perform any particular function.[29]

It seems to follow then that ideally the investigator would want to gather information on the seriousness and frequency of the crises and needs of the members of the social group under study, the resources at their disposal which they could mobilise to help them meet these needs and their attitudes to the various persons and organisations to which they could conceivably have turned for assistance. Kin are but one of these alternatives. We must therefore try to look at as many aspects of the social, physical and technical environment in which the population lived as is possible within the limitations of the availability of data. Environmental factors act as crucial constraints on possible family-relational patterns. The occupational structure of the community, occupational recruitment patterns, housing conditions, the attraction of migration and distance migrated, the efficiency and rules of the various social welfare organisations, working hours, the turnover of population in neighbourhoods, ideally one would like information on all these topics and many more besides. Unfortunately it is precisely in some of these areas that data are most likely to be lacking or of uncertain reliability. This does not mean that the attempt to collect it should not be made. It does mean that a cast-iron explanation of patterns of family behaviour will seldom be possible.

Finally it must be remembered that patterns of behaviour are not simply determined by the objective constraints of a situation, although these in poorer communities will seldom be far from people's minds. These constraints are only manifested in action after they have been mediated through people's normatively prescribed definitions of 'proper' or 'ideal' behaviour. It is in this area that the greatest problems arise in an historical context, for data on values, on affective behaviour, on how important people actually saw relationships to be, on their motivations for maintaining relationships and on their perceptions of alternatives, are seldom obtainable in any quantity and may often be very unreliable when they are found. Nevertheless all scraps of information on this area must be systematically collected. Out of these scraps some overall if slightly hazy jigsaw picture can usually be made up.

This leads then to a final introductory point, the importance of descriptive material of all kinds for a complete understanding of patterns of family relationships and of factors which influence them. While much time will be taken up with detailed and systematic work on samples from the census enumerators' books, many other kinds of data will also have to be used if an adequate picture is to be obtained. The enumerators' books, suitably used, can provide us with figures, some fairly precise others very sketchy, on such matters as where related families lived, age of marriage, household composition at different stages of the life cycle and at different ages, marital statuses and family sizes, the occupations of family members and their migration patterns. Other sources amenable to statistical treatment can also be used, either alone or in conjunction with each other, or with the enumerators' books. These will include firms' records of employees, workhouse and other poor-relief documents, registers of vital statistics, wills and published demographic information. Finally almost any contemporary document, tract, investigation or even novel may provide insights into areas which statistical data either do not cover or cover only in part. The uses of data of this kind are discussed later.

Before going on to describe in more detail the sources which may be available for students of family structure, and some of the techniques which can be used to tease the most information out of them, it may be worth while noting briefly some of the considerations which should be borne in mind when planning a study of this nature.

Most studies will need to use the enumerators' books of the Victorian censuses as a major data source. The availability of these for public inspection must inevitably influence the periods that can be studied. In England the complete documents are only available at present for the years 1841, 1851, 1861 and 1871 due to the 'hundred years rule'.[30] It has, however, proved possible in the past to have special tabulations made by the Registrar-General's office from the later census data,[31] and also to obtain photostats of enumerators' books with name and addresses erased.[32] Even where the costs of these special services are not considered prohibitive, however, these procedures may be less valuable for students of family structure than for some others. For example it is clearly impossible to use the bowdlerised photocopies to trace individuals from census to census or from census to other records, and techniques of this nature, particularly if the procedures can be computerised,[33] seem potentially to have an exciting pay-off both in their own right and as a check against conclusions from our one-shot data, by allowing us to study processes of change and their impact on the family.

There is also a further factor to be noted when considering the time span over which data should be collected. The enumerators' books taken alone do not provide all the information that we need. Supporting data, particularly of a descriptive kind is also needed unless our concern is exclusively with demographic, occupational or residential aspects of family structure. This descriptive material is, however, widely scattered so that one is forced to describe not family structure in, say, 1851, but family structure in the period 1841–61 or even 1831–71, in order to get enough background information to fill in descriptions and to support explanations. This implies the assumption that changes within the period reviewed were either very slow or, alternatively, proceeded in clearly defined and specified jumps. It is reasonable to assume that changes in family structure in the nineteenth century were in most places fairly slow, although obviously this is not so in areas subject to sudden major changes in the conditions of existence (e.g. the Irish famine) and is probably more true for some aspects of family behaviour (for example the effects of migration on relationships with kin left behind) than others (for example the relationships between father and son in cotton spinning).[34] Data from periods further from some centre point of a study must clearly be treated with caution. Nevertheless it seems pedantic and unrealistic to exclude them by some arbitrary line. To take a period extending twenty years on either side of the centre year (say 1851) seems not unreasonable, but this will depend greatly on the area and precise topic studied.

If, however, it is necessary to assume fairly long periods as homogeneous, this has other implications too. The most important is that it is unwise to attempt any study of gradual change in patterns of family behaviour over periods of less than about fifty years. Descriptive sources can usually only be used for work on very long-run or very major changes because otherwise the range of variation within the data for any period is almost as great as the changes overall. Attempts to make comparisons over short time periods are therefore to be viewed with great reservation. If analysis of change is to proceed beyond mere description of data from enumerators' books, trends must either be inferred from comparisons between areas more and less developed in terms of the independent variable *at a point in time* (e.g. 1851) or must, where data are available, be derived from the long-run data. There is little doubt that a comparative study taking listings for a year in the mid-eighteenth century and for, say, 1851 and 1970, combined with descriptive and supporting data for a period of twenty years on either side of the dates of the first two, and interview material for the last, might provide us with valuable insight into processes of change. If adequate descriptive material was available, many of the listings of the kind used by Laslett and his associates, particularly if they were combined with family reconstitutions to provide information on relationships between persons who were not co-residing, are detailed enough to make at least crude long-run comparisons possible. This is particularly so in rural areas where inconsistencies over definitions of houses and households are much less likely to cause difficulties.

In general then, to get an understanding of the family patterns we observe in nineteenth-century Britain, and of the factors at work on them, it is best to concentrate in detail on a small span of time, attempting to link individuals between censuses and to other data sources, and making an intensive search for literary background material. This is likely to prove more fruitful than attempts at comparison between one Victorian decade and another.

A few other observations may also be made on the censuses already available for public inspection. Firstly, and unfortunately, the enumerators' books of the 1841 census are of limited value for the study of family structure for they omit the all-important 'Relation to Head of Family' column. The other columns are also less detailed and frequently appear to be less carefully completed. Of the other censuses that of 1851 is from a technical point of view perhaps slightly superior, because the division of the enumerators' books into houses and census families, although undoubtedly subject to some error, is considerably clearer and probably more consistent than in 1861 and thereafter.[35]

Difficulties in many ways similar to those discussed above arise also in the choice of an area for study. Statistical material is more readily assessed and more easily assembled if it is for a single town chosen because it is believed to be typical of the region or of communities with a particular occupational base,[36] although a sample of several villages in an area is probably best for a rural study. On the other hand adequate descriptive evidence for one town will very seldom be found. Data from other similar towns seems admissible, however, although once again caution is necessary. One should always ask oneself whether differences in workbase, size, location, death rates, migration rates or other factors between these other communities and the chosen town have had effects on their family structure.

Finally since census data are available for almost the whole country,[37] choice of area and size of area will depend on the theoretical or historical problem in view, and on the availability of supporting data. For some areas this last is so scanty that interesting projects will be stultified. Here as always thorough exploratory work and pilot studies save much wasted time and effort.

Data of a statistical nature can only take the story so far. They must be filled out and supplemented by other descriptive material drawn from a wide range of sources.

A word of caution may be useful as a preliminary.[38] Great care must be taken when collecting and analysing descriptive material to ensure that one records not only data on the performance of any function by any family member of kinsman but also data on the performance of that function by any other individual or agency, and on the refusal by anyone to perform the function. If this is not done a totally one-sided picture will be built up in the research notes, and in the final analysis the importance of family relationships will be greatly overstressed. Moreover it should be remembered that the data themselves are likely to be somewhat one-sided. Just because a third of one's notes refer to kin performing any given function is no indication that kin performed this function in a third of all cases even if the number of references is large. Sometimes comment will be made because the action was seen by the observer as extraordinary. Often no comment will be made because the action was seen as unremarkable. Some cases of non-performance will anyway be missed. Even if all cases (of a fairly large number of cases) are either positive or negative, categorical statements cannot be made without a careful consideration of all possible explanations of this apparent unanimity. Above all one must ask whether or not it was likely that mention of deviant cases would be made at all. Wherever possible the data must be checked against quantifiable material for indications of their generality.[39]

Descriptive material fulfils two main functions. First it helps in the interpretation of quantitative data. Second it is the only type of source which will cover areas where statistical data are either entirely lacking or are of only limited and often tangential nature. This is particularly likely to be the case where one is interested in people's motivations and in the ways in which they themselves perceived their situation.

Under the first heading three points may be noted. Firstly descriptive data may often suggest hypotheses to be examined. Thus it was statements to the effect that the old in Lancashire were often provided for because they could perform useful functions when the wife was working away from home in factories,[40] which led me in my Lancashire study to see whether there was a relationship between the mother being in employment and the presence of a parent in the household. Such a relationship did indeed exist.[41] Secondly relationships suggested by statistical analysis (for example the finding that many single young immigrant lodgers came from the same village and were in the same occupation as the heads of their co-residing groups) can be filled out and the mechanisms by which such situations came about can be explored. In the case of the lodgers this involves looking at evidence describing the processes whereby young men were invited by those who had earlier emigrated from their village to come to the town and were then found jobs and provided with semi-permanent homes.[42] Most statistical data indeed will require some support from non-statistical evidence, particularly if processes are being examined. Illustrations of such processes from descriptive data also give life and credulity to the statistical assertions. Thirdly the motivations and underlying actions cannot usually be understood simply by reference to statistical data. For example it was found in Preston that if their mother was dead, children were much more likely to leave home than they were if their father had died. One possible explanation of this, suggested by theory and supported by much descriptive data, was that children perceived their mothers and fathers very differently. They tended to see their fathers as cruel and egoistic while their mothers were usually seen as self-sacrificing. As a result, bonds of affection and feelings of obligation to mothers were much stronger than bonds to fathers.[43]

Descriptive data also have a role uniquely their own. It is evident that there are many topics on which one would like information (because different aspects of family behaviour are intimately related and the understanding of any one needs some insight into all) but which cannot, in a historical situation, be investigated directly by statistical analysis. Since only descriptive data can be used, assertions can usually be made only with much less certainty.[44] It is unfortunately rarely possible to use any rigorous form of content analysis on the kinds of data used in the study of family structure[45] although always important to keep one eye open for data suitable for quantitative analysis in this way.

Descriptive data are the chief source of information on the

following: qualitative and emotional aspects of family relationships; authority patterns; socialisation; an actor's conception of the family and its meaning to him and the roles and obligations that membership imposes on him; his views on the relative strength of obligations to wife, children, parents, uncles, cousins, neighbours, friends, workmates, persons born in the same village, etc.; many of the functions family members perform for each other in everyday life and in crises, and why, how and when they do so. Data on these and many other topics must, in a historical context, come solely, or almost solely, from descriptive sources.

Descriptive materials useful for this subject can be divided into three broad categories; descriptions of how and why members of groups of other people in general behave; of how and why other individuals have behaved or behave; and of how and why they themselves behave or have behaved.

Tracts, reports of missionary and charitable societies, descriptions of crises, newspaper investigations into the condition of the people, parliamentary investigations and the evidence of some witnesses to them, speeches in parliamentary debates, and some aspects of novels and other works come under the first head. Descriptions of crises – epidemics and slumps for example – are often of particular value for it is at such times as these that the full services of a kinship system are likely to be mobilised.[46] Most of the above sources also contain examples which fall under the second head. Under the third head come on the one hand verbatim or semi-verbatim replies to inquiries or questions – particularly useful here are the occasions on which ordinary people gave evidence to parliamentary inquiries about themselves, above all when the same questions were asked to a large number of people. Biographies, autobiographies and diaries are another valuable source under this head. Such materials are the major source of evidence on motivations and on the more intimate aspects of family life. It must be remembered however when considering answers to questions, that these were usually recorded long-hand by members of the middle class who may have slightly altered the original words used and in doing so have often increased the sophistication or the affective content of the phraseology in such a way as to convey an incorrect impression of concern, attachment or motivation.

As always when interpreting data, attention must be paid to its probable reliability and generality. In particular three questions seem important for the study of family structure: did the reporter really know enough about a situation to report it accurately? was he biased? how far can his findings be generalised?

Under the first head two comments are important. Many of those who reported aspects of family behaviour, above all if they were dealing with the working class, were middle-class people with little real understanding of working-class life. They were, moreover, often visitors to the region in question, reporting superficial impressions or even basing their conclusions on selections from documentary material produced by others. For Lancashire Peter Gaskell, Ashley, Engels and a number of novelists (Tonna or Dickens for example) fall into this category. A second group consists of those who although more familiar with working-class life and reliable on some topics still fail to understand properly the constraints operating on people to bring about certain aspects of behaviour and thus impute incorrect motivations to them. Criticisms of working wives, of parents seeking employment for young children, and of unemployed fathers often fall under this head.[47]

The second head, that of bias, is less important in this field than in most areas of historical inquiry. Most of the topics covered by this kind of research were not the express concern of the investigator whose report is being considered. Evidence, rather, usually comes as by-products of such inquiries and from odd comments although certain topics – parental authority or the absence of care for kin in their old age for example – are sometimes of more direct concern to the authors, and the possibility of bias should be borne in mind. The disadvantages which result from the data being in this form have been noted earlier when the reasons why any piece of behaviour might or might not be the topic of comment were discussed. Moreover the scattered nature of so much of the evidence makes its gathering laborious – there is no one source for any topic – and makes classification and filing somewhat of a nightmare. It does help, however, to ensure its reliability particularly if information about behaviour can be cross-checked from a number of different kinds of source.

It is the third head that presents the most trouble. It was pointed out above that the literature always tends to report what struck the observer as out of the ordinary or shocking – Mayhew's costermongers, drunks, children who deserted their parents, cases of extreme self-sacrifice or devotion. A further problem is that many of the best sources from the point of view of detail and quantity of data are primarily concerned with social pathology, with the very poor, the delinquent and the criminal. sometimes, as for example with children who deserted their parents and went into lodgings, statistical data can be used to suggest that in spite of widespread comment in the literature, the frequency of such behaviour was in fact low[48] (although the forces which led to the cases where a break actually occurred may still have been active in changing the quality of relationships which continued). If statistical confirmation is not available, the extent to which data can be generalised must be carefully considered; whether or not the behaviour seems consistent with other forms of behaviour on which evidence is 'harder' is often a useful guide. Above all the pitfall of assuming that all behaved like a conspicuous minority, that for example all working-class husbands were wife-beating, callous, selfish drunkards must be rigorously avoided.

One point on the presentation of data may also be mentioned. It will never be possible to quote in full all references to any aspect of behaviour which one traces; indeed what is required is analysis, so overquotation should be avoided. Thus a long list of references in support of a point can be made to look very impressive, when in fact each one applies only to one isolated case. Conversely two supporting references to general statements by well-qualified and perceptive commentators are probably a far more valuable source. It is desirable that the type of source used on any topic and its assumed generality should be systematically indicated. Asterisks might for example be put to all references which are to single cases only. Statements supported by references thus marked can then be treated with a proper caution.

To conclude, it may be useful to suggest a number of possible lines of future research. More studies of the family in all its aspects in regions with different economic and social characteristics are highly desirable. London, the Midlands, mining areas, and some rural counties, as well as Ireland, all seem to offer scope for interesting work on a broad front and to have adequate descriptive data available. Studies of an area over time might also prove useful, for example the comparison of the kinship structure of a town in the 1850s and in the present day, particularly if economic change has been rather slower there than elsewhere, would be very worthwhile. Studies comparing areas of similar workbase but in different economic circumstances might also prove very interesting. A study of a town involved in a big strike or a slump at the time of the census compared with another not so affected, for instance, might throw interesting light on the reactions of the family to crises. Intensive studies concentrating on a group of villages and using registration and other locally available data; studies limited to middle-class groups to test the generality of Crozier's London findings; studies of migrants; of the relationship between marriage and the transfer of land; and many more, would be of considerable value. Above all a sure foundation of facts presented in such a way that comparability with other studies is ensured, and preferably orientated to theoretical considerations, will surely be a useful contribution to the furtherance of knowledge and the replacement of folk myth by fact.

11 Class Structure in Early Twentieth-century Salford*

Robert Roberts

We are the mob, the working class, the proletariat (*Song*).

No view of the English working class in the first quarter of this century would be accurate if that class were shown merely as a great amalgam of artisan and labouring groups united by a common aim and culture. Life in reality was much more complex. Socially the unskilled workers and their families, who made up about 50 per cent of the population in our industrial cities, varied as much from the manual elite as did people in middle station from the aristocracy. Before 1914 skilled workers generally did not strive to join a higher rank: they were only too concerned to maintain position within their own stratum. Inside the working class as a whole there existed, I believe, a stratified form of society whose implications and consequences have hardly yet been fully explored. Born behind a general shop in an area which, sixty years before, Frederick Engels had called the 'classic slum', I grew up in what was perhaps an ideal position for viewing the English proletarian caste system in all its late flower.

*Reprinted from Robert Roberts, *The Classic Slum: Salford Life in the First Quarter of the Century* (Manchester: University of Manchester Press, 1971) pp. 1-16, with the permission of the publishers and the author.

> All Salford [wrote Engels in 1844] is built in courts or narrow lanes, so narrow that they remind me of the narrowest I have ever seen, in the little lanes of Genoa. The average construction of Salford is, in this respect, much worse than that of Manchester and so, too in respect of cleanliness. If, in Manchester, the police, from time to time, every six or ten years, makes a raid upon the working-people's district, closes the worst dwellings, and causes the filthiest spots in these Augean stables to be cleansed, in Salford it seems to have done absolutely nothing.

For twenty years from 1850 Engels held interests in cotton mills on the western side of Manchester. This meant that on journeys between town and factory he had to pass through Salford; our 'village' was the greatest slum *en route*. One of his early mills (Ermen and Engels) stood in Liverpool Street, which ran through the heart of it. This is how Engels described our area in 1844:

> The working-men's dwellings between Oldfield Road and Cross Lane (Salford), where a mass of courts and alleys are to be found in the worst possible state, vie with the dwellings of the Old Town in filth and overcrowding. In this district I found a man, apparently sixty years old, living in a cow-stable. He had constructed a sort of chimney for his square pen, which had neither windows, floor nor ceiling, had obtained a bedstead and lived there, though the rain dripped through his rotten roof. This man was too old and weak for regular work, and supported himself by removing manure with a hand-cart; the dung heaps lay next door to his palace.

Through a familiarity so long and close, this district must have become for Engels the very epitome of all industrial ghettos, the 'classic slum' itself. He died in 1895 having seen that little world change, develop, 'prosper' even, yet stay in essence the same awful paradigm of what a free capitalist society could produce. By 1900 the area showed some improvement; his 'cow-stable' had doubtless been demolished together with many another noisesome den, but much that was vile remained.

Our own family was in the slum but not, they felt, of it; we had 'connections'. Father, besides, was a skilled mechanic. During the sixties of the last century his mother, widowed early with four children, had had the foresight to bypass a mission hall near the alley where she lived and send her three good-looking daughters to a Wesleyan chapel on the edge of a middle-class suburb. Intelligent girls, they did their duty by God and mother, all becoming Sunday-school teachers and each in turn marrying well above her station, one a journalist, another a traveller in sugar and a third a police inspector – an ill-favoured lot, the old lady grumbled, but 'you can't have everything'. The girls adapted themselves smoothly to their new milieu, paid mother a weekly danegeld and Carter's Court knew them no more. My father, years their junior, stayed working class; it was, in fact, always harder for a man to break into the higher echelons. At the age of eight he took up education and twelve months later, put it down, despite the newfangled 'Compulsion' Act, to find, his mother[1] said, 'summat a sight better to do at the blacksmith's'. At twenty-one father married a girl from a cotton mill.

As a child my mother had been something of a prodigy and was hawked from one local school to another to display her talents; but, her father dying, she got work at nine, helping in a weaving shed. Happily her family had 'expectations'. When the £900 legacy arrived it was laid out with skill and duly improved status: one sister married a clerk and two elder brothers opened little shops which prospered. They were on the way up! My father, a man given to envy, felt the call of commerce too and came home one evening twelve months after marriage to announce in tipsy triumph that he had, on borrowed money, just bought a grocery store for £40. Horrified, my mother inspected his 'gold mine' – in the heart of a slum – and refused point blank to go. But he cajoled and persuaded. In two or three years, he said, they could build it up, sell it for hundreds of pounds and buy a nice place in the country. She looked at the dank little premises and the grim kitchen behind. 'Two years', she told him, 'and no more! This is no place to bring up a family.' Solemnly he promised. In the little bedroom above the kitchen she bore him seven children and stayed thirty-two years – a life sentence.

Every industrial city, of course, folds within itself a clutter of loosely defined overlapping 'villages'. Those in Great Britain of seventy years ago were almost self-contained communities. Our own consisted of some thirty streets and alleys locked along the north and south by two railway systems a furlong apart. About twice that distance to the east lay another slum which turned on its farther side into a land of bonded warehouses and the city proper. West of us, well beyond the tramlines, lay the middle classes, bay-windowed and begardened. We knew them not.

In the city as a whole our village rated indubitably low. 'The children of this school', wrote one of King Edward VII's inspectors commenting on our only seat of learning, 'are of the poorest class; so, too, is the teaching.' With cash or on tick our villagers, about 3,000 in all, patronised fifteen beer-houses, a hotel and two off-licences, nine grocery and general shops, three greengrocers (for ever struggling to survive against the street hawker), two tripe shops, three barbers, three cloggers, two cook shops, one fish and chip shop (*déclassé*), an old clothes store, a couple of pawnbrokers and two loan offices.

Religion was served by two chapels (Primitive Methodist and Congregationalist), one 'tin' mission (Church of England) and one sinister character who held spiritualist séances in his parlour and claimed from the window to cure 'Female Bad Legs'. (Through overwork innumerable women suffered from burst varicose veins.) Culture, pleasure and need found outlet through one theatre (and later three cinemas), a dancing room ('low'), two coy brothels, eight bookmakers and a private moneylender.

The first of our public buildings reared its dark bulk near the railway wall. Hyndman Hall, home of the Social Democratic Federation (S.D.F.), remained for us mysteriously aloof and through the years had in fact about as much political impact on the neighbourhood as the nearby gasworks. The second establishment, our Conservative Club, except for a few days at election times didn't appear to meddle with politics at all. It was notable usually for a union jack in the window and a brewer's dray at the door.

Over one quarter of a mile of industry stood represented by a dying brickworks and an iron foundry. Several gasholders on the south side polluted the air sometimes for days together. Little would grow; even the valiant aspidistra pined.[2] We possessed besides two coal yards, a corn store, a cattle wharf and perhaps as closed an urban society as any in Europe.

In our community, as in every other of its kind, each street[3] had the usual social rating; one side or one end of that street might be classed higher than another. Weekly rents varied from 2*s* 6*d* for the back-to-back to 4*s* 6*d* for a 'two up and two down'. End houses often had special status. Every family, too, had a tacit ranking, and even individual members within it; neighbours would consider a daughter in one household as 'dead common' while registering her sister as 'refined,' a word much in vogue. (Young women with incipient consumption were often thought 'refined'.) Class divisions were of the greatest consequence, although their implications remained unrealised: the many looked upon social and economic inequality as the law of nature. Division in our own society ranged from an elite at the peak composed of the leading families, through recognised strata to a social base whose members one damned as the 'lowest of the low' or simply 'no class'. Shopkeepers, publicans and skilled tradesmen occupied the premier positions, each family having its own sphere of influence. A few of these aristocrats, while sharing working-class culture, had aspirations. From their ranks the lower middle class, then clearly defined, drew most of its recruits – clerks and in particular schoolteachers (struggling hard at that time for social position). Well before translation those striving to 'get on' tried to ape what they believed were 'real' middle-class manners and customs. Publicans' and shopkeepers' daughters for instance set the fashion in clothes for a district. Some went to private commercial colleges[4] in the city, took music lessons or perhaps studied elocution – that short cut, it was felt, to 'culture' – 2*s* an hour, their new 'twang' tried out later over the bar and counter earning them a deal of covert ridicule. Top families generally stood ever on the lookout for any activity or 'nice' connection which might edge them, or at least their children, into a higher social ambience. But despite all endeavour, mobility between manual workers, small tradesmen and the genuine middle class remained slight and no one needed to wonder why; before the masses rose an economic barrier that few men could ever hope to scale. At the end of the Edwardian period an adult male industrial worker earned £75 a year; the average annual salary of a man in the middle classes proper was £340.

That wide section beyond the purely manual castes where incomes ranged between the two norms mentioned was considered by many to be no more than 'jumped-up working class', not to be confused with the true order above; but the striving sought it nevertheless, if not for themselves, at least for their children. The real social divide existed between those who in earning daily bread dirtied hands and face and those who did not.

The less ambitious among skilled workers had aims that seldom rose above saving enough to buy the ingoing of a beer-house, open a corner shop or get a boarding house at the seaside. By entering into any business at all a man and his family grew at once in economic status, although social prestige accrued much more slowly. Fiascos were common; again and again one noticed in the district pathetic attempts[5] to set up shops in private houses by people who possessed only a few shillings' capital and no experience. After perhaps only three weeks one saw their hopes collapse, often to the secret satisfaction of certain neighbours who, in the phrase of the times, 'hated to see folk trying to get on'.

On the social ladder after tradesmen and artisans came the semi-skilled workers (still a small section) in regular employment, and then the various grades of unskilled labourers. These divisions could be marked in many public houses where workers other than craftsmen would be frozen or flatly ordered out of those rooms in which journeymen foregathered. Each part of the tavern had its status rating; indeed 'he's only a tap-room man' stood as a common slur. Nevertheless whatever the job the known probity of a person conferred at once some social standing. 'She was poor but she was honest' we sang first in praise, not derision. I remember neighbours speaking highly of an old drudge, 'poor but honest', who had sought charring work with a flash publican new to the district. 'I dunno,' he told her, 'but come tomorrer and fetch a "character".' She returned the next day. 'Well, yer brought it?' he asked. 'No,' she said 'I got yours an' I won't be startin'!'

Many women and girls in the district worked in some branch of the textile industry. Of these we accepted weavers as 'top' in their class, followed by winders and drawers-in. Then came spinners. They lacked standing on several counts: first the trade contained a strong Irish Catholic element, and wages generally were lower than in other sections. Again because of the heat and slippery floors, women worked barefoot, dressed in little more than calico shifts. These garments, the respectable believed, induced in female spinners a certain moral carelessness. They came home, too, covered in dust and fluff; all things which combined to depress their social prestige. Women employees of dye works, however, filled the lowest bracket: their work was dirty, wet and heavy and they paid due penalty for it. Clogs and shawls were of course standard wear for all. The girl who first defied this tradition in one of Lancashire's largest mills remembered the 'stares, skits and sneers' of fellow workers sixty years afterwards. Her parents, urgently in need of money, had put her to weaving where earnings for girls were comparatively good. They lived, however, in one of the newer suburbs with its parloured houses and small back gardens. To be seen in such a district returning from a mill in clogs and shawl would have meant instant social demotion for the whole family. She was sent to the weaving shed wearing coat and shoes and thereby shocked a whole establishment. Here was a 'forward little bitch' getting above herself. So clearly in fact did headwear denote class that in Glasgow separate clubs existed for 'hat' girls and 'shawl' girls. Nevertheless, before 1914 even, continued good wages in weaving and the consequent urge to bolster status had persuaded not a few to follow the lone teenager's example. By the end of the war, in the big town cotton mills at least, coats and shoes could be worn without comment.

Unskilled workers split into plainly defined groups according to occupation, possessions and family connection, scavengers and night-soil men rating low indeed. Following these came a series of castes, some unknown and others it seems already withered into insignificance in Professor Hoggart's Hunslet of the 1930s:[6] first the casual workers of all kinds – dockers in particular (who lacked prestige through the uncertainty of their calling), then the local street sellers of coal, lamp oil, tripe, crumpets, muffins and pikelets, fruit, vegetables and small-ware. Finally came the firewood choppers, bundlers and sellers and the rag and boners, often whole families. These people for some reason ranked rock-bottom among the genuine workers. It may have been that firewood sellers rated so very low socially because they competed in some districts with small teams of paupers who went about in charge of a uniformed attendant hawking firewood, chopped and bundled at the Union. Workhouse paupers hardly registered as human beings at all. Even late in the nineteenth century able-bodied men from some northern poorhouses worked in public with a large P stamped on the seat of their trousers. This not only humiliated the wearer but prevented his absconding to a street market where he could have exchanged his good pants for a cheap pair – with cash adjustment. The theft of 'workhouse property' was a common offence among the destitute.

Forming the base of the social pyramid we had bookies' runners, idlers, part-time beggars and petty thieves, together with all those known to have been in prison[7] whatever might be their ostensible economic or social standing. Into this group the community lumped any harlots, odd homosexuals, kept men and brothel keepers. Hunslet's sympathy with a prostitute, mentioned in *The Uses of Literacy*, seems unusual even during the thirties. In the proletarian world of my youth, and long after, the active drab was generally condemned out of hand, certainly by 'respectable' women. Their menfolk agreed or remained uneasily silent. Nor did retirement lead to social acceptance. I recall one street walker, ten years after ceasing her trade, blamelessly married, with a 'clean doorstep and a beautiful house of furniture', who was still cold-shouldered by her neighbours. Drunk one day, she could stand it no longer and burst in a passion through her doorway half pleading, half enraged. 'It's not what I was!' she screamed again and again, 'it's what I am now – a decent, clean-living woman.' This, over a knot of startled children playing in the street, to rows of closed condemnatory doors. The moralists found it hard to forgive and they never forgot. 'I wonder,' sniffed one old neighbour to another, after hearing of the outbreak of World War II, 'I wonder if Mrs J., with her husband away, will go on the game again like what she did last time?'

I don't recall, though, that any 'lost women' ever threw themselves off bridges in despair; as they grew older most found a complaisant male to marry or live with and dwelt, if not accepted, at least tolerated by most neighbours.

Drunkenness, rowing or fighting in the streets, except perhaps at weddings and funerals (when old scores were often paid off), Christmas or bank holidays could leave a stigma on a family already registered as 'decent' for a long time afterwards. Another household, for all its clean curtains and impeccable conduct, would remain uneasily aware that its rating had slumped since grandma died in the workhouse or cousin Alf did time. Still another family would be scorned loudly in a drunken tiff for marrying off its daughter to some 'low Mick from the Bog'. With us, of course, as with many cities in the north, until the coming of the coloured people, Irish Roman Catholic immigrants, mostly illiterate, formed the lowest socio-economic stratum. A slum Protestant marrying into the milieu suffered a severe loss of face. Such unions seldom occurred.[8]

At all times there were naturally many unsnobbish people in the working class who remained indifferent to the social effects of affluence or poverty on those about them and who judged others not at all by their place and possessions. On the whole though most families were well aware of their position within the community, and that without any explicit analyses. Many households strove by word, conduct and the acquisition of objects to enhance the family image and in so doing often overgraded themselves. Meanwhile their neighbours (acting in the same manner on their own behalf) tended to depreciate the pretensions of families around, allotting them a place in the register lower than that which, their rivals felt, connections, calling or possessions merited. In this lay much envy (envy was the besetting sin), bitterness and bad blood which, stored up and brooded over, burst on the community in drunken Saturday night brawls. Tiffs over children usually provided the opening skirmishes, but before the fighting proper began between the males, housewives shrieked abuse at one another, interspersed with 'case history' examples aiming to prove to the world that the other party and its kindred were 'low class' or no class at all. One waved for instance a 'clean' rent book (that great status symbol of the times) in the air, knowing the indicted had fallen in arrears. Now manners and morals were arraigned before a massed public tribunal; innuendoes long hinted at found blatant proof and shame fought with outraged honour screaming in the gutter; a class struggle indeed! Purse-lipped and censorious, the matriarchs surveyed the scene soaking it all in, shocked by the vulgarity of it all, unless of course their own family was engaged. Then later, heads together and from evidence submitted, they made grim readjustments on the social ladder.

As a child before World War I, I hardly knew a weekend free from the sight of brawling adults and inter-family dispute. It was then one saw demonstrated how deeply many manual workers and their wives were possessed with ideas about class; with some, involvement almost reached obsession. Yet in examining the standards of the Edwardian lower orders one has always to bear in mind that street disturbers, gutter fighters and general destroyers of the peace came from a comparatively small section of the community. Nevertheless in the 'dialogue' of street dissension one saw exposed all the social inhibitions of the more respectable.

One or two proletarian authors writing about these times and of the slump between the wars, appear to me to sentimentalise the working class: even worse, by too often depicting its cruder and more moronic members they end by caricaturing the class as a whole. In general women in the slums were far from being foul-mouthed sluts and harridans sitting in semi-starvation at home in between trips to the pub and pawnshop, nor were most men boors and drunken braggarts. People *en masse* it is true had little education but the discerning of the time saw abundant evidence of intelligence, shrewdness, restraint and maturity. Of course we had low 'characters' by the score, funny or revolting; so did every slum in Britain. Such types set no standards. In sobriety they knew their 'place' well enough. Very many families even in our 'low' district remained awesomely respectable over a lifetime. Despite poverty and appalling surroundings parents brought up their children to be decent, kindly and honourable and often lived long enough to see them occupy a higher place socially than they had ever known themselves: the greatest satisfaction of all. It is such people[9] and their children now who deny indignantly (and I believe rightly) that the slum life of the industrial north in this century, for all its horrors, was ever so mindless and uncouth as superficial play and novel would have a later generation believe.

Position in our Edwardian community was judged not only by what one possessed but also by what one pawned. Through agreement with the local broker the back room of our corner shop served as a depot for those goods pledged by the week which owners had been unable to redeem before nine o'clock on Saturday, when the local pawnshop closed. Our service gave women waiting on drunken or late-working husbands a few hours' grace in which to redeem shoes and clothing before the Sabbath, and so maintain their social stake in the English Sunday. Towards our closing time there was always a great scurrying shopwards to get the 'bundle'. Housewives after washday on Monday pledged what clean clothes could be spared until weekend and returned with cash to buy food. Often they stood in the shop and thanked God that *they* were not as certain others who, having no clothes but what they stood in, had sunk low enough to pawn ashpans, hearth rugs or even the 'pots off the table'. Other customers tut-tutted in disgust. News of domestic distress soon got around. Inability to redeem basic goods was a sure sign of a family's approaching destitution and credit dried up fast in local tick shops. Naturally the gulf between those households who patronised 'Uncle', even if only occasionally, and those who did not gaped wide. Some families would go hungry rather than pledge their belongings.

The interest charged on articles pawned was usually a penny in the shilling per week, one half being paid at pledging time (Monday) and the other on redemption of the goods (Saturday). Much trucking went on among neighbours and this often led to dispute. One woman, as a favour, would make up a bundle of her clothing for another to pawn. The pledger would then gradually gear her household economy to the certainty of hocking the same bundle every Monday morning. But the boon would be withdrawn with 'I don't know whose clothes they are – mine or hers!' Then came bitterness, recrimination and even a 'stack-up' street fight.

The great bulk of pledged goods consisted of 'Sunday best' suits, boots and clean clothing. Their lying with Uncle provided not only cash but also convenient storage for households with next to no cupboard and where that word 'wardrobe' was yet unknown. Among the body of 'white slaves', the washerwomen, there was always one notorious for pledging the clothes she had laundered professionally. Bold with booze from the proceeds of her crime, she would then send her client (usually a publican or shopkeeper) the pawn ticket and a rude verbal message ending her contract for ever. But even in those days washerwomen were hard to come by and the good one, although occasionally dishonest, could always find labour at two shillings *per diem*.

Behind his cold eye and tight lip our local broker, it was said, had a heart of stone. Only one customer, he boasted, had ever 'bested' him. An Irish woman he knew as a 'good Catholic' had presented him with a large bundle containing exactly the same washing week after week for months on end. At last he ceased to open it and paid her 'on sight'. Suddenly she disappeared and left the goods unredeemed. Weeks after a revolting smell from the store room forced him to open her pledge. He found, rotting gently among rags, an outsize savoy cabbage.

Few shopkeepers indeed would lend cash. Women customers at our shop very seldom asked for a loan but their husbands, banking on a wife's good name, would send children from time to time – 'Can yer lend me father a shilling, an' he'll give yer one an' three at the weekend?'

'Tell him this is a shop,' my mother would snap, 'not a loan office.'

This usually happened on the day of some big race. If the would-be punter's fancy won, he blamed mother bitterly for robbing him of his gains.

Only those in dire straits and with a certainty of cash cover to come patronised the local blood sucker; he charged threepence in the shilling per week. To be known to be in his clutches was to lose caste altogether. Women would pawn to the limit, leaving the home utterly comfortless, rather than fall to that level.

Though the senior members of a household would try to uphold its prestige in every way, children in the streets had the reprehensible habit of making friends with anyone about their own age who happened to be around, in spite of the fact that parents, ever on the watch, had already announced what company they should keep. One would be warned off certain boys altogether. Several of us for instance had been strictly forbidden ever to be seen consorting with a lad whose mother, known elegantly as the She Nigger, was a woman of the lowest repute. Unfortunately we could find nothing 'low' in her son. A natural athlete (he modelled his conduct on Harry Wharton of the *Magnet*), a powerful whistler through his teeth, generous, unquarrelsome, Bill seemed the kind of friend any sensible lad would pick. We sought him out at every opportunity but took very good care to drop him well away from home base. He accepted our brush-off meekly, but in the end protested with a dignity which left the other three of us in the group deeply embarrassed. 'Why', he asked, 'won't you be seen with me in the street?'

We looked at one another: 'It's – it's your old lady', I mumbled at last – 'You know!'

'I can't help what the old lady does, can I?' he asked.

'It's not us,' we explained lamely. 'It's them – you know – them at home. . . .'

He turned and walked away.

All of us were then within a few weeks of leaving school; no longer children. We went again to our common haunts but he came no more; the friendship was over.

Through our teens we saw him pass often but he ignored us. The break would have come in any case I told myself uneasily. He got a job after school as a mere chain horse lad; we had become apprentices of a sort; but a social barrier had risen for good.

The class struggle, as manual workers in general knew it, was apolitical and had place entirely within their own society. They looked upon it not in any way as a war against the employers but as a perpetual series of engagements in the battle of life itself. One family might be 'getting on' – two or three children out to work and the dream of early marriage days fulfilled at last. The neighbours noted it as they noted everything, with pleasure or envy. A second household would begin a slip downhill as father aged or children married. They watched, sympathetically perhaps, or with a touch of *schadenfreude.* All in all it was a struggle against the fates, and each family fought it out as best it could. Marxist 'ranters' from the Hall who paid fleeting visits to our street end insisted that we the proletariat stood locked in titanic struggle with some wicked master class. We were battling, they told us (from a vinegar barrel borrowed from our corner shop), to cast off our chains and win a whole world. Most people passed by; a few stood to listen but not for long; the problems of the 'proletariat', they felt, had little to do with them.

Before 1914 the great majority in the lower working class were ignorant of Socialist doctrine in any form, whether 'Christian' or Marxist. Generally those who did come into contact with such ideas showed either indifference or more often hostility. Had they been able to read a *Times* stricture of the day most would have agreed heartily that 'Socialist is a title which carries in many minds summary and contemptuous condemnation'. They would have echoed too its pained protests on the iniquities of the doctrine. 'To take from the rich', said a leader in 1903 *à propos* a mild tax proposal, 'is all very well if they are to make some more money, but to take from the rich by methods that prevent them replacing what is taken is the way to national impoverishment from which the poor, in spite of all doles and Socialist theories, will be the greatest sufferers.'

Meanwhile though the millennium for a socialist few might seem just around the corner, many gave up struggling. The suicide rate among us remained pretty high. There was Joe Kane for instance, an unemployed labourer who was found by a neighbour blue in the face with a muffler tied about his neck. Some time previously he had taken carbolic acid and bungled that attempt too. But the magistrate didn't think much of Joe's efforts.

'If the prisoner', he said, 'is anxious to get to heaven, one would have thought he could have managed it by some better means than that. He could, now, have thrown himself into the river, or something else.'

The prisoner was discharged. But several months later Joe took up the magistrate's thoughtful suggestion and drowned himself in the canal.

Throughout a quarter of a century the population of our village remained generally immobile: the constant shifts of nearby country folk into industrial towns, so common during the previous century, had almost ceased; although our borough was still growing at a diminished rate. A man's work, of course, usually fixed the place where his family dwelt; but lesser factors were involved too: his links, for instance, with local kith and kin. Then again he commonly held a certain social position at the nearby pub, modest perhaps but recognised, and a credit connection with the corner shop. Such relationships once relinquished might not easily be re-established. All these things, together with fear of change, combined to keep poor families, if not in the same street, at least in the same neighbourhood for generations. There was of course some movement in and out, and naturally we had the odd 'moonlight' flitting when a whole household, to dodge its debts, would vanish overnight. Everybody laughed about it except the creditors. What newcomers we got were never the 'country gorbies' whom my grandfather remembered as the 'butt of the workshops' in his youth, but families on the way up or down from other slums of the city: yet new neighbours or old, all shared a common poverty.

Even with rapidly increasing literacy during the second half of the nineteenth century, years were needed, sometimes decades, before certain ideas common to the educated filtered through to the very poor. By 1900, however, those cherished principles about class, order, work, thrift and self-help epitomised by Samuel Smiles and long taught and practised by the Victorian bourgeoisie, had moulded the minds of even the humblest. And slow to learn, they were slow to change. Whatever new urges might have roved abroad in Early Edwardian England, millions among the poor still retained the outlook and thought patterns imposed by their Victorian mentors. For them the twentieth century had not begun. Docilely they accepted a steady decline in living standards and went on wishing for nothing more than to be 'respectful[10] and respected' in the eyes of men. For them the working-class caste structure stood natural, complete and inviolate.

Part Five

Interpretative Procedures

12 Introduction and Further Reading

Martin Bulmer

> You have been told to go grubbing in the library, thereby accumulating a mass of notes and a liberal coating of grime. You have been told to choose problems wherever you can find musty stacks of routine records based on trivial schedules prepared by tired bureaucrats and filled out by reluctant applicants for aid or fussy do-gooders or indifferent clerks. This is called 'getting your hands dirty in real research'. Those who counsel you are wise and honourable; the reasons they offer are of great value. But one more thing is needful: first-hand observation. Go and sit in the lounges of the luxury hotels and on the doorsteps of the flophouses; sit on the Gold Coast settees and on the slum shakedowns; sit in the Orchestra Hall and in the Star & Garter Burlesk. In short, gentlemen, go get the seat of your pants dirty in *real* research (R. E. Park, quoted in Lofland [1971] p. 2).

Social-survey research and secondary analysis of already available unobtrusive measures usually treat the problem of the interaction between the subject of research and the researcher as relatively unproblematical. In the large survey organisation for example the various tasks of the research are subdivided, and it is possibly only the interviewer who will interact with the person providing the data upon which the subsequent analysis will be developed. The interviewer himself or herself may have little sociological understanding, performing what is essentially a routinised and technical task for which training has been provided. Social-survey research can of course take a different form if it is carried out on a smaller scale by sociologists themselves. For example *The Affluent Worker* research involved all members of the team in the interview programme, and although it used paid interviewers these were given an extensive prior training in the concepts and rationale of this study of social stratification. Sociology graduate students assisted in the coding of the data on crucial open-ended questions.

Whether large, medium or small-scale, social-survey research tends to distance the researcher from those whom he studies. Variability in norms, values, attitudes and cultural attributes generally are inferred from verbal or behavoural clues in standardised interviews or questionnaires. There is little direct contact with the groups being investigated, and no access to the social situations in which actors lead their day-to-day lives. The premium placed on hard quantifiable data contrasts with the strategy discussed in this section of interpretative involvement in ongoing social situations with a distinctly 'softer' outcome in terms of the kinds of data it yields.

Social-survey procedure, in its search for regularities, is typically based on random samples of individuals drawn from a large population, and therfore focused on social atoms studied as individuals ouside their social context. Since anthropologists first started doing field work, intensive research has been favoured as a means of studying social groups *in situ*, whether organisations, institutions, associations, informal groups or localities. It is argued that the in-depth study of one particular social setting yields a different and sometimes more useful perspective than a large-scale study of individuals from a whole population.

Why do sociologists adopt research procedures of this latter kind when (particularly in terms of representativeness and reliability) they are less rigorous than survey methods or the use of secondary sources? The reasons are several. One is the view that research procedures should reflect the nature of theoretical propositions in sociology. Since many such propositions refer to social *relationships*, research should try to look at actual patterns of social interaction not just verbalised reports or *post hoc* traces of such interaction.

Another is that sociology is concerned with the interpretative understanding of social action as well as with its causal explanation. It is therefore essential to study social action from the actor's point of view to provide some account of the actor's subjective 'definition of the situation' (to use a phrase made famous by W. I. Thomas).

A further reason relates to the nature of language and the quality of communication in standardised surveys. 'A large part of collective life is problematic to define because of its essentially oral tradition, and because even its formally stated written tradition is subject to the differential perception and interpretation of actors variously distributed in the social structures' (Cicourel [1964] p. 221).

The value of studying localities or social groups as *wholes* rather than atomised individuals has already been mentioned. This in turn is linked to a further advantage. Where there are topics which are elusive or intangible or sensitive to the survey researcher – whether the study of power structures, organisational settings, or criminal and deviant behaviour – then intensive field-work may provide a feasible and illuminating way of tackling the problem.

As a style of sociological research, interpretative procedures are popularly identified with the techniques of participant observation, and with a richness, colour and depth of description which few other social research methods allow for. W. F. Whyte's famous autobiographical account of his research in 'Cornerville' for *Street Corner Society*, or Alison Lurie's satirical novel about a sociologist's attempts to study a doomsday cult, *Imaginary Friends* [1967], convey some of this excitement, and of the personal element which is to the forefront in interpretative-style work. Nevertheless it is a mistake to see this type of sociological work simply in terms of depth, colour and richness of description. There are serious theoretical and methodological purposes behind the adoption of this style, which the extracts here are intended to convey.

This book is not concerned with techniques of data collection, and the inclusion of the article by Mark Benney and Everett Hughes [1956] on interviewing is something of an oddity. Moreover it could be argued that it is included in the wrong section and should properly be in that dealing with social-survey research. Its presence here is intended to convey the extent to which researcher-respondent interaction is a subtle and negotiable social encounter in which the respondent is presenting the self which he wants to present or thinks the sociologist wishes to see. Benney and Hughes bring out elegantly how interviewing is more than the brisk 30 to 45 minutes question-and-answer session with the lady from the market-research firm.

Irwin Deutscher takes this one stage further by emphasising the importance of context, cues, subculture and overall linguistic framework within which research is carried on. Very often in research, although we may think ourselves speaking the same language as our respondents, the assumption is not in fact a readily justifiable one. Both extracts highlight the value of interpretative procedures in penetrating into areas of social interaction and linguistic complexity which standard survey methods do not reach.

The final chapter on 'Concepts in the analysis of qualitative data' returns to themes treated in Chapter 1. It explicitly raises issues about the place of theory in qualitative research, and of how the categories which are used to organise data appear. It discusses various alternatives which have been proposed such as 'analytic induction' and 'grounded theory', and emphasises that conceptualisation is part of the warp and woof of sociological research. One of the little-recognised methodological features of case studies is that they can provide a basis for theoretical work just as much as can survey methods (cf. Mitchell [1983]). No doubt both tend to lapse rather easily into purely descriptive exercises – in the case of participant observation, through rich ethnography – but both can be and are used to further theoretical understanding.

Further Reading

Methodology

There is a large theoretical literature on interpretative understanding in sociology to which Weber [1947] Ch. 1, Winch [1958], Ryan [1973] and Wilson [1970] provide useful introductions. The practice of interpretative research has largely been discussed apart from this theoretical debate; the emphasis here is therefore more upon how to do research and the scientific problems which arise in doing so.

(1) G. J. McCall and J. L. Simmons (eds), *Issues in Participant Observation: A Text and a Reader* (Reading, Mass.: Addison-Wesley, 1969) is the best single collection of readings on participant

observation and is essential reading. It covers all aspects of research including field relations, entry to the research situation, data collection, the generation of hypotheses and a comparison with other methods.

(2) R. Burgess (ed.), *Field Research: A Sourcebook and Field Manual* (London and Boston: Allen & Unwin, 1982) and *In the Field* (London and Boston: Allen & Unwin, 1984). A reader and textbook providing a comprehensive introduction to all aspects of field research, with an emphasis on links to history and anthropology. The textbook draws on the author's own research in the sociology of education.

(3) M. H. Agar, *The Professional Stranger: An Informal Introduction to Ethnography* (New York: Academic Press, 1980). An insightful introduction to the playing of the participant observer role in field research.

(4) Hammersley, M. and Atkinson, P. *Ethnography: Principles in Practice* (London: Tavistock, 1983). A good general overview of the process of ethnographic research with attention to the role of theorising.

(5) I. Deutscher, *What We Say/What We Do: Sentiments and Acts* (Glenview, Illinois: Scott Foresman, 1973) is a fascinating discussion of the relationship between attitudes and actions in actual research, trying to answer the question: can we explain behaviour by giving evidence of attitudes? It includes a wide range of material from the classic articles by LaPiere [1934] and Blumer [1956] to more recent work by social psychologists and phenomenologists.

(6) M. Bulmer (ed.), *Social Research Ethics: An Examination of the Merits of Covert Participant Observation* (London: Macmillan, and New York: Holmes & Meier, 1982). Discusses by means of actual examples of field research the pros and cons of the observer concealing his role from those being studied.

Empirical studies

(1) E. Liebow, *Tally's Corner, Washington D.C.: A Study of Negro Street Corner Men* (Boston: Little, Brown, 1967) is both an illuminating study of the condition of lower-class black Americans and one of the finest accounts of a piece of field research to appear in the last twenty years. This book is also a disproof of the arguments of those who claim that a small number of cases cannot provide the basis for meaningful generalisation. For a more general discussion of the 'culture of poverty' see Valentine [1968] and Bonney [1975]).

(2) William F. Whyte, *Street Corner Society: The Social Structure of an Italian Slum* (3rd edn; Chicago University of Chicago Press, 1981). A classic study of an Italian quarter of Boston which is perhaps the most widely-read field study in sociology. The new edition contains a fascinating appendix by Whyte's key informant, 'Doc'.

(3) A. W. Gouldner, *Patterns of Industrial Bureaucracy* (New York: Free Press, 1955). A classic study of the industrial organisation of a gypsum plant and mine carried out by a student research team. Morris Stein's methodological Appendix is full of freshness and insight.

(4) A. V. Cicourel, *The Social Organisation of Juvenile Justice* (New York: Wiley, 1968). A seminal work dealing with encounters between juvenile offenders, probation officers, police and parents. Concerned particularly with unacknowledged differences in interpretation that exist between the sociologist, his subjects and his readers, it relies on extensive transcripts. Relevant also to the discussion of the production of official statistics in an earlier section.

(5) K. Pryce, *Endless Pressure* (Harmondsworth: Penguin Books, 1979). A recent British study, in the St Paul's area of Bristol, of the social situation of black youth. A flawed study, with a number of methodological imperfections, which nevertheless illustrates the potential usefulness of this type of research.

(6) S. Ball, *Beachside Comprehensive: A Case-study of Secondary Schooling* (Cambridge: Cambridge University Press, 1981). An empirical study in the sociology of education which exemplifies the use of interpretative methods.

13 Of Sociology and the Interview*

Mark Benney and Everett C. Hughes

Sociology has become the science of the interview, and that in two senses. In the first sense the interview has become the favoured digging tool of a large army of sociologists. The several branches of social study are distinguished from one another perhaps more by their predilection for certain kinds of data and certain instruments for digging them up than by their logic. While the essential features of human society have probably varied within fairly narrow limits in all times and places where men lived, certain of these features can be more effectively observed in direct contact with living people. Others may perhaps be best seen through the eyes of men who left documents behind them. Sociologists have become mainly students of living people. Some to be sure do still study documents. Some observe people *in situ*; others experiment on them and look at them literally *in vitro*. But by and large the sociologist of North America, and in a slightly less degree in other countries, has become an interviewer. The interview is his tool; his works bear the marks of it.

Interviews are of many kinds. Some sociologists like them standardised and so formulated that they can be 'administered' to large

* Reprinted from M. Benney and E. C. Hughes, 'Of Sociology and the Interview', *American Journal of Sociology*, 62 (July 1956) pp. 137–42,

groups of people. This can be done only among large homogeneous populations not too unlike the investigator himself in culture. Where languages are too diverse, where common values are too few, where the fear of talking to strangers is too great, there the interview based on a standardised questionnaire calling for a few standardised answers may not be applicable. Those who venture into such situations may have to invent new modes of interviewing. Some face problems of large-scale standardised interviews; others tell of the peculiar problems of interviewing special kinds of people.

In the second sense sociology is the science of the interview in a more essential way. The subject-matter of sociology is interaction. Conversation of verbal and other gestures is an almost constant activity of human beings. The main business of sociology is to gain systematic knowledge of social rhetoric; to gain the knowledge we must become skilled in the rhetoric itself. Every conversation has its own balance of revelation and concealment of thoughts and intentions: only under very unusual circumstances is talk so completely expository that every word can be taken at face value. The model of such exposition is the exchange of information among scientists. Each is pledged to tell all he knows of the subject in terms whose meanings are strictly denoted. Every member of any society knows from early childhood a number of such model situations and the appropriate modes of rhetoric. He knows them so well in fact that he can improvise new ones and can play at the game of keeping others guessing just what rhetoric he is using. We mention these subtleties of social rhetoric and social interaction not to spin out analysis of them, but to sharpen the point that the interview, as itself a form of social rhetoric, is not merely a tool of sociology but a part of its very subject-matter. When one is learning about the interview, he is adding to sociological knowledge itself. Perhaps the essence of the method of any science is the application, in quest of new knowledge, of what is already known of that science. This is certainly true of sociology: what we learn of social interaction – of the modes of social rhetoric – we apply in getting new knowledge about the same subject.

But the interview is still more than tool and object of study. It is the art of sociological sociability, the game which we play for the pleasure of savouring its subtleties. It is our flirtation with life, our eternal affair, played hard and to win, but played with that detachment and amusement which give us, win or lose, the spirit to rise up and interview again and again.

The interview is of course merely one of the many ways in which two people talk to each other. There are other ways. Some time ago a Miss Margaret Truman [daughter of former U.S. President, Harry S. Truman] was employed on Ed Murrow's *Person to Person* television show to interview her parents in their home, and the event proved to be a notable exercise in multiple role-playing. As a daughter Miss Truman asked the kinds of questions that any daughter might ask of a parent: 'Dad, how is the book coming?' As interviewer she asked questions that bore the unmistakable stamp of the newspaperman: 'So many people want to know what you do to relax, inasmuch as you don't fish, hunt or play golf.' And at the end of the interview she achieved a nice convergence of the two roles by asking, as interviewer, her parents' views about herself, as daughter. Now Miss Truman is by way of being both a professional daughter and a professional interviewer, and the happy idea that she should act in the one role in a situation and with people where the other role is conventionally to be expected takes us right to the centre of our concern.

If we look at the variety of ways in which people in our culture meet together and talk we will be struck not only by the range of expectations which subsume unique particular encounters under a rubric of reciprocal roles, but also by the different degrees of self-involvement that inform the playing of different roles. Much attention has been given to the range of intensity with which the individual plays his roles; much less attention has been paid to the degree of *expected* intensity. It is clear enough that along with more or less specific expectations of the appropriate behaviour in a given role go other expectations about the degree of self-involvement. The general expectation is that Miss Truman should be more involved in the role of daughter than of interviewer; and certainly she managed to underline the family ties by very frequent use of such terms of address as 'dad' and 'mommie' and also by occasionally prefacing a question with the phrase 'Ed Murrow wanted me to ask . . .'. These differences of expected intensity are to some extent codified for us in such terms as 'commandment', 'law', 'rule', 'standard', 'convention', 'fashion'. At the upper limits of intensity there is a total proscription of alternative roles – the priest must never be a lover, the citizen must never be a traitor: only minimal distinction is expected between the self and the role. At the lower limit there is still the expectation that when roles conflict the resolution shall favour one role rather than another, but by their very semantics such terms as 'convention' or 'fashion' operate in areas of life where ethical neutrality is acceptable and ambivalence frequent. Thus Miss Truman could abandon the role of interviewer for that of daughter without our feeling that violence has been done to our ethos; she could not, if the two roles conflicted, abandon the role of daughter so easily.

The role of the interviewer then is one governed by conventions rather than by standards, rules or laws; it is a role that is relatively lightly held even by professionals, and may be abandoned in favour of certain alternative roles if the occasion arises. *What* alternative roles is another matter. The interview is a relatively new kind of encounter in the history of human relations and the older models of encounter – parent-child, male-female, rich-poor, foolish-wise – carry role definitions much better articulated and more exigent. The interviewer will be constantly tempted, if the other party falls back on one of these older models, to reciprocate – tempted and excused.

For unlike most other encounters the interview is a role-playing situation in which one person is much more an expert than the other, and while the conventions governing the interviewer's behaviour are already beginning in some professional circles to harden into standards, the conventions governing the informant's behaviour are much less clearly articulated and known. Vidich and Bensman, discussing this aspect of the interview, give examples of the respondent's insecurity in his role:

> In a difficult joint interview between a husband and wife, which required them to discuss certain problems, respondents would remind their spouses of failures to fulfil the instruction to 'discuss' with the remark that 'this is not what they wanted!' When couples failed to fulfil the instructions and saw that they had failed, they frequently apologised for their 'ignorance' or ineptitude.[1]

Of course there is an enormous amount of preparatory socialisation in the respondent role – in schools and jobs, through the mass media – and more and more of the potential respondents of the Western world are readied for the rap of the clipboard on the door. (In some places perhaps overreadied. There was a charming story in the *News of the World* about a political canvasser who liked to demonstrate, on the backsides of young suburban mothers, how they could check the urge to delinquency in their offspring. During the ensuing prosecution it was suggested that the ladies had become, through their experiences with interviewers, so docile as subjects of experiments that they were surprised at nothing.) Probably the most intensive presocialisation of respondents runs in roughly the social strata from which interviewers themselves are drawn – the middle, urban higher-educated groups, while at the top and bottom, though for different reasons, the appropriate role of the informant is apparently much less known. At the moment it is enough to say that where the parties to an interview are unsure of their appropriate roles they are likely to have recourse to other more firmly delineated social roles that will turn the encounter into one where they feel more at home.

Two conventions characterise most interviews and seem to give this particular mode of personal encounter its uniqueness: these are the conventions of *equality* and *comparability*.

The view that information obtained under stress is likely to be unreliable is not universal even in our own culture as 'third degree' practices by the police and some popular techniques of cross-examination in the law courts indicate. But in the research interview at least – and we can regard this as archetypal – the assumption is general that information is the more valid the more freely given. Such an assumption stresses the voluntary character of the interview as a relationship freely and willingly entered into by the respondent; it suggests a certain promissory or contractual element. But if the interview is thought of as a kind of implicit contract between the two parties, it is obvious that the interviewer gains the respondent's time, attention and whatever information he has to offer, but what the respondent gets is less apparent. A great many people enjoy being interviewed, almost regardless of subject, and one must assume, from the lack of tangible rewards offered, that the advantages must be totally subjective. Here Theodore Caplow's suggestion [1956] that the interview profits as a communication device from the contrast it offers to conversation in less formal situations might satisfy us until further evidence is available: that by offering a programme of discussion and an assurance that information offered will not be challenged or resisted, self-expression is facilitated to an unusual degree and that this is inherently satisfying. In this sense then the interview is an understanding between the two parties that in return for allowing the interviewer to direct their communication, the informant is assured that he will not meet with denial, contradiction, competition or other harassment. As with all contractual relations, the fiction or convention of equality must govern the situation. Whatever actual inequalities of sex, status, intelligence, expertness or physique exist between the parties should be muted. Interviewing-training consists very largely of making interviewers aware of the kinds of social inequalities with which respondents are likely to be concerned and of teaching them how to minimise them. This is most important perhaps if the respondent is likely to see himself as inferior in some respect to the interviewer, and certainly this has been the most closely studied aspect of interviewer effect.

But what happens when, as increasingly happens, a run-of-the-mill middle-class interviewer encounters a member of some financial, intellectual or political elite? Our own impression is that such respondents contrive to re-establish equality in the interview by addressing themselves subjectively, not to the actual interviewer, but to the study director or even his sponsor. The different subjectives uses to which respondents put these ghostly figures is something that might very profitably be looked into; certainly people of superior status are more aware of them and make more use of them than others.

Evidently such a view of the interview has much in common with Simmel's view of sociability. Both in the interview as seen here and in the sociable gathering as seen by Simmel the convention of equality is a formal necessity and is achieved by excluding from immediate awareness all those attributes of the individual, subjective and objective, which make for inequalities in everyday life. But as Simmel stresses the objects of a sociable gathering can be achieved only within a given social stratum – 'sociability among members of very different social strata often is inconsistent and painful'.[2] The muting of minor social inequalities such as age, sex, wealth, erudition and fame can be accomplished only by the physical elimination of the grosser subcultural differences. But the interview was designed to provide a bridge for communicating between the social strata precisely of the kind that sociability cannot provide (if it could, interviewing would be unnecessary). And this fact brings out another important difference between the interview as practised and the sociable gathering as seen by Simmel – in the handling of affect. The identifications which bring people together easily in sociable gatherings are primarily established on an emotional basis, and as Simmel stresses any affective expression which runs counter to these emotional bonds is suppressed: it is says Simmel the essential function of *tact* 'to draw the limits, which result from the claims of others, of the individual's impulses, ego-stresses, and intellectual and material desires'.[3] The only emotional expression tolerable in the sociable gathering is that which heightens the emotional bonds already established within the group. Psychologically, however, exclusion from these shared affective responses constitutes social inequality; and if equality in the interview is to be established, it must at bottom be achieved by the interviewer's encouraging and accepting the affect as well as the information the respondent offers. (Hence the growing emphasis on 'rapport' in the technical manuals dealing with the interview.) The problem of establishing equality in the interview then depends on the expression rather than the suppression of affective responses, on some encouragement of the private, idiosyncratic and subjective dimensions of at least one of the personalities involved. True the interview *tends* toward the form of the sociable conversation in that once the interviewer has been 'cued' to the level of discourse a given respondent is capable of and has adapted himself to it, communication is expected to approximate that which would take place between actual equals, so that the information carried away is assumed to be such as a man might give when talking freely to a friend. Thus students of the dynamics of interviewing find that there is in general an early release of affect, followed by a more equable flow of information.

Interviewing then is distinguished by the operations of the convention that both parties to the encounter are equals, at least for the purposes and duration of the encounter. But there is another important characteristic of the interview which serves to differentiate it from other modes of human interaction – the convention of *comparability*. The first operates primarily for the advantage of the respondent; the second for the advantage of the interviewer and his employers. They are not completely compatible conventions, and the latent conflict between them is always threatening to become manifest.

Regarded as an information-gathering tool, the interview is designed to minimise the local, concrete, immediate circumstances of the particular encounter – including the respective personalities of the participants – and to emphasise only those aspects that can be kept general enough and demonstrable enough to be counted. As an encounter between these two particular people the typical interview has no meaning; it is conceived in a framework of other comparable meetings between other couples, each recorded in such fashion that elements of communication in common can be easily isolated from more idiosyncratic qualities. However vaguely this is conceived by the actual participants, it is the needs of the statistician rather than of the people involved directly that determine much, not only the content of communication but its form as well. Obviously this convention conflicts with the psychological requirements for equality of affective interchange and one can observe various attempts to resolve the problem, from interviewing in groups to interviewing in depth. At its most obvious the convention of comparability produces the 'standardised' interview, where the whole weight of the encounter is placed on the order and formulation of the questions asked and little freedom is permitted to the interviewer to adjust the statistician's needs to the particular encounter. The statistician indeed seldom uses *all* the material collected; few reports apparently make use of more than 30 to 40 per cent of the information collected. But less obtrusively it enters into almost all interviewing, even psychiatric interviewing, as the possibilities of statistical manipulation of 'data' force themselves on the attention of research-minded practitioners. Here technological advances such as the tape recorder are hastening the process – directly, by making available for comparison transcripts of psychiatric interviews hitherto unobtainable and, indirectly, by exposing more clearly to colleagues those purely personal and private (or 'distorting' and 'biasing') observations and interpretations which the practitioner brings into the interview with him. The very displacement of the older words 'session' or 'consultation' by the modern word 'interview' to describe what passes between the psychiatrist and his patient, is a semantic recognition of this spread of the convention of comparability.

All this amounts to a definition of the interview as a relationship between two people where both parties behave as though they are of equal status for its duration, whether or not this is actually so; and where also both behave as though their encounter had meaning only in relation to a good many other such encounters. Obviously, this is not an exhaustive definition of any interview; it leaves out any reference to the exchange and recording of information, to the probability that the parties involved are strangers, and to the transitory nature of the encounter and the relationship. In any formal definition of the interview these elements must have a place.

A relationship governed by the conventions just discussed can occur, it is clear, only in a particular cultural climate; and such a climate is a fairly new thing in the history of the human race. Anthropologists have long realised – if not always clearly – that the transitory interview held with respondents who do not share their view of the encounter is an unreliable source of information in itself. It is not until they have been in the society long enough to fit into one of its better-defined roles that they can 'tap' a valid communication system and hear the kind of messages that the others in the culture hear. Equally the climate which makes widespread interviewing possible in the West today is itself relatively novel. A century ago when Mayhew pioneered in the survey by interviewing 'some thousands of the humbler classes of society', the social distance between his readers and his subjects, although they largely lived in the same city, was such that he could best conceptualise his undertaking as an ethnological inquiry seeking to establish that 'we, like the Kaffirs, Fellahs and Finns, are surrounded by wandering hordes – the "Sonquas" and the "Fingoes" of this country'. Mayhew was a newspaperman and his survey was first published in a London newspaper. This fact serves to remind us that interviewing as we know it today was an invention of the mass-communications industry and as a mode of human encounter has much the same boundaries. On the other hand the interview has become something very like a medium of mass communication in its own right and one, on the whole, with less frivolous and banal concerns than related media. One might even make the point that newspapers, movies, radio and television have been encouraged to pursue their primrose paths by delegating to the survey researchers and their interviewers most of the more serious functions of social communication. If this is so the interviewer has ousted the publicist by virtue of the convention of comparability, and the ideological and social shifts which have made it possible for individuals willingly to populate the statistician's cells become as worthy of study as, say, the spread of literacy.

We can trace the spread of this convention from the time it was a radical idea in the mind of Jeremy Bentham and a few of his disciples until it became a habit of thought of all but the very top and bottom segments of our society. In like fashion we trace the growth of the convention of equality from the ideas of John Locke and his disciples to its almost total permeation of the American scene. To chart such changes in the way people relate themselves to one another is the historian's job rather than the sociologist's, and it is one requiring volumes rather than pages. But even a brief review of the course of such changes will lead to a sharper sense of the novelty and significance of the interview as a mode of human relationship and will perhaps aid in assessing its limits and potentialities in the future.

14 Asking Questions (and Listening to Answers): a Review of some Sociological Precedents and Problems*

Irwin Deutscher

This chapter is a second voyage of exploration and discovery. On the first trip my purpose was to locate critical points at which language becomes relevant to social research by examining situations in which such critical points are dramatically highlighted [1968].[1] It was an attempt to identify language-related problems in cross-cultural research, a situation in which the participants generally recognise that more than one language is involved and that something needs to be done about language. The present paper considers some of these same critical points in situations where they are more obscure i.e. where people proceed on the assumption that they are communicating in 'the same language'.

Let me begin with an example. In an even earlier paper I had raised the question (only half seriously) of whether one could safely assume that the dichotomy between a negative response and an affirmative response was as easily translatable as it seemed to be:

*'Asking Questions (and Listening to Answers)' by Irwin Deutscher, *Sociological Focus*, vol. 3, no. 2 (1969/70) pp. 13–32.

'Should we assume that a response of "yah", "da", "si", "oui", or "yes" all really mean exactly the same thing in response to the same question? Or may there be different kinds of affirmative connotations in different languages?' ([1966] p. 249). During the 1968 voyage I discovered that this was a more serious question than I had thought. I learned for example that 'a simple English "No" tends to be interpreted by members of the Arabic culture as meaning "yes". A real "No" would need to be emphasised; the simple "No" indicates a desire for further negation. Likewise a non-emphasised "yes" will often be interpreted as a polite refusal' (Glenn [1954] p. 164).[2] But this problem is not restricted to exotic languages and cultures. It occurred to me that part of the conventional wisdom of American college men is that when a girl says 'no' she may very well mean 'yes'. Even more revealing is David Riesman's finding that there is something of the Arab (or college girl) in English-speaking American professors. Riesman personally interviewed survey respondents to the Lazarsfeld and Thielens Teacher Apprehension Study. He asked the professors about their responses to precoded alternatives and concluded that 'It sometimes happens that people torn between "yes" and "no" will answer in one direction and then add qualifications in the other, showing for example that their "yes" doesn't quite mean "yes", and may even lean toward "no"' (Riesman [1958] p. 277, n. 11). Other elements of Riesman's analysis will be considered later in this paper. The present example is intended only to indicate that language problems which are apparent in dealing with strange languages may also be present in one's own language – although not nearly so apparent. Furthermore such problems may have serious methodological implications.

My 1968 paper concluded with a two-page section entitled 'The Local Scene'. It is to the local scene that the present paper addresses itself. The earlier paper focused on language as culture; the present one attempts (not always successfully) to hold culture constant, exploring some of the nuances of language and social research within a given cultural context.

Benjamin Lee Whorf assumed that the Indo-European languages with which most Westerners are familiar are so similar to one another that we aren't aware of the great impact which language can have on thought and behaviour. Whorf lumped all of these languages together into what he called 'Standard Average European' and made his empirical observations by contrasting them collectively with various unrelated languages, especially those of American Indians (Whorf [1956] p. 138).

Whorf, I suspect, was on to something more important than even he imagined. He suggested that differences in thought and behaviour were related to gross lingual differences. I am suggesting that these same differences may also exist (a) between related languages, including 'Indo-European' (for examples see Deutscher [1968]), and (b) even within what we normally refer to as 'a language'.[3] This last order of difference is more insidious since it is more subtle and less identifiable as a source of differential perceptions of the world and of other people. The example of the distinction between affirmative and negative responses is a case in point. Although probably distorted and exaggerated, the novelist Robert Gover [1963] describes a situation which provides some clues to the problem. The real tragedy of the one-hundred dollar misunderstanding is not so much that Kitten and Howland couldn't understand each other but rather that *they did not know* that they couldn't understand each other. This is what it means to have a 'misunderstanding' and I submit that there may be many such misunderstandings between interviewer and respondent in our own domestic research.

The potential for semantic breakdown or 'misunderstanding' between the 'English speaking' teenage black prostitute and the 'English speaking' Babbitt-like college sophomore differs only in degree from what occurs when an American who speaks French interviews a Moroccan whose French was learned on the streets of Casablanca (Blanc [1956] p. 207).[4] C. Wright Mills has observed the tendency in a fragmented multigroup society such as our own for people to 'talk past one another. We interpret the "same" symbols differently. Because the coordinated social actions sustaining the meaning of a given symbol have broken down, the symbol does not call out the same response in members of one group that it does in another, and there is no genuine communication' (Mills [1939] pp. 435–6). What are the linguistic concomitants to such social fragmentation – to living in a society in which various activities are organised within group contexts and groups have limited contacts with each other? Dell Hymes insists that 'The case is clear in bilingualism; we do not expect a Bengali using English as a fourth language for certain purposes of commerce to be influenced deeply in world view by its syntax.' But, he continues, '*What is necessary is to realise that the monolingual situation is problematic as well.* People do not all everywhere use language to the same degree, in the same situations, or for the same things' (Hymes [1964] p. 20, italics added).

It is hard to say how much misunderstanding occurs since, by the nature of it, it frequently passes unrecognised. Aaron Cicourel has advised that 'The sociologist . . . when interviewing, cannot afford to treat his own language from the perspective of a native speaker, but must adopt the position of a cryptanalyst approaching a strange language' (Cicourel [1964] p. 175). This is a fair description of the stance taken by David Riesman in his analysis of the interviewing of a national sample of college professors for *The Academic Mind* (i.e. the Teacher Apprehension Study referred to above). After interviewing both survey interviewers and survey respondents, Riesman allows that 'for the most part, our methods lack the subtlety to catch the myriad ways in which (as in the novels of Henry Green) people can talk past each other, while believing themselves to be understood – or vice versa' ([1958] p. 273).

This paper then is devoted to the proposition that language is important not only cross-culturally but *within* our (or any other) society as well, where we are prone to assume that everyone is speaking the same language. In fact Anderson goes so far as to define problems of interviewer–interviewee relations as translation problems: 'translation is involved whenever our research requires us to ask the "same" question of people with different backgrounds' (Anderson [1967]).

Language and Domestic Research

There is empirical evidence that phonetic (sound) differences exist among social classes and among various speech contexts in New York City (Labov [1966]) and furthermore that these are influenced by interactional contexts (Crockett and Levine [1967]). There is also evidence that syntactic styles vary among different classes of Arkansan and Londoner (Schatzman and Strauss [1955]; Bernstein [1966]). In addition semantic variations have been found between black and white American college students (Barth [1961]), although no such differences were observed between American sailors and college students (Heise [1966]). Within a society, as well as between societies, the sociologist seeks information from and about people who operate verbally with different vocabularies, different grammars and different kinds of sounds. In effect we address our interests to publics who vary from the rest of us in their everyday lexicon, syntax and phoneme in certain important and potentially revealing ways.

The phonetic data suggest the existence of excellent indicators of socioeconomic status, social mobility, aspirations and reference group orientations – indicators which have been largely ignored by sociologists.[5] The syntactic data on the other hand transcend methodological considerations since they contain important implications for role-taking ability and thus for role playing and interpersonal competence. The semantic data highlight the importance to the researcher of sensitising himself to the private language used by his respondents.

Do we find within our own society different lexicons in operation and different meanings attached to the same word? Consider this dialogue between a principal in a Pittsburgh slum school and a teenage black pupil (Brewer [1966] p. 32):

> *Principal*: Why are you stretched so thin by joy? Are you flying backwards?
> *Pupil*: My special pinetop is smoking and wants to eyeball you fast.
> *Principal*: I'm stalled. What is this all about?
> *Pupil*: I wasted one of the studs for capping me. Teach blasted at me and told me to fade away to the hub and fetch you.
> *Principal*: Don't put your head in the bowl and pull the chain.

The principal reports this incredible conversation in good faith and even if exaggerated there is enough truth to the notion that ghetto children speak a different language to lend credence to the idea of teaching English as a 'second language' to such American children (see for example Stewart [1964]). What is remarkable is that the English rules of syntax are followed in the sentences quoted (they are grammatical sentences) and all of the words are commonly used in English (with the possible exception of 'capping' which would be understood only by nurses and then differently from its usage here). Yet it is doubtful that many of the 'English speaking' peoples of the world outside the American ghetto can understand or translate much of that dialogue.[6]

This is the language which Cohen and Hodges [1963] put to work to reveal the world view of the lower classes. Words and phrases like 'playing it cool', 'trouble', and 'conning' provide insight into the concept of self and others held by those who commonly employ them. Differences in the understanding of the same words are attributed to both race and class by Barth ([1961] p. 71). His data reveal differences in word connotations between middle-class black and white college students for the words 'colour' and 'minority', but not for the words 'slum' and 'policeman'. He suggests that the latter set is more class-related than race-related and that control of the class dimension would reveal differences in connotations of these words too.[7]

Barth's interpretation receives some support from Heise, who suggests that some subgroups in the society are compelled to create a private language because of the strong differences in value attached to certain terms. He explains private languages as arising to reduce dissonance created by connotations of words in the standard language (Heise [1966] p. 230):

> Consider the case of a slum boy coping with the problem of policemen. In his own experience, police are bullying and persecuting; but the words 'policeman' or 'officer' connote respect and even admiration. . . . The referent category for lawmen is linked not to 'policeman' or 'officer' but to synonyms such as 'cop', 'the Man', or 'fuzz', whose connotations are more in line with the boy's personal feelings.

Putting aside the unnecessary determinism implied by the invocation of a functional balance theory to explain the genesis of a private language,[8] it is in fact unlikely that Barth's middle-class Seattle subjects, living in integrated neighbourhoods and attending integrated schools all of their lives, would have been confronted with as much *overt discrimination* as is found in most urban ghettos. It follows that they would be less likely to use synonyms for some terms than would lower-class blacks. Other terms however which carry connotations reminiscent of the *covert prejudices* confronting all blacks could be expected to be viewed differently from whites – regardless of social class.

Nevertheless it remains difficult to explain the fact that Heise found no difference semantically between two classes of sailors or between sailors and college students. Heise is convinced that in our society the connotation of words is generally uniform across groups, with synonyms being developed in place of differential connotations being attached to the same word ([1966] p. 238). Such a position is not inconsistent with Hertzler's argument that throughout the modern world a process of semantic 'uniformation' is taking place. According to Hertzler 'the very extension and the increasing intensity of social intercourse over ever wider areas makes for even wider uniformity of both – language and speech'. This is true, he says, not only internationally but within nations where one finds 'the increasing sway of the "standard" language of the language community while local or regional dialects, the occupational jargons, the plural lingualism of ethnic groups, and the social class and other "special" sublanguages weaken or even disappear' (Hertzler [1966] p. 305; see also Hertzler [1965] Ch. 8). Comparisons among three nations by Hunt and his colleagues lend support to Hertzler's thesis. They conclude for example 'that subcultural differences in basic attitudes and outlook made for greater differences in access within each system than broader cultural differences among the various systems of the Western world' (Hunt *et al.* [1964] p. 61). In terms of a comparative historical process Hertzler is undoubtedly correct, but the evidence reviewed in this paper (and in Deutscher [1968]) suggests that differentiation remains so great both between nations and within them that it is impossible to understand human behaviour or interaction without taking account of it.

The United States appears to be engaged in a constant and deliberate process of magically changing phenomena by changing their names through the application of euphemism or epithet. Politicians, social reformers and social scientists commonly employ what Everett Hughes has called a form of 'exorcism'. As he puts it, 'a considerable part of sociology consists of cleaning up the language in which common people talk of social and moral problems. We make great effort to make bad things better by changes of names, and we try, too, to make things disappear by giving them bad names' (Hughes and Hughes [1952] pp. 131, 137–8). In this manner youthful crime became 'juvenile delinquency' and we move from old age to 'later maturity', from race relations to 'intergroup relations', from birth control to 'family planning', from insane asylums to 'mental hospitals' and from lunacy to insanity to 'mental illness' and, sometimes, to 'mental health'. In recent decades the valued concept of 'peace' has become for many Americans a tainted emblem of the 'international communist conspiracy'. Is it possible to retain a concept when the word which symbolises it has become an epithet and no synonym has developed?

The reverse question must also be asked. Does the incorporation of a synonym into the everyday vocabulary necessarily suggest the development of a new concept? When 'The Man' manages to learn to call 'the nigger' a black does the nigger in fact cease to exist? Perhaps such magic does occur – to a degree, for some people, under some conditions. Hughes reminds us that when a new vitamin was discovered it was correctly surmised that few people would be induced to consume a daily dose of 'nicotinic acid'. The adoption of a euphemism, in this case a simple capital letter with a numerical subscript (Vitamin B_1), permitted nicotinic acid to become almost as common in the American household as table salt. 'He who gets into social politics would be very stupid if he should allow himself to be a purist, insisting that all things be called by scientifically valid names rather than by terms which mobilise people for action' (Hughes and Hughes [1952] p. 138).[9] Connecting Hughes's insight with Heise's observation of the creation of 'synonyms' for the word 'policeman', we can see how names do indeed mobilise people for action – or inaction. People call upon policemen and cops for assistance. The fuzz or the pigs are certainly not types who are called or from whom one can expect assistance.

Cicourel, true to his own dictates, asks if the variations observed in cross-cultural kinship terminology may not be an important factor in understanding intrasocietal differences as well. He finds the study of law cases to be of particular interest because of the self-conscious quest of legalists for semantic comparability. 'Law cases, for example, seek to show how people labelled or named "mother" or "father" or "child" or "uncle", and the like, are or are not "really" "mothers", "fathers", and so on . . .' (Cicourel [1967]). In studying the law it becomes imperative for the sociologist to identify and pursue meanings of key words – words which carry weight in reaching decisions. What for example is meant by an 'unstable' family, an 'indifferent' mother or a child's 'needs'? (Cicourel [1967]).[10]

Differences within a language and within a culture are not restricted to the United States. It has been observed for example that the word 'divorce' is employed in four Spanish-speaking Catholic countries to denote the same phenomenon. But the connotations of the term and the consequences of the act differ radically among those countries in spite of their common language and common cultural heritage (Cicourel [1967]). Among Tamil-speaking Indians there are important caste differences in the connotations of the 'same' words. For example the Brahman uses the terms *tiirto* and *tanni* to refer respectively to 'drinking-water' and 'non-drinkable water' while the non-Brahman uses the identical words to distinguish between 'holy water' and all other kinds of water (Bright [1966] p. 316). The ancients were well aware that language carried within itself, not only through words but through phonetic indicators, the mark of who a man is:[11] Then said they unto him, say now Shibboleth: and he said Sibboleth: for he could not frame to pronounce it right. Then they took him and slew him ... (*Judges* 12:6).

Although they are not usually this dramatic, there are frequently important lines of action leading from linguistic differentiation within a society. Unlike the trend toward lingual uniformation posited by Hertzler, Brown points out that in a complex society specialised subcommunities develop, with concomitant linguistic specialisation: 'there is a special lexicon to meet special cognitive needs' (Brown [1958] p. 256).

Some Methodological Implications for Interviewing and Field Work

When Benney and Hughes (above, p. 216) suggest that the interview as a form of social rhetoric is not merely a tool of sociology but part of its very subject matter, they are reminding us that the peculiar thing about human interaction is its symbolic nature and, in large part, the symbols employed are linguistic ones. It is possible that many of the kinds of errors in translation and interpretation – the semantic slip-ups – which occur in cross-lingual situations also occur between interviewer and interviewee within our own society. In his unique analysis of the interviewing process in a domestic survey Riesman [1958] indentifies many of the communication problems I discovered in international research (Deutscher [1968]). Like some European legislators and Middle East 'traditionalists' (Lerner [1956] p. 191; see also Hunt *et al.* [1964]), some American academicians appear to reject 'role playing' questions: they are 'too "iffy" to make sense' (Riesman [1958] p. 275).[12] Yet these very types of questions which met resistance in one kind of college proved to be 'just what the doctor ordered' in another kind (Riesman [1958] p. 316, n. 55). What I referred to as Riesman's discovery of a bit of the Arab in American professors (in the opening example in this paper) suggests not only that 'yes' may mean 'no' but also that there may be degrees of 'yesness' and 'noness'. If this is true then one cannot assume a simple dichotomy and furthermore one cannot assume a symmetrical scale with 'no' and 'yes' at points equidistant from the centre. Asymmetry in scale distributions as analysed by Jordan points up the fact that what appears to be a strong 'no' is not necessarily as strong as a strong 'yes' (Jordan [1965]).

Critics of surveys in the developing countries have argued that there may be no 'public opinion' in those countries or that 'opinion' may be restricted only to certain areas (Mitchell [1965] pp. 67–3; Wuelker [1963] p. 37). The logic of this position as applied to the domestic scene was developed years ago by Herbert Blumer [1948] and has been empirically verified by Converse [1964] who found that even issues considered to be salient to wide segments of the American population had relatively small publics. The Blumer thesis is further documented by Riesman: 'We see here one of the problems of a national survey, namely, that coverage and comparability mean that the same questions will be asked of those who are virtually "know-nothings" and those who could write a book on each theme' (Riesman [1958] p. 360). He concludes that 'on a national survey there is always danger in the assumption that we are in fact one country, and that issues relevant to one part of the population are or could become meaningful to another' (Riesman [1958] p. 365; see also n. 9 on pp. 275–6).

Throughout his analysis of an American national survey, Riesman is sensitive to the role of 'politeness' as it enters into the interview situation – a phenomenon reminiscent of the 'courtesy bias' observed in South-east Asia interviews (Jones [1963]; Mitchell [1965] p. 681). Finally he provides us with an illustration of the manner in which 'cultural' differences between an English-speaking interviewer and respondent can impinge upon the interview situation on the domestic scene. The case in point is the inability of a northern faculty member in a southern college to take the role of his southern interviewer accurately:

> 'Southern charm' is, however, a two-way street. Interviewers who might, in old Southern fashion, emphasise their kin connections to gain entree, might also evoke the gallantry of otherwise fearful administrators and respondents; this was perhaps especially likely where an apparently well-born interviewer could talk to the intellectual elite with freedom from demagogic cliches on the race question: class pride, in the South especially, can link Jeffersonian traditions of academic freedom to good manners in expressing such traditions. Obviously enough, such nuances of communication might well be lost on a City College graduate teaching his first year of anthropology at a state-controlled institution in the Deep South (Riesman [1958] p. 332).

This example provides an instance of what are essentially social structural interferences with communication in a presumably monolinguistic situation (are such interferences of the same order as those which would obtain as a result of cultural differences between an Englishman and American?). Earlier in this paper it was suggested that these are types of interference which derive from social structural differentiation within the population, as well as those microcosmic interferences resulting from the particular situations and social interactions in which people find themselves involved. Definitions from all of these levels can enter into the construction of the interaction between interviewer and interviewee.

Benney and Hughes ([1956] p. 142) define an interview, in part, as a relationship between two people where both parties behave as though they are of equal status for its duration whether or not this is actually so. This kind of fiction is obviously going to come off better in some cultures than in others and among some segments of a society than in others. In the following statement one can substitute for the word 'culture' either 'social structure' or 'situation':

> Anthropologists have long realised – if not always clearly – that the transitory interview, held with respondents who do not share their view of the encounter, is an unreliable source of information in itself. It is not until they have been in the society long enough to fit into one of its better-defined roles that they can 'tap' a valid communication system and hear the kind of messages that the others in the culture hear. Equally, the climate which makes

widespread interviewing possible in the West today is itself relatively novel (Benney and Hughes [1956] p. 2).

Riesman ([1958] p. 281) describes his college professor respondents as very American in their willingness to trust strangers and their unwillingness to 'play it close to the chest', as well as in their consequent fear of having talked too much. It remains for the analysts of transcripts of interviews with Arkansans following a disaster to draw clear social structural distinctions in the definition of the interview situation. The meaning of the interview for middle-class respondents is posed like this (Schatzman and Strauss [1955] pp. 336–7):

> Although the interviewer is a stranger, an outsider, he is a well-spoken educated person. He is seeking information on behalf of some organisation, hence his questioning not only has sanction but sets the stage for both a certain freedom of speech and an obligation to give fairly full information.... At the very least he has had some experience in talking to educated strangers.... So he becomes relatively sensitive to communication *per se* and to communication with others who may not exactly share his view-points or frames of reference.

In contrast the lower-class person infrequently meets a middle-class person in a situation anything like the interview:

> Here he must talk at great length to a stranger about personal experiences, as well as recall for his listener a tremendous number of details. Presumably he is accustomed to talking about such matters and in such detail only to listeners with whom he shares a great deal of experience and symbolism, so that he need not be very self-conscious about communicative technique. He can, as a rule, safely assume that words, phrases and gestures are assigned approximately similar meanings by his listeners. But this is not so in the interview, indeed, in any situation where class converses with class in non-traditional modes.

Cicourel [1966] sees the interview situation in Goffmanesque terms as a managed performance on the part of both actors where, regardless of social class or other structural differences, 'each seeks to bargain with the other implicitly about what will be tolerated, how each seeks to convey or blur some image of themselves, their relative interest in each other as person and so on'. His sensitivity to linguistic and paralinguistic nuances of interaction and the manner in which they enter into the interview 'findings', provokes him into designing an alternate strategy to conventional survey interviewing. This strategy, derived from the phenomenology of Alfred Schutz, leads to a concentration on the routine grounds for making sense of communication. What is not said becomes as important as what is said. Linguistic codes and their switching become data. Standard techniques such as the 'probe' (e.g. 'What do you mean by that?') are prohibited since they strip the respondent of 'the kind of vague or taken for granted terms and phrases [he] characteristically uses as a competent member of the society' (Cicourel [1966]).

Although primitive, this approach provides a refreshing glimpse of language and its use in the interview as a central datum. From Cicourel's perspective formal precoded instruments become anathema, imposing a role of passive compliance upon the respondent – compliance to the preconceived categories of those who write the questions. Clearly the problems of measurement reaction which are of increasing concern to the social psychologist engaged in laboratory experiments with human subjects, are endemic in the field interview situation as well.[13] But the very recognition of such problems reduces their problematic aspects. It becomes possible then to view the interview as an exchange in which one or another variety of reality is negotiated or socially constructed by the interviewer and the respondent (for the general argument see Scheff [1968]).

Evidence concerning the great varieties of classification and categories employed in different languages (Deutscher [1968] pp. 326–9) suggests the possibility of problems of this order arising in a monolingual society. It is possible that, as one research team suggests, the lower-class respondent 'cannot talk about categories of people or acts because, apprently, he does not think readily in terms of classes' (Schatzman and Strauss [1955] p. 333). On the other hand these same scholars are aware that, as middle-class observers, they may be unable to recognise lower-class classifications. The latter explanation seems more credible. Secondary analyses of previously published 'scales' do suggest that sometimes the categories imposed by the investigators are indeed unlike those in the minds of the subjects (Jordan [1965]). In order to detect the 'scales' people may carry around in their heads, Hamblin [1966] has followed a lead from psychophysics. He suggests that social scientists employ ratio measures which are based on whatever ranges or intervals are used by respondents.

Linguistic research is increasingly providing clues for needed methodological innovations in social-science field research. Researchers need to keep in mind the fact that communication styles do vary, for example among the social classes. Schatzman and Strauss [1955] are convinced, on the basis of transcripts of interviews, that lower-class respondents are interpersonally incompetent – relatively unable to take the role of the other. Cohen and Hodges appear to verify this position and conclude that 'interview and questionnaire techniques are more likely, when applied to [lower class] respondents than when applied to respondents to the other social strata, to produce caricatures ...' ([1963] p. 333). In commenting on the lack of role-taking ability manifested in the interviews of lower-class people, Cohen and Hodges concede that this does not deny its existence and remind us of the 'peasant shrewdness' of the lower classes as for example in their 'conning' ability ([1963] p. 332).

A solution to this field communication problem is suggested by Basil Bernstein, who also observes this social-class relationship between verbal fluency and role-taking ability. The middle class switch easily between an 'elaborated' coding of English and a 'restricted' code while the lower classes are limited to the restricted code. Bernstein provides a clue to methods of tapping lower-class communication channels when he observes that 'In restricted codes, to varying degrees, the extra-verbal channels become objects of special perceptual activity; in elaborated codes it is the verbal channel' (Bernstein [1964] p. 63). It would seem to follow then that in order to 'interview' successfully users of restricted codes (such as lower-class persons), the field worker must shift his detection devices from verbal indicators to nonverbal indicators. Extensive vocabulary and syntactic refinements become meaningless. The semantics of the situation, which is what the field worker seeks to grasp, are revealed through other kinds of communication channels. As one insightful survey expert understates it: 'Since those who prepare questionnaires are typically from the middle and upper classes, the instruments they produce are likely to be somewhat inappropriate for large segments of the population' (Mitchell [1965] pp. 678–9).

The field interview is a peculiar form of conversation occurring in a peculiar situation. Possibilities of distortion arising out of differential definitions of that peculiar situation have already been alluded to. Cicourel [1967] is interested in 'how conversational materials and their properties become trasformed when they become interviews, questionnaires, and written reports ... interview and questionnaires', he says, 'usually are removed from the actual conditions of social interaction in which conversations occur ... and therefore [are] in doubtful correspondence [seldom established empirically] with the actual activities to which the interview and questionnaire items refer'. The 'doubtful correspondence' between verbal statements and overt acts has been clearly established empirically (for some of the evidence see Deutscher [1973]). But what Cicourel is talking about is the variation in degree of 'management' or verbalisations under varying conditions. And if there is any doubt about the ability and inclination of ordinary people to shift their style of speaking along with the context in which the speech occurs, Labov's data should dispel it. His tables show a consistent shift among all social classes toward more phonetic 'correctness' as the context shifts from informal conversation ('casual speech') to the interview ('careful speech') and finally to highly formalised contexts (reading style and word lists) (Labov [1966]).

It would appear that a great deal remains to be learned about how to communicate with those we seek to understand – about interviews, questionnaire construction and the nonverbal dimensions of language among other things. And it would appear that a sociological sensitivity to language can provide a key to at least some of this learning. It is remarkable that sociologists have managed to so great a degree to avoid consideration of linguistic phenomena. The unique quality of human conduct is its symbolic mediation through language – both verbal and nonverbal. Sociologists generally understand that this is the heart of George Herbert Mead's imagery of human nature. Perhaps we have failed to understand that no thoughtful observer of human conduct can reach any other conclusion. Pavlov, for example, whose brilliant researches have been so badly distorted by sycophantic followers, was impressed by what he called a 'second signal system' in human beings. The physical stimuli to which all animals respond and which are the focal concern of

Pavlov's conditioning experiments, are the 'first signals'. 'Second signals' are primarily *words*: 'The word created a second system of signals of reality which is peculiarly ours, being the signal of signals. On the one hand, numerous speech stimuli have removed us from reality.... On the other, it is precisely speech which has made us human' (Pavlov [1927] p. 357). It is this existence of language in himan beings which, according to Pavlov, makes inappropriate any generalisation from the behaviour of experimental animals to the behaviour of human beings. 'Of course,' Pavlov insists, 'a word is for man as much as a real conditioned stimulus as are other stimuli common to men and animals, yet at the same time it is so all-comprehending that it allows of no quantitative or qualitative comparisons with conditioned stimuli in animals' (Pavlov [1927] p. 407).

15 Concepts in the Analysis of Qualitative Data*

Martin Bulmer

Definitive and Sensitising Concepts

The question arises: do problems of concept-formation in such research differ from those in quantitative social research? It has often been maintained that this is so. While in quantitative social research concepts tend to be pre-formed and fixed (it is argued), in qualitative research they tend to be fluid and emergent. Herbert Blumer's classic paper, 'What is wrong with social theory?' (1954), in which he distinguished between *definitive* and *sensitising* concepts provides a clear statement of this view.

Blumer identified three main deficiencies of contemporary sociological theory. It was divorced from the empirical realm, compartmentalised into a world of its own; when applied to empirical data it ordered the data to fit the theory rather than amending the theory to fit the data. Theory, moreover, provided little guidance for research; propositions were rarely stated in a form facilitating direct investigation to see whether they were true. And the development of social theory was almost entirely divorced from

*Reprinted from *The Sociological Review*, vol. 27 (4), November 1979, pp. 653–77.

the growing amount of social data, 'facts' derived from empirical observation and inquiry.

The diagnosis of this critical state of affairs Blumer traced to the concept. 'Theory is of value in empirical science only to the extent to which it connects fruitfully with the empirical world. Concepts are the means, and the only means, of establishing such connections, for it is the concept that points to the empirical instances about which a proposal is made.' Terms like social institution, reference group, value, social system, urbanisation or social control rest on vague sense, not on a precise specification of attributes in terms of which empirical instances of the concept may be identified. The ambiguity and vagueness of its concepts is the basic deficency of social theory. Even though an understanding of concepts is built up over time through use, apt illustration and the sharing of a common universe of discourse, they lack clarity and sufficiently definite empirical reference. How can this be achieved?

Two solutions are possible, Blumer argues. One is the development of fixed and specific procedures designed to isolate a stable and definitive empirical content, with this content constituting the definition of the concept. Such *definitive* concepts refer with precision to what is common in a class of objects, by the aid of a clear definition in terms of attributes or fixed bench-marks. Examples of ways of developing such concepts include the use of operational definitions, factor analysis, and the construction of reliable quantitative indices. His main example is the I.Q. score as a stable and discriminating empirical measurement which provides a means of linking data to theory in an effective and rigorous manner, by means of an operational definition.He then goes on to criticise roundly definitive concepts in social theory, using this example of intelligence.

The alternative solution to the problem of concept-formation is therefore to develop concepts which are both more adequate theoretically and also more faithful to the empirical social world than definitive concepts. Blumer argues that many of the concepts of the social sciences are *sensitising* concepts, which satisfy both of these criteria. Whereas definitive concepts provide definitions which serve as a means of clearly identifying the individual instance in terms of the concept, sensitising concepts lack such specification of attributes and do not permit the user to move directly to the instance. Instead, sensitising concepts give the user a general sense of reference and guidance in approaching empirical instances. 'While definitive concepts provide prescriptions of what to see, sensitising concepts merely suggest direction along which to look.' Concepts such as social structure, culture and personality rest on a general sense of what is relevant rather than on a clear-cut prior specification.

The sensitising concept is more responsive to empirical data. One of the justifications for its use is the researcher's need to be attuned to the distinctive, particular character of every object of consideration in the natural social world of everyday experience. Sensitising concepts provide a means of moving from the concept to the concrete distinctiveness of a particular empirical case, rather than (as with definitive concepts) embracing the instance within the abstract framework of the concept. 'Since what we infer does not express itself in the same fixed way, we are not able to rely on fixed objective expressions to make the inference.'

Blumer has exercised a considerable influence on symbolic interactionist qualitative research in the United States (cf. Williams [1976]). His contrast between definitive and sensitising concepts is frequently quoted to justify the use of sensitising concepts in qualitative work. How adequate as a whole is his account of the variable nature of scientific concepts, and in particular how convincing his typification of definitive concepts? Implied contrasts between 'soft' and 'hard' social science are not infrequently made in terms of 'fluid' and 'fixed' concepts.

One may endorse wholeheartedly Blumer's view that theory, enquiry and empirical data are necessarily closely interwoven, and that their interplay is the means by which an empirical science develops, without accepting his picture of the nature of concepts. In particular, important qualifications need to be made to his account of definitive concepts. Blumer places great emphasis on their definition in terms of observables. This refers to the property that any statement, however abstract, can be transformed into an equivalent statement in terms of observations. Such an emphasis does play a central role in certain types of scientific concept formation. The operationism of the physicist P. W. Bridgman, for example, took this form. 'We mean by any concept nothing more than a set of operations; the concept is synonymous with the corresponding set of operations' [1948 p. 5]. Thus the concept of 'intelligence' can be defined by the observations 'what intelligence tests measure'.

C. G. Hempel, in his classic discussion of scientific concept-formation has criticised this view as too narrow [1952, p. 44 ff.]. Many of the terms with which the natural and social sciences are concerned are not directly observable characteristics but are *dispositions*. For example, the term 'magnetic' does not refer to directly observable characteristics, but to a disposition on the part of certain physical objects to display specific reactions (such as attracting iron). A term such as 'introvert' in psychology is similarly a disposition term, referring to a tendency to act in a particular way under certain conditions. Terms may therefore be given partial or conditional definitions, not only in terms of observables, but also in terms of specified conditions.

A third, more abstract, type of concept may also be distinguished, which involves naming both observables *and* non-observables. Hempel and others have distinguished between operational definitions and disposition concepts on the one hand, and theoretical *constructs* on the other, not derived in the first instance from empirical data. Such constructs are introduced jointly, at both theoretical and empirical levels, by setting up a theoretical system formulated in terms of them, and by giving this system an interpretation in terms of observables, which confers empirical meaning on the theoretical constructs.

Examples of such constructs in natural science include 'mass' and 'force' in classical mechanics; 'absolute temperature', 'pressure' and 'volume' in thermodynamics; 'electron' and 'proton' in quantum mechanics. Such highly abstract terms have a central theoretical role in those disciplines, but their use depends on not only their theoretical relevance but the fact that empirical observations make sense in terms of these concepts. 'Comprehensive, simple and dependable principles for the explanation . . . of observable phenomena cannot be obtained merely by summarising and inductively generalising observational findings. A hypothetico-deductive-observational procedure is called for. . . . Guided by his knowledge of observational data, the scientist has to invent a set of concepts – theoretical constructs, which lack immediate experiential significance, a system of hypotheses couched in terms of them, and an interpretation of the resulting theoretical network; and all this in a manner which will establish explanatory . . . connections between the data of direct observation (Hempel [1952] pp. 36–7).

Interdependence of Theory and Data

It is clear, in the light of this distinction between operational definitions, disposition terms, and theoretical constructs, that Blumer's definitive concept is both overdrawn and in significant respects misleading. His prototype of conventional solutions to the problem of how to form scientific concepts, with which sensitising concepts are then contrasted, is something of a caricature of the philosophy of science.

It is by no means necessary to adopt Hempel's standpoint as a whole in order to criticise Blumer. Indeed, some philosophers of science have questioned postulates such as the distinction between a theoretical language and an observational language. Differences in the nature of concepts are not ontological, as though observational terms name other kinds of things than theoretical terms. A theory-free description, it is argued, is a misplaced objective. In Hanson's words, 'people, not their eyes, see. Cameras, and eyeballs, are blind' [1958, p. 6]. However, this does not render all observation relative to the standpoint of the observer. The way to approach the paradox of categorisation is to focus on the *interdependence* of theory and observation in concept-formation.

A way of appreciating this is to think of differences between different kinds of concepts along an empirical-theoretical continuum. Some terms in social science are based on relatively simple and direct observation, such as the report of a dream or the marking of a ballot. Or perhaps the vital events of birth, marriage and death lend themselves most readily to treatment as such *observational terms.* Other types of observational data are more complex. Is an observation of the act of prayer direct, for instance? (cf. Wilson [1970]).

Observing someone at prayer may be a case of *indirect observation,* using a term whose application involves relatively subtle and complex perception in which inference plays a part. The inference that a person kneeling in a place of worship is at prayer involves assumptions about the social significance of posture, the locale in which this act is taking place, and the relationship between that locale and religious belief. As Kaplan, echoing Hanson, rather vividly puts it, 'Do we see genes when we look into a pair of blue eyes?' (Kaplan [1964] p. 55). Very similar problems often arise in qualitative social research in connecting observations and interpretation.

Some terms, however, cannot be inferred directly from observations even though they refer to phenomena definable at least in principle in terms of observables. Actions of individuals, for example, do not enable one to define the concept of 'government'. The *construct* 'government' implies more than a collection of individually observable acts. Similarly terms like 'taboo' or 'money' do not derive their meaning from particular observations directly, even though they do so ultimately. Witness the proverbial Martian in the English bank who used to feature in debates about methodological individualism and holism.

Constructs, however, at least in principle, derive their meaning in terms of particular empirical observations. *Theoretical terms*, on the other hand, cannot be defined even in principle in terms of observables. Concepts such as the 'protestant ethic' or 'marginal utility' derive their meaning from the part they play in the theory in which they are embedded, and from their role in that theory itself. 'This systematic quality is what makes the analysis of theoretical terms so difficult; what begins as an effort to fix the content of a single concept ends as the task of assessing the truth of a whole theory. The meaning of a theoretical term is fixed by horizontal as well as vertical members of the conceptual structure, and only the structure as a whole, at best, rests firmly on empirical ground' (Kaplan [1964] p. 57).

Blumer's picture of scientific concepts does not recognise this variety. The image of the definitive concept is that of the measuring-rod. The scientist constructs this and then goes out into the world to make measurements. In extreme form the measuring-rod *is* the concept. The ruler *is* length, or intelligence *is* the I.Q. score. It may be more helpful to use a different analogy of the zip-fastener to characterise the relationship between concepts and observations.

Consider certain natural scientific concepts like 'electron' or 'gene'. These derive their meaning not only from the role they play as a construct or theoretical term in a theory, but also from observational evidence in experiments, etc. Braithwaite's analogy of the zip-fastener [1953] or Hanson's 'semantical zipper' [1969] suggest that scientific conclusions may be reached, not by working from premisses to conclusions but by working back from conclusions to premisses. The conclusions of electrical theory, for example, express propositions about observable flashes of light or pointer readings of a measuring instrument. These, coming together at the bottom of the zip-fastener, are the results of actual observations used to test consequences of the theory. The meaning of the terms derives from their use in that context. These meanings are then transferred back up through the steps of the theory (the zip) by a kind of 'reverse deduction', until at last the zip reaches the top. At this point the much-travelled terminology used in empirical observations reaches the high-level term 'electron'.

This indirectness of meaning poses considerable problems. The terms are theoretical, yet 'experience must, one way or another, enter into this determination; for otherwise the symbols would not stand for empirical concepts at all, and what we took to be physics would turn out to be pure mathematics. The question is in what way a theoretical concept like an electron is an empirical concept; it cannot be answered by denying that an electron is an empirical concept at all' (Braithwaite [1953] p. 52).

The way out of this dilemma is to avoid a direct definition of the concept. Many concepts in science apart from electron have this character. Just as the search for an explicit definition of 'life' in biology is a misconception, no physicist would choose to answer the question: what is Schrodinger's wave-function, Ψ? Does it really exist? He would prefer to give an indirect definition by explaining how it is used in his calculus. He does not, however, start with deductive propositions which are 'about' a concept which he denotes with Ψ, and then go on to represent these propositions in the deductive system by formulae in a calculus. Rather he starts with a calculus whose derived formulae can be interpreted as the empirical generalisations which he is concerned to explain. To think about Ψ is to use the symbol Ψ in an appropriate way in his calculus. Once the status of a term within the calculus has been expounded, there is no further question as to the ontological status of that theoretical term. That term appears to have no meaning apart from the context of its representation in a scientific system.

Concept and observation are thus interdependent, but in a quite specific sense. Concepts are not just developed out of observations, but neither are they imposed *a priori* categories. Rather their use is justified in terms of their context in a particular theory and particular observations which that theory seeks to explain. This is a quite different picture from Blumer's account of definitive concepts, and a more convincing one. For 'theories are not developed deductively or inductively, but *both* deductively and inductively. There is constant interplay between the observation of realities and the formation of concepts, between research and theorising, between perception and explanation. The genesis of any theory is best described as a reciprocal development of observational sophistication and theoretical precision' (Lachenmeyer [1971] p. 61).

The logic of such a procedure may be formalised, in the terms suggested by N. R. Hanson [1958] as *retroduction*. The form of such inference is:

1. Some surprising phenomenon, *P*, is observed.
2. *P* would be explicable as a matter of course if *H* were true.
3. Hence there is reason to think that *H* is true.

Such a sequence is distinctively different both from induction (generalising from particular cases) or deduction (moving from the general to the particular). In a retroductive explanation, one starts from the observation of a phenomenon, *P*. *P* would be explicable as a matter of course if a certain general statement, *H*, were true. So let us suppose that *H* obtains. The reasoning is from data to hypothesis, not vice versa. But neither is it inductive generalisation, since it involves conjecture. It is the working of one's way up the zip-fastener. 'Theories provide patterns within which data appears intelligible. They constitute a "conceptual Gestalt". A theory is not pieced together from observed phenomena; it is rather what makes it possible to observe phenomena as being of a certain sort, and related to other phenomena. Theories put phenomena into systems. They are built up "in reverse" – retroductively. A theory is a cluster of conclusions in search of a premise. From the observed properties of phenomena, the [scientist] reasons his way to a keystone idea from which the properties are explicable as a matter of course. The [scientist] seeks not a set of possible objects, but a set of possible explanations (Hanson [1958] p. 90).

The hypothetico-deductive method seeks well-formulated solutions to problems stated in the form of testable hypotheses. The striking lack of examples of, for instance, Popperian method in British sociology has many causes, but one is undoubtedly the difficulties of theory construction (a realm which Popper relegates to psychology). Hanson, on the other hand, has suggested that 'the hypothetico-deductive account seems illuminating *vis-à-vis* our ideas of hypothesis-testing, and terse expositions of the results of that testing' – or, as he puts it, *ex post facto* logical reconstructions of the 'argument-anatomy' of Finished Research Reports. 'The retroductive emphasis, however, is more centred on the conceptual aspects of problem solving' (Hanson [1971] pp. 65–6). Its aim is to clarify the premisses – the concepts and theoretical propositions – from which a particular empirical datum follows.

The application of these ideas to the analysis of qualitative sociological data, which may not be immediately apparent, arises from the connections, between an emphasis on the interplay of concepts and empirical data, and several methodological attempts to clarify the logic of analysis in qualitative sociology, by Blumer, Znaniecki, Lazarsfeld and Barton, and Glaser and Strauss. All propose means of developing concepts out of qualitative sociological data. Of the four, Blumer's account of sensitising concepts is the most sketchy.

The emphasis in Blumer's discussion of sensitising concepts is congruent with a number of the points made earlier about the interdependence of data and concept. Regrettably, very little guidance is provided about how this is done in practice. Not only is 'What is wrong with social theory?' programmatic, it is also singularly unspecific. Blumer admits that the procedure lends itself to abuse. 'The great vice, and the enormously widespread vice, in the use of sensitising concepts, is to take them for granted – to rest content with whatever element of plausibility they possess. Under such circumstances, the concept takes the form of a vague stereotype and it becomes only a device for ordering or arranging empirical instances' (Blumer [1954] p. 9). Blumer recommends the avoidance of this trap principally by 'patient, careful and imaginative life-study' of the natural social world, remaining in close and continuing relations with it. Little further specification is provided. Short of an analysis of the empirical monographs of his students, one is left with little concrete guidance as to how to proceed.

Analytic Induction

Florian Znaniecki, however, in his much-neglected classic *The Method of Sociology*, first adumbrated procedures for generating categories from sociological data, which he called 'analytic induction'. This procedure he contrasted with enumerative induction, '*inductio per enumerationem simplicem*,' the procedure of collecting a large number of cases, and when they are assembled, formulating categories and empirical generalisations strictly on the basis of the data available. Data dredging procedures in social survey research are of this type (Selvin and Stuart [1966]). Analytic induction, by contrast, is as the name implies a more guided procedure, intended to maintain faithfulness to the empirical data while abstracting and generalising from a relatively small number of cases. Its aim is to 'preserve plasticity' by avoiding prior categorisation. No definition of a class or category of data precedes the selection of data to be studied as the representative of that class. The data analysis begins before any general formulations are proposed (i.e. the procedure is inductive rather than deductive). However, whereas enumerative induction abstracts by generalising, analytic induction generalises by abstracting. It abstracts from a given concrete case the features that are essential, and generalises them.

First (a) discover which characters in a given datum of a certain class are more, and which less, essential. Then (b) abstract these characters and assume that the more essential are the more general than the less essential and must be found in a wider variety of classes. Follow this by (c) testing this hypothesis by investigating classes in which both the former and the latter are found. Finally, (d) establish a classification, i.e. organise all these classes into a scientific system based on the functions the respective characters play in determining them (Znaniecki [1934]).

This somewhat abstract procedure can be illustrated from its use in empirical studies (a) to develop classifications and types and (b) to propound explanatory hypotheses. R. C. Angell's study *The Family Encounters the Depression* [1936] exemplifies the former aim. He set out to examine the effects of a sudden and lasting decrease in income upon American families, using 50 personal documents. The analysis was 'an almost perfect example of the muddling, tentative way in which the so-called scientific mind gets ahead'. The main points to highlight are the emergence of the classification out of analysis of a relatively small number of cases, the rigorous search for negative evidence (indicated by disagreement between two or three judges) in the construction of the classification, and the way in which a new theoretical conception (that of adaptability) emerged in the course of research. This use of analytic induction upon 'subjective' data to construct empirical types exemplifies the method as a means of classification.

The use of analytic induction to produce explanatory propositions is shown in Lindesmith's study of opiate addiction [1947], based on about seventy in-depth interviews with addicts. The problem was to explain why some people exposed to morphine and heroin become addicts, while others so exposed do not. The analytic method followed is best described as study of a series of critical cases, leading to successive revisions of the guiding theory. The research strategy involved identifying a limited and specific problem and analysing it as exhaustively as possible using case-study data. The procedure, described as analytic induction, was to formulate propositions which applied to all the cases studied without exception. Such propositions were then subjected to empirical test, *any* negative evidence requiring *their* reformulation. Theory and evidence are closely articulated one with another in the process, for whatever a provisional hypothesis may be, it must be changed to conform with evidence which contradicts it.

The following sequence of analysis resulted. First the hypothesis was considered that individuals who do not know what they are receiving (if they are in fact receiving morphine or heroin) do not become addicted. This was immediately abandoned because of negative evidence. A second hypothesis was therefore put forward that people become addicts when they recognise symptoms of withdrawal distress which they are experiencing, on coming off the drug. If they do not recognise withdrawal distress, they do not become addicts. Further negative evidence counter to this was found, but the approach was more fruitful, leading to a third hypothesis. This was that people become addicted after experiencing withdrawal symptoms, for the purpose of alleviating the distress which they have experienced. No negative evidence was found to refute this.

Lindesmith's aim was to produce *universal* generalisations, which would apply to *all* the cases that he studied. The search for negative evidence was so rigorous, following this procedure, that finding a single negative case necessitated either reformulating the hypothesis, or redefining the phenomenon. The latter is possible because the process is one of building types or classifications out of the data. These are built up as one goes along, rather than being established *a priori.*

Critics of analytic induction such as W. S. Robinson [1951] and R. H. Turner [1953] have questioned whether its logic of explanation is original, and whether it permits the development of universals from case studies. Its relevance to the development of concepts and propositions in close conjunction with empirical evidence is, however, apparent. Even W. S. Robinson agreed that Lindesmith's two solutions when negative evidence confronted a provisional hypothesis were acceptable. The first – to alter the hypothesis – is the method of the working hypothesis, trying out propositions which, even if falsified, suggest more fruitful lines forward. Paying particular attention to deviant cases is especially fruitful as a self-correcting procedure. The second – to redefine the phenomenon when faced with negative evidence – is of particular interest here. The limitation of the scope of the universal is carried out to ensure causal homogeneity, but it also emphasises that conceptual refinement is an integral and active part of the process of theory construction. Thus, Lindesmith used the procedure to distinguish between true addiction and habituation. Cressey [1953] thereby distinguished between violation of financial trust undertaken in good faith, and acceptance of trust for the express purpose of violating it.

The concepts developed are closely integrated into their associated causal generalisations. The generalisations are derivable from the definitions. Thus Lindesmith worked out side-by-side his concept of addiction and the essential stages of becoming addicted. Critics have suggested that the method has rarely worked to produce the kinds of generalisations in which its adherents were interested, instead tending to encourage the development of typologies (Williams [1976] p. 135). Nevertheless, analytic induction is a fruitful way of delimiting and defining a causally homogeneous category of phenomena (cf. Mitchell [1983]). 'The operation in practice is one which alternates back and forth between tentative cause and tentative definition, each modifying the other so that in a sense closure is achieved when a complete and integral relation between the two is established' (Turner [1953] p. 609).

The distinction between qualitative and quantitative data is in reality an artificial one. An interesting parallel approach to the problem of concept-formation is that of Paul Lazarsfeld, who was intensely interested in problems in systematically analysing qualitative data (Lazarsfeld [1972]). In later papers, he and Barton discussed how to make the transition from concepts to indicators, having once formed general concepts and categories (Lazarsfeld and Barton [1955]; Lazarsfeld [1958]). In an important earlier paper, however, they tackle the question of how one forms such categories in the first place. Given the state of theory, much research is explanatory, aimed at qualitative answers to questions such as: what goes on in a certain situation? what influences people in behaving in a particular way? how do people justify holding a certain set of beliefs? In exploratory research, the investigator is faced with an array of raw data for which ready-made theoretical categories do not exist. 'The job of finding out what theoretical categories are applicable to the given field of behaviour will be a long one, and will involve switching back and forth between concrete categories closely adapted to the data themselves, and general categories able to tie in with other fields of experience, until both concrete applicability and generality are obtained' (Lazarsfeld [1972] p. 226).

The first stage is to find some preliminary means of classification. Lazarsfeld and Barton suggest four principles to follow as guidelines in this: the requirements of articulation, logical correctness, adaptation to the structure of the situation, and adaptation to the respondent's frame of reference.

Articulation, first, is a means of putting a very large number of observations into smaller groups – each more or less alike in relation to the phenomenon being studied – without premature closure. The latter can result from having to choose between forming a few very broad groups (the elements in which are not very similar) and a larger number of smaller categories (which retain important distinctions but are too numerous to be handled easily). Articulation provides a solution to this dilemma. Classification should proceed from the general to the particular, so that material (such as answers to open-ended questions) can be examined in terms of broad groupings or detailed categories whichever are more appropriate for a given purpose.

Logical correctness, second, requires that at each stage of articulation, the categories formed at each step should be both exhaustive and mutually exclusive. Exhaustiveness implies that categorisation should cover the full range of data and not put into a residual category elements which are distinctive. Mutual exclusiveness means that there should be one and only one place to put an item in a given classification system. Confusion may arise in two ways. Either categories may be used which embrace other categories within them (e.g. visiting friends/mass media/playing sport – watching TV – the latter is a subcategory of mass-media). Or categories may be constructed which mix different aspects of objects in a single-dimension classification scheme (e.g. combining political allegiance and social beliefs). Each dimension should, initially at least, have a separate classification system. These can be combined later if appropriate.

If the form of the classification is thus dealt with, content is more problematical and intractable. The formation of categories in terms of content should be adapted to the material and the problem being studied. Categories are an aid to understanding and generalisation. In the long run, this must involve relating such categories to a more general system, in order to contribute to social theory. The investigator may use the customary terms of everyday life or his own categories. The latter is more common. If the latter, then the classification should be adapted to the structure of the situation being studied. The situation or process is then divided into its various 'natural parts' on the basis of experienced personal judgement or general theoretical directives. This involves a two-way process, moving from the data to the categories into which they might fit, but at the same time dividing these categories into finer categories.

As their fourth principle, Lazarsfeld and Barton recommend the need to adapt to the respondent's frame of reference, to present as clearly as possible the respondent's own definition of the situation. Very frequently, the model held by the researcher (e.g. in studies of the state of the economy or voting behaviour) may be different from that held by the respondent – for instance, people may not see economic problems in terms of a model of the entire economy. Such empirical findings must not be overlooked, or subsumed under the social scientist's own categories – rather the categories must be made responsive to the respondent's frame of reference, his focus of attention and categories of thought. Lazarsfeld and Barton's incisive contribution is generalisable to the problems of analysing a wide range of qualitiative data.

Grounded Theory

The most influential recent attempt to provide guidance on how to analyse case study data, *The Discovery of Grounded Theory* by B. G. Glaser and A. L. Strauss [1967], bears some broad resemblance to Znaniecki's programme a generation earlier. Glaser and Strauss distinguish between substantive, grounded theories and formal, more abstract theories. Cross-cutting this is a model of the research process in terms of a progression from raw data to categories, to their properties, and then to hypotheses. 'Categories' and 'the properties of categories' are equivalent to concepts in the present discussion. Thus, for example, they distinguish between the *category* of nursing care: social loss of a dying patient, and the *property of that category*: the loss rationales used by nursing staff.

Their approach to theory generation places a heavy emphasis on induction and openness to the data. New conceptualisation from one's data is encouraged at the early phases of the research. Low-level categories are generated out of a process of constant comparison in the early phases of data collection. The sociologist is urged to avoid forcing round data into square categories; rather categories should emerge in the course of analysis. Categories and their properties should be *analytic* – i.e. sufficiently generalised to designate *characteristics* of entities, rather than the entities themselves – and *sensitising* (in Blumer's terms). Relations between categories and their properties are then formulated in hypotheses, which are in principle subject to verification. The aim of the procedure is primarily to generate theory.

As in analytic induction, the collection, coding and analysis of data are all inextricably bound up with each other. 'They should blur and intertwine continually, from the beginning of an investigation to the end.' In other respects, however, grounded theory differs from analytic induction. The use of the constant comparative method to generate categories, properties and hypotheses about one's problem is different from the process of generalising by abstracting. The focus on formal as well as substantive theory is more general; on the other hand grounded theory is not seen as producing total explanations, nor is it pre-eminently concerned with proof. Developing grounded theory is seen as a stage prior to verification, whereas Znaniecki sought an alternative to it.

In some respects, it is more of a rhetorical evocation of qualitative research than a clear and tightly written specification, but the authors could justifiably argue that this reflects the character of much interpretative research, involving immersion in the natural social world. It is difficult to provide a clear specification for this osmotic process. Other criticisms, however, have more substance.

Their *tabula rasa* view of inquiry is open to serious doubt. In the development of categories, they urge the investigator 'at first, (to) literally ignore the literature of theory and fact on the area under study, in order to assure that the emergence of categories will not be contaminated by concepts more suited to different areas. Similarities and convergences with the literature may be established after the analytic core of categories has emerged.' Glaser and Strauss apparently believe that the chicken and egg can be separated. Logically such a claim is doubtful. Deductivists such as Popper have made damaging attacks on induction on logical grounds, but proponents of retroduction, while critical of hypothetico-deduction, are also critical of pure induction, which Glaser and Strauss seem to espouse. (Analytic induction avoids their extreme claims.) The zip-fastener analogy emphasises the interdependence of observation and concepts rather than the temporal priority of one or the other.

Empirically, prior blankness of mind, if conceivable, may be easier in hitherto unresearched areas. Glaser and Strauss, for instance, cite loneliness, brutality, resistance, debating, bidding systems and diplomacy as such *terrae incognitae.* But to keep one's mind altogether free from presuppositions or prior conceptualisations in well-researched areas of sociology such as the family, mental illness or social stratification is surely much more difficult.

A second difficulty is when to stop the process of category development. Analytic induction does specify a fairly tight relation between categories and hypotheses. Grounded theory has a somewhat uncontrolled air about the proceedings, wherein the constant comparative analyst is rushing hither and thither gaining new insights, while also trying to build up from data to categories and their properties to substantive theory and then formal theory. When are his categories sufficiently formed to stop the process?

Thirdly, there is very considerable imprecision as to what Glaser and Strauss mean by 'theory', as has been pointed out by Brown and Williams. Brown [1973, p. 6] is justifiably worried that they fail to specify the nature of the link between theory and data (Williams [1976] pp. 135–6); that they use 'theory' to refer both to properties and their categories *and* to hypotheses. Paradoxically, these criticisms suggest that the method may be more successful in generating concepts than in generating testable hypotheses. Like analytic induction, its very success in improving categorisation seems to inhibit movement to verification. Critics of analytic induction have made much the same point as Brown does of grounded theory: 'The type of material best given to the development of grounded theory – in the sense of theory which can be held with considerable assurance without formal testing – is that commonly associated with the classificatory kind of activity or some kinds of processual analysis' (Brown [1973] p. 8).

Empirical Studies

Sensitising concepts, analytic induction and grounded theory all do considerably less than justice to the process of double-fitting which goes on in the process of developing concepts out of case-study material. As an alternative to searching the literature for convincing reconstructions of the 'context of discovery', what appear to be the sources from which concepts and categories are drawn in the empirical studies in the symposium in which this chapter originally appeared (Blaxter [1979])? The following generalisations are offered in further support of the argument that the development and justification of social science concepts is a process which is not readily reducible to simple formulae.

(a) One important source of sociological concepts lies in objective facticity, in the presentation to the observer of phenomena so real that he cannot ignore them. 'Social class' is a concept of this kind, particularly as it is used in official statistics. In other contexts, 'religion' or 'race' may present themselves in this way.

(b) The logical analysis of a process may yield fruitful concepts, echoing Lazarsfeld's point that concepts should be adapted to the structure of the situation.

(c) Professional definitions of objective facticity provide a further source of concepts in social research.

(d) The literature in particular areas may be a further source of concepts. This is probably true of all fields where there has been significant prior research.

(e) The social scientist's own prior experiences may be a further source of conceptual guidance.

(f) The social scientist's values are clearly another source of conceptualisation.

(g) Once research has commenced, concepts may be formed by working back from regularities in the data, which form empirically convenient demarcations. The definition of the concept may be derived from an empirically convenient grouping which delimited the data in a workable way.

(h) 'Common-sense' constructs widespread in the society provide guidance in conceptualisation. An example, mentioned earlier, is the Registrar-General's concept of social class. Interestingly, the development of this concept by government statisticians seems to have owed little or nothing to social science and a great deal to common-sense ideas about social differentiation and their consequences for the life chances of different occupational groups (cf. Stevenson [1928], Leete and Fox [1977]).

(i) An important source of conceptualisation in the research reported here are members' own concepts and definitions, which are elicited in the course of research. Such concepts emerge from research as it proceeds.

(j) Overlapping with this, but distinct from it, is the abstraction of concepts from life experiences as recorded in life histories.

Ten different sources of concepts have been identified. Which of them feature in a particular study is clearly contingent on more than the individual character of the researcher. One factor is the investigator's general sociological orientation.

Another source of variation is the richness of the existing literature. Research on organisational structure or decision-making, for instance, has a much more considerable background of scholarship to draw on than, for example, the sociology of sexual deviance or of paranormal phenomena. Part of this background is formed of the existing concepts in a particular field. Even if not used directly, these are quite likely indirectly to inform concept-formation as the research develops.

A third source of variation is the nature of the phenomena being studied. It is a commonplace that interpretative research has developed further in some areas – deviance, locality studies and complex organisations – than in others – mass media, politics, attitude change. Not all phenomena lend themselves to intensive study by means of drawing out members' own categories. 'Some phenomena involve much greater discontinuity in either time or space or in the level of the system studied. In such circumstances close contact with the phenomenon may not produce much by way of "theory". . . .' Grounding an analysis in members' own perspectives is probably easier where one is concerned with 'relatively short-term processes, sequences of behaviour that are directly observable or can be easily reported upon, and behaviour which has a repetitive character' (Brown [1973] pp. 6, 8). It is less easy where relevant behaviour is not observable or easily reported upon, for instance relationships between mentally-ill persons and their families. Critical data can only be obtained by questioning after the event. It is not easy by this means for the investigator to get an intuitive feel of the factors influencing the relatives' definitions of the situation, which would enable him to ground the analysis in their categories. Routes to the formation of concepts in the analysis of qualitative data are therefore empirically variable, according to the general sociological orientation of the researcher, the richness of existing literature, and the nature of the phenomena being studied.

Conclusion

The 'paradox of categorisation' has not been resolved, though certain solutions to it, particularly the distinction between definitive and sensitising concepts, have been criticised as inadequate. It is also clear that members' own concepts are insufficient as a basis for analysis, though they may form a starting-point. Some conclusions may, however, be stated negatively, both to cast doubt on some of the more rhetorical statements in the literature and to pose questions for future researchers.

The first negative conclusion is that there is a widespread failure to distinguish clearly between concepts and explanatory propositions – there is fuzziness about what people mean by 'theory'. The two are clearly distinct. Concepts are means of organising data; propositions or hypothesis, means of stating relationships between concepts, which are empirically testable and which may be true or false. Justifications for the logic of interpretative research in terms of analytic induction or grounded theory tend to blur the distinction, and even lead to premature crystallisation at the stage of conceptformation, rather than going on to produce explanatory theory. Though some sociologists see their work as preliminary to the latter task, others appear to be satisfied with description, or conveying a sense of 'understanding', or in illustrating a general orientation. To what extent is a strategy of data-grounded generalisation from case study material inimical to the production of testable propositions?

The second negative conclusion is to doubt the salience of 'emergence' in data analysis. Both Blumer and Glaser and Strauss place great emphasis on this, yet in practice concepts do not merely form themselves out of the data. The postulated emergence of sensitising concepts seems more of a programme than an account of research practice. On the other hand, a model such as Lazarsfeld's of moving from imagery to concept to indicator to composite index is not supported either in the research reported here. What seems much more characteristic is the *interplay* of data and conceptualisation, the 'flip-flop' between ideas and research experience. Whether the notion of the 'semantical zipper' can be applied with the same degree of plausibility to sociology as it can to modern physics is debatable. But at least it serves a negative purpose in suggesting that the interpretative sociologist is neither a man with a measuring-rod nor an embodiment in conceptual terms of the bucket theory of the mind.

A third negative conclusion, particularly surprising in view of recent sociological trends, is the relative lack of emphasis on members' own accounts as a source of concepts, and the reliance on other sources. Given recent theoretical ferment, one might have expected more of an attempt, not just to ground concepts in 'the data' but in the categories of members. Perhaps this stems from the linguistic ambiguities with which sociologists grapple (Starr [1974] pp. 404–7). Ditton brings this out in discussing ([1977] p. 13) whether to treat 'fiddling' as a natural phenomenon or not, quoting A. MacIntyre: 'We use certain criteria to identify this or that as gold or as amino acid or a Christmas pudding. If certain characteristics are present and others absent, then this will suffice in all normal circumstances for the identification. But what if the standard criteria are satisfied and then it turns out that this otherwise normal gold emits radiation . . . or that this Christmas pudding talks? . . .'. It has been argued, for example by Rock [1973], that a thoroughgoing phenomenalism which does not reach beyond actors' own categories will be left in a descriptive posture resistant to explicit analysis. The symposium (Blaxter [1979]) suggested an awareness of this problem and a reluctance to rely solely on the world as seen by the subjects of research.

A fourth negative conclusion is the inappropriateness of the epithet 'qualitative' in relation to the forms of conceptualisation described here. To rule measurement out in principle in research of this type is an error, particularly given the fact that so much social measurement is only nominal or ordinal. Sociologists whose preferred styles of research differ as markedly as Paul Lazarsfeld and Howard Becker show a considerable degree of convergence when discussing the coding and analysis of qualitative data. One-sided views of research methods are particularly misleading in suggesting a necessary connection between qualitative data, sensitising concepts and theory generation on the one hand; quantitive data, definitive concepts and theory testing on the other. The relationship is only contingent. One step in the right direction would be to talk of 'interpretative research' rather than 'qualitative' data.

Fifthly and finally, how are concepts justified and validated? Interpretative procedures tend to be weak in providing justifications for particular conceptualisations. There is often a shared assumption that the concepts used are fruitful and make sense in the context of the particular analysis being done. Blumer's main solution to the problem of validating concepts is to ensure that they are faithful to the data, that there is a good fit between them. This is extremely important, but it leaves on one side the issue of the *inter-subjective* validity of concepts. Would another social scientist studying the same problem find the same concepts equally fruitful? Is it possible that error may occur in the process of conceptualisation? The resolution of this question lies not in further conceptual analysis, but in the testing and falsification of explanatory propositions employing particular concepts. As already noted, the possible falsification of theories is not greatly emphasised here. As Brown has argued in relation to grounded theory, it may nevertheless be necessary. 'Alternative explanations may come readily to mind that cannot be settled by the investigator's greater immersion in the situation. . . . A theory may arise from first-hand observation (or at least be compatible with it) but alternative explanations will be obvious. . . . Theory will at times be so equivocal that it will not be profitable to pursue research without taking account of methodological issues – questions of how one can decide between alternative theories – at a very early stage' (Brown [1973] pp. 6, 7).

The sociologist is thus left to strike a balance in concept-formation between faithfulness to his data and premature closure. If induction is implausible and sensitising concepts particularly prone to vagueness, a model of the deductive testing of propositions embodying precisely specified definitive concepts is even more inappropriate to the research reported here. Ambiguity and a degree of indeterminateness is the result, reflected in five negative conclusions. The 'paradox of categorisation' suggests that this is unavoidable. 'There is a certain kind of behavioural scientist who, at the least threat of an exposed ambiguity, scurries for cover like a hermit crab into the nearest abandoned logical shell. But there is no ground for panic. That a cognitive situation is not as well structured as we would like does not imply that no inquiry made in that situation is really scientific. On the contrary, it is the dogmatisms outside science that proliferate closed systems of meaning; the scientist is in no hurry for closure. Tolerance of ambiguity is as important for creativity in science as it is anywhere else' (Kaplan [1964] pp. 70–1).

Part Six

Theory, Method and Substance

16 Introduction and Further Reading

Martin Bulmer

> Be a good craftsman. Avoid any rigid set of procedures. Above all, seek to develop and use the sociological imagination. Avoid the fetishism of methods and technique. Urge the rehabilitation of the unpretentious intellectual craftsman, and try to become such a craftsman yourself. Let every man be his own methodologist; let every man be his own theorist; let theory and method again become part of the practice of a craft (C. Wright Mills [1959] p. 224.)

It is appropriate now to revert to the theme of Chapter 1 and to ask what one can say in general about the relationship between theory, method and substance in sociological research. Two types of answer are possible, and these will be considered in turn. The first is in terms of the logic of scientific explanation, the second in terms of the practice of theorising.

There are several systematic accounts available of the logic of explanation which demonstrate the connections between theory and research. Three distinctive accounts are widely supported.

The *hypothetico-deductive* approach briefly discussed above suggests that social science progresses by testing empirically deductions made from universal statements and specific initial conditions, and using the results of the test to verify or falsify the original theory (leading to its confirmation or modification). Thus Durkheim, having observed that Catholics had a lower suicide rate than Protestants, was concerned to provide an explanation of the observed difference. This led him to postulate an explanation of egoistic suicide in terms of social cohesion and to formulate the hypothesis that suicide rates are a function of unrelieved anxiety states and stresses. In R. K. Merton's reformulation ([1957] p. 97) the argument has the following structure:

(1) Social cohesion provides psychic support to group members subjected to acute stresses and anxieties.
(2) Suicide rates are functions of unrelieved anxieties and stresses to which persons are subjected.
(3) Catholics have greater social cohesion than Protestants.
(4) Therefore lower suicide rates should be anticipated among Catholics than among Protestants.

The last term is a deduction made from the preceding terms, which is then the subject of empirical test. This account of the logic of social science has been influentially stated by R. B. Braithwaite, K. Popper, E. Nagel, C. G. Hempel and others; it provides the philosophical underpinning of a model of research in terms of stages discussed in the Introduction.

However there are objections. The *practice* of research seems to involve a more active interplay of theory and data than this model allows. The *origin* of hypotheses in conjecture is left unexplicated, yet this is crucial for the fruitfulness of the development of research. And the role of induction is ignored.

> As a description of most sociological research, the process just outlined is far from satisfactory and many of us doubt whether it should be seen as some distant grail which we should all pursue. There are many reasons for this. Most scientists agree that inductive processes play a larger part than simply the modification of theory to account for some observed discrepancy. In sociology the state of theoretical development is such that research is very largely inductive, and much research activity consists of making inductive inferences from data (Bechhofer [1973] p. 72.)

Two alternative perspectives upon the process of theorising give greater weight to the role of induction. *Analytic induction* was first suggested by Znaniecki [1934] and developed by Robinson [1951], Turner [1953], Glaser and Strauss [1967] and Denzin [1970]. In this view, generalisations are drawn out of empirical case studies by means of a process of refinement, abstraction and generalisation. (Analytic induction is quite distinct from enumerative induction, the collection of a very large number of cases or items of data followed at the end by the formulation of empirical generalisations strictly on the basis of the data available.) In analytic induction the procedure is as follows. Having chosen one's problem (e.g. opiate addiction in Lindesmith's study using this method [1947, 1968]), a hypothetical explanation of that phenomenon is formulated. A few cases are then studied in depth to derermine whether the hypothesis fits the data. If the hypothesis does not fit the data, either the hypothesis is reformulated or the phenomenon to be explained is redefined. If the hypothesis does fit, further cases are examined in a search for disconfirming evidence and the search continues until a universal relationship is established. The empirical test of the hypothesis is particularly rigorous, even a single negative case requiring reformulation of the hypotheses or redefinition of the phenomenon.

The same interplay of theory and data is characteristic of *retroduction* or *abduction.* Derived from the work of the American philosopher C. S. Pierce, the logic of this account of scientific procedure has been most fully worked out by Hanson [1958] in a classic discussion of the discovery of scientific ideas (as opposed to their verification). In this view the first step is that some observations are made which cannot be accounted for by existing knowledge. The scientist then reasons back from the data to develop a theory which will account for the observations. Provided that the theory fully accounts for the initial observations, then there is reason to think that the theoretical inference is correct.

> A theory is not pieced together from obseved phenomena; it is rather what makes it possible to observe phenomena as being of a certain sort, and as related to other phenomena. Theories put phenomena into systems. They are built up 'in reverse' – retroductively. A theory is a cluster of conclusions in search of a

> premiss. From the observed properties of phenomena, the physicist reasons his way towards a keystone idea from which the properties are explicable as a matter of course. The physicist seeks not a set of possible objects, but a set of possible explanations (Hanson [1958] p. 90.)

The conflict between the deductive, analytic inductive and retroductive accounts of theorising can to some extent be resolved by the familiar distinction between the psychology and logic of explanation; between the origin and validity of a proposition. Popper [1957] argues that 'it is irrelevant whether we have obtained our theories by jumping to unwarranted conclusions or merely by stumbling over them (that is, by "intuition") or else by some inductive procedure. The question: "How did you first *find* your theory?" relates, as it were, to an entirely private matter, as opposed to the question, "How did you test your theory?" which alone is scientifically relevant.'

To place such a heavy emphasis on the distinction between the context of discovery and the context of justification is however not warranted in the present state of sociology. The *source* of theoretical ideas is highly relevant for the development of the subject and deserves the fullest explication. The interplay of theory and data is a continuous one. The sociological imagination deserves to be encouraged from whatever source, and in whatever logical form it is expressed. There are different ways of bringing sociological theory and research into close and fruitful intercourse. A primary purpose of the material collected here is to explore and open up for discussion the different ways in which sociologists may 'theorise' in the course of empirical work.

Indeed, a paradox haunts sociological methodologists. The principles and logic of scientific explanation are codified and clearly set out in classic texts (cf. Braithwaite [1953], Popper [1959]). Yet as the later chapers in this book have from time to time suggested, the practice of sociological explanation seems to be rather different. Sociology has few universal statements which are recognised as having the status of general laws, although there are many well-established empirical generalisations. Theories too are often stated in a form that does not meet the ideal criteria of a science (cf. P. S. Cohen [1968] pp. 6–11). The paradox is that how sociologists theorise does not necessarily conform to how philosophers of social science say they should do so. In the search for intelligibility, pattern and organisation in social events and processes, the ways in which theory and inquiry interrelate to each other are more subtle than a commitment to deductive verification or falsification allows for. A number of accounts of the craft of social research, notably those contained in Phillip Hammond's collection *Sociologists at Work*, emphasise the extent to which there is continual interplay between theory and method.

An example from that collection will demonstrate the point. S. M. Lipset there describes the history of the research for *Union Democracy* (see further reading for Part 2) in which he, M. Trow and J. Coleman investigated the internal system of government of the International Typographical Union in New York. Their starting-point was the apparent contradiction between Michels's 'iron law of oligarchy' ('he who says "organisation" says "oligarchy"') and the internal political system of the I.T.U. which was run on a two-party oppositional basis, with a significant turnover of officials at national and local levels. Lipset's first attempt to explain this contradiction between theory and observation postulated that it was explicable in terms of the self-maintaining mechanism of a two-party system. A unique set of historical circumstances had set in motion a process by which two roughly equal groups fought each other within the union over a period of years, and in so doing institutionalised a number of features of representative government.

Michels had also hypothesised that membership of oligarchic organisations tended to be incompetent or unwilling to participate in the affairs of the organisation. So Lipset tried to explain the exceptionality of the I.T.U. in terms of the self-maintaining processes of the party system, opposition within the union serving to stimulate recruitment and train printers for internal party politics.

The striking point about Lipset's account of the evolution of this research, however, is that in the course of initial work in the field interviewing members of the New York Local of the union, Lipset largely revised his theoretical explanation of the phenomenon of internal self-government, and this in turn gave the inquiry a new direction. The reformulation took place when he realised the importance for the political system of the pattern of leisure relations among printers, and particularly the large number of voluntary associations – social clubs, athletic clubs, ex-army groups and so on – exclusively for printers. One way in which this came to his attention was through reading a number of bi-weekly newspapers published by printers for printers, but without any formal relationship to the union, which had a long history stretching back to about 1900.

Thus the earlier theoretical formulations were entirely revised to suggest that the men were tied to printing through their leisure activities, which in turn aided recruitment to the union political system; that these leisure activities fostered leadership and organisational skills outside union politics; and that they allowed the opportunity for interaction and political discussion outside the control of the union bureaucracy. The features were later summed up in the concept of 'occupational community', the defining characteristic of which was an overlap between the social relationships of work and the social relationships of leisure time.

This example supports the view that the search for intelligibility and pattern in the social world is a complex one in which the interplay of theory and data can not only test theories but lead to their complete reformulation. Had Lipset proceeded along strict verificationist lines it is conceivable that he would not have come up with the concept of 'occupational community' at all. Just as at the empirical level the findings of research may lead to questions about what is to be taken as obvious, at the theoretical level discoveries may be made which cannot be fitted into the verificationist account of the relationship between theory and investigation.

Edward Shils [1957] has shown how the interplay between his own research experience and established theory led him to discard, reformulate and rethink the different theories with which he was concerned as his experience with different sets of data brought into perspective different elements in the theories of Toennies, Cooley, Mayo, Schmalenbach, Lenin, Weber, Parsons and Sorel with which he was concerned. The process was a disjointed one.

> I have dared to tell this rambling tale of my intellectual wanderings because I have thought that it might help sociologists to obtain a more just conception of the collaboration of research and theory. I think that the prevailing conceptions of this collaboration are usually erroneous. The earlier view of a steady progress from particular facts to general theories has now been replaced by the more sophisticated image of a hypothesis, derived from a general theory, being tested by a systematic scrutiny of

particular facts: then the theory is either disconfirmed by the facts and is replaced by one more adequate to them or the hypothesis and corresponding theory are confirmed and the problem is settled. There are variations and complications of this latter schema but in all essentials this account of it is correct. It sees the relationship as an orderly process of truth. But in reality nothing could be less truthful than this picture of scientific growth.

The growth of knowledge is a disorderly movement. It is full of instances of things known and overlooked, unexpected emergencies, and rediscoveries of long-known facts and hypotheses which in the time of their original discovery had no fitting articulation and which found such articulation only after a considerable time. . . . It is an interesting question as to why sociologists hold this incorrect view of the relations between theory and research. Part of the difficulty arises from an erroneous conception of the nature of the growth of truth in physics, chemistry and the other well-established and esteemed sciences. Part of the error arises, however, from the position of the sociologists in the scientific community.

Sociologists are at present, despite their increased numbers and prosperity, a depressed class. They feel themselves outside the pale of the more reputable sciences and they wish very much to be within it. They look for their elevation to 'a theory' which will compel their general recognition. At the same time the theories which command attention in sociology are very abstract, very difficult to understand and even more difficult to use in the understanding of the world as we know it from our experience. They are especially difficult and probably impossible to use at present in the way in which sociologists think a scientific theory ought to be used.

These impediments do not make them valueless in advancing our understanding. Far from it. In order, however, for these theories to improve our understanding they must be deprived of their salvationary and even of their awe-inspiring character. Sociologists must cease to look upon them as finished products, waiting to be applied *in toto* in an orderly and systematic way. They must be taken as general guides and not as specific directives. They must be brought into operation only on the basis of a feeling of personal intimacy. They must be used only after an osmotic assimilation which involves discriminating acceptance

> and rejection, which rests on the sense of fitness and appropriateness rather than on any formal test. Although this counsel is full of pitfalls, I would say that sociologists will learn to use theory when they have also learned to trust their unconscious discriminatory powers. These might often be wrong, but without them there is little hope. Theory will bear fruit in sociology only when it has been assimilated into the perception of concrete and particular events and not as long as it is thought to be something which comes before and emerges from research (Shils [1957] pp. 144–5).

The context of the *discovery* of theoretical ideas, as distinct from their verification, is thus an important but neglected aspect of the research process. Research problems encountered in the sociology can be understood if a main theme of research is seen to be the struggle to make intelligible the complexities and contradictions of the empirical social world through theoretical insight and formulations developed out of or grounded in the subject-matter of their research. As Hammond [1964] observes: 'a common experience of social researchers is the sense of struggling with data so that conceptual schemes can be imposed. It is this imposition of conceptual order that distinguishes research from cataloguing. . . . Good specimens [of contemporary social inquiry] involve theory and research bound up as one.'

A number of autobiographical accounts of the conduct of sociological research confirm the picture provided by the contributors to Hammond's collection. These include Vidich, Bensman and Stein's *Reflections on Community Studies* [1964] (which also contains W. F. Whyte's classic account of his research for *Street Corner Society* [1981]), a special issue of *Sociological Inquiry* [1967] on 'The Craft of Sociology', *Sociological Self-Images*, edited by I. L. Horowitz [1970] (contains further autobiographical statements by well-known sociologists), and J. Fichter's reflections [1973] upon the research experiences of a Catholic sociologist. Among British sociologists, Basil Bernstein has provided ([1971] pp. 1–20) a fascinating autobiographical account of the development of his theoretical ideas about the sociology of language and learning, while Bell and Newby (eds) [1977] have attempted to produce a British version of Hammond. Banks [1979] has reflected on the links between theory and method in his own work. One chapter in this section focusses upon the discovery of theoretical ideas. Baldamus discusses the relationship between theoretical and empirical work and informal and formal processes, suggesting that significant interaction occurs between them, requiring the modification of conventional accounts of the processes of sociological research. In later work [1972, 1976] Baldamus has discussed the nature of discovery in social science using material from Hammond's collection.

Coser's chapter which closes the collection emphasises the interconnectedness of theory and method in a rather different way. It was given as his Presidential Address to the American Sociological Association. He points out, correctly, that methods are not ends in themselves but means to the end of greater sociological understanding of substantive issues. Methods of whatever kind should not be reified over and above their subject-matter. Good sociological work retains a concern with substantive significance, no matter how sophisticated the research strategies and techniques which are being employed. And this indeed is a highly appropriate note on which to end this collection. Theory, method and substance, ideas and research, are bound up one with another and cannot easily be separated. For pedagogical purposes, research methods may be treated as a separate topic of study. In the last analysis, however, the logic and procedures of research are an integral part of the sociological imagination which have to be used in conjunction with theories that are appropriate to the study of a particular substantive issue.

Further Reading

(1) N. R. Hanson, *Patterns of Discovery: An Inquiry into the Conceptual Foundations of Science* (Cambridge: Cambridge University Press, 1958). A discussion of the role of observation, fact, causality and theories in microphysical thinking which is of wide applicability and general interest. The clearest statement available of the logic of 'retroductive' explanation.

(2) P. E. Hammond (ed.), *Sociologists at Work: Essays on the Craft of Social Research* (New York: Basic Books, 1964). Thirteen sociologists chronicle in their own words their research experiences, with special attention being paid to the development of their theoretical ideas through the process of empirical investigation. Most styles of research – including historical and macroanalysis –

are represented. The collection is a uniquely important source for understanding the dynamics of the research process and what it means to call sociology a *craft.*

(3) Colin Bell and Howard Newby (eds), *Doing Sociological Research* (London: Allen & Unwin, 1977). An attempt to produce a British version of *Sociologists at Work.* Contains a lot of interesting insights, but overall the emphasis is too anecdotal and not enough attention is paid to the process of theorising.

(4) Burgess, R. G. (ed.), *The Research Process in Educational Settings: Ten Case Studies* (Lewes, Sussex: Falmer Press, 1984). First-hand autobiographical accounts by a group of sociologists of education about how they went about their own research, including attention to the process of theorising.

(5) J. Porter, 'Research Biography of a Macro-sociological Study: *The Vertical Mosaic*', in J. S. Coleman (ed.) *Macrosociology: Research and Theory* (Boston: Allyn & Bacon, 1970). A rare autobiographical account by Porter of the genesis of his major historical and comparative study of Canadian social structure *The Vertical Mosaic.* Particularly useful because few sociologists who have conducted empirical studies of whole societies or of macro-problems within or between societies have bothered to write about how they actually carried out the research.

(6) Edward Shils, 'The Calling of Sociology', in *The Calling of Sociology and Other Essays on the Pursuit of Learning* (Chicago: University of Chicago Press, 1980). A magisterial overview in essay form of the domain of sociology and the different types of sociology within it. Emphasises strongly the enduring connections between theory, method and substance.

(7) John Barnes, *Who Should Know What?: Social Science, Privacy and Ethics* (Cambridge: Cambridge University Press, 1980). A valuable study of the ethical and political context of social research. These issues have not (as indicated in the Preface) been considered here, but they are of fundamental importance. See also Sjoberg [1967], Diener and Crandall [1978], and Beauchamp *et al.* (eds) [1982]. Case studies of Project Camelot (Horowitz (ed.) [1967]) and of the Moynihan Report (Rainwater and Yancey [1967]) provide further key reading on the subject. The organisation of social research is discussed in Roth [1966], O'Toole [1971] and specifically in relation to British sociology by Platt [1975] and Shipman (ed.) [1976].

Finally, three rather different works are useful in their own way to the sociologist interested in method.

(8) Gerry Rose, *Deciphering Sociological Research* (London: Macmillan, 1982) provides a clear guide to how to read and analyse a piece of published research. A refreshing approach to the teaching of research methods.
(9) Patrick McC. Miller and Michael Wilson, *A Dictionary of Social Science Methods* (Chichester: Wiley, 1983). Useful reference work covering the whole field of research methods, with a somewhat quantitative and statistical bias in its coverage.
(10) M. Bulmer and R. G. Burgess (eds), *The Teaching of Research Methodology*, special issue of *Sociology*, vol. 15, no. 4, November 1981, pp. 477–602. The proceedings of a conference on problems of teaching research methods to British postgraduate students in sociology, which covers a wide range of topics: course content, assessment, effectiveness for employment and how to teach different styles of research. Includes a 12-page bibliography.

17 The Category of Pragmatic Knowledge in Sociological Analysis*

W. Baldamus

(1) Sociological Analysis[1]

There have been a number of new developments in the methodology of social science. One of them is the emergence of a new field, vaguely called 'sociological analysis'. The aim of this chapter is to contribute towards a sharper delineation of this field. The present usage of the term is still very uncertain and therefore difficult to summarise. One could say, however, in general that all discussions of this kind are in one way or another striving towards a closer integration of theory and research. Many attempts have been made to find out how general theory could be made more realistic. The words 'realistic', 'social reality', 'real structure', 'real type' are used in such discussions with increasing frequency and also with a sense of urgency. But the boxes thus labelled are as yet rather empty. For example the concept of real-type analysis is used to suggest some sort of contrast to the method of theory building by means of ideal-type constructs. Although there has been much controversy about ideal-type theory[2] the one thing that is unquestionable about

*Reprinted from *Archives for the Philosophy of Law and Social Philosophy*, 53 (1967) pp. 31–49, with the permission of the publishers and the author.

Weber's intentions is that an ideal type is *not* a statistical mode representing a cluster of observable real entities in a given frequency distribution.[3] One accepts therefore that real types will turn out to be something in the nature of clustered entities that *are* observable (statistically or otherwise). Hence, while ideal types are fictitiously constructed in the 'imagination' of the social scientist,[4] it is believed that real types can be found or discovered in the real world. But all this is dubious and, as we shall see, it needs to be examined carefully whether 'discoveries' are possible at all in the social sciences.[5] I am taking the view that even real types involve necessarily an element of subjective meaning (in Weber's sense) and that therefore they are not in diametrical contrast to the construction of ideal types.[6] This is so because all the concepts of the social scientist are ultimately derived from concepts of pragmatic knowledge.

In general the emancipation of sociological analysis as a separate approach seems largely a consequence of the growing recognition that there is no longer a clear difference between empirical and theoretical modes of sociological inquiry.[7] We may recall that the traditional hostility between theoreticians and empiricists has been more violent in the development of modern sociology than in any other social science. It reached a climax and also a turning-point about 1959 when C. Wright Mills attacked simultaneously and with equal force both 'grand theory' (illustrated by Talcott Parsons's work), and 'abstracted empiricism' (with reference to Lazarsfeld's research). Eloquently, if somewhat naïvely on epistemological grounds, he demonstrated the increasing sterility of the controversy. By stressing the creative aspects of scientific work he was among the first to place a new emphasis on value commitments and relevance as against the conventional concern with formalistic methodology. As often happens in social development an apparently insoluble conflict had thus been removed by making it irrelevant in the light of other developments superseding or bypassing it. To many the old debate seemed suddenly to have lost most of its importance. The ancient habit of contrasting general theory and empirical work, although deeply institutionalised in the traditional organisation of teaching and investigation, had lost its vitality. Much of the impact of Mills's exhortations, of course, was due to the fact that *in the practice* of sociological investigation the crucial interaction between fact-finding and theorising had never been seriously questioned.

But despite the growing concern with questions of sociological analysis and the growing conviction that a new 'style' of sociological thinking is emerging, much of it remains obscure and ineffective on account of a number of technical difficulties which persist to confuse the discussion. For example, there is as yet an excessive emphasis on philosophical and epistemological side-issues. Above all, although those interested in the new development agree, negatively, that there cannot be an essential difference between theoretical and empirical sociology, nobody seems to be able to state in positive and exact terms what precisely the two approaches have in common. Nor is there any agreement about how such an intangible and immensely complicated subject could be taught. Traditionally the manner in which research procedures as well as techniques of theory-construction are taught amounts to little more than treating the student as a sort of apprentice who is expected to acquire the skills of the trade by way of constant practice, that is to say, intuitively and mechanically.

Among the ideas that were – by the end of the fifties – relatively well established was the notion that relevance, both theoretical and empirical, depended very much on the intrusion of *noncognitive* or nonrational factors such as unexpressed value premises. Thus the apparent elusiveness of the common substance of theoretical and empirical methods was then mainly connected with the difficulty of identifying the exact nature of the process by which such elements are infused into the social scientist's work. Hardly any progress has been made in this area. While the commitment to values is admitted to be indispensable, no answer has been found to the question as to how the distorting effect of values on scientific work may be traced and controlled. There is merely a tenuous notion that somehow, ultimately, the hard facts of 'reality' will assert themselves over the kind of biased perception which stems from value-orientations. But since the distinction between 'fact' and 'theory' has become blurred, no solution can be expected on this basis. Evidently the value-problem must be postponed until we have achieved a better understanding of the interaction between theorising and fact-finding. The enormous difficulties created by the present position should not be underestimated: if there was really no substantial difference between theoretical and empirical inquiry, then we could no longer expect empirical studies to be value-free, moreover we could no longer appeal to 'the facts' in trying to demonstrate the distorting effect of values on theory.

The nature of these questions explains why, almost suddenly, a fresh interest in the sociology of knowledge has arisen.[8] I am referring particularly to the remarkable expansion of a special distinctively empirical field to which sociologists and social anthropologists have made important contributions - the sociology of science.[9] Although, oddly enough, these studies restrict themselves to the *natural* sciences, their main concern does in fact turn on the role of noncognitive factors. For instance they focus on questions such as the simultaneity of discoveries, on the large complex of the social and cultural context of the origin and the diffusion of inventions, on the determinants of scientific 'productivity' or 'creativity', on an explanation of differential rates of scientific development, career patterns of scientists and technologists and studies on the self-conception of scientists.

(2) Organisation and Social Inquiry

If we extrapolate these trends we should have to extend the sociology of science into sociological studies on the *social* sciences. This points to a formidable task of quite unexpected proportions, a task which is certainly unmanageable at present. Would it lead to a sociology of sociology where sociologists interview each other about the values they project into their own investigations? Would it be possible to develop methods of sociological analysis that are equally applicable to the natural and the social sciences, thus exploring their common grounds? The most obvious danger here is the temptation to trespass into epistemology and logic. It should be noted, however, that this danger has so far not been very serious: the sociology of science developed independently of, and side by side with, the philosophy of science.[10]

In groping my way towards this new task I shall begin by making use of an approach borrowed from organisation theory. It is obvious, at least superficially, that scientific work has something in common with processes of administrative organisation. We might therefore use these as a sort of model to visualise the more obscure aspects of the noncognitive factors mentioned earlier. That is to say, empirical research activity and theory construction alike may be seen to be a specific form of *discontinuous trial-and-error processes* similar to the kind of decision-making activities with which we are familiar in the realm of administration in business, government and so on. For example a great deal is now known about the connection between formal and informal organisation. This opens up the possibility of representing the unknown connection between cognitive (=formal) and noncognitive (=informal) aspects of 'mental production processes' in a similar manner. Above all a further implication of this model is that both fact-finding and theory-construction might be approached not as things or finished end-products, but as a *process through time.* In so far we are in fact dealing with the 'work'-process of scientific inquiry. As a result we shall move towards an approach that is quite different from the conventional methodology of social science where the main emphasis has always been on the manifest, formalised, objective, observable end-products, not on the actual production process of theorising and researching itself.

Although the dichotomy of formal and informal process has recently come under criticism in organisation theory, I think it will still be useful as a point of departure in the context of social-science work activities. Its application is very simple. I shall treat the published result of theoretical and empirical work – in so far as it is controlled by articulated procedural rules – as 'formal' aspects, the preparatory and exploratory stages of such work, on the other hand, as 'informal' aspects. As regards the latter, we shall be able to lean to some extent on the sociology of (natural) science. We can ask for instance: in which sense has there been any cumulative 'progress' in sociology or in the social sciences generally? Are there 'discoveries' and if so how do they come about? Thus as soon as one begins to look at the social scientist's work process as a phenomenon worth investigating, questions come into view that seem to threaten a great deal of what hitherto has been taken for granted. Among them is the problem of scientific 'creativity'. Again it is very odd that while this question has become increasingly important in the sociology of natural science[11] no systematic empirical work has been done on creative work in the *social* sciences. It is probable therefore that this kind of question will lead to a revision of current opinon concerning the difference and the similarity of natural and social science.[12]

It need hardly be stressed that even if we manage to keep out philosophy we are facing stupendous difficulties. At the moment we barely know how to formulate the questions. My first objective will be to simplify the main issues. For the rest I shall pursue a few

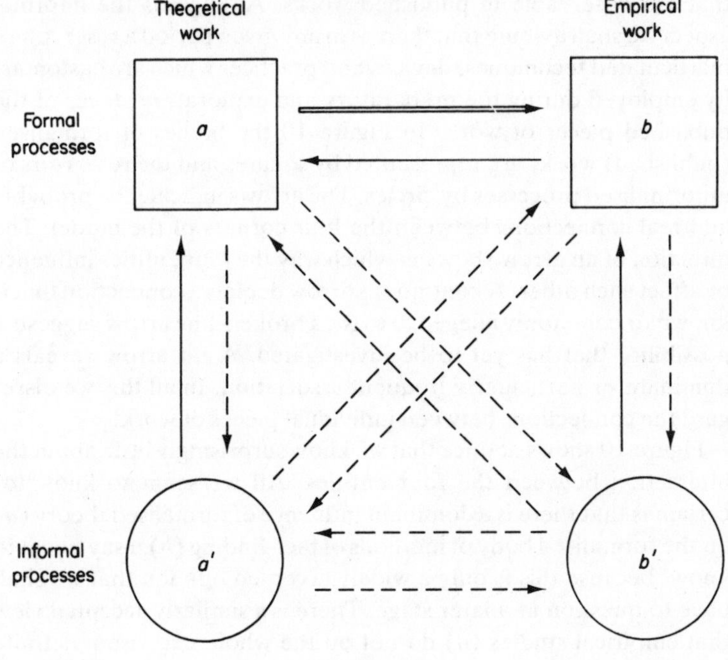

FIGURE 10

selected lines of inquiry that would seem reasonably manageable with available resources. The organisational model (Figure 10) will be used only to map out the overall problem area, it will have to be discarded later on.[13] In terms of graph theory the model depicts the possible connections between two sorts of criteria (a) the conventional distinction between 'theoretical' and 'empirical' work – it reflects the widely accepted belief that there exists a division of labour between those social scientists who specialise in the production of general theories and those who devote themselves to empirical investigations; (b) the dichotomy of 'formal' and 'informal' process mentioned earlier on. The model links together, for a given period, the existing body of theoretical work and the corresponding body of empirical work, each comprising the contributions of numerous individual scientists. At the same time we note that these bodies have a formal as well as an informal aspect. The formal one may be visualised as the procedures of theorising and fact-finding that are observable in published works. As regards the informal aspect we shall assume that there is in any given period a reservoir of inarticulated techniques, devices and practices which are customarily employed during the preparatory and exploratory stages of the published pieces of work. In Figure 10 the bodies of formalised (published) works are represented by squares and the reservoirs of unformalised processes by circles. The arrows indicate the probable and real connections between the four corners of the model. The direction of an arrow shows in which way the four entities influence or affect each other. A continuous arrow depicts a connection that is known or commonly alleged to exist; a broken-line arrow suggests a possibility that has yet to be investigated. A fat arrow reveals a dominant or particularly frequent association. In all this we disregard the connections between individual pieces of work.

Figure 10 shows at once that we know surprisingly little about the interaction between the four entities. All we seem to know for certain is that there is a dominant influence of formalised theory (a) on the formalised body of methods of fact-finding (b). I say 'seem to know' because this is only a widely accepted opinion that we shall have to question at a later stage. There is a similarly accepted view that empirical studies (b) do not on the whole exercise a definite influence on general theory (a). The other two unbroken arrows express the fact that the informal preparatory activities (a' and b') influence or determine the finished end-products as they appear in publications (a, respectively b). The right broken-line arrows suggest various possibilities that will have to be explored as we go along. It is possible for instance that certain informally used techniques of fact-finding exercise some influence on formal theory (b' affects a). Or one might plausibly argue that informal theorising (a'), such as intuitively performed conceptualisation, contributes to the shaping of published empirical studies (b). It is feasible that there is some sort of interaction between informal theorising (a') and informal fact-finding (b'). All this is hypothetical and vague. The matter is further complicated by the possibility of multiple connections: b' may affect b, and b in turn may have an influence on a; a' might determine b', and b' could impinge upon b and so on. To find out what relevance might be attached to these hypothetical connections we shall have to identify the nature of the four processes. In view of the size of this task I can only pursue a few lines of exploration, those that seem to me most profitable. To start with I shall concentrate on a crucial element in informal fact-finding (b'), the role of *'pragmatic knowledge'*. This element impinges, as we shall see, to some extent also upon b, a' and a. Initially the main direction of the analysis will be from the right-hand bottom corner of Figure 10 toward the left-hand corner at the top.

(3) Common Sense and Pragmatic Knowledge

I am taking my clue from an apparently very simple idea which is much taken for granted in discussion on general theory, the contrast between common sense and scientific thinking. It is often assumed that the purpose of a sophisticated scientific theory is to supersede common-sense thought. It is thereby implied that the latter is a sort of inferior knowledge or even something that cannot be classified as knowledge at all. It has been known however for a long time that the concepts used in everyday life involve a considerable degree of abstraction and are by no means simple. With special relevance to the social sciences, A. Schutz has demonstrated convincingly that our theoretical concepts are necessarily founded upon 'the thought objects constructed by the common-sense thought of man living his everyday life among his fellowmen'; thus we are in fact using 'constructs of the second degree, namely constructs of the constructs made by the actors on the social scene . . .'.[14] This means that the raw material out of which the social scientist builds his conceptual framework is given to him already in a prefabricated form. He does not deal with pure 'facts' but always only with interpreted facts. We can therefore utilise this observation as a first step towards dissolving the misleading dichotomy of 'theory versus fact'.

For it follows that formal theory, to obtain its data, does not depend on formal empirical studies: it can make use of common-sense observations. Indeed in a sense it is even preferable for the theorist to operate with common-sense knowledge instead of utilising material from empirical works because the concepts developed in such works are themselves derived from common-sense thoughts and would present, inside the theoretical frame, merely third-order categories. Recalling our model we may say that the path from b' to a is preferable to the path b' b a for it offers a more direct connection. As it happens this supposition is confirmed by actual practice. If we take Talcott Parsons's *The Social System* as a prominent example of a highly formalised general theory, we find that the use of common knowledge and common-sense experience is far more frequent and more important than any reference to specific empirical investigations. It is clear therefore on this basis why formal theory is on the whole not built upon the results of formal empirical studies. Such results may be used, however, after they are translated back into common-sense expressions.

By a similar argument we should expect that the constructs of general theory have only a limited usefulness to the empirical researcher. If theory is founded upon common-sense experience it would seem to be safer, as it were, for him to go directly to the sources of the theorist, instead of taking over his concepts. But this conclusion can be mentioned here only in passing. It contradicts so radically the conventional view of the relation between theory and research – depicted by the fat arrow from left to right in the upper part of Figure 10 – that it will have to be examined more closely at a later stage.

I hope it is clear by now that my approach is sociological and not epistemological. I am trying to look at the *behaviour* of social scientists in terms of mutual influence, interaction and so on. That the bulk of such interaction happens to be impersonal (through the medium of scientific vocabularies) does not invalidate my method. Nevertheless the peculiar nature of these interaction processes creates certain difficulties. We cannot fully understand them from their external appearances unless we take also the content into account. That is to say we can only restrict, but not altogether omit, problems which arise from variations in the validity of concepts. If the scientist's raw material consists of common-sense interpretations of the real world, we must concede that these are sometimes in some sense valid. We must assume that common-sense views contain, at least potentially, an element of truth. But this is all we need. We shall assume, in other words, that the theoretician's and the researcher's conceptions are merely a refinement, for example a more rigorous statement of common-sense notions. This implies that the available stock of common-sense thought includes certain types of 'knowledge'.[15] One of them is what I propose to call 'pragmatic knowledge'.

The idea occurred to me a few years ago in connection with operations research in its application to business administration. It appeared that in the case of comparatively simple problems, under favourable circumstances, the results of administrative trial-and-error processes are identical to those obtained by mathematical methods (such as linear programming).[16] Here the only difference between common-sense thought and scientific procedure lies in the degree of systematisation. Subsequently I found the concept of pragmatic knowledge indispensable in describing larger areas of organisational decision-making, so as to grasp the importance of purely cognitive processes fused into administrative action.[17] Recently I noticed that a similar concept, 'practical knowledge', has been developed by Hans Neisser in his essay *On the Sociology of Knowledge* ([1965] pp. 24–8, 34–50). He shows that the definition of this concept is beset with a number of unexpected difficulties. Tentatively it approximates the 'human know-how' that though obtained pragmatically rather than through scientific method yet reveals a sufficient degree of 'certainty' to distinguish it from marginal knowledge (p. 24). Neisser's concern with practical knowledge stems from his aim to extend the scope of the sociology of knowledge beyond its traditional subject matter, the analysis of political-ideological knowledge. While this new point of departure appears to me immensely fruitful, my own interest in the phenomenon of practical knowledge is somewhat different, and in order to indicate this I will use the narrower term 'pragmatic knowledge'. It refers to the stock of knowledge in *modern* society that is generated as a latent (unintended) *by-product* of organisational behaviour. Scientific knowledge, by contrast, originates within social institutions the manifest function of which is the production and diffusion of knowledge. On this basis it will be possible to avoid the difficult criterion of certainty or degree of certainty.

It is significant, I think, that the new interest in practical and pragmatic knowledge has shown itself first in a roundabout way: in the analysis of *ignorance*.[18] While sociological theory normally disregards the actor's knowledge, because knowing is different from acting, it *has* concerned itself with the actor's ignorance since this is related to false or biased beliefs etc. It is in this sense that Moore and Tumin suggest that 'ignorance must be viewed not simply as a passive or dysfunctional condition, but as an active and often positive element in operating structures and relations'.[19] But if ignorance may have a positive or negative function surely the same goes for its opposite, namely knowledge? In an incisive discussion on the role of ignorance in sociological theory Louis Schneider recognises this possibility: 'As, let us say, actors follow their self-interest, they apply such knowledge pertinent to problem-solution as they can discover. This knowledge becomes "built-into" their behaviour. Its background in original problem solution is often forgotten, and the behaviour founded on knowledge is then transmitted from one generation to another simply as normative: so one must do.'[20] I would merely add here that we should expect pragmatic knowledge of this kind becoming increasingly important with the growth and the complexity of rational organisation in modern society.[21]

Returning to the model, it follows that pragmatic knowledge cannot be part of the interaction processes between the four points. As soon as it becomes assimilated by any one of these processes it has changed into scientific knowledge. Pragmatic knowledge surrounds the model, so to speak, from outside. It belongs to the external environment supporting the production of theoretical and empirical inquiries. It is the chief medium through which the scientist gains access to social reality. The role of this environment may be studied in a number of ways. I shall confine myself to what I think is its most important aspect: the effects of *changes* in the content of pragmatic knowledge, including particularly the innovating effect of new conceptions and experiences. Even this limited objective is bound to be vague and uncertain at the present stage. To make it more tangible I shall begin with a concrete example.

(4) Non-normative Constraints

The most central aspect of current sociological theory is still the concept of social norms. Although in recent years sociologists have become increasingly sceptical about the dominant place assigned to this concept (or its related elements such as roles, expectations, rule of conduct etc.),[22] it is as yet widely maintained that the main achievement of modern (functional) theory lies in the discovery that the stability of a given social order derives from the constraining power of norms to define morally approved conduct. It is true, if we gauge the progress of sociological theory over sufficiently long periods, that the idea of normative order as a conceptual tool has proved to be remarkably incisive. However on closer inspection considerable difficulties appear as soon as the concept is used in (formal) empirical studies. The reason for this is that in the theory one particular element of normatively controlled conduct is deliberately overemphasised: the function of conformity to normally approved rules of conduct. This is done of course to isolate the specifically sociological paradigm of inquiry (as different, for example, from the socio-psychological approach). Obviously in the real world a situation may have a number of other stability-generating properties. As these are not the object of sociological inquiry they have to be disregarded even if on common-sense grounds they seem important.

The analysis of pragmatic knowledge permits us to examine this question in a new light. As indicated earlier on, an understanding of common-sense thought requires lower levels of abstraction than established theory. At first sight this might seem to be a simple matter of making the general theory more specific by adding, step by step, additional elements until the necessary degree of concreteness is reached. Or as G. Poggi in a recent critique of Parsonian theory has put it: we would have to introduce certain 'extra-unit' conceptions so as to obtain a relevant definition of the kind of social action that is determined by pragmatic knowledge.[23] However, Poggi appears to be aware that the problem is far more difficult than that. What the difficulties are can best be seen if we try the method as far as it goes.

We could argue that whatever the nature of pragmatic knowledge will turn out to be, the term suggests that it is in some way concerned with the actor's definition to a concrete situation; it will be a kind of knowledge or experience that incorporates what is sometimes called 'external' or 'situational' constraints. At the same time, as for the moment we want to maintain the logical connection with functional-structural theory, it must also contain social normative elements. Now it is surprisingly (and suspiciously) easy to think of examples that seem to fulfil these conditions. They are evidently in the nature of normative definitions of the situation. Indeed some of the earliest and most striking observations on social norms come readily to mind, such as the famous rules of the bank-wirers in the Western Electric experiments. The rule 'you must not be a rate-buster' expresses the normative aspect by the word "must" in conjunction with the social stigma attached, in the circumstances of work groups, to the word 'rate-buster'. The situational element reveals itself in the underlying concept of wage-rates or wage system, for it is obvious that the context of appropriate, fair or acceptable piece-rates. The participants in this situation can maintain the behaviour prescribed by the rule only in so far as they have sufficient knowledge of how the wage-system works – including the process of so called 'rate-cutting'. Not only that, this piece of pragmatic knowledge must be correct. This shows that the stability of social interaction under such conditions is by no means determined solely by the normative element, as one would assume on the basis of orthodox theory; the situation derives already a certain amount of stability owing to the existence of a particular kind of wage regulation. In other words the notion of 'rate-busting' represents a crossing-point between the internal social system of the work group and the external economic system of the wage mechanism. Thus what seemed to be a pure social norm turns out to be in fact a *mixture* of social and economic constraints on behaviour.

Many other examples come readily to mind. Clearly non-normative constraints are not confined to the economic system. A similar and equally important area of mixed normative and non-normative controls on behaviour is the legal system. Here, as a matter of fact, the fusion of the two aspects in practical affairs is so pervasive that sociologists have only gradually become aware of it.[24] The situation is very much the same in respect of the interlocking between technological constraints and social norms. The most tangible evidence of this can be found wherever the praxis is concerned with technological optima. The definitions of 'optimum' capacity, operation, size, speed, efficiency and so on. Again only recently have sociologists begun to look into this direction.[25] It is obvious that here the relation between normative and non-normative constraints is far more complex than in my example of work behaviour. I have chosen deliberately a comparatively simple illustration to make the implications more striking.

This is not the place to attempt a substantial analysis of the problem. I am discussing here only the methodological aspect. Even so it should be fairly obvious from the foregoing that a great deal of contemporary theory is less relevant to empirical studies than the frequent and all too convenient reference to its central constructs would suggest.

The question arises now, what is in fact the function of social norms if it is not solely and simply one of maintaining social order? Let us look once more at the example of the bank-wirer's norms. To discover the net effect of the normative element we would have to find out what would happen if the stability of the situation was supported merely by the wage system. This assumes that the wage earners have no knowledge of what constitutes, in the light of their sectional interests, the appropriate wage rate. Hence they would have to change their behaviour continuously in order to test, as it were, different experiences pragmatically. One might visualise this as a kind of lengthy and confusing process of learning which involves a certain amount of erratic movements. The situation as a whole and in the long run would still be stable on account of the wage mechanism. But the operation of this mechanism would be cruder and slower than it would be with the help of normative factors. Briefly, therefore, we can say that the function of social norms is a refinement of the situational (economic, technological etc.) constraints.

The importance of this difference will be underestimated unless the full complexity of a normatively structured situation is taken into account. A number of investigations on work-group behaviour have shown that a strategic variable in the context of industrial relations is the conception of 'fairness' or 'justice' as applied to the prevailing conditions of work and the amount of pay.[26] All wage payments, disregarding whether the method is piece rates or time rates, are defined as acceptable or unacceptable in respect of the amount and the technical and administrative conditions of work. Jobs as a whole, or particular features of the work situation (such as specific wage rates, hours of work, pace of work etc.) are defined as 'good' or 'bad' according to how the balance between rewards and deprivations is interpreted. A good deal about this has come to light through studies on restriction of output, strikes, absenteeism and other forms of instability, and it is widely accepted that these phenomena are manifestations of stresses which are caused by a maladjustment in the relationship of rewards and work deprivations. It is however not recognised that a more precise treatment is required in order to assess the stabilising net effect of the normative factors.

For an adequate analysis of this problem we must observe that the relevant norms do no more than set minimum or maximum boundary conditions for the 'appropriate' action. In the case of industrial work situations there are in general four different normative boundaries of this kind:

(1) the actor has some idea as to what constitutes the minimum money income required for his standard of living;

(2) there is also a norm, although usually less clearly articulated, about the maximum income which he ought not to exceed;

(3) his conduct in terms of acceptable working conditions – rate of work, average effort, amount and distribution of hours and so on – is restricted by an upper limit;

(4) there is also a minimum norm about exertion, effort and so on which expresses some sense of duty towards other workers, his employer or society at large.

It is unquestionable that in each of these basic norms there is an objective, external, situational element present. They are not 'pure' social norms but normative interpretations of the technical, physical, legal and economic properties of the situation. Moreover there is evidently a connection between them. According to our accustomed analytical thinking, we would look at all this as a 'social system'; we would argue that the various norms are so interrelated with each other as to secure the stability and the solidarity of the work group. On closer inspection, however, the kind of 'system' which emerges here is in fact no more than an upshot of the industrial environment of the group. In other words as soon as we analyse what appears to be a typical group phenomenon into its constituent elements, we find that the structuring mechanism is essentially *not* a social process but one that is rooted in the larger external system.

This observation has a number of implications for the questions which we set out to tackle. Going back to the classical tradition of sociological theorising, the emphasis on 'subjective meaning' as a fundamental element in social action reveals itself as an idealisation: a deliberate overemphasis for the sake of securing a logically coherent, specifically sociological, frame of analysis.

It is a procedure that eventually comes up against residual phenomena that remain inexplicable within its chosen conceptual framework. But as we have seen these residuals are not randomly distributed. They have a logic of their own, they are interconnected by some other system, a non-sociological system. In so far as it is usual and justified to describe a given theory as a form of idealisation, and its limitations according as lack of realism, we obtain here a first glimpse of what we are looking for: the kind of 'real structure' that we wish to associate with the notion of real-type analysis.

But there is another implication in the connection between normative definitions and pragmatic knowledge. What seems to be happening here is that the relevant elements of the situation are, from the viewpoint of the investigator, observable, non-subjective factual properties. They are in the nature of 'hard facts'. But they are in common-sense forms experienced and described by the actors in such a way that a normative evaluation is projected into them. The conception of an appropriate standard of consumption, a fair wage, a decent standard of living, a reasonable profit margin is at once a cognitive definition and a moral judgement. That is to say it manifests itself as a kind of knowledge. This is quite clear from the way in which these definitions are acquired: they are learned in the process of socialisation where the newcomer or the apprentice absorbs a certain vocabulary in which knowledge and values, knowing and believing, are fused into each other.

Moreover the cognitive element is more pronounced than the normative evaluation; as a rule the latter will barely be conscious at all.

If that is so the question arises whether this sort of knowledge has any degree of explanatory validity. At this point it will be most difficult to free ourselves from the habitual approach of the professional sociologist. The frame of mind of scientific inquiry presupposes from the outset that there cannot be any explanatory system (within a given discipline) other than that which the scientist brings to bear on his observations. The possibility that the very subjects whose behaviour we observe, measure or analyse, do maintain explanatory views does not arise, at least not as a relevant proposition. Indeed there is a tendency to assume that if there is such explanatory knowledge its latent characteristic is to be false in the sense of prejudice, convention, bias, lore, ideology and so on. The very notion of 'subjective meaning' of action implies a non-realistic, more or less distorted interpretation of the actor's world.

To overcome this tendency of restricting the concept of knowledge to scientifically testable knowledge, we should bear in mind that the recent trend in research theory emphasises the dynamic, trial-and-error, essentially heuristic aspect of scientific work. In so far, therefore, the contrast to pragmatic knowledge is no longer so marked. The same is true on account of the fact that the pursuit of scientific knowledge is now increasingly seen as a form of activity rather than a contemplative state of mind, an activity that includes non-rational impulses, value-orientations and prejudice. The only important difference to pragmatic knowledge that remains is the use of specially designed methods and techniques of knowledge-generating observation.

Our discussion points to the conclusion that the scientific status of social science is less secure than its recent growth and prestige would suggest. This applies particularly to sociology. We have drawn attention to four main reasons for the growing uneasiness about this situation.

(1) There is no longer a reliable difference between theory construction and empirical work. A great deal of what has hitherto been taken for granted about scientific procedure is therefore uncertain.

(2) It has become increasingly noticeable that in the practice of sociological work formal methods of theorising and fact-finding are invariably supplemented by informal devices of trial and error. If we combine the two distinctions: theory-research and formal–informal, into a model of social (scientific) inquiry, a number of important methodological questions arise that are at present unanswerable.

(3) Among them is the role of constructs derived from common sense and pragmatic knowledge. These phenomena set up a barrier between scientific thought and observation on the one hand and social reality on the other.

(4) A re-examination of the central concept of social norms suggests the existence of cognitive processes in the realm of pragmatic knowledge which appear to have been neglected in the past. Hence the prerogative of sociological science to produce social knowledge is in doubt.

Of course these conclusions are tentative. They are meant to direct current methodology into unexplored avenues. The most urgent need seems to me this. If it is true that much of social science is less scientific than neo-positivistic views would have us believe, then we are faced with a paradox. Looking at the long-term development of any one of the social sciences, we can be reasonably certain that it manifests something in the nature of overall advancement. Although difficult to measure, sufficient evidence could be assembled to demonstrate that this trend does exist at least in a number of important problem areas. Our doubts about the objectivity and fruitfulness of orthodox scientific procedures conflict therefore with what we seem to know on other grounds. One way or another we are forced to find an explanation for these grounds.

18 Two Methods in Search of a Substance*

Lewis A. Coser

I am perturbed about present developments in American sociology which seem to foster the growth of both narrow, routine activities, and of sect-like, esoteric ruminations. While on the surface these two trends are dissimilar, together they are an expression of crisis and fatigue within the discipline and its theoretical underpinnings. I shall attempt to express bluntly certain of my misgivings and alarms about these recent trends in our common enterprise; let the chips fall where they may.

Building on other students of science, Crane [1972] has argued that scientific disciplines typically go through various stages of growth accompanied by a series of changes in the characteristics of scientific knowledge and of the scientific community involved in the study of the area. In stage one, important discoveries provide models for future work and attract new enthusiastic scientists. In the next stage, a few highly productive scientists recruit and train students, set priorities for research and maintain informal contacts with one another. All this leads to rapid growth in both membership and publications. But in later stages the seminal ideas become

*Non-exclusive permission to reprint the following material: Lewis A. Coser, 'Presidential Address: Two Methods in Search of a Substance', *American Sociological Review*, vol. 40 (1975) pp. 691–700.

exhausted and the original theories no longer seem sufficient. At this point a gradual decline in both membership and publication sets in, and those who remain develop increasingly narrow, specialised, though often methodologically highly refined, interests. Unless fresh theoretical leads are produced at this point to inspire new growth, the field gradually declines.

Such stages of growth and decline are, of course, not limited to the sciences. In other spheres of culture, religion and the arts for example, similar phenomena have been observed (cf. O'Dea [1966]; Weber [1963]; Kroeber [1957]). One need only think of the creative effervescence in the communities of Christ's immediate disciples and their direct successors in contrast to quotidian routines and ritualised devotions of the later stages in what had now become the Church of Rome. Or consider the art of Byzantine icon painting where, after the early creative period, the same motives, even techniques, were endlessly repeated so that it takes a specialist to distinguish between paintings executed not just decades but even centuries apart. In religion and the arts, however, innovation is not a necessary condition for flowering and appeal, but in the sciences, when no innovation is forthcoming *rigor mortis* is not far away.

The findings of Crane and others in the sociology of science typically refer not to a whole branch of knowledge but only to sub-fields within such branches. It would therefore be wrong to apply these findings to sociology as a whole, composed as it is of a wide variety of sub-areas each with its own pattern and rhythm of growth. Yet permit me nevertheless roughly, and perhaps rashly, to sketch what I consider the present condition of sociology as a whole.

By and large, we are still in the second stage of growth, the stage of lively development, of creative ability, and innovative effervescence. Yet there now appear a number of danger signs suggesting that the fat years of the past may be followed by lean years, by years of normal science with a vengeance, in which not only the mediocre minds but even the minds of the best are hitched to quotidian endeavors and routine activities. This seems portended by the recent insistence among many sociologists on the primacy of precise measurement over substantive issues.

The germ of the idea for this chapter came to me when a friend of mine, the editor of a major sociological journal, explained with some pride that, no matter what the substantive merits of the chapter might be, he would refuse to accept contributions using old-fashioned tabular methods rather than modern techniques of regression and path analysis. I gather, for I have respect for his opinion, that he meant that he would not accept articles requiring modern methods of data analysis that do not make use of such techniques. Yet, though his intentions are undoubtedly excellent, I submit that such an orientation is likely to have a dynamic of its own and that, inadvertently perhaps, it will lead to a situation where the methodological tail wags the substantive dog, where as Bierstedt [1974, p. 316] once put it, methods would be considered the independent and substantive issues the dependent variable.

My friend's voice is, of course, not a lonely one. In fact, he expressed what is tacitly assumed or openly asserted by a growing number of our colleagues. Fascinated by new tools of research, such as computers, that have come to be available in the last decades, and spellbound by the apparently irresistible appeal of techniques that allow measures of a precision hitherto unattainable, many of our colleagues are in danger of forgetting that measurements are, after all, but a means toward better analysis and explanation. If concepts and theoretical notions are weak, no measurement, however precise, will advance an explanatory science.

The fallacy of misplaced precision consists in believing that one can compensate for theoretical weakness by methodological strength. Concern with precision in measurement before theoretical clarification of what is worth measuring and what is not, and before one clearly knows what one is measuring, is a roadblock to progress in sociological analysis. Too many enthusiastic researchers seem to be in the same situation as Saint Augustine when he wrote, on the concept of time, 'For so it is O Lord, My God, I measure it but what it is I measure I do not know' (Saint Augustine [1953] p. 35).

No doubt, modern methods of research have immeasurably advanced sociological inquiry. Only sociological Luddites would argue that computers be smashed and path diagrams outlawed. What I am concerned with is not the uses but rather the abuses of these instruments of research. They serve us well in certain areas of inquiry, but they can become Frankenstein monsters when they are applied indiscriminately and, above all, when their availability dictates the problem choices of the investigator so that trivial problems are treated with the utmost refinement.

The sheer availability of new methods encourages their use and seems to release the user from the obligation to decide whether his problem or findings are worthy of attention. By way of illustrating this let me quote from the summary of a recent paper by Oksanen and Spencer [1975] in one of the official journals of our Association, *The American Sociologist*: 'A rather large degree of explanatory power has been achieved by our regression model, in terms of overall goodness of fit and in terms of significant variables. It is of considerable interest to learn that high school performance is an invariably significant indicator of "success" in the [college] courses examined.' Kaplan's [1964, p. 28) delightful formulation of the Law of the Instrument comes to mind here: 'Give a small boy a hammer, and he will find that everything he encounters needs pounding.'

The fact is that, though in principle these new methods and technologies could help us achieve greater theoretical sophistication, they are used as 'magic helpers', as a shortcut to, or even replacement for, theoretical analysis rather than as a means for furthering it. An insistence on the use of these refined methods, no matter what, makes it fall prey to Kaplan's law.

It would be easy, and perhaps entertaining, to go on quoting similar instances, but each of us can easily supply other examples. Let me instead return to the serious problems now faced by our discipline, many of which have been created, or at least accentuated, by the revolution in methodology and research technology.

Our new methodological tools may well be adaptable to deal with a great variety of topics and problems, and I hope they are. However, the data needed for path or regression analyses are much harder to come by in some areas than in others, and in many of them it would take a great deal of sophistication to discover and handle useable indicators. Consequently; under the pressure to publish to avoid perishing, or to gain promotion, or simply to obtain the narcissistic gratification that comes from seeing one's name in print, it is more attractive to do what is quick and easy. This is so in every scholarly field and even in the healing arts. In psychiatry, for example, it leads to prescribing drugs instead of psychotherapy, often not as a result of deliberate choice between alternative diagnoses and prognoses, but simply because drug therapy is easy to administer and promises quick results, superficial though they may be. In the world of scholarships, moreover, not only the choice of technique but even the choice of the problem tends to be determined by what is quick and easy rather than by theoretical considerations or an evaluation of the importance of the questions that are raised. Moreover, the uses of a sophisticated technological and methodological apparatus gives assurance, but often deceptive assurance, to the researcher.

Sociology is not advanced enough solely to rely on precisely measured variables. Qualitative observations on a small universe can provide theoretical leads that may at a later stage become amenable to more refined statistical treatment. To refrain from using descriptive data because they may lend themselves only to tabular presentation will not only diminish our theoretical powers but will retard the refinement of statistical analysis as well.

Training the new generation of sociologists not to bother with problems about which data are hard to come by, and to concentrate on areas in which data can be easily gathered, will result, in the worst of cases, in the piling up of useless information and, in the best of cases, in a kind of tunnel vision in which some problems are explored exhaustively while others are not even perceived.

There is at least some evidence that we tend to produce young sociologists with superior research skills but with a trained incapacity to think in theoretically innovative ways. Much of our present way of training as well as our system of rewards for scientific contributions encourages our students to eschew the risks of theoretical work and to search instead for the security that comes with proceeding along a well-travelled course, chartered though it may be by ever more refined instruments of navigation. McGrath and Altman [1966] have shown this in instructive detail for small-group research, but it applies in other areas as well.

Careers, especially those of people with modest ambitions, can be more easily advanced through quantity rather than quality of publication. This leads to an emphasis on methodological rigor, not on theoretical substance. One way to publish rapidly is to apply 'the [same] procedure, task, or piece of equipment over and over, introducing new variables or slight modification of old variables, and thereby generate a host of studies rather quickly' (McGrath and Altman [1966, p. 87]. The formulation of theories, moreover, is time consuming, and may not lend itself easily to publication in journals increasingly geared to publishing empirical research, and to reject 'soft' theoretical papers. There exist, then, a number of factors in our present systems of training and of rewards that exercise pressures on incoming generations of sociologists to refine their methods at the expense of developing innovative lines.

This is not inherent in methods *per se*, but it is, let me emphasise again at the risk of repetition, a temptation for lesser minds. And here as elsewhere inflation has set in. However, it is important to note that even the better minds, those who have been able to use the new methods innovatively, are *nolens volens* geared to deal with problems, important as they may be, for which these methods promise quick results. Even in the serious work that is being done with the help of the new statistical techniques there lurks the danger of one-sided emphasis.

Stratification studies of recent years will illustrate this point. This field has benefited a great deal from modern path analytical methods whose power is perhaps shown at its best in Blau and Duncan's *The American Occupational Structure* [1968]. Path analysis allows these authors systematically to trace the impact of such factors as father's occupation, father's educational attainments, and son's education and first job on the son's placement in the occupational hierarchy. It allows for the first time the assessment in precise detail of the ways in which occupational status in a modern industrial society is based on a combination of achieved and ascribed characteristics. It permits, in fact, the assessment of the contributions of social inheritance and individual effort in the attainment of socioeconomic status.

Yet, to use an important distinction by Goldthorpe [1972], this research contributes to the understanding of the *distributive*, not to the *relational* aspects of social class. The focus is predominantly on the impact on individual careers of differences in parental resources, access to educational institutions and the like, or they centre attention upon individual characteristics of people variously placed in the class structure. There is no concern here with the ways in which differential class power and social advantage operate in predictable and routine ways, through specifiable social interactions between classes or interest groups, to give shape to determinate social structures and to create differential life chances. The first and only entry under path analysis in the 1966–1970 Index to *The American Sociological Review* (vols 31–5) refers to a paper by Hodge and Treiman [1968] tracing the effects of the social participation of parents on that of their offspring. There were only two papers analysing problems in social stratification with the aid of path analytical methods in the 1973 (vol. 38) volume of *The American Sociological Review*, and both (Kelley [1973] and Jackman and

Jackman [1973]) deal with the *distributional* aspects of social stratification or with the characteristics of individuals in the class hierarchy.

The 1974 volume of *The American Sociological Review* published three papers on stratification using path analysis, two of which (Porter [1974]; Alexander and Eckland [1974]) deal again with distributional aspects. The *Rose Monograph Series* published by the A.S.A. had issued twelve titles up to the end of 1974. Of these, four, that is one-third, deal with problems of stratification and use highly sophisticated research methods. Their titles speak for themselves: 'Socioeconomic Background and Educational Performance' (Hauser [1972]); 'Attitudes and Facilitation in the Attainment of Status' (Gasson *et al.* [1972]); 'Looking Ahead: Self-conceptions, Race and Family as Determinants of Adolescent Orientation to Achievement' (Gordon [1972]); and 'Ambition and Attainment: A Study of Four Samples of American Boys' (Kerckhoff [1974]). It would appear as if authors and editors of the series are fixated on the problems of making it.

Yet a class system is not only a distributive system, in which individuals are assigned to their respective niches in terms of background and training, nor is its analytical significance exhausted by individual characteristics of people who make their way within it; it is also a system that is shaped by the interaction between various classes and interest groups differentially located within the social structure. It is a system, moreover, in which command and coercion play major parts. Classes and other socioeconomic groups use their resources so as effectively to maintain or advance their positions and to maximise the distribution of material and social benefits to their advantage. Exclusive concern with the distributive aspects of stratification directs attention away from the socio-political mechanisms through which members of different strata monopolise chances by reducing the chances of others. Max Weber (Gerth and Mills [1948]), building on Karl Marx, saw this with exemplary clarity when he stated that, 'It is the most elemental economic fact that the way in which disposition over material property is distributed among a plurality of people ... in itself creates specific life chances. According to the law of marginal utility this mode of distribution excludes the non-owners from competing for highly valued goods. ... It increases ... the power [of the propertied] in price wars with those who, being propertyless, have nothing to offer but their labor....'

One need not accept Marx's dichotomous scheme of class analysis in order to agree that classes are linked in asymmetrical relationships. The notion of a class of owners of means of production is dialectically bound to the notion of a class of non-owners. Just as in the classical Indian caste system, as Dumont [1970] has shown, the purity of the Brahmans is inseparable from the impurity of the Untouchables, so the central characteristics of the class systems is not that there are propertied and the propertyless but that they are mutually interdependent. Collins, arguing against a narrowly defined sociology of poverty, puts the matter well when he writes, 'Why some people are poor is only one aspect of the same question as to why some people are rich: a generalized explanation of the distribution of wealth is called for if one is to have a testable explanation of either particular' (Collins [1975] p. 17).

A system of stratification consists in relationships between groups or categories of men and women which sustain, or alter their respective access to life chances. It is one thing to investigate the ways in which, for example, people manage to attain the status position of medical practitioners in American society, it is quite another to analyse the institutions that help the American Medical Association to monopolize the market for health care by restricting access. What needs analysis is not merely the ladder to medical success but those institutional factors that contribute to the maintenance of a system of medical service that effectively minimises the life chances of the poor (Kelman [1974]).

Analysis of the distributional aspects of stratification systems can dispense with considerations of social and political power; concern with the relational aspects, however, directs attention to the power contentions that make for the relationships which establish differential class privileges, and create patterned conflicts between unequally benefited contenders. When no question is asked about who benefits from existing social and political arrangements, stratification research, no matter how sophisticated its methodological tools, presents a 'bowdlerised' version of social reality. When the causes and consequences of differential location in the class structure remain unanalysed, the whole area of research so brilliantly opened up by Merton's [1968, Chs 6 and 7] seminal anomie paradigm remains unexplored.

I am not arguing, let this be clearly understood, that concern with the structures of power and exploitation is necessarily better than preoccupation with the pathways to individual mobility. There is surely a need for both types of studies. I believe, however, that the methodological tools that are available help focus on the latter. It must be added – lest I be accused of technological determinism – that such restrictions are also rooted in the prevailing American ideology of individual achievement. But taken together, the ideology combined with the use of statistical methods in limited areas, prevents the growth of our discipline and curtails our ability to strive for a full accounting and explanation of the major societal forces that shape our common destiny and determine our life chances. If the computer and the new methodological tools we possess now are not yet adequate for handling some of the issues I have raised, then let us at least press forward with theoretical explorations even if they should later have to be refined or modified by more precise empirical research. Let us not continue on a path about which one may say with the poet Roy Campbell [1955 p. 198]: 'They use the snaffle and the curb all right. But where is the bloody horse.'

Another symptom of the decline of a discipline, as Crane [1972] indicates, is exclusive insistence on one particular dimension of reality and one particular mode of analysis by cliques or sects who fail to communicate with the larger body, or with one another. Under such conditions, a community of scholars will gradually dissolve through splitting up into a variety of camps of ever more restricted esoteric and specialised sects, jealously fighting each other and proclaiming that they alone possess the keys to the kingdom, while others are not just in error, but in sin. Under such conditions the only dialogue between antagonistic camps is a dialogue of the deaf. Such tendencies have also become apparent in the last few years of the history of our discipline. This brings me to my second topic of examination, the assessment of ethnomethodology.

If I understand correctly, ethnomethodology aims at a descriptive reconstruction of the cognitive map in people's minds which enables them to make sense of their everyday activities and encounters. It is a method that endeavours to penetrate to the deeper layers of the categorical and perceptual apparatus that is used in the construction of diverse realities. The method also aims at a rigorous description of ordinary linguistic usage and speech acts. As such it seems aggressively and programmatically devoid of theoretical content of sociological relevance. Limiting itself by a self-denying ordinance to the concrete observation of communicative codes, subjective categorisations, and conversational gestures, it underplays the behavioural aspects of goal directed social interaction. It focuses instead on descriptions of definitions of the situation, meaning structures, conversational exchanges and the mutual modifications of images of self in such interchanges. Ignoring institutional factors in general, and the centrality of power in social interaction in particular, it is restricted to the descriptive tracing of the ways in which both individual actors and students of their activities account for their actions.

Ethnomethodologists put particular stress on the contextuality of accounts and meanings, their imbeddedness in the interactive context, their 'situated' nature. Given the constitutive situatedness of any act, it is asserted that no objective generalising approach is possible in the social sciences which by their very nature can only provide ideographic description. In some versions of ethnomethodology, inter-subjectivity is consciously neglected so that one ends up with a view of individual actors as monads without windows enclosed in their private and unshareable universes of meaning.

As distinct from path analysis and similar methods, ethnomethodology has not found ready acceptance within our discipline, in fact it has never sought such acceptance. It has consciously limited its appeal to devoted followers united in the knowledge that they possess a special kind of insight denied to outsiders.

Ethnomethodology claims access to types of knowledge not accessible to the sociological *vulgus*. Write Zimmermann and Pollner [1970], for example, on the ethnomethodological reduction, one of the mainstays of the method: 'The reduction does not generate research that may be regarded as an extension, refinement, or correction of extant sociological inquiry. . . . The reduction constitutes as its phenomenon an order of affairs that has no identifiable counterpart in contemporary social science.' More typically still than the oft-repeated insistence that ethnomethodology has a unique subject matter is the esoteric and particularistic nature of the pronouncements of its practitioners. Consider, for example, a paper by Sudnow [1972] entitled 'Temporal Parameters of Interpersonal Observation' which turns out to deal with the glances people exchange with one another or direct at the passing scene. It is concerned, as the author elegantly puts it, with 'the issue of glance timing importance' [1972, p. 273]. 'Let us consider', he states, 'the situation of "walking across the street", where an orientation to be clearly so seen is held by virtue of the noted presence of a rapidly approaching vehicle. Here a familiar traffic situation may be regularly imagined where a mere and single glance is expected, where the sufficiency of the mere and single glance is criterial for bringing off safe passage ... and where, as a consequence, the concern for a correspondence between the "details" of what we are doing and what we are seen at a single glance to be doing, may be of paramount concern' [1972, p. 269]. When I try to explain to my four-year old grandson that he should always be careful when crossing a street, I say to him, 'Always watch for passing cars.' I do not think that Sundow's jargon conveys anything more. Each field, to be sure, must construct its own defined terms, but what is developed here is a restricted code of communications rather than open scientific vocabulary (Bernstein [1971]).

It is much too facile simply to poke fun at a group of people who profess central concern with linguistic aspects of interactive processes and yet seem unable to handle the vernacular. But the fact is that such language diseases have sociological significance in the development of particularistic communities of True Believers. To begin with, esoteric language erects barriers against outsiders and confirms to the insiders that they have indeed a hold on some special truth. But there is more, such jargon, as the philosopher Susanne Langer puts it, 'is language which is more technical than the ideas it serves to express' [1973, p. 36], so that it can successfully camouflage relatively trivial ideas. Moreover, esoteric jargon may serve to bind the neophyte to his newfound anchorage. People tend to value highly those activities in which they have invested a great deal. Having invested considerable time and energy in mastering an esoteric vocabulary, people are loath, even when some disillusionment has already set in, to admit to themselves that what has cost them so much, might, after all be devoid of genuine value. Hence the particularistic vocabulary is not due to happenstance; it serves significant functions in marking boundaries and holding members.

Yet another characteristic with obvious functional value that ethnomethodologists share with similar close groupings in other scholarly areas, is the characteristic habit to limit their footnote references almost exclusively to members of the in-group or to non-sociologists, while quoting other sociologists mainly in order to show the errors of their way. There is, in addition, a peculiar propensity to refer to as yet unpublished manuscripts, to lecture notes and research notebooks.

It will be recognised that the characteristics I have outlined are those of a sect rather than of a field of specialisation. I here define a sect as a group that has separated in protest from a larger body and emphasises an esoteric and 'pure' doctrine that is said to have been abandoned or ignored by the wider body. Sects are typically closed systems, usually led by charismatic leaders and their immediate followers. They attempt to reduce communication with the outside world to a minimum while engaging in highly intense interactions between the True Believers (Coser [1974]). Sects develop a special particularistic language, distinctive norms of relevance, and specialised behaviour patterns that effectively set off the believers from the unconverted, serve as a badge of special status, and highlight their members' differentiation from the larger body of which they once formed a part.

Yet what is functional for the sect is, by the same token, dysfunctional for those who are not among the elect. Blockage of the flow of communication is among the most serious impediments of scientific developments. A science is utterly dependent on the free exchange of information between its practitioners. Preciseness and economy in information flow makes for growth, and blockages lead to decline (cf. Crane [1972]). But the language of ethnomethodology, as Coleman ([1968, p. 130]) once put it, makes for, 'an extraordinarily high ratio of reading time to information transfer'. More generally, an esoteric language can only serve to dissociate a body of people who were once united in common pursuits. As in the story of Babel in Genesis, 'And the Lord said, "Behold they are one people, and they have one language; and this is only the beginning of what they will do. . . . Come, let us go down, and there confuse their language, that they may not understand one another's speech".'

Even though the sect is still quite young, the splits and fissions that typically beset sectarian developments have already set in. I do not profess to be knowledgeable about the detailed grounds of these developments (see Attewell [1974] for an excellent mapping and critique), but shall only sketch some of them very roughly. At present, the ethnomethodology of Garfinkel [1969] differs significantly from that of Sacks which, in turn, is far removed from the concerns of Blum or the researches of Cicourel. Some versions are, in fact, solipsistic, others attend to intersubjective meanings, some admit the existence of invariant rules and procedures that transcend situations, others deny the possibility of any analysis that is not situation-specific. Some find philosophical anchorage in the German idealistic tradition and its Husserlian offshoots, others make use of British linguistic philosophy and seem to have replaced the guidance of Alfred Schuetz by that of Ludwig Wittgenstein. Some concentrate on the analysis of unique events, others attend to invariant properties of situated actions. The only thing all of them still seem to hold in common is the rejection of the possibility of an objective study and explanation of society and history, and a celebration of that long-dead warhorse of German idealistic philosophy, the transcendental ego.

Concern with the hypertrophy of wordage among ethnomethodologists and their other sectarian characteristics should, however, not preempt all of our attention. It is axiomatic among sociologists of knowledge that the origin of ideas does not prejudice their validity. It is possible that important and fruitful ideas may indeed develop in sectarian milieus. This has, in fact, often been the case, from the inception of puritanism to the emergence of psychoanalysis in the Viennese sect of Freud's immediate disciples.

Yet, when one turns to the problems that ethnomethodology tries to illuminate one is struck, for the most part, by their embarrassing triviality. We have already encountered Sudnow's 'glancing research', Schegloff [1968] has spent productive years studying the ways in which people manage to begin and end their telephone conversations. I am not denying that 'Studies of the Routine Grounds of Everyday Activities' (Garfinkel [1967]) may uncover significant and valuable matters, but in my considered judgement what has so far been dug up is mostly dross or interminable methodological disquisitions and polemics. Bittner's [1967] fine studies of the police or Cicourel's [1968] analysis of juvenile justice and a very few other good studies are not enough to justify the enormous ballyhoo surrounding ethnomethodology.

In general, it would seem to me, that we deal here with a massive cop-out, a determined refusal to undertake research that would indicate the extent to which our lives are affected by the socioeconomic context in which they are embedded. It amounts to an orgy of subjectivism, a self-indulgent enterprise in which perpetual methodological analysis and self-analysis leads to infinite regress, where the discovery of the ineffable qualities of the mind of analyst and analysand and their private construction of reality serves to obscure the tangible qualities of the world 'out there'. By limiting itself to trying to discover what is in the actors' minds, it blocks the way to an investigation of those central aspects of their lives about which they know very little. By attempting to describe the manifest content of people's experiences, ethnomethodologists neglect that central area of sociological analysis which deals with latent structures. The analysis of ever more refined minutiae of reality construction, and the assertion that one cannot possibly understand larger social structures before all these minutiae have been exhaustively mapped, irresistibly brings to mind Dr Johnson's pregnant observation that, 'You don't have to eat the whole ox to know that the meat is tough.'

Path analysis, as has been shown, is a method that found quick acceptance among wide circles in the sociological discipline because it provided technical means for more precise measurements hitherto unavailable; ethnomethodology in contrast, found acceptance only among a small number of practitioners huddled around a charismatic leader and his apostles. The first was widely communicated through the various informational networks, both personal and impersonal, available to sociologists; the second developed particularistic codes of communication that effectively restricted access to all but the insiders. Yet what both have in common is a hypertrophy of method at the expense of substantive theory. The first has been used as an encouragement to neglect important areas of inquiry even while it has brought about greater precision of measurement in other areas, some important, some trivial. The second lends itself at best to atheoretical mappings of cognitive categories, and deliberately eschews concern with most of the matters that sociology has been centrally concerned with ever since Auguste Comte. In both cases, I submit, preoccupation with method largely has led to neglect of significance and substance. And yet, our discipline will be judged in the last analysis on the basis of the substantive enlightenment which it is able to supply about the social structures in which we are enmeshed and which largely condition the course of our lives. If we neglect the major task, if we refuse the challenge to answer these questions, we shall forfeit our birthright and degenerate into congeries of rival sects and specialised researchers who will learn more and more about less and less.

Notes and References

Chapter 3

1. Blalock [1964].
2. It is often possible to test the assumption that both variables are indicators of the same concept through methods of internal consistency, scaling (Guttman, Likert and Thurstone scales), factor analysis, etc. Such symmetrical relationships may thus represent a first step towards the clarification of dimenisons and the improvement of measurement.
3. Durkheim [1947].
4. Merton [1957] Ch. 1; Davis [1959].
5. Blalock [1964] pp. 56–7.
6. It is important to know, of course, whether each variable equally affects the other or whether one variable has the more important influence. Fortunately this issue can be solved through panel analysis. See for example the discussion of mutual interactions in Lazarsfeld [1948]; Rosenberg and Thielens, 'The Panel Study', in Jahoda *et al.* [1951] vol. 2, pp. 587–609; and Pelz and Andrews [1964].
7. Attempts have been made by Blalock [1964] and Simon [1957] to establish the direction of causal relationships by means of statistical models. By examining the fit of the empirical data to alternative models, one is in a position to establish causal priorities among variables. This is a promising method, but the statistical principles are too advanced for the present discussion. The panel technique, through the study of temporal sequences or mutual interaction analysis, also helps one to deal with the causal problem.
8. Bunge [1959] Part 3.
9. Ibid. pp. 305–6.
10. Ibid. Part 1.
11. In social sciences it must be noted such determination is

virtually never invariable. Relationships are based on statistical trends, so that the relationships reflect tendencies. The independent variable then is the one which 'tends to determine' the dependent variable; the former might be said to 'influence' the latter. Nagel [1961] pp. 505–9 has noted that one reason why social science deals with statistical relationships whereas physical science deals with absolute laws is that the social-science laws are stated as though applicable to real situations rather than ideal ones. In order to apply to the real world, for example, the law of falling bodies would have to be stated in statistical terms since the law holds only in a vacuum which never occurs in the real world (cited in Blalock [1964] pp. 16–17).

12. P. F. Lazarsfeld, 'Interpretation of Statistical Relations in a Research Operation; in Lazarsfeld and Rosenberg [1955] p. 120.
13. Middleton [1963].
14. Almond and Verba [1963] Ch. 4.
15. Srole *et al.* [1962] p. 20.
16. Bunge [1959] p. 170.
17. Himmelweit *et al.* [1958].
18. Hempel [1952]; Weissman [1965].
19. Adorno *et al.* [1950] Ch. 7.
20. Rosenberg [1956].
21. Lott and Lott [1963] p. 608.
22. Weissman [1965].
23. Michels [1949].
24. Bunge [1959] p. 19.

Chapter 9

1. See Bierstedt [1959], which constitutes one of the most thoroughgoing attempts to differentiate history and sociology on the basis of the idiographic-nomothetic distinction.
2. For a penetrating critique of the idiographic-nomothetic distinction see Nagel [1952].
3. Cf. Lazarsfeld [1959].
4. Lazarsfeld [1957] p. 244.
5. See the provocative chapter 'The Uses of History', in Mills [1959]. Mills ranks among the great creators of the classic tradition – for example, such sociologists as Marx, Spencer, Weber, Mannheim and Schumpeter. To these one could add the names of many important pioneers in special branches of sociology, for example Ostrogorski, Mosca and Michels in political sociology, Veblen and Hobson in industrial sociology.

6. For a useful sample of papers showing recent tendencies in sociological theory, structural-functional and otherwise see McKinney and Tiryakian (eds) [1970]. See also Dawe [1970].

7. For example Cicourel [1964].

8. Cf. the essays on methodology brought together in Weber [1949]; also Weber's essay on Roscher and Knies (Weber [1975]).

9. Two valuable collections of work in this genre are Dyos (ed) [1968] and Thernstrom and Sennett (eds) [1969]. See also Wrigley (ed.) [1972] and Swierenga (ed.) [1970].

10. As one recent illustration, see Anderson [1971].

11. As examples see Bellah [1964] and Dunning [1967].

12. For the crucial role of this notion of immanence in theories of social evolution or development past and present, see the excellent book by Robert Nisbet, *Social Change and History* [1969].

13. See, for example, Perry Anderson's call for a 'totalising history of modern British society, which will provide the basis for an understanding of the dialectical movement of our society' [1965]. See also the reply of a historian, albeit a Marxist-orientated one: E. P. Thompson, 'The Peculiarities of the English' [1965].

14. Goldthorpe [1971].

15. Parsons [1966, 1971].

16. See especially Popper [1957] and Gellner [1964].

17. Nisbet [1969] p. 233.

Chapter 10

1. Dahrendorf [1964] p. 257.

2. Mayhew's *London Labour and the London Poor*, for example, is mainly about London costermongers, a distinctive minority if only because hardly any of them were legally married to their 'spouses' (Mayhew [1851] vol. 1, p. 20). This does not, however, stop Young and Willmott citing him for evidence on family behaviour 'in the old days' (Young and Willmott [1957] p. 8).

3. Goode [1963] pp. 6–7. Note how little hard statistical data on the family of the past used by, for example, Rosser and Harris in *The Family and Social Change* or in Young and Willmott's *Family and Kinship*. Cf. for a similar criticism of Rosser and Harris's book Scharf [1968] p. 286.

4. E.g. Rosser and Harris [1965]; Young and Willmott [1957]; Hoggart [1957].

5. Ibid.

6. Laslett [1965]; Laslett and Harrison [1963]. Note also, for example, Williams [1963] esp. pp. 140–4, 217–19.

7. For a list of some of the studies that have been done see notes 9–16 below. Note also McGregor [1961]. There are also a number of studies mainly with a demographic focus (e.g. Banks, *Prosperity and Parenthood*) or studies of certain processes or limited aspects of family behaviour (e.g. McGregor, *Divorce in England*).

8. Sample data on Preston suggest that the earlier that men could support a wife and family at their customary standard of living or reached their peak earning capacity, which ever came first, the earlier they married.

9. Habakkuk, 'Family Structure and Economic Change in Nineteenth Century Europe,' in Bell and Vogel [1960].

10. Collier [1965].

11. Smelser [1959] esp. Chs 9–13.

12. Hewitt [1953, 1959].

13. Pinchbeck [1930].

14. Particularly important of those known to me are those of Armstrong [1974] and Drake (unpublished work).

15. Crozier [1965].

16. Firth [1964].

17. Foster [1974].

18. Anderson [1971].

19. For Lancashire for example much useful material can be gleaned from Davies [1963].

20. *Select Committee on Education*, Parliamentary Papers (1837–8) VII, p. 102.

21. Crozier [1965].

22. Three thought-provoking discussions are by Back [1965]; Goode [1963–4]; and Lancaster [1961].

23. Cf. for example 'Labour and the Poor', *Morning Chronicle Supplements*, pp. 28–9.

24. This topic is discussed more fully in Anderson [1971] Ch. 7.

25. Ibid. esp. Chs 8, 9.

26. Ibid. esp. Chs 4, 9.

27. Cf. Back [1965] and Lancaster [1961].

28. Cf. Fox [1967] for a useful discussion of this point.

29. One example of this is Townsend [1965].

30. In Scotland the enumerators' books for the whole of the nineteenth century are already open to public inspection.

31. Hewitt [1953, 1959] are partly based on data obtained in this way.

32. Dyos and Baker [1968] discuss data obtained in this way.

33. Michael Drake's team at the University of Kent at Canterbury have already made considerable strides in the development of techniques for this purpose.

34. See the discussion in Smelser [1959] Ch. 9.

35. See Wrigley [1972] pp. 90–105 for a discussion of this problem. The inconsistencies between the two censuses in this matter seriously reduce the value of comparisons between the years 1851 and 1861.

36. This can be verified to some extent by reference to the published census tables of occupations, birth places and ages for the town compared with others in the area. A careful search of contemporary descriptive literature also helps to verify points such as this. Nevertheless it is obvious, and this should always be pointed out, that data assembled on this basis have no statistically valid claim to representativeness.

37. It is, however, well worth while to check before committing oneself too heavily to a region that the data have not been destroyed or become illegible, and also that special events – strikes, fairs and the like – were not affecting the region at the time the census was taken. Local newspapers and directories will often be useful here.

38. For an important discussion of the uses, problems and limitations of descriptive data see Angell [1947].

39. It can, for example, fairly easily be established that in spite of the outcry at the time and in spite of the fact that almost all the literature seems to imply that it was widespread, at any one point in time 2 per cent at an absolute maximum of all infant children in the industrial districts of Lancashire were being left during the day with professional child-minders, with all the social problems which were alleged to ensue. (For a full discussion see Anderson [1971] pp. 182–3; the figures are partly based on Hewitt [1953] pp. 271–5.)

40. E.g. *Employment of Children in Factories*: *First Report*, Parliamentary Papers (1833) XX, D2, 3; *State of the Population of Stockport*, Parliamentary Papers (1842) XXXV, 7.

41. For further discussion see Anderson [1971] pp. 267–72.

42. Ibid. pp. 287–303.

43. Ibid. Ch. 5.

44. I think it may be quite fairly asserted that Smelser, whose *Social Change in the Industrial Revolution* [1959] is based almost wholly on descriptive data, has not been as cautious as he might in drawing conclusions from them. This is particularly the case when he is discussing changes in the proportion of children in factories employed and recruited by relatives. On the basis of some limited statistical evidence I gathered in my Lancashire study, it would seem that he has definitely exaggerated the size of the change. (See Anderson [1971] Ch. 6.)

45. Among the more useful introductions to content analysis is

Berelson's paper 'Content Analysis' [1952], in Lindzey [1954]. For a critical discussion of some of the difficulties and restrictions of content analysis and consequently of all use of qualitative materials in historical sociology (particularly for the imputing of motives or affective states) see Cicourel [1964] Ch. 6.

46. For useful discussions of this topic in modern times see for example Litwak [1965]; Loudon [1961]; Young [1954].

47. On this topic, Mrs Gaskell might be a good example of a writer of this kind.

48. For a full discussion see Anderson [1971] pp. 101–5, 216–30.

Chapter 11

1. Grandma indeed seemed a realist all round. When for instance her husband, like Charles II, stayed lingering over his demise, solicitous neighbours were met with a cool 'I don't care how soon he's either better or worse'! She herself reached the age of ninety-three and died only moderately lamented.

2. To encourage the Adam in us our local park sold 'garden soil' at a penny a bucket. At home, expending twopence, we once tried a window-box 'for flowers' in the back-yard. A few blooms struggled up then collapsed. 'So!, said my mother loud in her husband's hearing, 'you can rear a child, it seems, on coal gas, but it does for geraniums!'

3. The railway company which owned most of our streets kept its houses in a moderate state of disrepair. Two workmen haunted the properties, a crabby joiner and, trailing behind him with the hand-cart, his mate, a tall frail consumptive. This pair were known to the neighbourhood unkindly as 'Scrooge' and 'Marley's Ghost'.

4. Since the state education system was doing little to train the mass of cheap female labour that commerce and the civil service drew upon after 1900, private 'colleges' sprang up in all the larger towns teaching shorthand, typing, book-keeping and foreign languages. One of these in the city, typical of many, opened in two small rooms, soured to prosperity through the inter-war years with more than 1,000 students annually ('20 lessons, 20 shillings!'), then collapsed in the sixties when the state finally got round to provide commercial education for all who needed it. In the years of mass unemployment after World War I some of these private establishments used to 'guarantee' their students a post after training. Desperate for work, many borrowed or used savings to pay fees,

only to be offered in the end one of those numberless jobs in commerce always to be had at starvation salaries.

5. 'CURRANT CAKES 3 FOR *2d*' advertised one neighbour on a little pile of grey lumps in her house window. Nobody bought. We children watched them growing staler each day until the kitchen curtain fell again on the venture like a shroud.

6. Hoggart [1957].

7. A common topic of shop and beerhouse was who, among the lower orders, had just gone into or come out of Strangeways.

8. Engels pointed out how, in the 1840s, the million or more brutalised Irish immisgrants pouring into English slums were depressing native, social and economical standards. Little integration, however, seems to have followed upon the influx. Even up to the outbreak of World War I differences in race, religion, culture and status kept English and Irish apart. The Irish poor, already of course deeply deferential to the church, remained, in sobriety, even more than their English counterparts, respectful to the point of obsequiousness to any they considered their social superiors.

9. Some professional inquirers into the past have persuaded the elderly both to reminisce and to complete lengthy questionnaires covering aspects of their lives in youth. This can of course yield valuable information, social and historical. But a certain caution is needed. During the thirties and forties I often talked with people who were already mature by 1914. They criticised the then fairly recent past, faculties alert, with what seemed some objectivity. But by the sixties myths had developed, prejudices about the present had set hard; these same critics, in ripe old age, now saw the Edwardian era through a golden haze!

10. Harry Quelch, proletarian leader in the S.D.F. who knew the common people if ever a man did, called the English working class of that day the 'most reverential to the master class' of any in Europe. In London in 1889 at the time of the dockers' and gasworkers' strikes Engels wrote:

> The most repulsive thing here is the bourgeois 'respectability' which has grown deep into the bones of the workers. The division of society into innumerable strata, each recognised without question, each with its own pride, but also inborn respect for its 'betters' and 'superiors', is so old and firmly established that the bourgeoisie find it fairly easy to get their bait accepted.

Engels seemed to find the workers' leaders little better. 'Even Tom Mann,' he complained, 'whom I regard as the best of the lot, is fond of mentioning that he will be lunching with the Lord Mayor' (Lenin [1934]).

Chapter 13

1. Vidich and Bensman [1954].
2. Wolff (trans.) [1950] p. 47.
3. Ibid. P. 45.

Chapter 14

1. In that same collection of essays William F. Whyte and Robert R. Braun describe how, in learning a language, one can also learn a culture (Whyte and Braun [1968]). Goffman's little piece 'The Neglected Situation', which also appears in that volume, is directly relevant to some of the issues considered in the present paper (Goffman [1964]).

2. See also Hunt *et al.* [1964] p. 66 who were informed by an Austrian respondent that 'every "yes" has its "however" and every "no" its "if".' They also report that 'it was not possible to find a French equivalent for "may or may not" as a check-list response'.

3. I am not of course the only observer to whom logical extensions of the Whorf hypothesis have occurred. See for example Hymes [1966]. Hymes's point is that Whorf's concepts can be extended to apply to language behaviour, that is to the different ways that language is used in various societies. Bright [1966] p. 314 suggests another kind of extension: 'although Whorf's comparisons involved widely differing linguistic communities . . . we may equally well undertake comparisons between parts of a single community, such as those parts which are characterised by differing linguistic structures and/or differing patterns of linguistic behaviour'.

4. When I suggest a difference 'in degree' between the two cases, I do not pre-judge which of the two has the highest potential for misunderstanding.

5. In some of his research Roger Brown has paid considerable attention to the impact of phonology on cognition (see especially Brown [1962]).

6. For further sociological analysis of this form of non-standard English see Cohen *et al.* [1968]. The extent to which the dialogue could be understood outside *Pittsburgh* is open to question. How much overlap is there in the language of children in widely dispersed

ghettos? If those in New York and St Louis and Chicago do speak the same dialect as those in Pittsburgh, how come?

7. An adequate test of the hypothesis suggested by Barth would require comparisons between each of the six possible subsamples derived from a race-class contingency table, i.e. middle-class blacks compared with lower-class blacks and with both lower- and middle-class whites; lower-class blacks compared with both middle- and lower-class whites; and lower-class whites compared with middle-class whites. I suspect that different sets of differences in word connotations would appear in each of these six comparisons.

8. Ned Polsky [1971] has pointed out some of the weaknesses in arguments suggesting the functionality of argots.

9. For the application of Hughes's notion of 'naming' to an empirical problem, see Seeman's study of the 'intellectual' in which the 'chief finding' is that 'the "naming trouble" is an essential part of the status involved' (Seeman [1958] pp. 27, 32).

10. Cicourel's choice of the application and interpretation of family law is an example of a principle I have heard Everett Hughes expound in response to the question: 'In the sociology of work, what governs the choice of occupations to be studied? Why one and not another?'. Among other criteria Hughes suggests that in different occupations one finds in exaggerated and dramatic form various processes which are common to all human behaviour. Cicourel has selected an occupation which requires a maximisation of commonly understood meanings for words.

11. This quotation was first brought to my attention by Nathan Goldman. It appears as a lead to Elbridge Sibley's 'A Note on the Pronounciation of "Shibboleth"' (Sibley [1965]).

12. Riesman comments at another point 'I was struck by the many similarities between the attitudes of Frenchmen, as Lerner [1956] met them, and certain types of respondents in this American survey' (Riesman [1958] n. 27, pp. 295–6). Riesman also notes problems of differences in connotations of the same words among different segments of the academic population. See for example his discussion of the reaction to such phrases as 'protest vigorously' (Riesman [1958] pp. 336–7).

13. The position taken here is that there is essentially no difference between the problems of interviewer effect, experimenter effect and instrument reactivity. Each is a variant of the same species. Attempts in social psychology to confront this issue have for the most part endeavoured to avoid verbal sources of evidence rather than to treat conversations as data in themselves.

Chapter 17

1. In writing this chapter I had the benefit of constructive criticism and countless valuable suggestions from Dr John C. McDonald of the Canadian Ministry of Manpower, Ottawa. Some of the ideas developed here are taken further in my chapter 'The Role of Discoveries in Social Science', in T. Shanin (ed.), *The Rules of the Game* (1972) pp. 276–302, and in my book *The Structure of Sociological Inference* [1976].

2. Among earlier treatments the most thorough is von Schelting [1934]; for recent discussions compare Kaufmann [1958]; Brown [1963] pp. 177–85; and von Friedeburg [1965] pp. 265–77.

3. Cf. Max Weber [1951] p. 191.

4. Ibid. p. 192.

5. This is the subject of my chapter 'The Role of Discoveries in Social Science', in Shanin [1972] pp. 276–302.

6. On this account I am using the concept of real type in a wider sense than is suggested by Neisser [1965].

7. Cf. Elias [1956]; Mills [1959] pp. 119–31 *passim*; Brown [1963] pp. 26–44; E. Shils, 'The Calling of Sociology', in Parsons *et al.* (eds) [1961] vol. 2, p. 1441; Cicourel [1964] pp. 189–244.

8. Cf. for example Dahrendorf [1958]; Madge [1964]; Neisser [1965]; Feuer [1962].

9. Notably Merton [1957] pp. 531–628; for a representative selection of relevant studies see Barber and Hirsch [1962].

10. Cf. for example Toulmin [1961]; Kuhn [1962].

11. Cf. Taylor and Barron [1963]. Psychologists, too, are engaged in this problem; I am indebted to Mr J. M. Innes for introducing me to this field.

12. This is followed up in my paper 'The Role of Discoveries in Social Science [1972].

13. It should be noted that this model is, like all models, tautological; it contains no more than is already implied by the meaning of the two criteria used. Cf. generally M. Brodbeck, 'Models, Meanings and Theories', in Gross (ed.) [1959]; and Allen [1960].

14. Schutz [1953] p. 3.

15. Common sense is therefore a component of what C. Madge describes as 'general eidos'. The approach which I am using is distinctively narrower; I am attempting to focus on knowledge to the exclusion of belief.

16. Cf. for instance Baumol [1961] pp. 64–133; Duckworth [1962] p. 22 *passim*.

17. In a study on 'Organisational Autonomy' to be published shortly.

18. Cf. Moore and Tumin [1949]; Schneider [1965].

19. Moore and Tumin [1949] p. 795.

20. Schneider [1965] p. 499.

21. This aspect of pragmatic knowledge is patently relevant to the process of democratisation as an object of political sociology. Cf., for example, from the point of view of industrial democracy, Ross [1966]. To pursue the larger question of rationality in political behaviour it seems to me necessary to shift the traditional emphasis from the normative toward the cognitive element in attitudes.

22. Cf. Rex [1961] pp. 102–14; Dahrendorf [1963]; Cicourel [1964] pp. 197–212; Poggi [1965].

23. Poggi [1965] p. 284.

24. Evan [1960–1, 1962].

25. Cf. Woodward [1958]; Baldwin [1964].

26. Whyte [1955]; Gouldner [1955a and b]; Behrend [1957]; Furstenberg [1958]; Baldamus [1961] pp. 81–122; Hickson [1961]; Flanders [1964] pp. 238–56.

Bibliography

ABRAMS, M. [1951], *Social Surveys and Social Action* (London: Heinemann).

—[1964], 'Rewards of Education', *New Society*, 93, p. 26.

ABRAMS, P. [1968], *The Origins of British Sociology* (Chicago: University of Chicago Press).

— (ed.) [1978], *Work, Urbanism and Inequality: U.K. Society Today* (London: Weidenfeld & Nicolson).

— *et al.* (eds) [1981], *Practice and Progress: British Sociology 1950–1980* (London: Allen & Unwin).

— [1982], *Historical Sociology* (Shepton Mallet, Somerset: Open Books).

ADORNO, T. W. *et al.* [1950], *The Authoritarian Personality* (New York: Harper).

AGAR, M. H. [1980], *The Professional Stranger: An Informal Introduction to Ethnography* (New York: Academic Press).

ALEXANDER, K. and ECKLAND, B. [1974], 'Sex Differences in Educational Attainment Process', *American Sociological Review*, 39, pp. 668–82.

ALKER, H. T. [1962], 'A typology of Ecological Fallacies', in M. Doggan and S. Rokkan (eds.), *Quantitative Ecological Analysis in the Social Sciences* (Cambridge Mass: M.I.T. Press) pp. 69–86.

ALLEN, R. G. D. [1960], 'The Structure of Macro-economic Models', *Economic Journal*, 70, pp. 38–56.

ALMOND, G. and VERBA, S. [1963], *The Civic Culture* (Princeton, N. J.: Princeton University Press).

ANDERSON, M. [1971], *Family Structure in Nineteenth Centrury Lancashire* (Cambridge: Cambridge University Press).

ANDERSON, P. [1965], 'The Origins of the Present Crisis', in *Towards Socialism*, ed. P. Anderson and R. Blackburn (London: Fontana).

ANDERSON, R. B. W. [1967], 'On the Comparability of Meaningful Stimuli in Cross-cultural Research', *Sociometry*, 30, pp. 124–36.

ANGELL, R. C. [1936], *The Family Encounters the Depression* (New York: Scribners).

— [1947], 'A Critical Review of the Development of the Personal Document Method in Sociology 1920–40', in Gottschalk [1947] pp. 175–232.

Annals of the American Academy of Political and Social Science [1978], *America in the Seventies: Some Social Indicators*, vol. 435, January, pp. 1–294.

— [1981], *Social Indicators: American Society in the Eighties*, vol. 453. January.

ARMSTRONG, A. [1974], *Stability and Change in an English Country Town: A Social Study of York, 1801–51* (Cambridge: Cambridge University Press).

ASHBY, M. K. [1961), *Joseph Ashby of Tysoe* (Cambridge: Cambridge University Press; paper edition London: The Merlin Press, 1974).

ATKINSON, A. B. [1972], *Unequal Shares* (Harmondsworth: Penguin Books).

— and HARRISON, A. J. [1978], *Distribution of Personal Wealth in Britain* (Cambridge: Cambridge University Press).

— *et al.* [1978], *Wealth and Personal Income* (Oxford: Pergamon).

ATKINSON, J. M. [1968], 'On the Sociology of Suicide', *Sociological Review*, 16, pp. 83–92.

— [1971], 'Societal Reactions to Suicide', in S. Cohen (ed.), *Images of Deviance* (London: Penguin Books pp. 165–91.

— [1973], 'Suicide, Status-integration and Pseudo-science', *Sociology*, 7, pp. 437–45.

ATTEWELL, P. [1974], 'Ethnomethodology and Garfinkel', *Theory and Society*, 1.

BABCHUK, N. and BATES, A. P. [1962], 'Professor or Producer: The Two Faces of Academic Man', *Social Forces*, 40, pp. 341–8.

BACK, K. W. [1965], 'A Social Psychologist Looks at Kinship Structure', in Shanas and Streib [1965].

BACKSTROM, C. and HURSH-CESAR, G. [1981], *Survey Research*, 2nd edn (New York: Wiley).

BAGLEY, C. [1972], 'Authoritarianism, Status Integration and Suicide', *Sociology*, 6, pp. 395–404.

— [1974], 'On the Validity and Meaning of Suicide Statistics', *Sociology*, 8, pp. 313–16.

BAILEY, K. D. [1978], *Methods of Social Research* (New York: Free Press).

BALDAMUS, W. [1961], *Efficiency and Effort* (London: Tavistock).

— [1972], 'The Role of Discoveries in Social Science', in T. Shanin (ed.), *The Rules of the Game* (London: Tavistock), pp. 276–302.

— [1976], *The Structure of Sociological Inference* (London: Martin Robertson).

BALDWIN, J. and BOTTOMS, A. [1976], *The Urban Criminal* (London: Tavistock).

BALDWIN, W. L. [1964), 'The Motives of Managers, Environmental Restraints and the Theory of Managerial Enterprise', *Quarterly Journal of Economics*, 78, pp. 238–56.

BALL, S. [1981], *Beachside Comprehensive: A Case Study of Secondary Schooling* (Cambridge: Cambridge University Press).

BANKS, J. A. [1954], *Prosperity and Parenthood* (London: Routledge).

— [1978], 'The Social Structure of Nineteenth Century England as seen through the Census', in Lawton, ed. [1978] pp. 179–223.

— [1979], 'Sociological Theories, Methods and Research Techniques – A Personal Viewpoint', *The Sociological Review*, 27 (3) pp. 561–78.

BARBER, B. and HIRSCH, W. [1962], *The Sociology of Science* (New York: Free Press).

BARNES, J. A. [1963], 'Some Ethical Problems of Modern Fieldwork', *British Journal of Sociology*, 14, pp. 118–34.

— [1980], *Who Should Know What? Social Science, Privacy and Ethics* (Cambridge: Cambridge University Press).

BARRINGTON MOORE JUN. [1969], *The Social Origins of Dictatorship and Democracy* (London: Penguin Books).

BARTH, E. [1961], 'The Language Behaviour of Negroes and Whites', *Pacific Sociological Review*, 4, pp. 69–72.

BARTON, A. H. and LAZARSFELD, P. F. [1955), 'Some Functions of Qualitative Analysis in Social Research', *Sociologica*, 1, pp. 321–61.

BATESON, N. [1984], *Data Construction in Social Surveys* (London: Allen & Unwin).

BAUMOL, W. J. [1961], *Economic Theory and Operations Analysis* (Englewood Cliffs, N. J.: Prentice-Hall).

BEAUCHAMP, T. L. *et al.* (EDS) [1982], *Ethical Issues in Social Science Research* (Baltimore: Johns Hopkins University Press).

BECHHOFER, F. [1967], 'Too Many Surveys', *New Society*, 245, pp. 838–9.

— [1973], 'Current Approaches to Empirical Research', in Rex (ed.) [1973] pp. 70–91.

BECKER, H. S. [1963], *Outsiders* (New York: Free Press).

— [1971], *Sociological Work* (London: Allen Lane).

— and GEER, B. [1957], 'Participant Observation and Interviewing', *Human Organisation*, 16, pp. 28–32.

BECKER, H. S. *et al.* [1961], *Boys in White* (Chicago: University of Chicago Press).

BECKER, H. S. *et al.* (eds) [1968], *Institutions and the Person* (Chicago: Aldine).

BEHREND, H. [1957], 'The Effort Bargain', *Industrial and Labor Relations Review*, 10, pp. 503–15.

BELL, C. and NEWBY, H. [1972], *Community Studies* (London: Allen & Unwin).

— — (eds) [1977], *Doing Sociological Research* (London: Allen & Unwin).

BELL, N. W. and VOGEL, E. F. (eds) [1980], *A Modern Introduction to the Family* (Glencoe, Ill.: Free Press).

BELLAH, R. N. [1964], 'Religious Evolution', *American Sociological Review*, 29, pp. 358–74.

BELLAMY, J. [1978], 'Occupation Statistics in Nineteenth Century Censuses', in Lawton [1978] pp. 165–78.

BENJAMIN, B. [1968], *Demographic Analysis* (London: Allen & Unwin).

— [1970], *The Population Census* (London: Heinemann for S.S.R.C.).

BENNETT, J. [1981], *Oral History and Delinquency: The Rhetoric of Criminology* (Chicago: University of Chicago Press).

BENNEY, M. and HUGHES, E. C. [1956], 'Of Sociology and the Interview', *American Journal of Sociology*, 62, pp. 137–42.

BERELSON, B. [1952], *Content Analysis in Communication Research* (Glencoe: Free Press).

BERNSTEIN, B. [1964], 'Elaborated and Restricted Codes', *American Anthropologist*, 66, pp. 55–69.

— [1967], 'Elaborated and Restricted Codes: An Outline', *Sociological Inquiry*, 36, pp. 254–61.

— [1971), *Class Codes and Control*, vol. 1: *Theoretical Studies Towards a Sociology of Language* (London: Routledge).

BERNSTEIN, B. [1973], 'Sociology and the Sociology of Education', in Rex (ed.) [1973] pp. 145–59.

BERRY, D. [1978], 'Review of Abrams (ed.) (1978)', *The Times Higher Education Supplement*, 1 December, p. 17.

BERTAUX, D. (ed.) [1981], *Biography and Society: The Life History Approach in the Social Sciences* (London: Sage).

BIERSTEDT, R. [1949], 'A Critique of Empiricism in Sociology', *American Sociological Review*, 14, pp. 584–92.

— [1959], 'Toynbee and Sociology', *British Journal of Sociology*, 10, pp. 95–104.

— [1974], *Power and Progress* (New York: McGraw-Hill).

BINGHAM, W. V. D. *et al.* [1959], *How to Interview*, 4th edn (New York: Harper).

BITTNER, E. [1967], 'The Police on Skid-row', *American Sociological Review*, 32, pp. 699–715.

BLALOCK, H. M. [1960], *Social Statistics* (New York: McGraw-Hill).

— [1964], *Causal Inferences in Non-experimental Research* (Chapel Hill, North Carolina: University of North Carolina Press).

— [1970], *An Introduction to Social Research* (Englewood Cliffs, N. J.: Prentice-Hall).

— (ed.) [1972], *Causal Models in the Social Sciences* (London: Macmillan).

— and BLALOCK, A. (eds) [1968], *Methodology in Social Research* (New York: McGraw-Hill).

BLANC, H. [1956], 'Multilingual Interviewing in Israel', *American Journal of Sociology*, 62, pp. 206–9.

BLAU, P. [1957], 'Formal Organisations: Dimensions of Analysis', *American Journal of Sociology*, 63, pp. 58–67.

— and DUNCAN, O. D. [1968], *The American Occupational Structure* (New York: Wiley).

— and SCHOENHERR, R. [1971], *The Structure of Organisations* (New York: Basic Books).

BLAUNER, R. [1964], *Alienation and Freedom* (Chicago: University of Chicago Press).

BLAXTER, M. [1976], 'Social Class and Health Inequalities', in Carter and Peel [1976], pp. 111–25.

— (ed.) [1979], 'The Analysis of Qualitative Data: A Symposium', *The Sociological Review*, 27 (4) pp. 649–827.

BLUMER, H. [1939], *An Appraisal of Thomas and Znaniecki's 'The Polish Peasant in Europe and America'* (New York: S.S.R.C.).

— [1948], 'Public Opinion Polls and Public Opinion Polling', *American Sociological Review*, 13, pp. 342–9.

— [1954], 'What is Wrong with Social Theory?', *American Sociological Review*, 19, pp. 3–10.

— [1956], 'Sociological Analysis and the "Variable"', *American Sociological Review*, 21, pp. 683–90.

BONNEY, N. [1975], 'Work and Ghetto Culture', *British Journal of Sociology*, 26, pp. 435–47.

BOOTH, C. (ed.) [1989–1902], *Life and Labour of the People of London*, 17 vols (London: Macmillan).

BORING, E. G. [1963], *History, Psychology and Science* (New York: Wiley).

— and BORING, M. D. [1948], 'Masters and Pupils among the American Psychologists', *American Journal of Psychology*, 61, pp. 527–34.

BOTTOMORE, T. B. [1975], *Marxist Sociology* (London: Macmillan).

BOUDON, R. [1969], 'Secondary Analysis and Survey Research', *Social Science Information*, 8, pp. 7–32.

— [1971], *The Uses of Structuralism* (London: Heinemann).

BOWLEY, A. L. [1915], *The Nature and Purpose of the Measurement of Social Phenomena* (London: King).

— and BURNETT-HURST, A. L. [1915], *Livelihood and Poverty* (London: Bell).

BRAITHWAITE, R. B. [1953], *Scientific Explanation* (Cambridge: Cambridge University Press).

BRAMSON, L. (1961], *The Political Context of Sociology* (Princeton, N. J.: Princeton University Press).

BREWER, J. M. [1966], 'Hidden Language', *New York Times Magazine*, 25 December.

BRIDGMAN, P. W. [1948], *The Logic of Modern Physics* (New York: The Macmillan Co.).

BRIGGS, A. [1961], *A Study of the Work of Seebohm Rowntree* (London: Longmans).

BRIGHT, W. [1966], 'Language, Social Stratification and Cognitive Orientation', *Sociological Inquiry*, 36, pp. 313–18.

BROTHERSTON, J. [1976], 'Inequality: Is it Inevitable?', in Carter and Peel [1976].

BROWN, G. W. [1973], 'Some Thoughts on Grounded Theory', *Sociology*, 7, pp. 1–16.

— and HARRIS, T. [1978], *The Social Origins of Depression: A Study of Psychiatric Depression in Women* (London: Tavistock).

BROWN, R. [1958], *Words and Things* (Glencoe: Free Press).

— [1962], 'Language and Categories', in J. S. Bruner *et al.*, *A Study of Thinking* (New York: Science Editions).

— [1963], *Explanation in Social Science* (London: Routledge).

BROWN, R. K. [1978], 'Work', in Abrams [1978] pp. 55–159.

BULMER, M. [1972], 'Social Survey Research and Postgraduate Training in Sociological Method', *Sociology*, 6, pp. 267–74.

— [1974], 'Sociology and History: Some Recent Trends', *Sociology*, 8, pp. 137–50.

— (ed.) [1975], *Working Class Images of Society* (London: Routledge).

— (ed.) [1978], *Social Policy Research* (London: Macmillan).

— (ed.) [1979], *Censuses, Surveys and Privacy* (London: Macmillan).

— [1980a], 'Review of *Demystifying Social Statistics*', *Quality and Quantity*, 14, pp. 365–6.

— [1980b], 'On the Feasibility of Identifying "Race" and "Ethnicity" in Censuses and Surveys', *New Community*, 8 (1) pp. 3–15.

— (ed.) [1980c], *Social Research and Royal Commissions* (London: Allen & Unwin).

— [1982], *The Uses of Social Research* (London: Allen & Unwin).

— [1984], *The Chicago School of Sociology: Institutionalization, Diversity and the Rise of Sociological Research* (Chicago: University of Chicago Press).

— (ed.) [1982], *Social Research Ethics: An Examination of the Merits of Covert Participant Observation* (London: Macmillan).

— [1985], *Essays on the History of British Sociological Research* (Cambridge: Cambridge University Press).

— and BURGESS, R. (eds) [1981], 'The Teaching of Research Methodology', Special Issue of *Sociology*, 15 (4) pp. 477–602.

— and WARWICK, D. P. (eds) [1983], *Social Research in Developing Countries: Surveys and Censuses in the Third World* (Chichester, Sussex: Wiley).

BUNGE, M. [1959], *Causalty* (Cambridge, Mass.: Harvard University Press).

BURCHINAL, L. G. and CHANCELLOR, L. E. [1962], 'Ages at Marriage, Occupations of Grooms and Interreligious Marriage Rates', *Social Forces*, 40, pp. 348–54.

— — [1963], 'Survival Rates among Religiously Homogamous and Interreligious Marriages', *Social Forces*, 41 pp. 353–62.

— and KENKEL, W. F. [1962], 'Religious Identification and Occupational Status of Iowa Grooms', *American Sociological Review*, 27, pp. 526–32.

BURGESS, E. W. and NEWCOMB, C. [1931], *Census Data of the City of Chicago 1920* (Chicago: University of Chicago Press).

— — [1933], *Census Data of the City of Chicago 1930* (Chicago: University of Chicago Press).

BURGESS, R. (eds) [1982], *Field Research: A Sourcebook and Field Manual* (London and Boston: Allen & Unwin).

— [1984a], *In the Field* (London and Boston: Allen & Unwin).

— (ed.) [1984b], *Key Variables in Social Investigation* (London: Routledge).

— (ed.) [1984c], *The Research Process in Educational Settings: Ten Case Studies* (Lewes, Sussex: Fulone Press).

BURNETT, J. [1974], *Useful Toil: Autobiographies of Working People from the 1820s to the 1920s* (London: Allen Lane).

BUTLER, D. and STOKES, D. [1969], *Political Change in Britain* (London: Macmillan).

CAMPBELL, A. [1981], *The Sense of Well Being in America: Recent Patterns and Trends* (New York: McGraw-Hill).

CAMPBELL, D. T. and FISKE, D. W. [1959], 'Convergent and Discriminant Validation by the Multitrait-multimethod Matrix', *Psychological Bulletin*, 56, pp. 81–105.

— and STANLEY, J. C. [1963], *Experimental and Quasi-experimental Designs for Research* (Chicago: Rand McNally).

CAMPBELL, R. [1955], *Selected Poems* (Chicago: Regnery).

CAPLOW, T. [1956], 'The Dynamics of Information Interviewing', *American Journal of Sociology*, 62, pp. 165–71.

CARLEY, M. [1981], *Social Measurement and Social Indicators* (London Boston: Allen & Unwin).

CARR, E. H. [1961], *What is History?* (London: Macmillan; paper edition, London: Penguin Books, 1968).

CARTER, C. and PEEL, J. (eds) [1976], *Equalities and Inequalities in Health* (London: Academic Press).

CENTRAL STATISTICAL OFFICE [1978], *Guide to Official Statistics*, revised edn (London: H.M.S.O.).

CHRISTENSEN, H. T. [1960], 'Cultural Relativism and Premarital Sex Norms', *American Sociological Review*, 25, pp. 31–9.

CICOUREL, A. V. [1964], *Method and Measurement in Sociology* (New York: Free Press).

— [1966], 'Fertility, Family Planning and the Organisation of Family Life' (University of California, Santa Barbara) mimeo.

— [1967], 'Kinship, Marriage and Divorce in Comparative Family Law', *Law and Society Review*, 1, pp. 103–29.

— [1968] [1976], *The Social Organisation of Juvenile Justice* (New York: Wiley) (British edition: Heinemann, 1976).

CLARK, [1957], *America's Psychologists* (Washington, D.C.: American Psychological Association).

CLARK, W. H. [1955], 'A Study of Some Factors Leading to Achievement and Creativity', *Journal of Social Psychology*, 41, pp. 57–69.

C.O.D.O.T. [1972], *Classification of Occupations and Directory of Occupational Titles* (London: H.M.S.O.).

COHEN, A. K. and HODGES, H. M. [1963], 'Characteristics of the Lower Blue-collar Class', *Social Problems*, 10, pp. 303–34.

COHEN, P. S. [1968], *Modern Social Theory* (London: Heinemann).

COHEN, R. *et al.* [1968], 'The Language of the Hard-core Poor', *Sociological Quarterly*, 9, pp. 19–28.

COLEMAN, J. [1968], 'Review of H. Garfinkel, *Studies in Ethnomethodology*', *American Sociological Review*, 33, pp. 126–30.

COLEMAN, J. S. (ed.) [1970], *Macro-sociology: Research and Theory* (Boston: Allyn & Bacon).

COLEMAN, J. S. *et al.* [1966], *Inequality of Educational Opportunity* (Washington, D.C.: U.S. Government Printing Office).

COLLIER, F. [1965], *The Family Economy and the Working Classes in the Cotton Industry 1784–1833* (Manchester: Manchester University Press).

COLLINS, R. [1975], *Conflict Sociology* (New York: Academic Press).

CONVERSE, P. E. [1964], 'New Dimensions of Meaning for Cross-section Sample Surveys in Politics', *International Social Science Journal*, 16, pp. 19–34.

COSER, L. [1971], [1977], *Masters of Sociological Thought* (New York: Harcourt Brace Jovanovich) (revised edition, 1977).

— [1974], *Greedy Institutions* (New York: Free Press).

— [1975], 'Two Methods in Search of a Substance', *American Sociological Review*, 40, pp. 691–700.

COSTNER, H. L. (ed.) [1974], *Sociological Methodology 1973–74* (San Francisco: Jossey Bass).

CRANE, D. [1972], *Invisible Colleges* (Chicago: University of Chicago Press).

CRESSEY, D. [1953], *Other People's Money* (Glencoe Ill.: Free Press).

CROCKETT, H. J. and LEVINE, L. [1967], 'Friends' Influence on Speech', *Sociological Inquiry*, 37, pp. 109–28.

CROWALD, R. H. [1964], 'Soviet Grave Markers Indicate How Buried Rated with Regime', *El Universal*, 196, p. 12.

CROZIER, D. [1965], 'Kinship and Occupational Succession', *Sociological Review*, 13, pp. 15–43.

DAHL, R. [1964], *Who Governs?* (New Haven, Conn.: Yale University Press).

DAHRENDORF, R. [1958], 'Out of Utopia', *American Journal of Sociology*, 64, pp. 115–27.

— [1963], 'Soziologie', in A. Flintner (ed.), *Wege zur Pedagogischen Anthropologie* (Heidelberg).

— [1964], 'Recent Changes in the Class Structure of European Societies', *Daedalus*, 93, pp. 225–70.

— [1968], *Essays in the Theory of Society* (London: Routledge).

DALTON, M. [1959], *Men who Manage* (New York: Wiley).

— [1964], 'Preconceptions and Methods in *Men Who Manage*', in P. Hammond (ed.) [1964] pp. 50–95.

DAVIES, C. [1980], 'Making Sense of the Census in Britain and the U.S.A.: The Changing Occupational Classification and the Position of Nurses', *The Sociological Review*, 28 (3) pp. 581–609.

DAVIES, C. S. [1963], *North-country Bred: A Working Class Family Chronicle* (London: Routledge).

DAVIES, J. A. [1971], *Elementary Survey Analysis* (Englewood Cliffs, N.J.: Prentice-Hall).

— *et al.* [1961], 'A Technique for Analysing the Effects of Group Composition', *American Sociological Review*, 26, pp. 215–25.

DAVIES, K. [1959], 'The Myth of Functional Analysis', *American Sociological Review*, 24, pp. 757–82.

DAWE, A. [1970], 'The Two Sociologies', *British Journal of Sociology*, 21, pp. 207–18.

DECHARMS, R. and MOELLER, G. [1962], 'Values Expressed in American Children's Readers: 1800–1950', *Journal of Abnormal and Social Psychology*, 64, pp. 136–42.

DENZIN, N. [1970], *The Research Act* (London: Butterworth).

— [1971], 'The Logic of Naturalistic Inquiry', *Social Forces*, 50, pp. 166–82.

DEUTSCHER, I. [1966], 'Words and Deeds: Social Science and Social Policy', *Social Problems*, 13, pp. 235–54.

— [1968], 'Asking Questions Cross-culturally: Some Problems of Linguistic Comparability', in H. S. Becker *et al.* (eds) [1968] pp. 318–41.

— [1972], 'Public and Private Opinions', in S. Z. Nagi and R. G. Corwin (eds), *The Social Contexts of Research* (New York: Wiley) pp. 323–49.

— [1973], *What We Say/What We Do: Sentiments and Acts* (Glenview, Ill: Scott Foresman).

DIENER, E. and CRANDALL, R. [1978], *Ethics in Social and Behavioral Research* (Chicago: University of Chicago Press).

DITTON, J. [1977], *Part-time Crime* (London: Macmillan).

DOLLARD, J. [1935], *Criteria for the Life History* (New Haven, Conn.: Yale University Press).

DORE, R. P. [1969], 'Making Sense of History', *European Journal of Sociology*, 10, pp. 295–305.

DOUGLAS, J. D. [1967], *The Social Meanings of Suicide* (Princeton, N.J.: Princeton University Press).

DOUGLAS, J. W. B. [1964], *The Home and the School* (London: McGibbon & Kee).

— *et al.* [1968], *All Our Future* (London: Peter Davis).

DOYAL, L. [1979], 'A Matter of Life and Death: Medicine, Health and Statistics', in Irvine *et al.* [1979] pp. 237–44.

DUBIN, R. [1969], *Theory Building* (New York: Free Press).

DUCKWORTH, W. E. [1962], *A Guide to Operational Research* (London: Methuen).

DUMONT, L. [1970], *Homo Hierarchicus* (Chicago: University of Chicago Press).

DUNNING, E. [1967], 'The Concept of Development: Two Illustrative Case Studies', in P. I. Rose (ed.), *The Study of Society* (New York: Random House).

DURAND, J. [1960], 'Mortality Estimates from Roman Tombstone Inscriptions', *American Journal of Sociology*, 65, pp. 365–73.

DURKHEIM, E. [1947], *The Division of Labour in Society* (Glencoe: Free Press) (English translation; original French edition 1893).

— [1951], *Suicide* (London: Routledge) (English translation; original French edition 1897).

— [1964], *The Rules of Sociological Method* (Glencoe: Free Press) (English translation; original French edition 1895).

DYOS, H. J. (ed.) [1968], *The Study of Urban History* (London: Arnold).

— and BAKER, A. [1968], 'The Possibilities of Computerising Census Data', in Dyos (ed.) [1968).

EDWARDS, B. [1974], *Sources of Social Statistics* (London: Heinemann).

ELDER, G. H. Jr [1974], *Children of the Great Depression* (Chicago: University of Chicago Press).

ELIAS, N. [1956], 'Problems of Involvement and Detachment', *British Journal of Sociology*, 7, pp. 226–52.

EVANS, W. M. [1960–1], 'Conflict and the Emergence of Norms: The "Springdale" Case', *Human Organisation*, 19, pp. 172–3.

— (ed.) [1962], *Law and Sociology* (New York: Free Press).

FARIS, R. E. L. (ed.) [1964], *Handbook of Modern Sociology* (Chicago: Rand McNally).

FERRIS, A. L. *et al.* [1978], 'Review Symposium on *Social Indicators 1976*', *Contemporary Sociology*, 7, pp. 712–24.

FEUER, L. [1962], 'What is *Alienation?*: The Career of a Concept', *New Politics*, 2, pp. 116–34.

FICHTER, J. [1973], *One-man Research: Reminiscences of a Catholic Sociologist* (New York: Wiley).

FIENBERG, S. E. [1977], *The Analysis of Cross-Classified Categorical Data* (Cambridge, Man.: M.I.T. Press).

FILMER, P. *et al.* [1972], *New Directions in Sociological Theory* (London: Collier-Macmillan).

FILSTEAD, W. J. (ed.) [1970], *Qualitative Methodology* (Chicago, Markham).

FIRTH, R. [1964], 'Family and Kinship in Industrial Society', in P. Halmos (ed.), *The Development of Industrial Societies* (Keele, Sociological Review Monographs).

FLANDERS, A. [1964], *The Fawley Productivity Agreements* (London: Faber).

FLINN, M. W. and SMOUT, T. C. (eds) [1974], *Essays in Social History* (London: Oxford University Press).

FORD, J. [1969], *Social Class and the Comprehensive School* (London: Routledge).
— [1975], *Paradigms and Fairytales* (London: Routledge).
FOSTER, J. [1974], *Class Struggle and the Industrial Revolution* (London: Weidenfeld & Nicolson).
FOX, J. [1977], 'Occupational Mortality 1970–72', *Population Trends*, 9.
FOX, R. [1967], *Kinship and Marriage* (London: Penguin Books).
FRIEDEBURG, L. VON [1965], 'Wissenschaftstheoretische Uberlegungen zur Methodologie Max Webers', in *Max Weber und die Sociologie heute* (Tübingen: Mohr) pp. 265–77.
FRIEDMAN, N. J. [1967], *The Social Nature of Psychological Research* (New York: Wiley).
FRY, C. L. [1933], 'The Religious Affiliations of American Leaders', *Scientific Monthly*, 36, pp. 241–9.
FURSTENBERG, F. [1958], *Probleme der Lohnstruktur* (Tübingen: Mohr).
GALTON, F. [1870], *Hereditary Genius* (New York: Appleton).
— [1872], 'Statistical Inquiries into the Efficacy of Prayer', *Fortnightly Review*, 12, pp. 125–3.
GALTUNG, J. [1967], *Theories and Methods of Social Research* (London: Allen & Unwin).
GARFINKEL, H. [1967], *Studies in Ethnomethodology* (Englewood Cliffs, N.J.: Prentice-Hall).
GASSON, R. M. *et al.* [1972], *Attitudes and Facilitation in the Attainment of Status* (Rose Monograph Series) (Washington, D.C.: American Sociological Association).
GELLNER, E. [1964], *Thought and Change* (London: Weidenfeld & Nicolson).
GERTH, H. H. and MILLS, C. W. (eds) [1948], *From Max Weber* (London: Routledge).
G.H.S. [1972], *The General Household Survey, 1971* (London: H.M.S.O.).
G.H.S. [1975], *The General Household Survey, 1972* (London: H.M.S.O.).
GIDDENS, A. [1971], *Capitalism and Modern Social Theory* (Cambridge: Cambridge University Press).
GILBERT, N. [1981], *Modelling Society: An Introduction to Loglinear Analysis for Social Researchers* (London and Boston: Allen & Unwin).
GITTUS, E. (ed.) [1972], *Key Variables in Social Research*, vol. 1: *Religion, Housing, Locality* (London: Heinemann for B.S.A.).
GLASER, B. G. and STRAUSS, A. L. [1965], *Awareness of Dying* (Chicago: Aldine).

— — [1967], *The Discovery of Grounded Theory* (London: Weidenfeld & Nicolson).

GLASER, N. [1959], 'The Rise of Social Research in Europe', in D. Lerner (ed.), *The Human Meaning of the Social Sciences* (Cleveland: World Publishing Co.) pp. 43–72.

GLENN, E. S. [1954], 'Semantic Differences in International Communication', *A Review of General Semantics*, 11, pp. 163–80.

GLENN, N. *et al.* [1978], 'Review Symposium on General Social Surveys', *Contemporary Sociology*, 7, pp. 532–49.

GOFFMAN, E. [1964], 'The Neglected Situation', *American Anthropologist*, 66, pp. 133–6.

GOLDTHORPE, J. H. [1971], 'Theories of Industrial Society: Reflections on the Recrudescence of Historicism and the Future of Futurology', *European Journal of Sociology*, 12, pp. 263–88.

— *et al.* [1968], *The Affluent Worker: Industrial Attitudes and Behaviour* (Cambridge: Cambridge University Press).

— *et al.* [1968], *The Affluent Worker: Political Attitudes and Behaviour* (Cambridge: Cambridge University Press).

— *et al.* [1969], *The Affluent Worker in the Class Structure* (Cambridge: Cambridge University Press).

— [1972], 'Class, Status and Party in Modern Britain', *European Journal of Sociology*, 13, pp. 342–72.

GOODE, W. J. [1963–4], 'The Process of Role Bargaining in the Impact of Urbanisation and Industrialisation', *Current Sociology*, 12, pp. 1–13.

GORDEN, R. L. [1975], *Interviewing: Strategy, Techniques and Tactics*, rev. edn (Arundel: Irwin–Dorsey).

GORDON, C. [1972], *Looking Ahead* (Rose Monograph Series) (Washington, D.C.: American Sociological Association).

GOTTSCHALK, L. *et al.* [1947], *The Uses of Personal Documents in History, Anthropology and Sociology* (New York: S.S.R.C.).

GOULDNER, A. W. [1955a], *Wildcat Strike* (London: Routledge).

— [1955b], *Patterns of Industrial Bureaucracy* (New York: Free Press).

GOVER, R. [1963], *The One-hundred Dollar Misunderstanding* (New York: Ballantine).

GREENWOOD, E. [1945], *Experimental Sociology* (New York: Kings Crown Press).

GREER, S. [1969], *The Logic of Social Inquiry* (Chicago: Aldine).

GROSS, L. (ed.) [1959], *Symposium on Sociological Theory* (New York: Harper).

HAKIM, C. [1980a], 'Census Reports as Documentary Evidence; The Census Commentaries 1801–1851', *The Sociological Review*, 28 (3) pp. 551–80.

— [1980b], 'Social Aspects of Employment: Data for Policy Research', *Journal of Social Policy*, 9, pp. 77–98.

— [1982], *Secondary Analysis in Social Research* (London and Boston: Allen & Unwin).

HALSEY, A. H. (ed.) [1972], *Trends in British Society since 1900* (London: Macmillan).

HAMBLIN, R. L. [1966], 'Ratio Measurement and Sociological Theory', (Washington University, St Louis) mimeo.

HAMMERSLEY, M. and ATKINSON, P. [1983], *Ethnography: Principles in Practice* (London: Tavistock).

HAMMOND, P. E. (ed.) [1964], *Sociologists at Work: Essays on the Craft of Social Research* (New York: Basic Books).

HANSON, N. R. [1958], *Patterns of Discovery: An Inquiry into the Conceptual Foundations of Science* (Cambridge: Cambridge University Press).

— [1969], *Perception and Discovery* (San Francisco: Freeman).

HARGREAVES, D. [1970], *Social Relations in a Secondary School* (London: Routledge).

HART, N. [1980], *Health and Inequality* (Colchester: Department of Sociology, University of Essex) mimeo.

HAUSER, R. M. [1970], 'Context and Consex: A Cautionary Tale', *American Journal of Sociology*, 75, pp. 645–64.

— [1972], *Socioeconomic Background and Educational Performance* (Rose Monograph Series) (Washington, D.C.: American Sociological Association).

HAWTHORN, G. [1970], *The Sociology of Fertility* (London: Collier-Macmillan).

HEBERLE, R. [1931], 'Soziographie', in A. Vierkandt (ed.), *Handworterbuch der Soziologie* (Stuttgart: Enke).

HEER, D. M. [1975], *Society and Population*, 2nd edn (Englewood Cliffs, N.J.: Prentice-Hall).

HEISE, D. R. [1966], 'Social Status, Attitudes and Word Connotations', *Sociological Inquiry*, 36, pp. 227–39.

— [1975], *Causal Analysis* (New York: Wiley).

HELLEVIK, O. [1984], *Introduction to Causal Analysis: Exploring Survey Data by Crosstabulation* (London and Boston: Allen & Unwin).

HEMPEL, C. G. [1952], *Fundamentals of Concept Formation in Empirical Science* (vol. 7, no. 2, International Library of Unified Science, University of Chicago Press).

HERTZLER, J. O. [1965], *A Sociology of Language* (New York: Random House).

— [1966], 'Social Uniformation and Language', *Sociological Inquiry*, 36, pp. 298–312.

HEWITT, M. [1953], 'The Effect of Married Women's Employment in the Cotton Textile Districts on the Home in Lancashire, 1840–80' (London University, Ph.D. thesis).

— [1959], *Wives and Mothers in Victorian Industry* (London: Rockliff).

HICKSON, D. J. [1961], 'Motives of Workpeople who Restrict their Own Output', *Occupational Psychology*, 35.

HIMMELWEIT, H. *et al.* [1958], *Television and the Child* (London: Oxford University Press).

HINDELGANG, M. J. *et al.* [1931], *Measuring Delinquency* (Beverly Hills: Sage).

HINDESS, B. [1973], *The Use of Official Statistics in Sociology* (London: Macmillan).

HIRD, C. and IRVINE, J. [1979], 'The Poverty of Wealth Statistics', in Irvine *et al.* (eds) [1979] pp. 190–211.

HIRSCHI, T. [1969], *The Causes of Delinquency* (Berkeley: University of California Press).

— and SELVIN, H. [1967], *Delinquency Research: An Appraisal of Analytic Methods* (New York: Free Press; republished in paper edn 1973 as *Principles of Survey Analysis*).

HODGE, R. W. and TREIMAN, D. J. [1968], 'Social Participation and Social Status', *American Sociological Review*, 33, pp. 722–40.

HOGGART, R. [1957], *The Uses of Literacy* (London: Chatto & Windus).

HOMANS, G. [1964], 'Contemporary Theory in Sociology', in R. E. L. Faris (ed.), *Handbook of Modern Sociology* (Chicago: Rand McNally), pp. 951–77.

HOPE, K. (ed.) [1972], *The Analysis of Social Mobility* (London: Oxford University Press).

HOROWITZ, I. L. (ed.) [1967], *The Rise and Fall of Project Camelot* (London: M.I.T. Press).

— (ed.) [1970], *Sociological Self-images* (Oxford: Pergamon).

HORTON, J. [1964], 'The Dehumanisation of Anomie and Alienation', *British Journal of Sociology*, 15, pp. 283–300.

HUDSON, D. [1972], *Munby: Man of Two Worlds* (London: John Murray).

HUGHES, E. C. and HUGHES, H. M. [1952], *Where Peoples Meet: Racial and Ethnic Frontiers* (Glencoe: Free Press).

HUGHES, H. S. [1959], *Consciousness and Society* (London: MacGibbon & Kee).

HUNT, W. H. *et al.* [1964], 'Interviewing Political Elites in Cross-cultural Comparative Research', *American Journal of Sociology*, 70, pp. 59–68.

HUNTER, A. [1974], *Symbolic Communities* (Chicago: University of Chicago Press).

HUNTER, F. [1953], *Community Power Structure* (Chapel Hill, North Carolina: University of North Carolina Press).

HYMAN, H. [1954], *Interviewing in Social Research* (Chicago: University of Chicago Press).

— [1972], *Secondary Analysis of Sample Surveys* (New York: Wiley).

HYMES, D. [1964], 'Introduction: Toward Ethnographies of Communication', *American Anthropologist*, 66, pp. 1–34.

— [1966], 'Two Types of Linguistic Relativity', in W. Bright (ed.), *Sociolinguistics* (The Hague: Mouton).

IANNI, F. A. J. [1957–8], 'Residential and Occupational Mobility as Indices of the Acculturation of an Ethnic Group', *Social Forces*, 36, pp. 65–72.

IRVINE, J., MILES, I. and EVANS, J. (eds) [1979], *Demystifying Social Statistics* (London: Pluto).

JACKMAN, M. R. and JACKMAN, R. W. [1973], 'An Interpretation of the Relation between Objective and Subjective Social Status', *American Sociological Review*, 38, pp. 569–82.

JACOBY, E. [1973], 'Three Aspects of the Sociology of Toennies', in W. Cahnmann (ed.), *Ferdinand Toennies* (Leidan: Brill) pp. 70–102.

JAHODA, M. *et al.* [1951], *Research Methods in Social Relations* (New York: Dryden Press).

JOHNSON, P. [1963], 'The New Men of the Soviet Sixties', *Reporter*, 28, 9 May.

JONES, E. L. [1963], 'The Courtesy Bias in South-east Asian Surveys', *International Social Science Journal*, 15, pp. 70–6.

JORDAN, N. [1965], 'The "Asymmetry" of "Liking" and "Disliking"', *Public Opinion Quarterly*, 29, pp. 315–22.

KAHN, R. F. and CANNELL, C. F. [1957], *The Dynamics of Interviewing* (New York: Wiley).

KAPLAN, A. [1964], *The Conduct of Inquiry* (San Francisco: Chandler).

KAUFMANN, F. [1958], *The Methodology of the Social Sciences* (London: Thames & Hudson).

KELLEY, J. [1973], 'Causal Chain Models for Socioeconomic Career', *American Sociological Review*, 38, pp. 481–93.

KELMAN, M. [1974], 'The Social Costs of Inequality', in L. A. Coser (ed.), *The New Conservatives* (New York: Quadrangle) pp. 151–64.

KENT, R. [1982], *A History of British Empirical Sociology* (Farnborough, Hants: Gower).

KERCKHOFF, A. C. [1974], *Ambition and Attainment* (Rose Monograph Series) (Washington, D.C.: American Sociological Association).

KITUSE, J. I. and CICOUREL, A. V. [1963], 'A Note on the Uses of Official Statistics', *Social Problems*, 11, pp. 131–9.

KNIGHT, R. [1967], 'Changes in the Occupational Structure of the Working Population', *Journal of the Royal Statistical Society*, **a**, 130, pp. 408–22.

KOLAKOWSKI, L. [1972], *Positivist Philosophy* (London: Heinemann).

KRIPPENDORF, K. [1980], *Content Analysis* (Beverly Hills: Sage).

KROEBER, A. L. [1957], *Style and Civilisations* (Ithaca, N.Y.: Cornell University Press).

KUHN, T. S. [1962], *The Structure of Scientific Revolutions* (Chicago: University of Chicago Press).

LABOV, W. [1966], 'The Effect of Social Mobility on Linguistic Behaviour', *Sociological Inquiry*, 36, pp. 186–203.

LACHENMEYER, C. [1971], *The Language of Sociology* (New York: Columbia University Press).

LANCASTER, L. [1961], 'Some Conceptual Problems in the Study of Family and Kin Ties in the British Isles', *British Journal of Sociology*, 12, pp. 317–33.

LANGER, S. K. [1973], *Mind*, vol. 1 (Baltimore: John Hopkins University Press).

LAPIERE, R. T. [1934], 'Attitudes versus Actions', *Social Forces*, 13, pp. 230–7.

LASLETT, P. [1965], *The World We Have Lost* (London: Methuen).

LASLETT, P. and HARRISON, J. [1963], 'Clayworth and Cogenhoe', in H. E. Bell and R. L. Ollard (eds), *Historical Essays 1600–1750 Presented to David Ogg* (London: Black).

LAWTON, R. (ed.) [1978], *The Census and Social Structure* (London: Frank Cass).

LAYARD, R. *et al.* [1978], *The Causes of Poverty* (Royal Commission on the Distribution of Income and Wealth: Background Study no. 5) (London: H.M.S.O.).

LAZARSFELD, P. F. [1948], 'The Use of Panels in Social Research', *American Philosophical Society Proceedings*, 92, pp. 405–10.

— [1949], '*The American Soldier* – An Expository Review', *Public Opinion Quarterly*, 13, pp. 378–80.

— [1957], 'The Historian and the Pollster', in M. Komarovsky (ed.), *Common Frontiers of the Social Sciences* (Glencoe: Free Press).

— [1958], 'Evidence and Inference in Social Research', *Daedalus*, 87, pp. 99–130.

— [1959], 'Problems of Methodology', in R. K. Merton *et al.* (eds), *Sociology Today* (New York: Basic Books).

— [1961], 'Notes on the History of Quantification in Sociology', in H. Woolf (ed.), *Quantification* (New York: Bobbs-Merrill) pp. 147–203.

— [1972], *Qualitative Analysis: Historical and Critical Essays* (Boston: Allyn & Bacon).

— and BARTON, A. H. [1955], 'Some Functions of Qualitative Analysis in Social Research', *Frankfurter Beitrage zur Soziologie*, Band 1, pp. 321 ff. (reprinted in McCall and Simmons [1969] pp. 163–96).

— and MENZEL, H. [1961], 'On the Relationship between Individual and Collective Properties', in A. Etzioni (ed.), *Complex Organisations* (Englewood Cliffs, N.J.: Prentice-Hall) pp. 422–40.

— and ROSENBERG, M. (eds) [1955], *The Language of Social Research* (Glencoe: Free Press).

LEETE, R. and FOX, J. [1977], 'Registrar-General's Social Class: Origin and Uses', *Population Trends*, 8, pp. 7–8.

LEHMAN, H. C. and WITTY, P. A. [1931], 'Scientific Eminence and Church Membership', *Scientific Monthly*, 36, pp. 544–9.

LENIN, V. I. [1934], *On Britain* (London: Lawrence).

LERNER, D. [1956], 'Interviewing Frenchmen', *American Journal of Sociology*, 62, pp. 187–94.

LEVINE, D. N. *et al.* [1976], 'Simmel's Influence on American Sociology', *American Journal of Sociology*, 81, pp. 813–45 and 1112–32.

LEWIS, O. [1961], *The Children of Sanchez* (London: Secker & Warburg).

— [1967], *La Vida: A Puerto Rican Family in the Culture of Poverty* (London: Secker & Warburg).

LIBBY, W. I. [1963], 'Accuracy of Radio-carbon Dates', *Science*, 140, pp. 278–80.

LIEBOW, E. [1967], *Tally's Corner, Washington D.C.: A Study of Negro Street Corner Men* (Boston: Little, Brown).

LINDBLOM, C. and COHEN, D. K. [1979], *Usable Knowledge* (New Haven, Conn.: Yale University Press).

LINDESMITH, A. [1947], *Opiate Addiction* (Bloomington, Ind.: Principia Press).

— [1968], *Addiction and Opiates* (Chicago: Aldine).

LINDSEY, C. (ed.) [1954], (Reading, Mass.: *Handbook of Social Psychology* Addison-Wesley).

LIPPMANN, W. [1955], *The Public Philosophy* (New York: New American Library).

LIPSET, S. M. [1968], 'History and Sociology: Some Methodological Considerations', in Lipset and Hofstadter (eds) [1968] pp. 20–58.

— and HOFSTADTER, R. (eds) [1968], *Sociology and History: Methods* (New York: Basic Books).

— *et al.* [1956], *Union Democracy* (Glencoe: Free Press).

LITWAK, E. [1965], 'Extended Kin Relations in an Industrial Democratic Society', in Shanas and Streib (eds) [1965].

LOCK, G. F. [1976], *General Sources of Statistics* (London: Heinemann).

LOETHER, H. J. and MCTAVISH, D. C. [1974], *Descriptive and Inferential Statistics for Sociologists*, 2 vols (Boston: Allyn & Bacon).

LOFLAND, J. [1971], *Analysing Social Settings* (Belmont, Calif.: Wadsworth).

LOTT, A. J. and LOTT, B. E. [1963], 'Ethnocentrism and Space-superiority Judgements Following Cosmonaut and Astronaut Flights', *Public Opinion Quarterly*, 27, pp. 604–11.

LOUDON, J. B. [1961], 'Kinship and Crisis in South Wales', *British Journal of Sociology*, 12, pp. 333–50.

LUKES, S. M. [1967], 'Alienation and Anomie', in P. Laslett and W. Runciman (eds), *Philosophy, Politics and Society: Third Series* (Oxford: Blackwell) pp. 134–56.

LURIE, A. [1967], *Imaginary Friends* (London: Heinemann).

MCCALL, G. J. and SIMMONS, J. L. (eds) [1969], *Issues in Participant Observation: A Text and a Reader* (Reading, Mass.: Addison-Wesley).

MCGRATH, J. E. and ALTMAN, I. [1966], *Small Group Research* (New York: Holt, Rinehart & Winston).

MCGREGOR, O. R. [1957], *Divorce in England* (London: Heinemann).

— [1961], 'Some Research Possibilities and Historical Materials for Family and Kinship Study in Britain', *British Journal of Sociology*, 12, pp. 310–17.

MACK, J. [1978], 'A Question of Race', *New Society*, 5 January, pp. 8–9.

MCKINNEY, J. C. and TIRYAKIAN, E. A. (eds) [1970], *Theoretical Sociology: Perspectives and Developments* (New York: Appleton-Century-Crofts).

MACRAE, D. [1954], 'Some Underlying Variables in Legislative Roll-call Votes', *Public Opinion Quarterly*, 18, pp. 191–6.

MADGE, C. [1964], *Society in the Mind* (London: Faber).

MANN, M. [1978], 'Review', *Times Literary Supplement*, 24 February, p. 235.

MARSH, C. [1979], 'Opinion Polls: Social Science or Political Manœuvre?', in J. Irvine *et al.*, *Demystifying Social Statistics* (London: Pluto).

— [1982], *The Survey Method: The Contribution of Surveys to Sociological Explanation* (London and Boston: Allen & Unwin).

MARSH, R. M. [1961], 'Formal Organisation and Promotion in a Pre-industrial Society', *American Sociological Review*, 26, pp. 547–56.

MARSHALL, T. H. [1963], *Sociology at the Crossroads* (London: Heinemann).

MARX, K. [1964] [1867], *Capital* (Moscow: Foreign Languages Press).

MATZA, D. [1969], *Becoming Deviant* (Englewood Cliffs, N.J.: Prentice-Hall).

MAYHEW, H. [1851], *London Labour and the London Poor*, 2 vols (London).

MEDAWAR, P. [1969], *Induction and Intuition in Scientific Thought* (London: Methuen).

MERTON, R. K. [1957] [1968], *Social Theory and Social Structure*, 2nd edn (Glencoe: Free Press) (2nd edn, 1968).

— *et al.* [1957], *The Student Physician* (Cambridge, Mass.: Harvard University Press).

— [1959], 'Notes on Problem-finding in Sociology', in R. K. Merton *et al.* (eds) [1959], *Sociology Today* (New York: Basic Books), pp. ix–xxxiv.

MICHALOS, A. C. [1980–2] *North American Social Report: A Comparative Study of the Quality of Life in Canada and the U.S.A. from 1964 to 1971* (Dentrecht: D. Reidel, 5 vols).

MICHELS, R. [1949], *Political Parties* (Glencoe: Free Press).

MIDDLETON, R. [1960], 'Fertility Values in American Magazine Fiction, 1916–56', *Public Opinion Quarterly*, 24, pp. 139–43.

— [1963], 'Alienation, Race and Education', *American Sociological Review*, 28, pp. 973–7.

MILES, I. and IRVINE, J. [1979], 'The Critique of Official Statistics', in J. Irvine *et al.* [1979] pp. 113–29.

MILLER, P. and WILSON, M. [1983], *A Dictionary of Social Science Methods* (Chichester, Sussex: Wiley).

MILLS, C. WRIGHT [1939], 'Language, Logic and Culture', *American Sociological Review*, 4, pp. 670–80.

— [1959], *The Sociological Imagination* (New York: Oxford University Press).

MITCHELL, J. C. [1969], *Social Networks in Urban Situations* (Manchester: Manchester University Press).

— [1983], 'Case and Situation Analysis', *The Sociological Review*, 31 (2) pp. 187–211.

MITCHELL, R. E. [1965], 'Survey Materials Collected in the Developing Countries: Sampling, Measurement and Interviewing Obstacles to Intra- and International Comparisons', *International Social Science Journal*, 17, pp. 665–85.

MOORE, W. E. and TUMIN, M. M. [1949], 'Some Social Functions of Ignorance', *American Sociological Review*, 14, pp. 787–95.

MORGENSTERN, O. [1963], *On the Accuracy of Economic Observations*, rev. edn (Princeton, N.J.: Princeton University Press).

MORRIS, M. D. [1979], *Measuring the Condition of the World's Poor* (New York and Oxford: Pergamon Press for the Overseas Development Council).

MOSER, C. [1978], 'Social Indicators: Systems, Methods and Problems', in Bulmer (ed.) [1978] pp. 203–14.

MOSER, C. A. and KALTON, G. [1971], *Survey Methods in Social Investigation* (London: Heinemann).

MOSTELLER, F. and MOYNIHAN, D. P. [1972], *On Equality of Educational Opportunity* (New York: Random House).

MUELLER, J. H. *et al.* [1970], *Statistical Reasoning in Sociology* (New York: Houghton Mifflin).

MULLINS, N. [1975], 'New Causal Theory: An Elite Specialism in Social Science', *History of Political Economy*, 7, pp. 499–529.

MYRDAL, G. [1961], 'Value-loaded Concepts', in H. Hegeland (ed.), *Money, Growth and Methodology* (Gleesup) pp. 273–88.

NAGEL, E. [1952], 'The Logic of Historical Analysis', *Scientific Monthly*, 74.

— [1961], *The Structure of Science* (London: Routledge).

NAROLL, R. [1956], 'The Preliminary Index of Social Development', *American Anthropologist*, 58, pp. 687–715.

— [1960], 'Controlling Data Quality', *Symposia Study Series*, 4, pp. 7–12.

— [1961], 'Two Solutions to Galton's Problem', *Philosophy of Science*, 28, pp. 15–39.

— [1962], *Data Quality Control* (Glencoe: Free Press).

NEISSER, H. [1965], *On the Sociology of Knowledge* (New York: Heinemann).

NETTLER, G. [1974], *Explaining Crime* (New York: McGraw-Hill).

NEWCOMB, C. and LANG, R. [1934], *Census Data of the City of Chicago* (Chicago: University of Chicago Press).

NICHOLS, T. [1979], 'Social Class: Official, Sociological, Marxist', in Irvine *et al.* [1979] pp. 152–71.

— and ARMSTRONG, P. [1976], *Workers Divided* (London: Routledge).

NISBET, R. [1967], *The Sociological Tradition* (London: Heinemann).

— [1969], *Social Change and History* (New York: Oxford University Press).

NORTH, R. C. *et al.* [1963], *Content Analysis* (Evaston, Ill.: Northwestern University Press).

OBERSCHALL, A. [1965], *Empirical Social Research in Germany, 1848–1914* (The Hague: Mouton).

— (ed) [1972], *The Establishment of Empirical Sociology: Studies in Continuity, Discontinuity and Institutionalisation* (New York: Harper).

O'DEA, T. [1966], *The Sociology of Religion* (Englewood Cliffs, N.J.: Prentice-Hall).

OKSANEN, E. H. and SPENCER, B. G. [1975], 'On the Determinants of Student Performance in Introductory Courses in the Social Sciences', *The American Sociologist,* 10, pp. 103–9.

O'NEILL, J. (ed.) [1973], *Modes of Individualism and Collectivism* (London: Heinemann).

O.P.C.S. [1970], *Classification of Occupations* (London: H.M.S.O.).

O.P.C.S. [1978], *1981 Census of Population,* Cmnd 7146 (London: H.M.S.O.).

OPPENHEIM, A. N. [1966], *Questionnaire Design and Attitude Measurement* (London: Heinemann).

Oral History [1971], The journal of the Oral History Society, vol. 1, 1971, to date, Department of Sociology, Essex University.

O'TOOLE, R. (ed.) [1971], *The Organisation, Management and Tactics of Social Research* (Cambridge, Mass.: Schenkman).

PARSONS, C. (ed.) [1972], *America's Uncounted People* (Washington, D.C.: National Academy of Sciences).

PARSONS, T. [1937], *The Structure of Social Action* (New York: McGraw-Hill).

— [1951], *The Social System* (Glencoe: Free Press).

— [1966], *Societies: Evolutionary and Comparative Perspectives* (Englewood Cliffs, N.J.: Prentice-Hall).

— [1970], 'On Building Social Systems Theory: A Personal History', *Daedalus,* 99, p. 830.

— [1971], *The System of Modern Societies* (Englewood Cliffs, N.J.: Prentice-Hall).

— *et al.* [1961], *Theories of Society* (New York: Free Press).

PAVLOV, I. P. [1927], *Conditioned Reflexes* (London: Oxford University Press).

PAYNE, G. *et al.* [1981], *Sociology and Social Research* (London: Routledge).

PAYNE, S. L. [1951], *The Art of Asking Questions* (Princeton, N.J.: Princeton University Press).

PELZ, D. C. and ANDREWS, F. M. [1964], 'Detecting Causal Priorities in Panel Study Data', *American Sociological Review*, 29, pp. 836–48.

PETERSEN, W. [1975], *Population*, 3rd edn (New York: Macmillan).

PFAUTZ, H. (ed.) [1967], *Charles Booth on the City* (Chicago: University of Chicago Press).

PHILLIPS, D. L. [1971], *Knowledge from What?* (Chicago: Rand McNally).

PINCHBECK, I. [1930], *Women Workers and the Industrial Revolution, 1750–1850* (London: Routledge).

PLATT, J. [1975], *Realities of Social Research: An Empirical Study of British Sociologists* (London: Chatto & Windus for Sussex University Press).

— [1981], 'Evidence and Proof in Documentary Research', *The Sociological Review*, 29 (1) pp. 31–66.

PLUMMER, K. [1983], *Documents of Life: An Introduction to the Problems and Literature of a Humanistic Method* (London: Allen & Unwin).

POGGI, G. [1965], 'A Main Theme of Contemporary Sociological Analysis: Its Achievements and Limitations', *British Journal of Sociology*, 16, pp. 283–94.

— [1972], *Images of Society* (Stanford, Calif.: Stanford University Press).

POLSBY, N. W. [1963], *Community Power and Political Theory* (New Haven, Conn: Yale University Press).

POLSKY, N. [1971], *Hustlers, Beats and Others* (London: Penguin Books).

POPPER, K. [1957], *The Poverty of Historicism* (London: Routledge).

— [1959], *The Logic of Scientific Discovery* (London: Hutchinson).

— [1972], *Objective Knowledge* (London: Oxford University Press).

PORTER, J. [1965], *The Vertical Mosaic* (Toronto: University of Toronto Press).

— [1970], 'Research Biography of a Macro-sociological Study: *The Vertical Mosaic*', in J. S. Coleman (ed.) [1970].

PORTER, J. N. [1974], 'Race Socialization and Mobility', *American Sociological Review*, 39, pp. 303–16.

PRESTON, B. [1974], 'Statistics of Inequality', *Sociological Review*, 22, pp. 103–18.

PRYCE, K. [1979], *Endless Pressure* (Harmondsworth: Penguin Books).

RAINWATER, L. and YANCEY, W. L. [1967], *The Moynihan Report and Politics of Controversy* (London: M.I.T. Press).

RAZZELL, P. E. [1977], 'Diet', *New Society*, 6 January, p. 31.

REGISTRAR-GENERAL'S DECENNIAL SUPPLEMENT [1977], *Occupational Mortality 1970–72* (London: H.M.S.O.).

REID, I. [1977], *Social Class Differences in Britain* (London: Open Books).

REISS, A. J. [1968], 'Stuff and Nonsense about Social Surveys and Observation', in H. S. Becker *et al.* (eds) [1968] pp. 351–67.

REX, J. A. [1961], *Key Problems in Sociological Theory* (London: Routledge).

— (ed.) [1973], *Approaches to Sociology* (London: Routledge).

RICHARDSON, S. A. *et al.* [1965], *Interviewing: Its Forms and Functions* (New York: Basic Books)).

RIESMAN, D. [1958], 'Some Observations on the Interviewing', in P. F. LAZARSFELD and W. THIELENS, *The Academic Mind* (Glencoe: Free Press) pp. 266–370.

RIKER, W. and NIEMI, D. [1962], 'The Stability of Coalitions on Roll Calls in the House of Representatives', *American Political Science Review*, 56, pp. 58–65.

ROBERTS, R. [1971], *The Classic Slum: Salford Life in the First Quarter of the Nineteenth Century* (Manchester: Manchester University Press).

— [1976], *A Ragged Schooling: Growing Up in the Classic Slum* (Manchester: Manchester University Press).

ROBINSON, W. S. [1950], 'Ecological Correlations and the Behavior of Individuals', *American Sociological Review*, 15, pp. 351–7.

— [1951], 'The Logical Structure of Analytic Induction', *American Sociological Review*, 16, pp. 812–18.

ROCK, P. [1973], 'Phenomenalism and Essentialism in the Sociology of Deviance', *Sociology*, 7, pp. 17–30.

ROGOW, A. A. and LASSWELL, H. D. [1963], *Power, Corruption and Rectitude* (Englewood Cliffs, N.J.: Prentice-Hall).

ROSE, D. *et al.* [1977], 'Land Tenure and Official Statistics', *Journal of Agricultural Economics*, 28, pp. 69–75.

ROSE, G. [1982], *Deciphering Sociological Research* (London: Macmillan).

ROSENBERG, M. [1956], 'Misanthropy and Political Ideology', *American Sociological Review*, 21, pp. 690–5.

— [1968], *The Logic of Survey Analysis* (New York: Basic Books).

ROSENTHAL, R. [1966], *Experimental Effects in Behavioral Research* (New York: Appleton-Century-Crofts).

ROSS, N. [1966], *Workshop Bargaining: A New Approach* (London: Fabian Society).

ROSSER, C. and HARRIS, C. C. [1965], *The Family and Social Change* (London: Routledge).

ROTH, J. [1966], 'Hired-hand Research', *The American Sociologist*, 1, pp. 190–6.

ROWNTREE, B. S. [1902], *Poverty: A Study of Town Life* (London: Longmans).

ROYAL COMMISSION ON THE DISTRIBUTION OF INCOME AND WEALTH [1975–9], *Reports on the Standing Reference* (London: H.M.S.O.).

RYAN, A. (ed.) [1973], *The Philosophy of Social Explanation* (London: Oxford University Press).

RYDER, N. B. [1965], 'The Cohort as a Concept in the Study of Social Change', *American Sociological Review*, 30, pp. 843–61.

SAINT AUGUSTINE [A.D. 401] [1953], *Confessions* (New York: Fathers of the Church).

SCHARF, B. R. [1968], 'Review of Rosser and Harris', *Population Studies*, 33, pp. 285–6.

SCHATZMAN, L. and STRAUSS, A. L. [1955], 'Social Class and Modes of Communication', *American Journal of Sociology*, 60, pp. 329–38.

— — [1973], *Field Research: Strategies for a Natural Sociology* (Englewood Cliffs, N.J. Prentice-Hall).

SCHEFF, T. J. [1968], 'Negotiating Reality', *Social Problems*, 16, pp. 3–17.

SCHEFFLER, I. [1967], *Science and Subjectivity* (Indianapolis: Bobbs-Merrill).

SCHEGLOFF, E. [1968], 'Sequencing in Conversational Openings', *American Anthropologist*, 70, pp. 1075–95.

SCHELTING, A. VON [1934], *Max Weber's Wissenschaftslehre* (Tübingen: Mohr).

SCHNEIDER, L. [1965], 'The Role of the Category of Ignorance in Sociological Theory: An Exploratory Statement', *American Sociological Review*, 30, pp. 492–508.

SCHUTZ, A. [1953], 'Common-sense and Scientific Interpretation of Human Action', *Philosophy and Phenomenological Research*, 14, pp. 1–37.

SCOTT, R. A. and SHORE, A. R. [1979], *Why Sociology Does Not Apply* (New York: Elsevier).

SEEMAN, M. [1958], 'The Intellectual and the Language of Minorities', *American Journal of Sociology*, 64, pp. 27–32.

SELLTIZ, C. *et al.* [1965], *Research Methods in Social Relations*, rev. edn of Jahoda [1951] (London: Methuen).

SELVIN, H. [1965a], 'Training for Social Research', in J. Gould (ed.), *Penguin Survey of the Social Sciences 1965* (London: Penguin Books) pp. 73–95.

— [1965b], 'Durkheim's *Suicide*: Further Thoughts on a Methodological Classic', in R. Nisbet (ed.), *Emile Durkheim* (Englewood Cliffs, N.J.: Prentice-Hall) pp. 113–36.

— and STUART, A. [1966], 'Data Dredging Procedures in Survey Analysis', *The American Statistician*, 20, pp. 20–3.

SENNETT, R. and COBB, J. [1973], *The Hidden Injuries of Class* (New York: Vintage).

SHANAS, E. and STREIB, G. B. (eds) [1965], *Social Structure and the Family: Generational Relations* (Englewood Cliffs, N.J.: Prentice-Hall).

SHANIN, T. (ed.) [1972], *The Rules of the Game* (London: Tavistock).

SHARPE, L. J. [1978], 'The Social Scientist and Policy-making in Britain and America: A Comparison', in Bulmer [1978] pp. 302–12.

SHAW, C. [1966], *The Jack Roller* (Chicago: University of Chicago Press).

SHILS, E. [1957], 'Primordial, Personal, Sacred and Civil Ties: Some Particular Observations on the Relationships of Sociological Research and Theory', *British Journal of Sociology*, 8, pp. 130–45.

— [1980], *The Calling of Sociology and Other Essays on The Pursuit of Learning* (Chicago: University of Chicago Press).

SHIPMAN, M. (ed.) [1976], *The Organisation and Impact of Social Research* (London: Routledge).

SHYROCK, H. S. and SIEGEL, J. S. [1975], *The Methods and Materials of Demography*, 3rd edn, 2 vols (Washington, D.C.: U.S. Government Printing Office).

SIBLEY, E. [1965], 'A Note on the Pronunciation of "Shibboleth" ', *S.S.R.C. Items*, 19, p. 16.

SIEBER, S. D. [1973], 'The Integration of Fieldwork and Survey Methods', *American Journal of Sociology*, 78, pp. 1335–59.

SILLITOE, K. [1978a], 'Ethnic Origin: The Search for a Question', *Population Trends*, 13, pp. 25–30.

— [1978b], *Ethnic Origins 1, 2, 3* (London: O.P.C.S. Occasional Papers nos 8, 9 and 10).

SIMEY, T. S. and SIMEY, M. B. [1960], *Charles Booth, Social Scientist* (Oxford University Press).

SIMON, H. A. [1957], *Models of Man* (New York: Wiley).

SJOBERG, G. (ed.) [1968], *Ethics, Politics and Social Research* (London: Routledge).

— and NETT, R. [1968], *A Methodology for Social Research* (New York: Harper).

SKOCPOL, T. [1979], *States and Social Revolutions* (Cambridge: Cambridge University Press).

— and SOMERS, M. [1980], 'The Use of Comparative History in Macrosocial Inquiry', *Comparative Studies in Society and History*, 22 (2) pp. 174–97.

SLOBIN, D. I. [1967], 'Soviet Psycholinguistics', in N. O'Connor (ed.), *Present-day Russian Psychology* (Oxford: Pergamon).

SMELSER, N. J. [1959], *Social Change in the Industrial Revolution* (London: Routledge).

SMITH, J. M. [1972], *Interviewing in Market and Social Research* (London: Routledge).

Social Indicators 1976 [1978] (Washington, D.C.: U.S. Government Printing Office).

Social Indicators III [1980] (Washington, D.C.: U.S. Government Printing Office).

Social Trends, annually since no. 1, 1970 (London: H.M.S.O.).

— [1975], 'Social Commentary of Social Class' (London: H.M.S.O.) pp. 10–31.

Sociological Inquiry [1969], issue on 'The Craft of Sociology', vol. 39, no. 2, with contributions by P. M. Blau, L. Coser, P. M. Hauser, A. J. Reiss, and N. J. Smelser.

SPARKS, R. *et al.* [1978], *Surveying Victims: A Study of the Measurement of Criminal Victimisation* (Chichester, Sussex: Wiley).

SROLE, L. *et al.* [1962], *Mental Health in the Metropolis* (New York: McGraw-Hill).

STACEY, M. [1960], *Tradition and Change* (London: Oxford University Press).

— (ed.) [1969], *Comparability in Social Research* (London: Heinemann for B.S.A. and S.S.R.C.).

STARR, P. [1974], 'The Edge of Objectivity', *Harvard Educational Review*, 44, pp. 393–415.

STEIN, M. I. and HEINZE, S. J. [1960], *Creativity and the Individual* (Glencoe: Free Press).

STEIN, M. R. [1960], *The Eclipse of Community* (Princeton, N.J.: Princeton University Press).

STEINMETZ, S. R. [1952], *Inleiding tot de Sociologie* (Harlem: Bohn).

STERN, R. [1960], *Golk* (New York: Criterion).

STEVENSON, T. H. C. [1928], 'The Vital Statistics of Wealth and Poverty', *Journal of the Royal Statistical Society*, 91, pp. 207–30.

STEWART, W. A. [1964], 'Foreign-language Teaching Methods in Quasi-Foreign Language Situations', in W. A. Stewart (ed.), *Non-standard Speech and the Teaching of English* (Washington, D.C.: Centre for Applied Linguistics).

STINCHCOMBE, A. [1968], *Constructing Social Theories* (New York: Harcourt Brace & World).

— [1970], Review of 'Students in Conflict: L.S.E. in 1967', *British Journal of Sociology*, 21, pp. 455–8.

STOUFFER, S. A. [1950], 'Some Observations on Study Design', *American Journal of Sociology*, 55, pp. 355–61.

— *et al.* (eds) [1949], *The American Soldier*, 4 vols (Princeton University Press).

SUDNOW, D. [1972], 'Temporal Parameters of Interpersonal Observation', in D. Sudnow (ed.), *Studies in Social Interaction* (New York: Free Press) pp. 229–58.

SWIERENGA, R. P. (ed.) [1970], *Quantification in American History: Theory and Research* (New York: Atheneum).

TAYLOR, C. [1978], 'Interpretation and the Sciences of Man', in R. Beehler and A. R. Drengson (eds), *The Philosophy of Society* (London: Methuen).

TAYLOR, C. W. and BARRON, F. [1963], *Scientific Creativity* (New York: Wiley).

THERNSTROM, S. and SENNETT, R. (eds) [1969], *Nineteenth Century Cities* (New Haven, Conn.: Yale University Press).

THOMAS, W. I. and ZNANIECKI, F. [1918–20], *The Polish Peasant in Europe and America*, vols 1, 2 (Chicago: University of Chicago Press); vols 3–5 (Boston: Badger).

THOMPSON, E. P. [1965], 'The Peculiarities of the English', in R. Miliband and J. Savile (eds), *The Socialist Register 1965* (London: Merlin).

— and YEO, E. (eds) [1971], *The Unknown Mayhew: Selections from the 'Morning Chronicle' 1849–50* (London: Merlin; paper edn Harmondsworth: Penguin Books, 1973).

THOMPSON, P. [1975], *The Edwardians* (London: Weidenfeld & Nicolson).

THORNDIKE, E. L. [1939], *Your City* (New York: Harcourt Brace).

THORNER, D. and THORNER, A. [1962], *Land and Labour in India* (London: Asia Publishing House).

TIRYAKIAN, E. A. (ed.) [1971], *The Phenomenon of Sociology* (New York: Appleton).

TOULMIN, S. [1961], *Foresight and Understanding* (Bloomington, Indiana: Indiana University Press).

TOWNSEND, P. [1965], 'The Effects of Family Structure on the Likelihood of Admission to an Institution of Old Age', in Shanas and Streib [1965].

— and DAVIDSON, N. [1982], *Inequalities in Health: The Black Report* (Harmondsworth: Penguin Books).

TROW, M. [1957], 'Comment on "Participant Observation and Interviewing" by Becker and Geer', *Human Organisation*, 16, pp. 33–5.

TUKEY, J. W. [1977], *Exploratory Data Analysis* (Reading, Mass.: Addison-Wesley).

TURNER, R. H. [1953], 'The Quest for Universals in Sociological Research', *American Sociological Review*, 18, pp. 604–11.

— (ed.) [1967], *Robert E. Park on Social Control and Collective Behavior* (Chicago: University of Chicago Press).

UDY, S. H. [1964], 'Cross-cultural Analysis: A Case Study', in Hammond [1964] pp. 161–83.

VALENTINE, C. A. [1968], *Culture and Poverty* (Chicago: University of Chicago Press).

VALLIER, I. (ed.) [1971], *Comparative Methods in Sociology: Essays on Trends and Applications* (Berkeley: University of California Press).

VAN DOORN, J. [1956], 'The Development of Sociology and Social Research in the Netherlands', *Mens en Maatschappij*, 31, pp. 189–217.

VANSINA, J. [1965], *Oral Tradition* (London: Routledge; paper edn London: Penguin Books, 1973).

VIDICH, A. J. and BENSMAN, J. [1954], 'The Validity of Field Data', *Human Organisation*, 13, pp. 20–7.

— — [1968], *Small Town in Mass Society*, rev. edn (Princeton, N.J.: Princeton University Press).

— — and STEIN, M. (eds) [1964], *Reflections on Community Studies* (New York: Wiley).

WAKEFORD, J. (ed.) [1979], *Research Methods Syllabuses in Sociology Departments in the U.K.* (Lancaster: Department of Sociology, University of Lancaster) mimeo.

WALIZER, M. H. and WIENIR, P. [1978], *Research Methods and Analysis* (New York: Harper).

WALKER, N. [1971], *Crimes, Courts and Figures* (Harmondsworth: Penguin Books).

WALLACE, W. [1969], *Sociological Theory* (London: Heinemann).

WARNER, W. L. [1959], *The Living and the Dead* (New Haven, Conn.: Yale University Press).

WARWICK, D. P. [1983], 'On Methodological Integration in Social Research', in Bulmer and Warwick [1983] pp. 275–97.

— and LININGER, C. [1975], *The Sample Survey: Theory and Practice* (New York: McGraw-Hill).

— and OSHERSON, S. (eds) [1973], *Comparative Research Methods* (Englewood Cliffs, N.J.: Prentice-Hall).

WAX, R. [1972], *Doing Fieldwork: Warnings and Advice* (Chicago: University of Chicago Press).

WEBB, E. J., CAMPBELL, D. T., SCHWARZ, R. D. and SECHREST, L. [1966], *Unobtrusive Measures: Non-reactive Research in the Social Sciences* (Chicago: Rand McNally).

WEBER, M. [1947], *The Theory of Economic and Social Organisation* (Glencoe: Free Press).

— [1949], *The Methodology of the Social Sciences* (Glencoe: Free Press).

— [1951], *Gesammelte Aufsatze zur Wissenschaftslehre*, 2nd edn (Tübingen: Mohr).

— [1963], *The Sociology of Religions* (Boston: Beacon).

— [1975], *Roscher and Knies: The Logical Problems of Historical Economics* (New York: Free Press).

WECHSLER, H. [1961], 'Community Growth, Depressive Disorders and Suicide', *American Journal of Sociology*, 67, pp. 9–16.

WEINBERG, A. and LYONS, F. [1972], 'Class Theory and Practice', *British Journal of Sociology*, 22, pp. 51–65.

WEISS, C. H. [1980], *Social Science Research and Decision-making* (Columbia University Press).

WEISS, R. S. [1968], *Statistics in Social Research* (New York: Wiley).

WEISSMAN, D. [1965], *Dispositional Properties* (Southern Illinois University Press).

WESTERGAARD, J. H. and RESLER, H. [1975], *Class in a Capitalist Society* (London: Heinemann).

WHORF, B. L. [1956], *Language, Thought and Reality* (New York: Wiley).

WHYTE, W. F. [1981], *Street Corner Society: The Social Structure of an Italian Slum*, 3rd edn (Chicago: University of Chicago Press).

WHYTE, W. F. *et al.* [1955], *Money and Motivation* (New York: Harper).

— and BRAUN, R. R. [1968], 'On Language and Culture', in H. S. Becker *et al.* (eds) [1968] pp. 119–38.

WILES, P. [1975], 'Criminal Statistics and Sociological Explanations of Crime', in W. G. Carson and P. Wiles (eds), *The Sociology of Crime and Delinquency in Britain*, vol. 1 (London: Martin Robertson) pp. 198–219.

WILLIAMS, R. [1976], 'Symbolic Interactionism: The Fusion of Theory and Method?', in D. C. Thorns (ed.), *New Directions in Sociology* (Newton Abbot: David & Charles) pp. 115–38.

WILLIAMS, W. M. [1963], *A West Country Village: Ashworthy* (London: Routledge).

WILSON, B. (ed.) [1970], *Rationality* (Oxford: Blackwell).

WILSON, W. J. [1970], *The Declining Significance of Race* (Chicago: University of Chicago Press).

WINCH, P. [1958], *The Idea of a Social Science* (London: Routledge).

WINSTON, S. [1932], 'Birth-control and Sex-ratio at Birth', *American Journal of Sociology*, 38, pp. 225–31.

WIRTH, L. (ed.) [1938], *Chicago Local Community Fact Book* (Chicago: Chicago Community Inventory).

WOLFF, K. (ed.) [1950], *The Sociology of Georg Simmel* (Glencoe: Free Press).

WOODWARD, J. [1958], *Management and Technology* (London: H.M.S.O.).

WORSLEY, P. [1964], *The Third World* (London: Weidenfeld & Nicolson).

WRIGLEY, E. A. (ed.) [1972], *Nineteenth Century Society* (Cambridge: Cambridge University Press).

WRONG, D. [1967], *Population and Society* (New York: Random House).

WUELKER, G. [1963], 'Questionnaires in Asia', *International Social Science Journal*, 15, pp. 35–47.

YOUNG, M. [1954], 'The Role of the Extended Family in a Disaster', *Human Relations*, 7, pp. 383–91.

— and WILLMOTT, P. [1957], *Family and Kinship in East London* (London: Routledge).

ZEISEL, H. [1968], *Say It with Figures*, 5th edn (New York: Harper).

ZEISL, H. [1933], 'Towards a History of Sociography', in M. Jahoda *et al.*, *Marienthal* (London: Tavistock, 1972, English edn) pp. 99–125.

ZELDITCH, M. [1962], 'Some Methodological Problems of Field Studies', *American Journal of Sociology*, 67, pp. 566–76.

ZETTERBERG, H. [1965], *On Theory and Verification in Sociology* (Totowa, N.J.: Bedminster Press).

ZIJDERVELD, A. C. [1966], 'History and Recent Development of Dutch Sociological Thought', *Social Research* 33, pp. 116–31.

ZIMMERMAN, D. and POLLNER, M. [1970], 'The Everyday World as a Phenomenon', in J. D. Douglas (ed.), *Understanding Everyday Life* (Chicago: Aldine).

ZITO, G. V. [1975], *Methodology and Meanings: Varieties of Sociological Inquiry* (New York: Praeger).

ZNANIECKI, F. [1934], *The Method of Sociology* (New York: Farrer & Rinehart).